GARY BUSBY

Microsoft® SQL Server™ 2000
Reporting Services

D1373009

About the Author

Brian Larson is a Phi Beta Kappa graduate of Luther College in Decorah, Iowa, with degrees in Physics and Computer Science. He has 19 years of experience in the computer industry and 15 years' experience as a consultant creating custom database applications. Brian is currently the Chief of Technology for Superior Consulting Services in Minneapolis, Minnesota, a Microsoft Consulting Partner for Reporting Services. Brian is a Microsoft Certified Solution Developer (MCSD) and a Microsoft Certified Database Administrator (MCDBA).

Brian served on the Reporting Services development team as a consultant to Microsoft. In that role, he contributed to the original code base of Reporting Services. Brian has mentored Fortune 500 companies and early adopters in the use and best practices of Reporting Services. Brian has been called upon by Microsoft to complete consulting assignments for several of its most important regional clients. He has been a leading spokesperson for Reporting Services, conducting numerous presentations, web casts, and classroom training sessions. In addition to writing this book, Brian co-authored the December, 2003 *SQL Server Magazine* cover article on Reporting Services.

Brian and his wife, Pam, have been married for 19 years. Pam will tell you that their first date took place at the campus computer center. Brian and Pam have two children, Jessica and Corey.

About the Technical Editor

Doug Harts is the Chief Technology Officer of Cizer Software Corporation. With 25 years of experience in software design and development and as a Microsoft Certified Systems Engineer, he manages the Joint Development Partnership between Cizer and Microsoft, creating browser-based authoring tools for Microsoft SQL Server Reporting Services. Doug holds a BSEE, an MBA, and a JD from the George Washington University Law School. Doug can be reached at dharts@cizer.com.

Microsoft® SQL Server™ 2000 Reporting Services

Brian Larson

McGraw-Hill/Osborne

New York   Chicago   San Francisco
Lisbon   London   Madrid   Mexico City   Milan
New Delhi   San Juan   Seoul   Singapore   Sydney   Toronto

The McGraw·Hill Companies

McGraw-Hill/Osborne
2100 Powell Street, 10th Floor
Emeryville, California 94608
U.S.A.

To arrange bulk purchase discounts for sales promotions, premiums, or fund-raisers, please contact **McGraw-Hill**/Osborne at the above address. For information on translations or book distributors outside the U.S.A., please see the International Contact Information page immediately following the index of this book.

Microsoft® SQL Server™ 2000 Reporting Services

Copyright © 2004 by The McGraw-Hill Companies. All rights reserved. Printed in the United States of America. Except as permitted under the Copyright Act of 1976, no part of this publication may be reproduced or distributed in any form or by any means, or stored in a database or retrieval system, without the prior written permission of publisher, with the exception that the program listings may be entered, stored, and executed in a computer system, but they may not be reproduced for publication.

1234567890 FGR FGR 01987654

ISBN 0-07-223216-1

Publisher	Brandon A. Nordin
Vice President & Associate Publisher	Scott Rogers
Editorial Director	Wendy Rinaldi
Acquisitions Editor	Nancy Maragioglio
Project Editors	Elizabeth Seymour, Carolyn Welch
Acquisitions Coordinator	Athena Honore
Technical Editor	Doug Harts
Copy Editor	Bart Reed
Proofreader	Stefany Otis
Indexer	Valerie Perry
Composition	Carie Abrew, Jean Butterfield, Dick Schwartz
Illustrators	Kathleen Edwards, Melinda Lytle, Jackie Sieben
Series Design	Peter F. Hancik
Cover Series Design	Pattie Lee

This book was composed with Corel VENTURA™ Publisher.

Information has been obtained by **McGraw-Hill**/Osborne from sources believed to be reliable. However, because of the possibility of human or mechanical error by our sources, **McGraw-Hill**/Osborne, or others, **McGraw-Hill**/Osborne does not guarantee the accuracy, adequacy, or completeness of any information and is not responsible for any errors or omissions or the results obtained from the use of such information.

This book is dedicated to my family.
To my children, Jessica and Corey, who gave up many
hours of "dad time" during the writing of this book.
And especially to my wife, Pam, who, in addition to
allowing me to commit to this project, gave countless hours
of her own time to make sure things were done right.

Contents at a Glance

viii Microsoft SQL Server 2000 Reporting Services

Part IV Appendixes

Appendix A **Report Item Reference** 515

Appendix B **Web Service Interface Reference** 553

Appendix C **Report Definition Language Reference** 603

Index 611

Contents

Foreword

The first time I met Brian Larson was in late 2001. At that time, our company had been working on Reporting Services for about a year. We were looking for someone to help write the PDF rendering extension as we were extremely busy with the core reporting processing engine and server infrastructure.

I had known Martin Voegele, Brian's coworker at Superior Consulting Services, from previous projects he had worked on for Microsoft. We contacted Marty and asked whether he and Brian would be interested in doing some work for a new product. The code had to be written in C# using the .NET Framework, both of which had been recently released. The catch was, as we were still over a year away from going public with Reporting Services, they wouldn't be able to talk about any of their work until we had announced the product. They agreed and started working on the extension.

Brian and Marty worked for over six months on the project before it was completed. This was a lot longer than we initially thought because the rendering APIs were still evolving at the time and we were learning about the PDF format. Also, we had written only the HTML rendering extension since so much of the page-oriented sizing and absolute positioning logic was new. By late 2002, we had finished integrating the code. Brian and Marty moved on to other projects, and we focused on different areas of the product.

Around the same time, we had been quietly showing the product to a small set of partners and customers. Although Reporting Services was originally scheduled to be released with the Yukon release of SQL Server, feedback from the early demos told us that we had something special on our hands that customers wanted sooner, not later. We decided to package what we had and release the product as an add-on to SQL Server 2000. In February 2003, we formally announced the existence of SQL Server Reporting Services and began work to deliver the early release.

Since then, it has been a whirlwind of activity and excitement. We released the first beta of the product in April 2003 and followed up with a second public beta in October of that year. Our initial goal for the second beta was 1,000 customers. By the time we closed the beta, we had over 14,000 customers signed up to participate.

The release of the product in January 2004 capped off three years of hard work and was the highlight of my professional career. I am very proud of the effort by the product team. Initial reaction to the product shows that we have exceeded many expectations.

As we wrapped up work on the early release and started working on Yukon, I was pleased to learn that Brian was writing a book on Reporting Services. Brian's in-depth knowledge of the product makes him an excellent resource, and his practical approach will ensure you are able to leverage all of the product's available features.

Reporting Services wouldn't be the same product without the support of folks like Brian, our early adopters, and the thousands of beta testers. It's been very gratifying to meet people who are doing amazing things with the product and pushing it in ways we never dreamed of. I encourage you to use the knowledge and techniques in this book to make Reporting Services work for you as well.

Enjoy!

Brian Welcker
Group Program Manager
Microsoft SQL Server Reporting Services

Acknowledgments

A journey of a thousand miles begins with a single step.

Perhaps this book project was not a journey of a thousand miles, although it seemed that way in the early hours of the morning with a deadline approaching. Be that as it may, it is possible to identify the first step in this whole process. A coworker of mine at Superior Consulting Services, Marty Voegele, was between assignments—"on the bench," in consultant-speak. He was bored, so he decided to take matters into his own hands. Marty had previously been a consultant for Microsoft and still had a few contacts in the SQL Server area. He made a few phone calls and before long, Marty was again consulting for Microsoft, this time creating something called Rosetta.

As additional work was added to the project, I had the opportunity to take on part of this assignment as well. It was both challenging and exciting working on code that I knew would be part of a major product from a major software company. What was perhaps the most exciting was the fact that Rosetta seemed to be a tool that would fill several needs we had identified while developing custom applications for our own clients.

As the beta version of what is now called Reporting Services was released, a brief introductory article on Reporting Services appeared in *SQL Server Magazine*. One of the sales representatives here at Superior Consulting Services, Mike Nelson, decided this would be a nice bit of marketing material to have as we trumpeted our involvement with Reporting Services. One thing led to another and before we knew it, Mike had offered Marty's and my services to write a more in-depth article for *SQL Server Magazine*. This article became the cover article for the December, 2003 issue. This has become known as the "Delightful" article (you'll have to read the first paragraph of the article to understand why) and it is now available on MSDN.

This was where I grabbed the map and compass and decided on the next path. Since the magazine article was received fairly well, I decided to write a book on the topic. Marty informed me that writing a 700-page book would probably make his fingers fall off, so I could take this next step on my own. And here I am today.

All of this is a rather lengthy way of saying that I owe a big "thank you" to Marty and Mike. I can say without a shadow of a doubt that this book would not have happened without them. In addition to the contributions already stated, I want to thank Marty for helping to keep me up to speed on Reporting Services information and newsgroup postings. We have learned a great deal preparing presentations on Reporting Services and providing Reporting Services solutions for clients. In addition to opening the door for the magazine article, I want to thank Mike for finding additional clients yearning for Reporting Services knowledge and solutions.

I also want to thank John Miller, the owner of Superior Consulting Services. He hired me as his first employee seven years ago to be Superior's Chief of Technology. John has supported our efforts on Reporting Services and made it a major area of focus at Superior Consulting. Without John's founding of Superior Consulting Services and his bringing together people such as Marty and Mike, none of this would have come into being.

I need to extend a big thank you to Brian Welcker and the rest of the Reporting Services development team. Their guidance and patience during development is much appreciated. The information they were able to provide during the creation of this book has enhanced the final product you are now holding.

I also want to thank the staff at McGraw-Hill/Osborne: Nancy Maragioglio, Elizabeth Seymour, Athena Honore, Carolyn Welch, Wendy Rinaldi, and Bart Reed, along with the technical editor Doug Harts from Cizer Software. Their assistance, guidance, professionalism, and humor have made this project much easier. The attention Osborne has given this project has been truly overwhelming.

Last, but certainly not least, I want to thank my wife, Pam, for all of her efforts and understanding. Not only did she agree to my taking personal time to write this book, she took it upon herself to proofread every page and work through every sample report. You, as a reader, are greatly benefiting from her efforts.

I also want to thank you, the reader, for purchasing this book. It is my hope that it will provide you with an informative overview, steady guide, and quick reference as you use Reporting Services.

Introduction

icrosoft SQL Server 2000 Reporting Services is an exciting product. Never has there been a product with so much potential for sharing business information with such ease of use and at such a reasonable price. Anyone who has ever struggled to find a way to efficiently share database information across an enterprise will see a reason to be delighted with this product.

Now I will admit that I may not be unbiased when expressing this opinion. I did have the opportunity to create a small piece of what has now become Reporting Services. But my excitement goes beyond that.

The main reason I get excited about Reporting Services is because I have been a database application developer for 15 years. I have fought with various reporting tools. I have struggled to find a way to efficiently share data between far-flung sales offices and their corporate headquarters. I have researched enterprise-wide reporting systems and started salivating when I saw the features they offered, only to have my hopes dashed when I looked at the licensing fees. I have shaken my fist at the computer screen and screamed, "There must be a better way!"

With Reporting Services, there is. During the past year, my colleagues and I at Superior Consulting Services have had the opportunity to incorporate Reporting Services into custom database solutions. We have worked with a number of organizations, helping them get up to speed on the product. We have seen how quickly and easily Reporting Services can improve the data analysis and data distribution capabilities within an enterprise.

At one client, we began implementing Reporting Services on Monday morning. By Wednesday afternoon, reports were being e-mailed around the company. Information was being shared as never before. On Thursday morning, the president of the company emerged from his office to see what all of the hoopla was about. As he stared at a newly created Reporting Services report, he began saying things like, "So that's why we're having a problem in this area" and "Now I see why our end-of-months totals went that direction." That is enough to make even the most cynical data processing professional sit up and take notice!

This book is designed to help you and your organization achieve those same results. As you work through the examples in this book, I hope you have several of those "ah-ha" moments. Not only moments of discovering new capabilities in Reporting Services, but also moments of discovering how Reporting Services can solve business problems in your organization.

This book is meant to be a hands-on process. You should never be far from your Reporting Services development installation as you read through the chapters. The book is based on the philosophy that people understand more and remember longer when the learning takes place in an interactive environment. Consequently, most of the book is based on business needs and the reports, code, and configurations you will create to fulfill those needs.

The book is dedicated to offering examples that demonstrate complete solutions. I have tried to stay away from code snippets as much as possible. There is nothing worse than seeing five lines of code and knowing they are exactly the solution you need, but being unable to implement them because you do not know what code is supposed to come before or after those five lines to make the whole thing work. With the examples in this book, along with the supporting materials available from the book's web site—www.osborne.com—you should always see a solution from beginning to end and be able to turn around and implement that solution to fulfill your organization's business needs.

I have also tried to have a little fun in the book when appropriate. That is why the business scenarios are based on Galactic Delivery Services (GDS), an interplanetary package delivery service. (You might call it the delivery service to the stars.) While GDS is a bit fanciful with its antimatter transports and robotic employees, the business needs discussed will ring true for most organizations.

I hope you find this book to be a worthwhile tool for getting up to speed on Microsoft's exciting new product. I hope you get a chuckle or two from its GDS examples. Most of all, I hope the book allows you to unlock the potential of Reporting Services for your organization.

Getting Started

Let's Start at the Very Beginning

IN THIS CHAPTER:

Sharing Business Intelligence

Report Authoring Architecture

Report Serving Architecture

Diving In

S QL Server 2000 Reporting Services is Microsoft's entry into the web-based reporting arena. Reporting Services allows you to easily share business information—what is commonly known as "business intelligence" these days—with management, co-workers, business partners, and customers throughout the world. In an interconnected workplace, it makes sense that your reporting solution should offer company-wide, nationwide, and even worldwide communication.

Reporting Services was code-named Rosetta during internal development at Microsoft. This name comes from the Rosetta Stone, a stone slab found in 1799 that contains an inscription in both Egyptian hieroglyphics and Greek. This stone provided the key piece of information necessary to unlock the mystery of Egyptian hieroglyphics for the modern world. Just as the Rosetta Stone brought key information across 1,400 years of history, Rosetta, or Reporting Services, is designed to bring key information across distances to unlock the mystery of succeeding at your business.

The Rosetta project was originally conceived as part of the next version of Microsoft's SQL Server database platform, code-named Yukon. However, as Microsoft told prospective customers about the features in Rosetta and demonstrated the first alpha versions, the reaction was very strong: "We need this product and we need it now!" Because of this reaction, Microsoft decided that Rosetta would not wait for the release of Yukon but rather would be made its own product and would work with SQL Server 2000.

Just what are the features of Reporting Services that got everyone so excited? Reporting Services provides an environment for creating a number of different types of reports from a number of different data sources. The reports are previewed and refined using this authoring tool. Once completed, the reports are deployed to a Report Server, which makes the reports available via the Internet in a structured, secure environment. Last, but not least, the report management and distribution portion of Reporting Services is free of charge to anyone with a SQL Server 2000 license.

Why did this set of features generate so much excitement? When you put them all together, the result is a product that facilitates the creation, management, and timely use of business intelligence.

Sharing Business Intelligence

Because you are reading this book, you are probably the keeper of some type of information that is important to your organization. You may have information on sales, finance, production, delivery—or one of a hundred other areas. All this information makes up the business intelligence necessary to keep today's corporate, academic, and governmental entities humming along.

The Need to Share

In addition to maintaining this information, you also have a need to share this information with others. This need to share may have come from an important lesson you learned in kindergarten ("The world would be a much happier place if we all learned to share.") or, more likely, this need to share your information was probably suggested to you by a manager or executive somewhere higher up the food chain. See if any of these situations sounds familiar.

The Production Manager

Your company's order-entry system automatically updates the inventory database every four hours. In your company's line of business, some orders can require a large quantity of a given product. Because of this, it is very important that the Production Manager knows about these changes in the inventory level in a timely manner so he can adjust production accordingly.

The Production Manager has asked you to provide him with an up-to-date inventory report that prints immediately following each update to the inventory database occurring during business hours. He would like this report to arrive on his PC as quickly as possible so that he can make changes to the production schedule within an hour of the updates. He would also like to be able to print this report so that he can add his own notations to the report as he works out his new production schedule.

One more fact to keep in mind: Your company's inventory system is in Cleveland, but the production facility is in Portland!

The Vice President of Sales

You are responsible for maintaining information on the amount of credit your company will extend to each of its clients. This information is updated daily in the company database. A report containing the credit information for all the clients is printed weekly at corporate headquarters and mailed to each sales representative.

The Vice President of Sales has requested that the credit information be made available to the sales staff in a timelier manner. He has asked that this report be accessible over the Internet from anywhere across the country. The sales representatives will print the report when they have access to the Internet, then carry it with them for those times when they cannot get online. He has also asked that this online version of the report be as up-to-date as possible.

The Chief Executive Officer

The Chief Executive Officer for your company has a very hands-on management style. She likes to participate in all facets of the decision-making process and therefore needs to stay well informed on all aspects of the company. This includes the corporate balance sheet, inventory and production, and the company's stock price.

The CEO expects all this information to be available on her desktop when she arrives for work each morning at 7:00 A.M. The information must be in a format that's appropriate to print and share with the corporate vice presidents at their meeting each morning at 9:00 A.M. As you search for solutions to this one, remember that there is no budget allocated for this project—and, of course, your job is on the line.

Possible Solutions

These situations, and a thousand others just like them, confront businesses each day. In our world of massive connectivity, these types of requests are not unreasonable. Even if that is the case, it does not mean that these requests are easy to fulfill.

An HTML Solution

The first candidate to explore when looking to move information across the Internet is, of course, HTML. You could use one of a number of tools for creating data-driven HTML pages. This would include Microsoft's Active Server Pages, Macromedia's ColdFusion, any of a number of Java environments, PHP—the list goes on and on.

Each of these environments is good at creating dynamic web content. However, they all take time and a certain level of programming knowledge. With deadlines looming, you may not have the time to create custom web applications to solve each of these problems. If you are used to manipulating data with Crystal Reports or Access reporting, you may not be ready to jump into full-blown application development and may not have a desire to do it at any time in the near future.

Even if you did create an application for each of these scenarios, one important requirement in each case is that the information must be printable. HTML screens can look great in a browser window but cause problems when printed. The content can be too wide to fit on the page, and there is no control of page breaks. In fact, the page can break right in the middle of a line of text, with the top half of the characters on one page and the bottom half of the characters on the next! These types of formatting issues could make the output difficult for the sales representatives and the production manager to read. Asking the CEO to take this type of a report to the executive meeting could get you fired.

Let's look for another option!

A PDF Solution

Because the ability to control the printed output is important, Adobe PDF should be considered. PDF files look good both on the screen and in print. You can control where the page breaks occur and make sure everything looks great. However, several issues need to be overcome with PDF files.

First of all, you will need some type of utility to produce output in a PDF format. This could be Adobe's full version of Acrobat or some other utility. Once this has been obtained, a document must be created that contains the desired database information. This is usually a report created with a reporting tool or development software. After this document is created, it is converted into a PDF document using an export function or a special printer driver.

Once the PDF document has been created, it can be copied to a website for access through the Internet. However, as soon as the PDF document is created, it becomes a static entity. It does not requery the database each time it is requested from the website. In order to remain up-to-date, the PDF document must be re-created each time the source data is changed. In addition, you may have to return to your programming environment to control access to the PDF documents on the website.

Perhaps there is a better way.

A Third-party Reporting Environment

There are certainly reporting environments from other companies that overcome the limitations of our first two options. These third-party products allow reports to be built without requiring large amounts of programming. They can also dynamically generate output in a format such as Adobe PDF that will perform well onscreen and in print.

The problem with third-party reporting environments is the cost. Some products can run into the thousands or tens of thousands of dollars. This can be enough to break the budget—if indeed there is a budget—for reporting projects such as the ones discussed previously.

Microsoft Reporting Services

Now you can begin to see why companies got so excited about Reporting Services. It provides an elegant solution for all three of your demanding users—the Production Manager, the Vice President of Sales, and the CEO. Reporting Services does not have the drawbacks inherent in the possible solutions considered previously.

No Programming Required

Reporting Services provides a simple, drag-and-drop environment for creating reports from database information. This report-authoring tool is contained within Microsoft Visual Studio .NET 2003. Even though this is the same integrated development environment used by programmers to create Visual Basic .NET and C# applications, no programming is required to create reports.

Later in this book we will look at some simple Visual Basic expressions that can be used to spice up your report's presentation. Note, however, that these expressions are not necessary to create useful reports. They are also simple enough that even those who are totally new to Visual Basic will be able to master them with ease.

A Server with a View

Reporting Services includes a report viewer that works with your browser. The viewer provides a high-quality presentation of each report using dynamic HTML. Reports are presented in multiple pages with "VCR-button" controls for navigating between pages.

Because the report viewer uses dynamic HTML, it does not require any additional programs to be downloaded on your PC. There is no ActiveX control to install, no Java applet to download. Any browser that supports HTML 4.0 can view reports.

Plays Well with Printers

In addition to presenting reports in your browser using dynamic HTML, Reporting Services can *render* a report in a number of additional formats. These include Adobe PDF, TIFF, and even a Microsoft Excel spreadsheet. All these formats look great onscreen when they are viewed or on paper when they are printed.

NOTE

When Reporting Services renders a report, it gathers the most recent data from the database, formats the data in the manner that the report's author specified, and outputs the report into the selected format (that is, HTML, PDF, TIFF, and so on).

Even when being output in the PDF or TIFF format, a report can be configured to requery the database every time it is accessed. This ensures that the report is always up-to-date.

Special Delivery

Reporting Services provides several different ways to deliver reports to end users. The Report Manager website allows users to access reports via the Internet. It also includes security features that ensure that users access only the reports they should.

Users can also subscribe to reports they would like to receive on a regular basis. Reporting Services will send out a copy of the report as an e-mail attachment to each subscriber on a regularly scheduled basis. Alternatively, a Reporting Services administrator can send out a copy of the report as an e-mail attachment to a number of recipients on a mailing list.

The Price Is Right

For anyone who has a licensed copy of SQL Server 2000, the price of Reporting Services is certainly right. Free! You will need to purchase a copy of Visual Studio .NET 2003 for creating reports, if you do not already have one. However, once you have obtained this, it will not cost you a penny to share your reports with others using Reporting Services.

Reporting Services to the Rescue

Let's take one more look at the three scenarios we considered earlier—the Production Manager, the Vice President of Sales, and the Chief Executive Officer. How can you use the features of Reporting Services to fulfill the requests made by each of them?

The Production Manager wants a report showing the current inventory. It is certainly not a problem to query the inventory data from the database and put it into a report. Next, he wants to get a new copy of the report every time the inventory is updated during business hours. The Production Manager can subscribe to your inventory report and, as part of the subscription, ask that a new report be delivered at 8:15 A.M., 12:15 P.M. and 4:15 P.M. Finally, the inventory system is in Cleveland, but the Production Manager is in Portland. Because a subscription to a report can be delivered by e-mail, the Reporting Services server can be set up in Cleveland, produce the report from the local data source, and then e-mail the report to Portland.

The solution for the Vice President of Sales is even more straightforward. He wants a report with credit information for each client. No problem there. Next, he wants the report available to his sales staff, accessible via the Internet. To achieve this, you can publish the report on the Report Manager website. You can even set up security so that only sales representatives with the appropriate user name and password can access the report.

Finally, the Vice President of Sales wants the report to look good when printed. This is achieved with no additional work on the development side. When the sales representatives retrieve the report from the website, it is displayed as HTML. This looks good in the browser, but may not look good on paper. In order to have a report that looks good on paper every time, the sales representatives simply need to export the report to either the PDF or TIFF format and then display and print the exported file. Now they are ready to go knocking on doors!

For the CEO, you can build a report or perhaps a series of reports that reflects the state of her company. This will serve to keep her informed on all facets of her business. To have it available on her desktop at 7:00 A.M., you can set up a subscription that will run the reports and e-mail them to her each morning at 6:15 A.M.

Finally, because she wants to print this report and share it with the corporate vice presidents, you can make sure that the subscription service delivers the report in either PDF or TIFF format. The best part is that, because you already have a copy of Visual Studio .NET 2003 for other development, the Reporting Services solution costs the company nothing. You have earned a number of bonus points with the big boss, and she will make you the Chief Information Officer before the end of the year!

Report Authoring Architecture

As mentioned previously, Reporting Services reports are created using Microsoft Visual Studio .NET 2003. Visual Studio contains all the tools to create a wide variety of reports for Reporting Services. Everything you need to select information from data sources, create a report layout, and preview the report to test your creation is right at your fingertips.

Visual Studio does not come with Reporting Services. Instead, you need to obtain one copy of Visual Studio .NET 2003 for each person who will be authoring reports. If you have a copy of Visual Studio that you are using to develop Visual Basic .NET, C#, or ASP.NET applications, you can use that same copy for creating reports. If you do not currently own a copy of Visual Studio, you will need to obtain a copy and install it before installing Reporting Services.

Visual Studio .NET 2003 is known as an *integrated development environment,* or *IDE.* Integrated development environments came into being when the people who create programming languages thought it would be more convenient if the editor, compiler, and debugger were packaged together. Prior to the advent of integrated development environments, creating and debugging software could be a long and tedious process. With an IDE, however, a programmer can be much more efficient while writing and testing an application.

Even though we will be creating reports rather than writing software, Visual Studio provides us with a very friendly working environment. We won't be editing, compiling, and debugging, but we will be selecting data, laying out the report, and previewing the end result. All of this is done quickly and easily within Visual Studio.

The Business Intelligence Project Type

Visual Studio can be used to build a wide variety of software solutions. It supports a number of different programming languages, from Visual Basic .NET to C#. It can create a number of different types of programs—from an application that runs on a single PC to a website that runs on a cluster of Internet servers.

To facilitate this variety, Visual Studio supports many different types of projects. These project types organize the multitude of programs that can be created within Visual Studio into related groups. Reporting Services reports are created using the Business Intelligence project type.

Project Templates

When you choose to create a new project in Visual Studio, you will see the New Project dialog box shown in Figure 1-1. The Project Types area shows all the various project types available through your installation of Visual Studio. This will vary depending on your version of Visual Studio and which programming languages have been installed.

The Business Intelligence project type contains two templates: Report Project Wizard and Report Project. Each of the templates will ultimately create a report

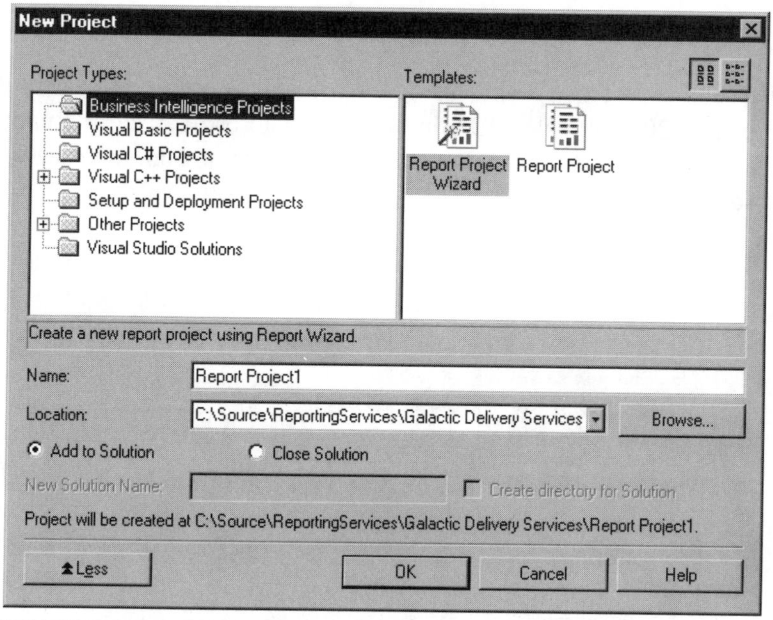

Figure 1-1 *The New Project dialog box*

project. The Report Project Wizard template uses the Report Wizard to guide you through the process of creating the first report in your new report project. The Report Project template simply creates an empty report project and turns you loose.

Report Structure

A report project can contain a number of reports. Each report contains two distinct sets of instructions that determine what the report will contain. The first is the data definition. The data definition controls where the data for the report will come from and what information will be selected from that data. The second set of instructions is the report layout. The report layout controls how the information will be presented on the screen or on paper. Both of these sets of instructions are stored using the Report Definition Language.

Figure 1-2 shows this report structure in a little more detail.

Data Definition

The data definition contains two parts: the data source and the dataset. The data source is the database server or data file that provides the information for your report. Of course, the data source itself is not included in the report. What is included is the set of instructions that the report needs to gain access to that data source. These instructions include the following:

▶   The type of source you will be using for your data (for example, Microsoft SQL Server 2000, Oracle, DB2, Informix, or Microsoft Access). Reporting Services will use this information to determine how to communicate with the data source.

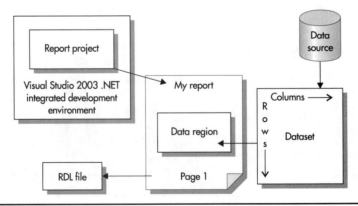

Figure 1-2   *Report structure*

▶   The name of the database server or the path to the data file.

▶   The name of the database.

▶   The login for connecting to this data source, if a login is required.

When the report is executing, it uses the data source instructions contained in the report to gain access to the data source. It then extracts information from the data source into a new format that can be used by the report. This new format is called a *dataset*.

The content of the dataset is defined using a tool within Visual Studio called the Query Builder. The Query Builder, as the name implies, helps you to build a database query. This query provides instructions to the data source telling it what data you want selected for your report. The query is stored in the report as part of the data definition.

The data that is selected by the query into the dataset consists of rows and columns. The rows correspond to the records that the query selects from the data source. The columns correspond to fields that the query selects from the data source. Information on the fields that will be selected into the dataset is stored in the report as part of the data definition. Only the information on what the fields will be called and the type of data they will hold is stored in the report. The actual data is not stored in the report definition but instead is selected from the data source each time the report is run.

Report Layout

The data that the report has extracted into a dataset is not of much use to you unless you have some way of presenting it to the user. You need to specify which fields go in which locations on the screen or on paper. You also need to add things such as titles, headings, and page numbers. All of this forms the report layout.

In most cases, your report layout will include a special area that interacts with the dataset. This special area is known as a *data region*. A data region displays all the rows in the dataset by repeating a section of the report layout for each row.

Report Definition Language

The information in the data definition and the report layout are stored using the Report Definition Language (RDL). RDL is an Extensible Markup Language (XML) standard designed by Microsoft specifically for storing report definitions. This includes the data source instructions, the query information that defines the dataset, and the report layout. When you create a report in Visual Studio, it is saved in a file with an .RDL extension.

If you have not worked with XML or are not even sure what it is, don't worry. Visual Studio and Reporting Services will take care of all the RDL for you. For those of you who want to learn more about RDL, we'll take a quick peek under the hood in Chapter 7. For the really hardcore, a reference to the RDL standard is included in Appendix C.

Visual Studio .NET 2003

Figure 1-3 shows the Visual Studio environment that we will be using for creating and editing reports. We will take a glimpse at some of Visual Studio's features now and discuss them in more detail in Chapter 5.

Design Window

The Design window, in the center of Figure 1-3, is where you create your report. You create both the data definition and the report layout here. This is also where you get to see your creation come to life!

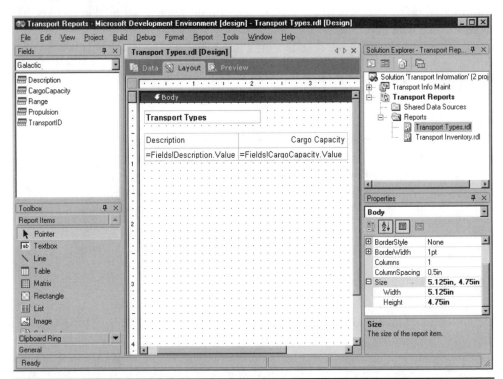

Figure 1-3 *Microsoft Visual Studio .NET 2003*

The Design window has three tabs. On the Data tab, you define the data source for the report. This is also where you use the Query Builder to create datasets.

On the Layout tab, you build the report layout. To do this, you utilize three of the other windows visible in Figure 1-3: the Fields window, the Toolbox, and the Properties window. You will learn how this works in the following sections.

On the Preview tab, you get to see the report layout and the data combined to create an honest-to-goodness report. The report preview allows you to see what the report will look like as HTML or when it is exported to any of the other data formats.

Fields

The Fields window, in the upper-left corner of Figure 1-3, provides a list of the database fields that can be used in your report. These are the fields you selected for your dataset using the Query Builder. Once the dataset has been defined in the Query Builder, the selected fields are displayed in the Fields window.

The Fields window makes it very easy to add database information to your report layout. Simply drag the desired field from the Fields window and drop it in the appropriate location on your report layout in the Design window. Visual Studio will take care of the rest.

Toolbox

The Toolbox, in the lower-left corner of Figure 1-3, contains all the report items you use to build your reports. These report items, sometimes called *controls,* are responsible for getting the text and graphics to show up in the right place on your reports. As with any construction project, you will be able to properly construct reports only after you have learned how to properly use the tools (report items) in the Toolbox. You will be learning how to use each of the report items in the Toolbox in Chapters 4, 5, and 6.

As with the fields in the Fields window, the report items in the Toolbox are placed on the report layout with a simple drag and drop. However, whereas fields are pretty much ready to go when they are dropped onto the report layout, report items almost always need some formatting changes to get them just the way you want them. This is done by changing the size, the color, the font, or one of many other characteristics of the report item.

Properties Window

The Properties window, in the lower-right corner of Figure 1-3, is the place where you control the characteristics of each report item. The Properties window always shows the characteristics, or *properties,* for the report item currently selected in the

Design window. You will see an entry in the Properties window for each and every aspect of this report item that you can control.

The top of the Properties window shows the name of the selected report item. In Figure 1-3, the body of the report is currently selected. The left column in the Properties window shows the name of each property that can be changed for that report item. The right column shows the current setting for each of those properties. For example, in Figure 1-3 you can see that the report body has a size of 5.125 inches by 4.75 inches.

Solution Explorer

The Solution Explorer, in the upper-right corner of Figure 1-3, manages all the objects you are working with in Visual Studio. Objects in the Solution Explorer are displayed in an outline that resembles an upside-down tree. There is a root entry at the top of the outline, and branch entries appear further down.

The entries in the outline can be expanded by clicking the plus (+) sign next to each entry. The entries can be contracted by clicking the minus (-) sign next to each entry. An entry in the outline that does not have a plus sign or a minus sign next to it does not have any additional entries beneath it. Expanding and contracting outline entries is useful for hiding portions of a complex outline so that you can concentrate on the area you are currently working on.

In Figure 1-3, the root entry is a solution called "Transport Information." Visual Studio uses solutions to group together a number of projects that all relate to solving the same business problem. Each solution contains one or more projects. This could be a report project, a Visual Basic programming project, or a project from any of the other project types shown in Figure 1-1.

In our example, the Transport Information solution contains two projects. The first is a Visual Basic project called "Transport Info Maint" that creates an application for entering and editing information. The second project is a report project called "Transport Reports" that creates reports to present that information.

A report project always contains two folders. The Shared Data Sources folder contains connections to different sources of data for your reports. As the folder name implies, these data sources can be shared by multiple reports in the report project.

The second folder in the report project is the Reports folder, which contains the reports you create in Visual Studio. In Figure 1-3, the Reports folder contains two reports: Transport Types and Transport Inventory.

When you are editing a report project in Visual Studio, the Design window and the Fields window display information for one report at a time. If your project has multiple reports, you can switch among them by double-clicking a report in the Solution Explorer window.

Report Serving Architecture

Once you have completed building your report and have it looking exactly the way you want, it is time to share that report with others. This is the time when your report moves from safe, childhood life inside a report project to its adult life on a Report Server. This is known as deploying the report. Let me assure you, reports pass through deployment much easier than you and I passed through adolescence!

Report Server

The Report Server is the piece of the puzzle that makes Reporting Services the product that it is. This is the software environment that allows you to share your report with the masses, at least those masses who have rights to your server. Figure 1-4 shows the basic structure of the Report Server.

Report Catalog

When a report is deployed to a Report Server, a copy of the report's RDL definition is put in that server's Report Catalog. The Report Catalog is a database used to store the definitions for all the reports available on a particular Report Server. It also stores the configuration and security information necessary for the operation of that Report Server.

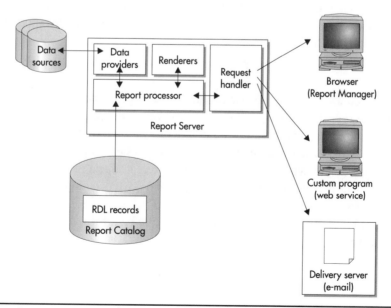

Figure 1-4   *Report serving architecture*

Even though you may use any ODBC or OLE DB–compliant data source to supply data to your reports, the Report Catalog database can only exist in SQL Server 2000. The Report Catalog database is created as part of the Reporting Services installation process. Except for creating regular backups of any Report Catalog databases, it is probably a good idea to leave the Report Catalog alone.

Report Processor

When a report needs to be executed, the report processor component of the Report Server directs the show. The report processor retrieves the RDL for the report from the Report Catalog. It then reads through this RDL to determine what is going to be needed for the report.

The report processor orchestrates the operation of the other components of the Report Server as the report is produced. It takes the output from each of the other components and combines them together to create the completed report.

Data Providers

As the report processor encounters dataset definitions in the report RDL, it retrieves the data to populate that dataset. It does this by first following the instructions in the report's data source for connecting to the database server or file that actually contains the data. The report processor selects a data provider that knows how to retrieve information from this type of data source.

The data provider then connects to the source of the data and selects the information required for the report. The data provider returns this information to the report processor, where it is turned into a dataset for use by the report.

Renderers

Once all the data for the report has been collected, the report processor is ready to begin processing the report's layout. To do this, the report processor looks at the format requested. This might be HTML, PDF, TIFF, or one of several other possible formats. The report processor then uses the renderer that knows how to produce that format.

The renderer works with the report processor to read through the report layout. The report layout is combined with the dataset, and any repeating sections of the report are duplicated for each row in the dataset. This expanded report layout is then translated into the requested output format. The result is a report ready to be sent to the user.

Request Handler

The request handler is responsible for receiving requests for reports and passing those requests on to the report processor. Once the report processor has created the requested report, the report handler is also responsible for delivering the completed report. In the next section, we will look at the various methods that the request handler uses for delivering reports.

Report Delivery

We have discussed how a report is created by the Report Server. What we have not discussed is where that report is going after it is created. The report may be sent to a server through the Report Manager website. It may be e-mailed to a user who has a subscription to that report. It may also be sent in response to a web service request that came, not from a user, but from another program.

Report Manager Website

One way for users to request a report from the Report Server is through the Report Manager website. This website is created for you when you install Reporting Services. Figure 1-5 shows a screen from the Report Manager website.

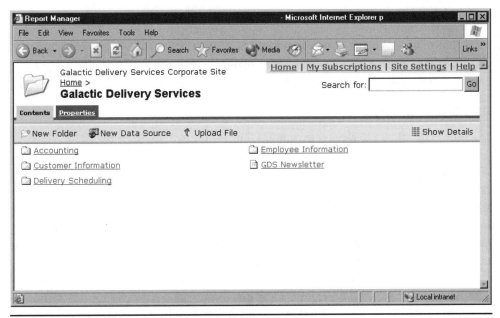

Figure 1-5   *The Report Manager website*

The Report Manager website organizes reports into folders. Users can browse through these folders to find the report they need. They can also search the report titles and descriptions to locate a report.

The Report Manager also includes security that can be applied to folders and reports. With this security, the site administrator can create security roles for the users who will be accessing the site. These security roles control which folders and reports a user is allowed to access. We will discuss security when we look at the Report Manager in Chapter 10.

In the Report Manager, reports are always displayed using the HTML format. Once a report has been displayed as an HTML page, the user can then export the report into any of the other available formats.

Subscription Delivery

If the users do not want to go to the report, the request handler can make the report go to them. In other words, users do not necessarily need to come to the Report Manager website to receive a report. They can have the report delivered to them through a subscription service. The Report Manager allows users to locate a report on the site and then subscribe to it so that it will be delivered to them in the future.

When users subscribe to a report, they provide an e-mail address to which the report will be delivered as an e-mail attachment. Users can specify the format for this attachment at the time they create their subscription.

The site administrator can also set up report subscriptions. These function like a mass mailing, using a list of e-mail addresses. Rather than requiring each user to access the Report Manager to create their own subscription, the site administrator can create one subscription that is delivered to every user in the list.

Web Service Interface

In addition to delivering reports to humans, either at their request or on a subscription basis, the request handler can deliver reports to other software applications. This is done through a series of web services. A *web service* is a mechanism that allows programs to communicate with each other over the Internet.

A program calls a web service on the Report Server, requesting a particular report in a particular format. The request handler relays this request to the report processor, just like any other request for a report. The completed report is returned to the program that originated the request as the response to the web service request.

Web services use a standard called the Simple Object Access Protocol (SOAP). SOAP is supported by both Windows and non-Windows environments. Therefore, a program running on a non-Windows computer that supports SOAP can receive a report created by Reporting Services.

Diving In

Now that you have been introduced to all the capabilities of Reporting Services, I hope you are ready to dive in and make it work for you. In the next chapter we will cover the installation and set up of Reporting Services. If Reporting Services has already been installed for you, you can skip ahead to Chapter 3.

In Chapter 3 we will make sure you have a firm understanding of database basics before getting to the actual building of reports in Chapter 4. Chapter 3 will also introduce you to Galactic Delivery Services (GDS), the company we will be using as a case study throughout the remainder of the book. Even if your database skills are tip-top, you should spend a few minutes in Chapter 3 to get to know GDS.

Putting the Pieces in Place: Installing Reporting Services

Before you can begin to enjoy all the benefits of Reporting Services discussed in Chapter 1, you, of course, have to install the Reporting Services software. This chapter will guide you through that process so that you can quickly move on to creating and managing reports.

In this chapter, we will look at the various types of Reporting Services installations and how to plan for each installation type. As part of that planning, we will note the software that must be in place prior to installing Reporting Services. After considering these preliminaries, we will walk through the installation process. Finally, we will look at some of the problems you may encounter during installation and some of their common remedies.

Preparing for the Installation

The most important part of the Reporting Services installation is not what you do as you run the setup program, but what you do before you begin. In this section, we will look at the knowledge you need and the steps you need to take to prepare for installation. With the proper plan in place, your Reporting Services installation will go smoothly and you will be creating reports in no time.

The Parts of the Whole

Reporting Services is not a single program that runs on a computer to produce reports. Instead, it is a series of services, web applications, and databases that work together to create a report development environment. As you plan your Reporting Services installation, it is important that you understand a little bit about each piece of the puzzle and how they all work together to create a complete system.

Figure 2-1 shows all the parts that make up a complete Reporting Services installation. Each part has a specific role to play in the development, management, and delivery of reports or in the management of the Reporting Services environment itself. Not all these items are installed with Reporting Services. Some are prerequisites and must be installed before you can begin the Reporting Services installation process.

Let's take a look at each part and see how it fits into the whole.

NOTE

Not all Reporting Services installations include all the items shown in Figure 2-1. The following sections of this chapter will discuss the various types of installations and which components they include.

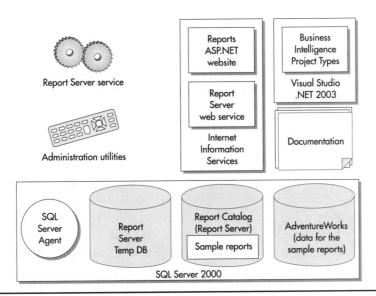

Figure 2-1   *Reporting Services component parts*

The Report Server Service

The Report Server service is the heart of Reporting Services and is, of course, installed as part of the Reporting Services installation. As you saw in Figure 1-4 of Chapter 1, the Report Server is responsible for processing any report requests. This includes fetching the report definition, retrieving the data used in the report, and rendering the report in the desired format.

The Report Server is a Windows service, and it makes its functionality available as web services. This means that it does not directly interact with the user. Instead, the Report Server Windows service runs in the background and handles requests made by other programs through the web services. Like other Windows services, such as SQL Server and Internet Information Services (IIS), the Report Server begins running when the computer starts up and continues running until the computer shuts down.

Because the Report Server service starts up on its own, it needs to have a valid username and password that it can use to log on to the server when it starts up. This login information, along with other information that determines how the Report Server will operate, is stored in the RSReportServer.config file. The content of this configuration file is determined by the choices you make during the setup process. We will talk more about this and other configuration files later in this chapter.

NOTE

Most of the information in the RSReportServer.config file is stored as plain text and can be modified using Notepad or a similar text editor. The login information, however, is encrypted when it is stored in this file. It cannot be changed except through one of the Administration Utility programs.

The Administration Utilities

The administration utilities are tools for managing the Report Server service and for making changes to its configuration. These utilities take care of tasks such as manually starting the Report Server service if it fails to start up automatically. The utilities can also be used to change the login information used by the service when it starts up.

These utility programs are run in a command window. There isn't a user interface with menus, buttons, and text boxes. Instead, the utilities use parameters specified as part of the command line that launches the program. These parameters determine what changes the utility program will make in the Reporting Services configuration.

The administration utilities can be run on the computer that is hosting the Report Server service to manage the configuration on that computer. Most of the administrative utilities can also be used to manage a Report Server service that is running on another computer. This is called *remote administration*.

The administration utilities are installed as part of the Reporting Services installation.

SQL Server 2000

SQL Server 2000 holds the database where Reporting Services stores its Report Catalog database. Reporting Services also uses the SQL Server Agent, which we will discuss shortly. In addition, databases in SQL Server 2000 can be used as data sources for Reporting Services reports.

The Reporting Services installation process creates several databases. For this reason, SQL Server 2000 must be installed before you begin the Reporting Services installation.

SQL Server Agent

SQL Server Agent is part of SQL Server 2000 and is created as part of the SQL Server 2000 installation process. It is used by SQL Server to execute jobs that are scheduled to run at a certain time. These jobs might back up a database or transfer information from one database to another. Jobs may be scheduled to run once or they may run on a regular basis, such as once a day or once a week.

Reporting Services also uses the SQL Server Agent to execute scheduled jobs. These jobs are used to run reports and distribute the results. In Chapter 1, we talked about users who subscribe to a report. When users subscribe to a report, they ask for it to be run and delivered to them on a regular basis. When a user creates a subscription, Reporting Services creates a SQL Server Agent job to handle that subscription.

For example, our Production Manager in Chapter 1 wanted an inventory report to be printed every four hours during the workday. He subscribes to the inventory report and creates a delivery schedule of 8:15 A.M., 12:15 P.M., and 4:15 P.M. When this subscription is created, Reporting Services creates a SQL Server Agent job scheduled to run at 8:15 A.M., 12:15 P.M., and 4:15 P.M. each day. The job takes care of running the report and e-mailing it to the Production Manager.

The Report Server and Report Server Temp DB Databases

During the Reporting Services installation process, two databases are created within SQL Server 2000: the Report Server and Report Server Temp DB databases. The Report Server database is used to store the Report Catalog. (Recall from Chapter 1 that the Report Catalog holds the information about all the reports that have been deployed to a Report Server.) The Report Server database also holds information about the Report Manager website. This includes such things as the folder structure of the website and the security settings for each folder and report.

As the name implies, the Report Server Temp DB database is used as temporary storage for Reporting Services operations. Information can be stored here to track the current users on the Report Manager website. Short-term copies of some of the most recently executed reports are also stored here in what is known as the *execution cache*.

Sample Reports and the AdventureWorks Database

As part of the Reporting Services installation process, you can choose to install several sample Reporting Services reports. These reports end up in the Report Catalog within the Report Server database. If you choose to install the sample reports, another database, called AdventureWorks 2000, is installed in SQL Server 2000. The AdventureWorks 2000 database serves as the data source for the sample reports.

Internet Information Services

Internet Information Services (IIS) is used to host Internet and intranet websites. It also serves as the host for web services. A website, of course, is used by a person to request information from a computer over the Internet or some other network. A web service is used by a computer to request information from another computer over the Internet or some other network.

When Reporting Services is installed, it creates a website and a web service hosted by IIS. Therefore, IIS must be installed before you begin the Reporting Services installation.

The Reports Website

The Reporting Services installation creates a website called Reports. The Reports website is what provides the Report Manager interface for Reporting Services. If Reporting Services is installed on a server named www.MyRSServer.com, then when you surf to www.MyRSServer.com/Reports, you will see the Report Manager home page.

The Reports website is built using ASP.NET. This means that ASP.NET support has to be enabled on IIS in order for the website to function. We will discuss how to do this in the "Installation Requirements" section of this chapter.

Report Server Web Service

A web service called Report Server is also created by the Reporting Services installation. The Report Server web service allows other programs to interact with and even administer Reporting Services. In addition, it allows other programs to request reports without having to go through the Report Manager interface. In short, the Report Server web service allows Reporting Services to be tightly integrated into other applications. Because web services work across an intranet or across the Internet, the web service interface allows Reporting Services to be integrated with applications running in the next room or in the next country.

The Report Server web service is also built using ASP.NET, so once again, ASP.NET support must be enabled on IIS in order for this feature to function.

Visual Studio .NET 2003

As discussed in Chapter 1, Reporting Services reports are created using Visual Studio .NET 2003. When Reporting Services is installed, it creates the Business Intelligence Project Types in Visual Studio. For this reason, if you are going to be creating reports on a particular computer, Visual Studio .NET 2003 needs to be installed on that computer before installing Reporting Services.

Business Intelligence Project Types

Reporting Services reports can only be created in Visual Studio projects that are initiated with one of the Business Intelligence Project Types. These project types are only created within Visual Studio if Visual Studio is found on the computer during installation.

Documentation

The final piece of Reporting Services is the documentation. The bulk of this documentation is Reporting Services Books Online. After Reporting Services is installed, you can view the Reporting Services Books Online through your Start menu. You'll find it under Programs | Microsoft SQL Server | Reporting Services | Reporting Services Books Online. In addition to this is a set of help screens for the Report Manager interface that can be accessed through the Reports website.

Editions of Reporting Services

Reporting Services is available in three editions: Standard Edition, Enterprise Edition, and Developer Edition. Reporting Services is licensed as part of your SQL Server 2000 license. Therefore, in a production environment, the Reporting Services edition you are licensed to use is the same as the SQL Server 2000 edition you are licensed to use. For example, if you have a Standard Edition of SQL Server 2000, you are only licensed for the Standard Edition of Reporting Services.

The Standard Edition

All editions of Reporting Services provide a rich environment for report authoring, report management, and report delivery. There are just a few of the more advanced features of Reporting Services that are not included in the Standard Edition. These advanced features are listed in "The Enterprise Edition" section that follows.

The Enterprise Edition

The following features require the Enterprise Edition of Reporting Services:

▶ **Security Extension API**   Create your own custom security structure rather than requiring Windows Integrated security for the Report Manager web application and the web service. The Security Extension API is discussed in Chapter 12.

▶ **Data-Driven Subscriptions**   Send a report to a number of users from a predefined mailing list. Data-driven subscriptions are discussed in Chapter 11.

▶ **Web Farm Configuration**   Configure several IIS servers running the Report Manager web application and the web service to point to a single SQL Server

2000 server hosting the report catalog. The web farm configuration is discussed in the "Types of Reporting Services Installations" section of this chapter.

▶ **Advanced Server Support**   Multiple symmetric multiprocessing to support more than four processors and additional memory support to handle more than 2GB of RAM.

The Developer Edition

The Developer Edition provides support for all the features of the Enterprise Edition. The Developer Edition does not, however, require that you have an Enterprise Edition license of SQL Server 2000. Of course, the Developer Edition is only for development and testing. It cannot be used in a production environment.

Types of Reporting Services Installations

The first decision you need to make when installing Reporting Services is which of the items mentioned in the previous section you want to include. Although you can choose to include or exclude items in any combination you like, in the end there are really just three combinations that make sense: the full installation, the server installation, and the report designer installation.

In addition to these are a couple specialized installation types. These are the distributed installation and the web farm installation. These installations are for high-end, high-volume Reporting Services sites. We will discuss these configurations briefly so you are familiar with the variety of ways that Reporting Services can be configured.

The Full Installation

The full installation, as the name implies, is the "everything including the kitchen sink" installation. All the items shown in Figure 2-1 and discussed in the previous section are included in this installation. Nothing is left out.

The full installation is most likely to be used in a development environment. This might be on a server that is used by a group of developers or on a power workstation used by a single developer. In either case, we want to have all the bells and whistles available to us as we figure out how to best use Reporting Services to suit our business needs.

The Server Installation

The server installation is most likely to be used when we're setting up Reporting Services on a production server. On a production server, we only want those items that are going to be used to deliver reports or help us manage Reporting Services. We don't want to include anything that will take up space unnecessarily. Figure 2-2 shows the items included in the server install.

The server installation includes the Report Server service and the administration utilities used to manage it. This type of installation also includes the Reports website and the Report Server web service for managing and delivering reports. In addition, Reporting Services will need the SQL Server Agent and the Report Server and Report Server Temp DB databases for its operations.

We won't be doing any development work on the production server, so we will not need Visual Studio or the Business Intelligence Project Types. It is possible that you would want the documentation on the production server for questions on managing Reporting Services. It is probably a better idea, however, to have the documentation handy on a development computer and keep the production installation as uncluttered as possible. The same can be said for the sample reports and the AdventureWorks database. You may want these on your production server for demonstration purposes, but again, it is probably better to do this on a different computer and reserve your production server for reports and data required by your users.

The Report Designer Installation

The report designer installation is for individuals who are creating Reporting Services reports but not doing heavy-duty development. These report designers may even be

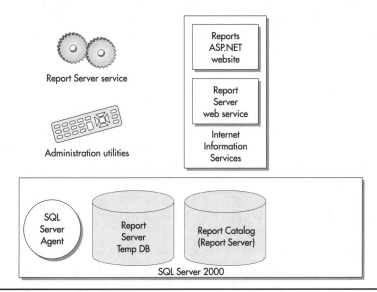

Figure 2-2   *The server installation*

creating ad hoc reports in order to find the answers to business questions as they arise. Report designers will not be creating full-blown applications that incorporate Reporting Services as part of a larger business system. The items included in the report designer installation are shown here.

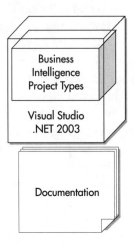

Report designers need the capability to create and preview reports. This capability is found within Visual Studio and the Business Intelligence Project Types. Report designers may also want access to the Reporting Services Books Online to look up information as they create reports. (Although, in my humble opinion, this book would serve as a better resource.) When report designers have completed their reports and are ready to have others use them, they will deploy the reports to a production Reporting Services server.

The Distributed Installation

In a distributed installation, the Reporting Services items we have discussed are not installed on a single computer. Instead, they are split between two computers that work together to create a complete Reporting Services system. One computer runs SQL Server 2000 and hosts the Report Server database. This is the database server. The other computer runs the Report Server service and IIS. This is the Report Server.

Figure 2-3 shows a distributed installation. Note that Figure 2-3 shows the servers and the report designer workstations. It does not show computers used for viewing reports.

The distributed installation has advantages when it comes to scalability. Because the workload of the three server applications—IIS, SQL Server, and the Report Server—is divided between two servers, it can serve reports to a larger number of

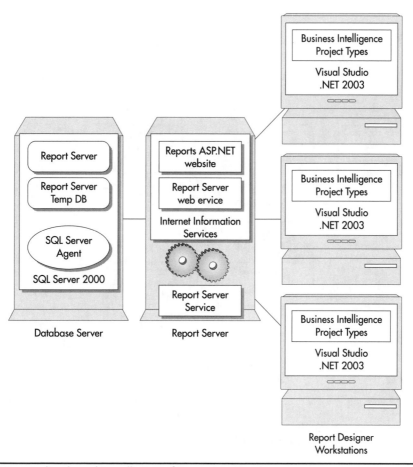

Figure 2-3   *A distributed installation of Reporting Services*

simultaneous users. The disadvantage of this type of installation is that it is more complex to install and administer. However, if you need a high-volume solution, it is certainly worth the effort to obtain a solution that will provide satisfactory response times under a heavy workload.

The Web Farm Installation

The web farm installation is a specialized form of the distributed installation, as shown in Figure 2-4. In a web farm, a single database server interacts with several Report Servers. Each of the Report Servers uses the same Report Server database for its information. By using additional Report Servers, we can handle even more

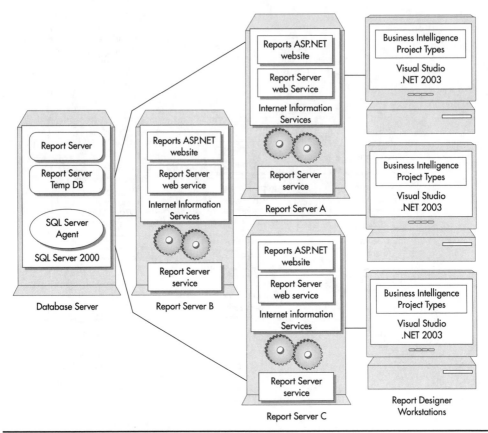

Figure 2-4 *A web farm installation of Reporting Services*

simultaneous users with the web farm installation than we could with the distributed installation.

Again, note that Figure 2-4 shows only the servers and the report designer workstations. It does not show computers used for viewing reports.

When report designers create reports, they can deploy them to any of the Report Servers. No matter which server is used, the reports will end up in the single Report Server database. Once the reports are in the Report Server database, they can be delivered by any of the Report Servers. In addition, because all the information about the Report Manager is stored in the Report Server database, any changes to the Report Manager configuration made on one server will take effect on all the servers.

For example, suppose an administrator uses the Reports website to access the Report Manager through Report Server A. The administrator creates a new folder in Report

Manager called "Sales Forecasts 2004," sets the security so the sales staff can access this folder, and places the Sales Forecast report in the folder. Immediately after the administrator is finished, a sales person brings up Report Manager through Report Server C. The sales person can browse the contents of the Sales Forecasts 2004 folder and will be able to run the Sales Forecast report.

As with the distributed installation, the web farm installation provides a way to handle a large number of simultaneous requests for reports. Even though the web farm uses a number of servers to deliver reports, it allows the Report Manager interface to be administered without duplication of effort. The web farm installation may take additional effort to get up and running, but once it is ready to go, it provides a very efficient means of serving a large number of users.

Installation Requirements

We have briefly touched on some of the required software for many of the Reporting Services items. In this section, we will itemize these requirements with respect to each of the three installation types. Before we get to that, however, let's take a look at the hardware requirements for Reporting Services.

Hardware Requirements

The first thing to keep in mind when considering what computer hardware to use for Reporting Services is "bigger and faster is better." With Reporting Services, we are dealing with a server application that will be handling requests from a number of users at the same time. In most installations, the Report Server service will be sharing processor time and computer memory with IIS and SQL Server 2000. We need to have enough server power so that all three of these systems can happily coexist.

Processor   Microsoft's stated minimum processor is a 500 MHz Pentium II. You should install Reporting Services on this type of computer only if you are a very patient person. A more realistic low end is probably a Pentium III at or near 1 GHz. This is true even for the report designer installation. Visual Studio .NET 2003 demands a fair amount of horsepower to keep it from being sluggish.

Computer Memory   Microsoft's minimum requirement for computer memory is 256MB with a recommendation of 512MB or more. In this case, you should treat the recommended amount as your minimum. If you are running Reporting Services on the same server with IIS and SQL Server, that minimum should probably go up to 1GB.

Disk Space   A server installation of Reporting Services requires a minimum of 50MB of disk space. This does not include the space required for SQL Server 2000 or IIS. Consult the Microsoft website for information on the disk space requirements for these items.

A report designer installation requires a minimum of 30MB of disk space. Plan on using an additional 145MB if you are installing the sample reports. Taken all together, you are going to need a minimum of 225MB of disk space for a full installation of Reporting Services.

Remember that these requirements are minimums. Also, keep in mind that they do not include the space required for reports to be deployed to the server or project files created by Visual Studio. A Reporting Services installation is not very useful if there is no room for reports.

Software Requirements

As we consider the software requirements, we will first look at the requirements for a server installation and then the requirements for the report designer installation. From these, you can determine the requirements for the other installation types.

Server Installation   The following software must be installed and running properly on your computer before you can complete a server installation:

- ▶ The latest service pack for your Windows version. (For Windows 2000, this is SP4. For Windows XP, this is SP1a.)
- ▶ SQL Server 2000 with Service Pack 3a.
- ▶ Internet Information Services (IIS) 5.0 or higher.
- ▶ The .NET Framework version 1.1. (This is installed as part of Windows 2003 or Windows XP. It must be installed separately on Windows 2000.)
- ▶ ASP.NET support must be enabled in IIS. (See the "Other Installation Considerations" section for more on this.)
- ▶ Microsoft Data Access Components (MDAC) 2.6 or higher.

Report Designer Installation   The following software must be installed and running properly on your computer before you can complete a report designer installation:

- ▶ Visual Studio .NET 2003.
- ▶ .NET Framework version 1.1. (If it is not already available on your computer, this is installed as part of the Windows Component Update that is done as the first step in installing Visual Studio .NET 2003.)

Other Installation Considerations

You need to keep several other tidbits of information in mind as you are planning your Reporting Services installation. Many of these items are listed here.

General Server Considerations

The following are some of the things to keep in mind as you are planning which server or servers to use for your installation:

► You cannot install more than one copy of the Report Server service on a single computer.

► Reporting Services cannot be installed on a Windows 2003 computer configured as a primary domain controller (PDC).

► If you create a distributed installation, the Reporting Services server, the IIS server, and the database server must all be in the same domain or in domains that have a trust relationship. If you create a web farm installation, all the report servers and the database server must be in the same domain or in domains that have a trust relationship.

Database Server Considerations

The following are some of the things to keep in mind as you are determining which server will host the Reporting Services databases:

► The Report Server and Report Server Temp DB databases must be hosted by SQL Server 2000. They cannot be hosted by an earlier version of SQL Server, SQL Server Personal Edition, or the Microsoft Data Engine (MSDE).

► If you do not wish to use the default name for the Reporting Services database (ReportServer), you can specify a different name. The database name you specify must be 117 characters or fewer.

IIS Server Considerations

The following are some of the things to keep in mind as you are determining which server will host the Reporting Services website and web service:

► You must be able to use http://<servername> to access the default website on the IIS server. For example, if the server is named MyRSServer, the default website on this server must have a URL of http://MyRSServer.

▶ The Reporting Services installation creates two virtual directories under the default website. The Reports virtual directory hosts the website that provides the Report Manager interface. The ReportServer virtual directory hosts the Report Server web service.

▶ If you do not wish to use the default names for these virtual directories (Reports and ReportServer), you may specify different names. The virtual directory names that you specify must be 50 characters or fewer.

E-Mail (SMTP) Server

If you are going to allow users to subscribe to reports and have them e-mailed, you will need to specify the address of an SMTP server during the Reporting Services installation. SMTP stands for Simple Mail Transfer Protocol. It is the standard for exchanging e-mail across the Internet. You need to specify the address of an e-mail server that will accept e-mail messages from the Report Server service and send them to the appropriate recipients.

In many cases, the address of your e-mail server is the same as the portion of your e-mail address that comes after the "@" sign, prefaced by "www.". For example, if your e-mail address is MyEmail@Galactic.com, your e-mail server's address is probably either www.Galactic.com or smtp.Galactic.com. Be sure to verify the address of your e-mail server with your e-mail administrator. Also, make sure that this e-mail server supports the SMTP protocol and that it will accept and forward mail originating from other servers on your network.

Enabling ASP.NET

Support for ASP.NET must be enabled in IIS before the Report Manager interface will work properly. You can check if ASP.NET support is enabled by doing the following:

1. Start the Internet Information Services Management Console from the Control Panel. (You may need to switch to Administrative Tools when in the Control Panel.)
2. Expand the Local Computer node.
3. Expand the Web Sites node.
4. Right-click the Default Web Site node and select Properties from the context menu.
5. Select the Home Directory tab of the Default Web Site Properties dialog box.

6. Click Configuration.

7. On the Mappings tab of the Application Configuration dialog box, you should see an entry for ".aspx" as shown in Figure 2-5. If this entry exists, ASP.NET is enabled in IIS.

8. Click and drag the line between the Executable Path and Verbs headings to widen the Executable Path column. You'll see a folder in this path that includes the version number of the .NET Framework. For example, the path may be

```
C:\WINDOWS\Microsoft.NET\Framework\v1.1.4322
```

where v1.1.4322 is the version of the .NET Framework.

NOTE

If you are using a version of the .NET Framework prior to v1.1.4322, you will have to upgrade to the current version of the .NET Framework. This can be downloaded from Microsoft at no charge.

9. Click Cancel to exit all dialog boxes; then exit the Internet Information Services Management Console.

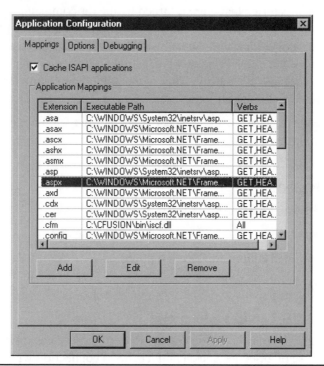

Figure 2-5   *Checking for ASP.NET support*

If there is not an entry for .aspx, use the following procedure to enable ASP.NET support:

1. Open a command window. (One way to open a command window is to select Start | Programs | Accessories | Command Prompt.)
2. Change to the C: drive if you are not already there.
3. If you are using Windows XP or Windows 2003, type

    ```
    cd \windows\microsoft.net\framework
    ```

    and press ENTER.

    If you are using Windows 2000, type

    ```
    cd \WINNT\microsoft.net\framework
    ```

    and press ENTER.
4. Type the following and then press ENTER:

    ```
    dir v*
    ```
5. Look at the directories that were returned by the dir command. One or more of these directories will have a "v" followed by a version number. For example, you may see a directory with the name v1.1.4322. These directories represent the versions of the .NET Framework installed on this computer. Determine which directory has the latest version of the .NET Framework (the directory with the biggest number after the "v").
6. Change to the directory with the latest version of the .NET Framework by typing a command similar to

    ```
    cd v1.1.4322
    ```

    and pressing ENTER.
7. Type the following and press ENTER:

    ```
    aspiis_regiis -i
    ```

    This program will enable ASP.NET support.
8. Type **exit** and press ENTER.

Encrypting Reporting Services Information

One of the options you may select during the Reporting Services installation process is to require the use of a Secure Sockets Layer (SSL) connection when accessing the Reports website and the Report Server web service. When an SSL connection is used, all the data transmitted across the network is encrypted so that it cannot be intercepted and read by anyone else. This is very important if your reports contain sensitive personal or financial information.

To use SSL on a server, the server must have a server certificate. Server certificates are purchased from a certificate authority and installed on your server. You can find information on certificate authorities on the Internet.

Each server certificate is associated with a specific URL. To use SSL with the Reports website and Report Server web service, your server certificate must be associated with the URL that corresponds to the default website on the server. If www.MyRSServer.com takes you to the default website on your server, then the server certificate must be associated with www.MyRSServer.com. If you are planning on requiring an SSL connection, you should obtain and install the appropriate server certificate prior to installing Reporting Services.

When you require the use of an SSL connection to access the Reports website and the Report Server web service, your users must specify a slightly different URL to access these locations. For instance, if the users would normally use http://www.MyRSServer.com/Reports to get to the Reports website, they will now have to use https://www.MyRSServer.com/Reports. The "https" in place of the "http" creates the SSL connection.

Microsoft Distributed Transaction Coordinator

The Reporting Services setup program uses the Microsoft Distributed Transaction Coordinator (MS DTC) to help control the setup process. You need to make sure that the MS DTC will be available to the setup program. To do this, go to the Control Panel and select Administrative Tools and then double-click Services. In the list of services, find the entry for Distributed Transaction Coordinator. The entry in the Startup Type column should be Manual or Automatic, as shown in Figure 2-6.

If the Startup Type is Disabled, use the following procedure:

1. Double-click the entry for Distributed Transaction Coordinator in the Services window.

2. Select Manual from the Startup Type drop-down box in the Distributed Transaction Coordinator Properties (Local Computer) dialog box (see Figure 2-7).

3. Click OK.

4. Close the Services window.

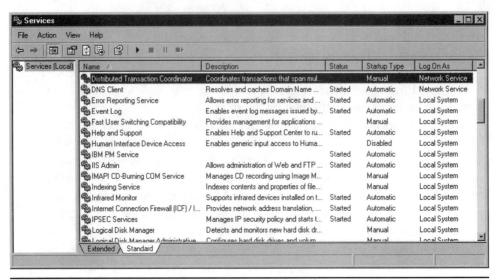

Figure 2-6   *The services entry for the Distributed Transaction Coordinator*

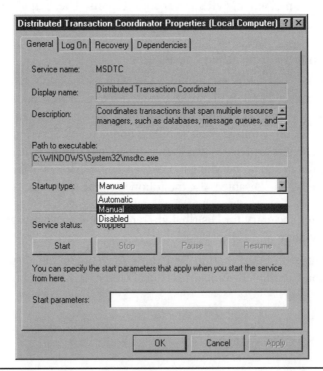

Figure 2-7   *The Distributed Transaction Coordinator Properties (Local Computer) dialog box*

Login Accounts

The login account you are logged in as when you run the setup program must have administrative rights on the computer where the installation is being done. If you are doing a distributed or web farm installation, the login account must have administrative rights on both the computer that will be the Report Server and the computer that will be the database server.

The login account you are logged in as must also have system administration rights in the SQL Server 2000 installation that will contain the Report Catalog. The setup program uses this login to access SQL Server and create the items necessary for the Report Catalog. You may specify a different login, either a SQL login or a Windows login for the Report Server to use when accessing the Report Catalog after the installation is complete.

You will be asked to specify several login accounts during the Reporting Services installation. Make your choices ahead of time and track down any passwords you may need before you begin the installation process.

The Report Server Service Login Account for Windows   First of all, you will be asked to specify the login account used by the Report Server service. You can choose from the following types of accounts:

▶   **The built-in account NT AUTHORITY\SYSTEM (also called the local system account)**   The local system account has access to almost all resources on the local computer and may or may not have access to resources on other computers in the network.

▶   **The built-in local service account**   This account exists on Windows 2003 servers for running services. This account cannot access other servers on the network. This choice will only be available if you are installing Reporting Services on Windows 2003.

▶   **The built-in network service account**   This account exists on Windows 2003 servers for running services. This account can access other servers on the network. This choice will only be available if you are installing Reporting Services on Windows 2003.

▶   **A domain user account**   This is a regular user account that exists in the domain in which this server resides.

Microsoft recommends that the local system account be used as the login for the Report Server service. Using the local system account ensures that the Report Server service has all the rights it needs on the local server.

The Report Server Web Service Login Account for Windows

The second login account required by the Reporting Services installation is used by the Report Server web service. If you are installing on any Windows platform other than Windows 2003, you do not have a choice here. The Report Server web service will be required to use the login account configured for ASP.NET on this computer.

If you are installing Reporting Services on Windows 2003, you will be able to choose between the network service account and the local system account for this login. The network service account is used by services to log on to the local machine. It has the added advantage of being able to log on to other computers in the network. When you're installing on Windows 2003, the network service account is the default for the Report Server web service login.

The Report Server Service Login Account for the Database Server

The third login account required by the Reporting Services installation is used by the Report Server service to log in to SQL Server and access the Report Server and Report Server Temp DB databases. As noted earlier, this login account is used after the installation is complete. It is not used to access SQL Server during the installation process.

You have four options:

▶   The login account used by the Report Server service to log in to Windows

▶   The built-in local system account

▶   A domain user account

▶   A SQL Server login

You will need to work with the database administrator of your SQL Server to determine which of these options to use.

NOTE

If a SQL Server login other than sa is used, the SQL Server login must be added to the RSExecRole role in the ReportServer, ReportServerTempDB, master and msdb databases.

Running the Reporting Services Setup Program

When you run the Reporting Services setup program, you need to run it under a login that is a member of the local system administrators group. In addition, your login will need to have administrator permissions in SQL Server so you can perform the following tasks:

- ► Create SQL logins
- ► Create SQL roles
- ► Create databases
- ► Assign roles to logins

The Installation Process

Now that you have worked through all the preparation, it is finally time to install Reporting Services. We will walk through the steps necessary to perform each type of Reporting Services installation.

The Full Installation and the Server Installation

The steps for performing a full installation are very similar to the steps for performing a server installation. This section covers both of these installations and points out the few differences as they occur in the procedure.

Begin the installation by inserting the Reporting Services installation CD into your CD or DVD drive. In most cases, the autorun process should start the setup program. If this does not happen automatically, navigate to the setup.exe program on the installation CD and execute it.

Preliminaries

The setup process begins by taking care of some housekeeping and checking to make sure all the prerequisite software is installed and properly configured.

The End User License Agreement Screen   The first step of the Setup Wizard is the End User License Agreement screen. Review the license agreement as needed. When you are comfortable with the terms of the license agreement, check the check box to accept the terms and click Next to continue.

The Component Update Screen   The next step is the Component Update screen. Here, the wizard will check your system to make sure it has all the components needed to run the setup itself. It is making sure that you have the following:

- ► Windows Installer 2.0
- ► Microsoft .NET Framework version 1.1

► Setup support files (any compressed files on the installation CD that need to be expanded before they can be used)

You may have to wait a moment or two while the Component Update screen checks to make sure these items are installed. If it discovers one or more of these components are not available, the Install button will appear on the screen. Click Install to install the missing components. You will need to wait again for the install to complete.

When the install is complete, or if all the components were found, the Next button will appear on the screen, as shown in Figure 2-8. Click Next to continue.

The System Prerequisites Check Screen   After the Component Update screen, you will see the System Prerequisites Check screen. Here, the wizard will check for the following:

► Internet Information Services is installed and running.

► The default website is enabled.

► ASP.NET support is enabled in IIS.

► Visual Studio .NET 2003 is installed.

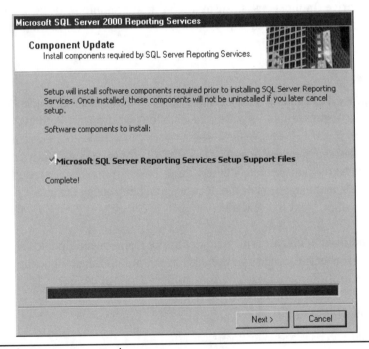

Figure 2-8   *The Component Update screen*

Any of these not found by the System Prerequisites Check screen will be marked with a red X, as shown in Figure 2-9.

If you are doing a full installation, all the required items should be found, as shown in Figure 2-10. If any of these items are not found, you need to cancel the setup, remedy the problem, and start the installation again. See the previous sections of this chapter if you need more information on these prerequisites.

If you are doing a server installation, Visual Studio .NET 2003 is not needed. If Visual Studio .NET 2003 is marked with a red X, you may ignore it. If any of the other items are not found, you need to cancel the setup, remedy the problem, and start the installation again. Again, see the previous sections of this chapter if you need more information on these prerequisites.

When all the required items for your type of installation have been found, click Next to continue.

The Installation Process

Now that the preliminaries are completed, the setup program collects the configuration information and completes the actual software installation.

The Welcome to Microsoft SQL Server 2000 Reporting Services Setup Screen   After you click Next on the System Prerequisites Check screen, the Preparing to Install… dialog box will appear briefly. This will be replaced by the Welcome to Microsoft SQL Server 2000 Reporting Services Setup screen. It may take a few moments for the Next button to appear on this screen as the setup finishes loading. When the Next button does appear, click it to continue.

The Registration Information Screen   The Welcome screen is followed by the Registration Information screen. Fill in the Name and Company items, if they are blank. Click Next to continue.

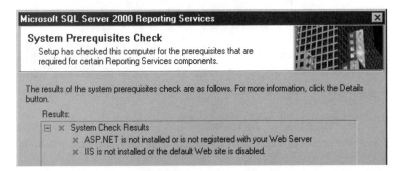

Figure 2-9   *The System Prerequisites Check screen with required software missing*

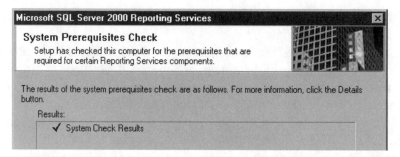

Figure 2-10 *The System Prerequisites Check screen with all required software detected*

The Feature Selection Screen for the Full Installation

NOTE

If you are doing a full installation, follow the instructions in this section. If you are doing a server installation, follow the instructions in the section "The Feature Selection Screen for the Server Installation."

The Feature Selection screen will appear next. By default, the Feature Selection screen will appear as shown in Figure 2-11. All the features that make up Reporting Services are marked for install except for Reporting Services Sample Reports and AdventureWorks database.

To perform a full installation of Reporting Services, click on each red X and select Will Be Installed on Local Hard Drive from the context menu. This is shown here.

When you have everything selected for a full installation, the screen will appear as shown in Figure 2-12. When you have all the features selected, click Next. Skip over the next section and continue with the section "The Service Account Screen."

The Feature Selection Screen for the Server Installation   The Feature Selection screen will appear next. By default, the Feature Selection screen will appear as shown in

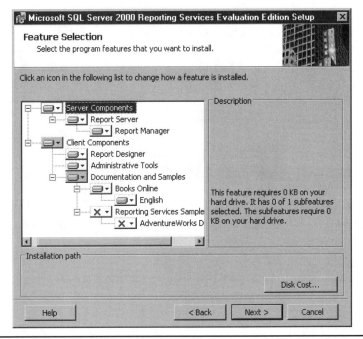

Figure 2-11   *The Feature Selection screen with the default configuration*

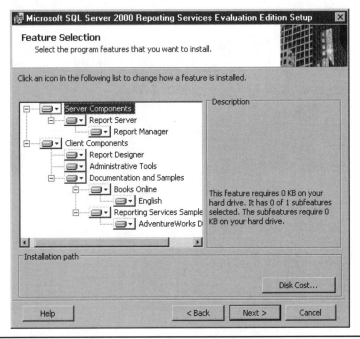

Figure 2-12   *The Feature Selection screen for a full installation*

Figure 2-11. All the features that make up Reporting Services are marked for install except for Reporting Services Sample Reports and AdventureWorks database.

To perform a server installation of Reporting Services, click the computer icon next to Client Components and select Entire Feature Will Be Unavailable from the context menu. This is shown here.

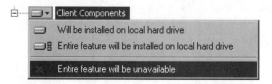

Next, click the X next to the Administrative Tools and select Will Be Installed on Local Hard Drive from the context menu. Your screen should now appear as shown in Figure 2-13. Click Next.

The Service Account Screen   Next you will see the Service Account screen, as shown in Figure 2-14. On this screen you will select the login account used by the Report Server service. If you are installing on Windows 2003, you will also be able to select

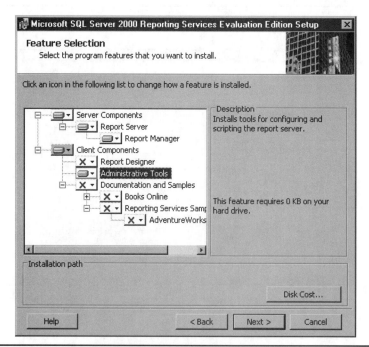

Figure 2-13   *The Feature Selection screen for a server installation*

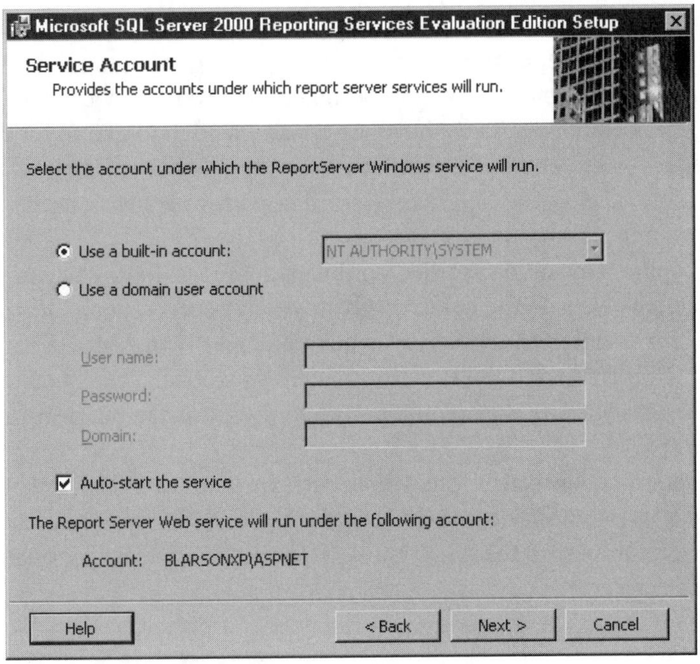

Figure 2-14   *The Service Account screen*

the login account used by the Report Server web service. If you are installing on any other version of Windows, the Report Server web service login account will be displayed in the lower part of the screen, as shown in Figure 2-14, and no selection will be necessary. If you have any questions on specifying either of the login accounts required on this screen, refer back to the "Login Accounts" section in this chapter.

The other option that must be specified on this screen is whether the Report Server service should start automatically each time the computer starts up. This is known as *auto-starting the service.* This option should be checked in almost all cases.

If you are doing a full installation of Reporting Services on a development computer where Reporting Services development will be done only occasionally, you may not want to have the Report Server service running all the time. In this case, the option should be unchecked. If the Auto-start the Service check box is unchecked, you will have to manually start the Report Server service any time you want to make use of it.

If you are doing a server installation, the Auto-start the Service check box should be checked. On a server machine, we want the Report Server service to run all the time so it is available to deliver reports.

Once you have made your selections on the Service Account screen, click Next.

The Reporting Services Virtual Directories Screen   The Reporting Services Virtual Directories screen will appear next. This screen is shown in Figure 2-15. On this screen you specify the names that will be assigned to the web service and the website used by Reporting Services. As we have discussed, the default name for the web service is ReportServer, and the default name for the website is Reports. These names should not be changed unless they conflict with websites or web services already in use on this computer.

Two other options must be specified on this page. First of all, you can make the Reporting Services website the default website on this server. For example, if you do so and the server is called MyRSServer, when you enter **http://MyRSServer** in your browser, you will be taken to the Reporting Services website. You should make the Reporting Services website the default website only if it is the main website hosted by this server.

The final option on this screen is to use Secure Sockets Layer (SSL) when retrieving data from the Reporting Services website and web service. If you have any questions on this option, refer back to the "Encrypting Reporting Services Information" section in this chapter.

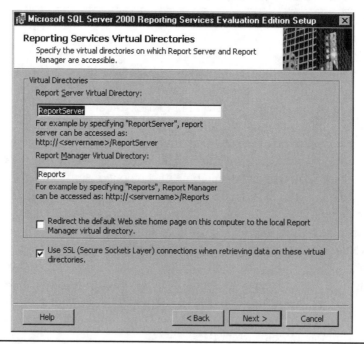

Figure 2-15   *The Reporting Services Virtual Directories screen*

The Use SSL (Secure Sockets Layer) Connections When Retrieving Data on These Virtual Directories check box is checked by default. If you wish to require an SSL connection and you have the appropriate server certificate installed on your server, you may leave this item checked. If, however, you do not have a server certificate installed, you must uncheck this item.

Once you have made your selections on the Reporting Services Virtual Directories screen, click Next. If you left the Use SSL... check box checked and you do not have the appropriate server certificate installed, you will see a warning dialog box when you click Next. If this occurs, click OK in the dialog box, uncheck the Use SSL... check box, and click Next again.

The Report Server Database Screen   Next you will see the Report Server Database screen. This screen is shown in Figure 2-16. It allows you to specify where the SQL Server databases used by Reporting Services will be created, what they will be called, and how they will be accessed.

For a full installation or a server installation, the SQL Server databases used by Reporting Services will reside on the computer on which you are running the setup. The name of this computer will be the default value for the SQL Server instance. We will discuss distributed and web farm installations later in this chapter.

Next, you will need to specify the name of the database. The default value is ReportServer. You should leave the default value unless this name conflicts with another database already installed on this computer.

Finally, you will need to specify the login account used to access this database. If you have any questions on specifying the login account required on this screen, refer back to the "Login Accounts" section in this chapter.

Once you have made your selections on the Report Server Database screen, click Next.

The Report Server Delivery Settings Screen   The Report Server Delivery Settings screen will be displayed next, as shown in Figure 2-17. If you plan on allowing users to have report subscriptions e-mailed to them, enter the address of the SMTP server that should be used by Reporting Services to deliver these e-mails. If you have any questions on specifying an SMTP server address, refer back to the "E-Mail (SMTP) Server" section in this chapter.

You can also specify the e-mail address that will be placed in the from field of any e-mails sent by Reporting Services. This does not need to be a valid e-mail address. However, in many cases, it is a good idea to use an address that is monitored by the person responsible for administering Reporting Services. That way, if a user has a

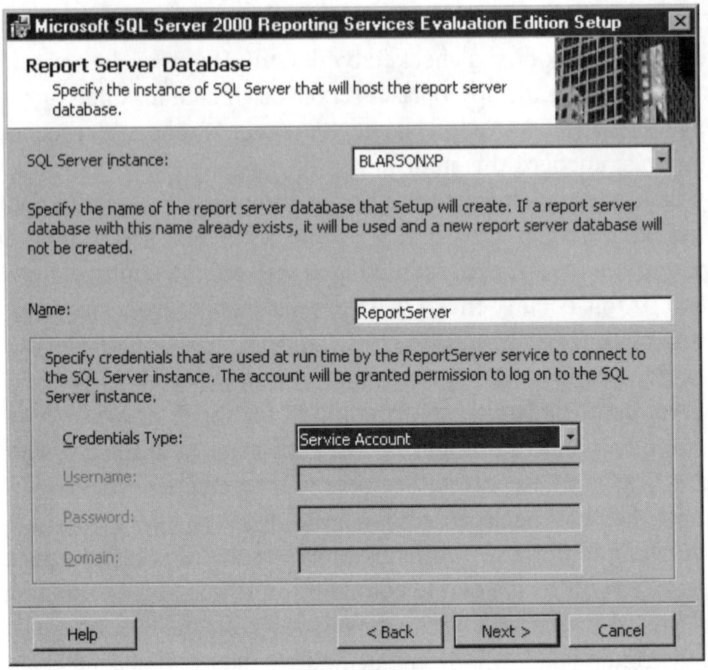

Figure 2-16 *The Report Server Database screen*

problem with a subscription report and sends a reply e-mail to the subscription, they will actually contact someone who can help them out.

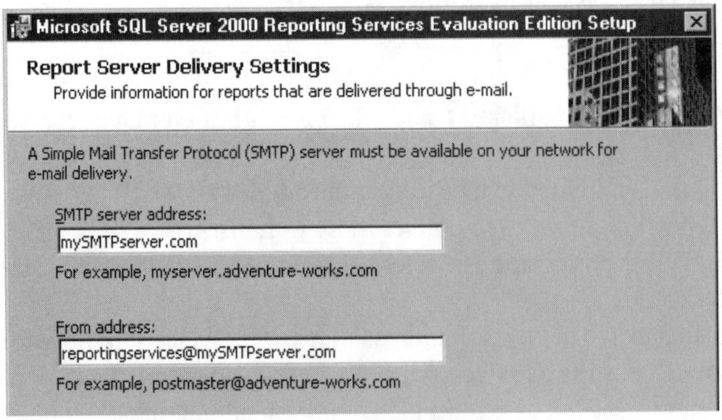

Figure 2-17 *The Report Server Delivery Settings screen*

If you do not want to enable e-mail subscriptions, you may leave all the items on this screen blank. Once you have made your selections on the Report Server Delivery Settings screen, click Next.

The Report Server Samples Setup Screen   If you are doing a full installation, you will see the Report Server Samples Setup screen. This is shown in Figure 2-18. If you are doing a server installation, skip to the section "The License Mode Screen."

Here, you can specify the SQL Server that will contain the AdventureWorks database used by the sample reports. For a full installation, the AdventureWorks database will reside on the computer on which you are running the setup. The name of this computer will be the default value for the SQL Server instance.

Once you have made your selection on the Report Server Samples Setup screen, click Next.

The Licensing Mode Screen   You will now see the Licensing Mode screen, as shown in Figure 2-19. The information you enter here should match the licensing you have for the SQL Server that is hosting the Reporting Services databases. For example, if the computer you are using for this full installation of Reporting Services has a per-processor license of SQL Server and has two processors, you should select the Per Processor License radio button and enter **2** in the Processors text box.

Once you have entered your licensing information, click Next.

Completing the Installation

The next screen is the Ready to Install screen. You have supplied all the necessary information for the setup program to complete the installation. Click Install.

The Installing Reporting Services screen appears. This screen shows you the progress of the installation process. This may take a few minutes. Once the

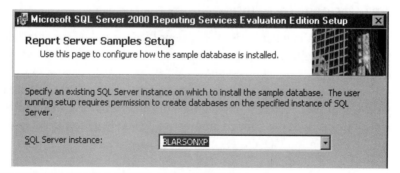

Figure 2-18   *The Report Server Samples Setup screen*

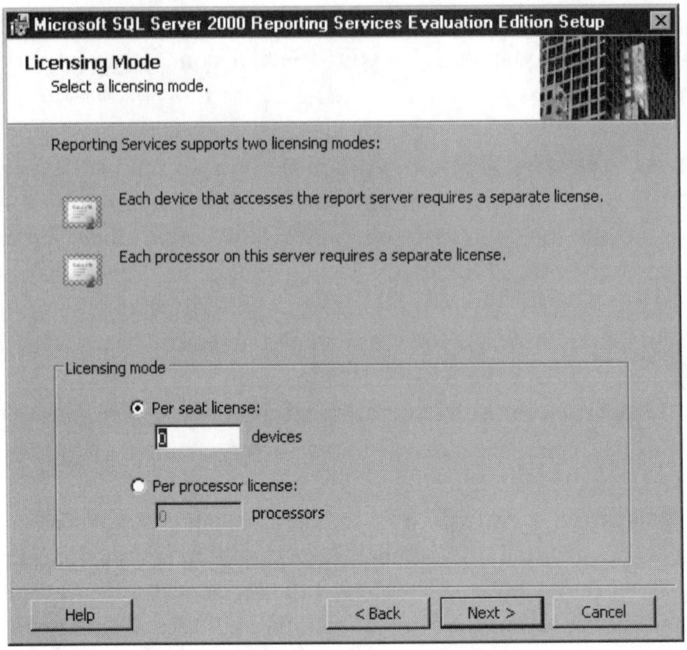

Figure 2-19   *The Licensing Mode screen*

installation process completes, the Completing the Microsoft SQL Server 2000 Reporting Services Setup screen appears. Click Finish.

Congratulations, you have successfully completed a Reporting Services installation. If you encountered problems during the installation process, refer to the "Common Installation Issues" section later in this chapter.

The Report Designer Installation

The report designer installation includes fewer steps than the full or server installations. Because we are not installing any databases, websites, or services, fewer configuration choices are required.

Begin the report designer installation by inserting the Reporting Services installation CD into your CD or DVD drive. In most cases, the autorun process should start the setup program. If this does not happen automatically, navigate to the setup.exe program on the installation CD and execute it.

Preliminaries

The setup process begins by taking care of some housekeeping and checking to make sure all the prerequisite software is installed and properly configured.

The End User License Agreement Screen   The first step of the Setup Wizard is the End User License Agreement screen. Review the license agreement as needed. When you are comfortable with the terms of the license agreement, check the check box to accept the terms and click Next to continue.

The Component Update Screen   The next step is the Component Update screen. Here, the wizard will check your system to make sure it has all the components needed to run the setup itself. It is making sure that you have the following:

- ▶ Windows Installer 2.0
- ▶ Microsoft .NET Framework version 1.1
- ▶ Setup support files (any compressed files on the installation CD that need to be expanded before they can be used)

You may have to wait a moment or two while the component update is being done. When the update is complete, as shown in Figure 2-20, click Next to continue.

The System Prerequisites Check Screen   After the Component Update screen, you will see the System Prerequisites Check screen, as shown in Figure 2-21. Here, the wizard will check for the following:

- ▶ Internet Information Server is installed and running.
- ▶ The default website is enabled.
- ▶ ASP.NET support is enabled in IIS.
- ▶ Visual Studio .NET 2003 is installed.

Since we are doing a report designer installation, some or possibly all of these items may not be found. The first three prerequisite items are not required for a report designer installation, so you may ignore those red X's and click Next to continue. However, if Visual Studio is not found, you will need to cancel the installation and install Visual Studio .NET 2003 before continuing.

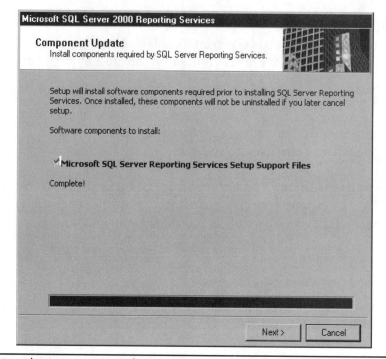

Figure 2-20 *The Component Update screen*

The Installation Process

Now that the preliminaries are completed, the setup program collects the configuration information and completes the actual software installation.

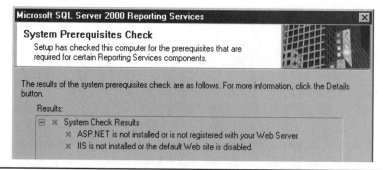

Figure 2-21 *The System Prerequisites Check screen for a report designer installation*

The Welcome to Microsoft SQL Server 2000 Reporting Services Setup Screen   After you click Next on the System Prerequisites Check screen, the Preparing to Install… dialog box will appear briefly. This will be replaced by the Welcome to Microsoft SQL Server 2000 Reporting Services Setup screen. It may take a few moments for the Next button to appear on this screen as the setup finishes loading. When the Next button does appear, click it to continue.

The Registration Information Screen   The Welcome screen is followed by the Registration Information screen. Fill in the Name and Company items, if they are blank. Click Next to continue.

The Feature Selection Screen   The Feature Selection screen will appear next. By default, the Feature Selection screen will appear as shown in Figure 2-22. All the features that make up Reporting Services are marked for install except for Reporting Services Sample Reports and AdventureWorks database.

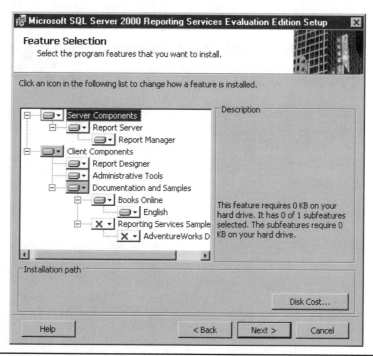

Figure 2-22   *The Feature Selection screen with the default configuration*

To perform a report designer installation of Reporting Services, click the computer icon next to Server Components and select Entire Feature Will Be Unavailable from the context menu. This is shown here.

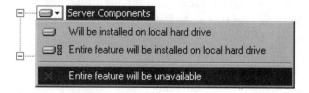

When your screen appears as shown in Figure 2-23, click Next.

Completing the Installation

The next screen is the Ready to Install screen. You have supplied all the necessary information for the setup program to complete the installation. Click Install.

The Installing Reporting Services screen appears. This screen shows you the progress of the installation process. Once the installation process completes, the

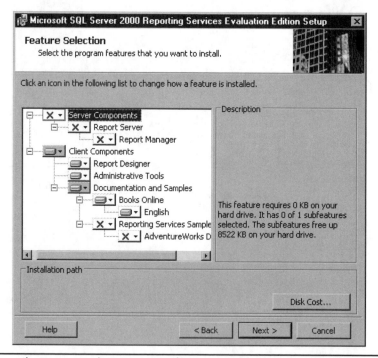

Figure 2-23   *The Feature Selection screen for a report designer installation*

Completing the Microsoft SQL Server 2000 Reporting Services Setup screen appears. Click Finish.

Congratulations, you have successfully completed a report designer installation. The Business Intelligence project types are now available in Visual Studio and the Reporting Services Books Online can be viewed on this computer. If you encountered problems during the installation process, refer to the "Common Installation Issues" section later in this chapter.

The Distributed Installation

The distributed installation is similar to the server installation. To create a distributed installation, run the setup program on the computer you will be using as a report server. Follow the procedures for a server installation except as specified in the following section.

The Report Server Database Screen for a Distributed Installation

When you reach the Report Server Database screen, you will not be using the default value for the SQL Server instance. Instead, enter or select the name of the server that you will be using for the database server. The database server should, of course, already have SQL Server 2000 installed and running on it.

Next, you will need to specify the name of the database. The default value is ReportServer. You should leave the default value unless this name conflicts with another database already installed on the database server.

Finally, you will need to specify the login account used to access this database. You will need to either use a SQL Server login or use a domain login that has rights on the report server and the database server.

Once you have made your selections on the Report Server Database screen, click Next.

The Web Farm Installation

The web farm installation is similar to the distributed installation. In fact, the way to create a web farm installation is to run the distributed installation on several computers that will be Report Servers. The key to creating a web farm is the selections you make each time you reach the Report Server Database screen.

The Report Server Database Screen for a Web Farm Installation

When you reach the Report Server Database screen, you will not be using the default value for the SQL Server instance. Instead, enter or select the name of the server that you will be using for the database server. The database server should, of course, already have SQL Server 2000 installed and running on it.

In order to create a web farm, you must specify the same server name each time you reach the Report Server Database screen. This will cause all your Report Servers to connect to the same database server to access the Report Server database.

Next, you will need to specify the name of the database. The default value is ReportServer. You should leave the default value unless this name conflicts with another database already installed on the database server.

Again, in order to create a web farm, you need to specify exactly the same name for the database each time. This will cause all your Report Servers to connect to the same Report Server database. When you install the first Report Server, the setup program will create the Report Server database on the database server. Each subsequent time you install a Report Server, the setup program will not create a new database but instead will configure Reporting Services to use the database that already exists.

Finally, you will need to specify the login account used to access this database. You will need to either use a SQL Server login or use a domain login that has rights on the Report Server and the database server.

Once you have made your selections on the Report Server Database screen, click Next.

The Report Server Web Farm Setup Screen

When doing a web farm installation, you will see a new screen after the Report Server Database screen. This is the Report Server Web Farm Setup screen, shown in Figure 2-24. In the Report Server text box, type the name of the Reporting Services server that originally created the Report Server database that this computer will be using. For example, if ReportServerA is the first server you installed in the web farm, this installation will create the database on the database server. When you do subsequent installations on computers that are joining the web farm, you will enter **ReportServerA** in the Report Server text box on the Report Server Web Farm Setup screen.

In the lower portion of the screen, enter a login account that has administrative rights on the computer whose name you entered at the top of the screen. For example, if you entered ReportServerA in the Report Server text box, you need to specify a login account that has administrative rights on ReportServerA.

Once the Report Server Web Farm Setup screen is complete, click Next. The setup will continue with the Report Server Delivery Settings screen.

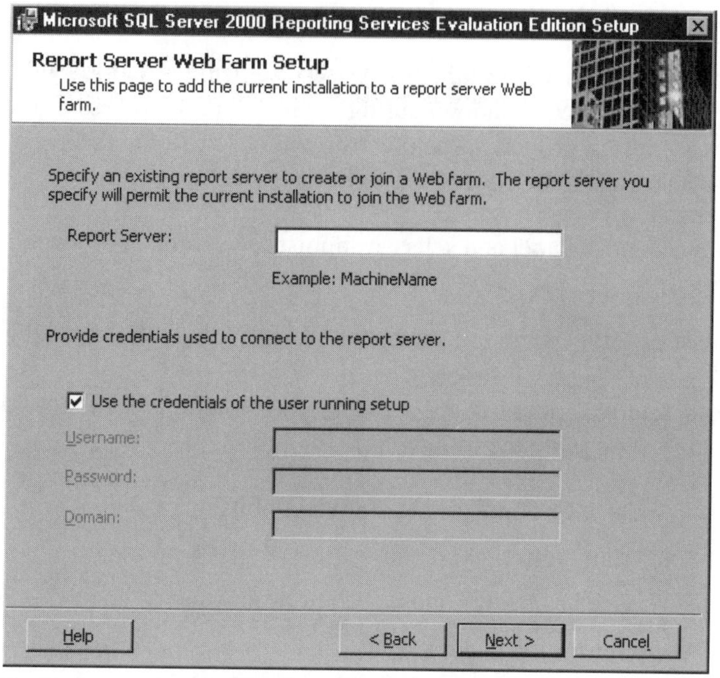

Figure 2-24   *The Report Server Web Farm Setup screen*

Common Installation Issues

This section lists some of the common problems you may encounter while installing Reporting Services. Suggested solutions are provided to help you resolve these problems.

The Setup Error Screen

If the setup program encounters an error during the setup process, it will display a screen alerting you to the error and ask you how to proceed. In most cases, you'll see a Retry button and an Ignore button, along with the other choices at the bottom of the screen.

Retry

Any computer professional worth their salt will not believe an error message the first time it occurs. Therefore, your first step in troubleshooting an installation error is to click Retry and see if the error screen returns.

Manually Start IIS

The setup program stops and restarts the IIS service (called "World Wide Web Publishing" in the Services window) during the installation process. If the IIS service does not restart properly, a setup error will occur. If you receive a setup error, check the status of the IIS service as follows:

1. Go to the Control Panel and select Administrative Tools.
2. Double-click Services.
3. In the list of services, find the entry for World Wide Web Publishing.

If the word "Started" does not appear in the Status column for the World Wide Web Publishing service, do the following:

1. Right-click the entry for World Wide Web Publishing.
2. Select Start from the context menu.
3. Once the service has started, close the Services window.
4. On the setup error screen, click Retry.

Ignore

If neither of the previous processes got rid of the error screen and the Ignore button is present, select it so that the setup will continue and, hopefully, run to completion. Once the setup is complete, you can use the information provided here and through other sources to correct the problem and get your installation up and running.

Administrative Rights

One of the biggest problems with the Reporting Services setup is not using login accounts that have the appropriate rights. If you encounter an error during installation, refer back to the "Login Accounts" section of this chapter and make sure you are using login accounts that have the appropriate rights.

If you discover you received a setup error because one of the login accounts you used was not adequate to the task, remove the failed installation of Reporting Services and try again. To remove the failed installation, select Add or Remove Programs from the Control Panel and choose to remove Reporting Services.

Server Components Not Shown on the Feature Selection Screen

If you are performing an installation that requires the server components, but they are not present on the Feature Selection screen, this is probably an indication that you are not up-to-date on your Windows service packs. Reporting Services is finicky about this. As stated earlier, the Reporting Services installation process requires Service Pack 4 if you are using Windows 2000 and Service Pack 1a if you are using Windows XP Professional.

If you encounter this problem, cancel the installation, install the latest service pack for your version of Windows, then start the installation process again.

Installation Error 1603

You may receive Error 1603 if you are doing a Report Designer Installation of Reporting Services on a computer that is not running Internet Information Services. The Reporting Services installation looks for a user called ASPNET. This user is created by the .NET Framework installation on computers running IIS. If there is not IIS running, no ASPNET user is created.

This problem is solved by creating a local user called ASPNET on the computer where you are doing the Report Designer Installation. This user does not need to have any particular password or any particular rights on the computer. For a Report Designer installation, a user with this name simply needs to exist on the computer.

Installation Error 2755

You may receive Error 2755 if you are installing Reporting Services using a Terminal Server session. This will occur if you are using a mapped drive to access the setup files. The Windows Installer service that actually performs the setup operation is running in a different Windows session, so it may not have the same drive mappings. The error occurs because certain files needed by the installer cannot be found.

To remedy this problem, use a UNC path to access the setup files rather than a mapped drive. Alternatively, you may put the installation CD in a drive that is local to the computer on which you are performing the installation or copy the setup files to a drive local to that computer.

Manually Activating Reporting Services

In some cases, the only problem with the Reporting Services installation is that it did not activate properly at the end of the setup process. You can try to manually activate

Reporting Services to remedy this problem. In situations where you ignored a setup error and the setup ran to completion, but Reporting Services does not appear to work, you should try a manual activation.

To manually activate Reporting Services, do the following:

1. Open a command window. (One way to open a command window is to select Start | Programs | Accessories | Command Prompt.)

2. Change to the C: drive if you are not already there.

3. Type the following and then press ENTER:

   ```
   cd \Program Files\Microsoft SQL Server\80\Tools\binn
   ```

4. Type the following on one line, where {username} and {password} represent a login account that has administrative rights, and then press ENTER:

   ```
   RSActivate -c "c:\Program Fields\Microsoft SQL
   Server\MSSQL\Reporting Services\Report
   Server\RSReportServer.config" -u {username} -p {password}
   ```

The RSActivate utility program will attempt to activate the Reporting Services installation specified by the RSReportServer.config file. The results of running RSActivate will be displayed in the command window.

Making the Reports Website Available Outside of Your Network

The Reporting Services setup program assumes that you will be accessing the Reports website using an address similar to http://MyRSServer/Reports. This works fine inside your network, but it probably isn't going to work well if you want to make the Reports website available from outside your network. For instance, if you want to allow users to access the Reports website using an address such as http://www.MyRSServer.com/Reports, you will need to make a change to the configuration created during setup.

To make this change, you will need to find the RSWebApplication.config file. The default location for this file is C:\Program Files\Microsoft SQL Server\MSSQL\ Reporting Services\Report Manager. Open the RSWebApplication.config file with a text editor. The first few lines of the file will be similar to the following:

```
<Configuration>
  <UI>
    <ReportServerUrl>http://MyRSServer/ReportServer</ReportServerUrl>
  </UI>
```

Replace the text between <ReportServerUrl> and </ReportServerUrl> with the complete address that should be used to access the Reports website. In our example, the modified RSWebApplication.config file would look like this:

```
<Configuration>
 <UI>
  <ReportServerUrl>http://www.MyRSServer.com/ReportServer</ReportServerUrl>
 </UI>
```

You will need to restart the IIS service for this change to take effect. Do the following:

1. Go to the Control Panel and select Administrative Tools.
2. Double-click Services.
3. In the list of services, find the entry for World Wide Web Publishing.
4. Right-click this entry and select Restart from the context menu.
5. Close the Services window.

Installing on a SharePoint Server

Reporting Services can be installed on a server that is running SharePoint Services. However, you may encounter activation errors during the installation process. You can ignore these errors and complete the installation. Once the installation is complete, follow the steps in the Reporting Services ReadMe file under "Installing Reporting Services with Windows SharePoint Services" to properly activate Reporting Services.

The Installation Log File

If none of these suggestions solves your installation issues, you may want to consult the installation log file for more information. This log file is a bit tricky to track down. The reason it is hard to find is because it is created inside a CAB file. This makes it easier to send the file to Microsoft support when you ask them to help solve an installation problem. It may make things more efficient for Microsoft support, but it makes it tough for you, if you are looking for a LOG extension as opposed to a CAB extension.

The default location for the log file is:

```
C:\Program Files\Microsoft SQL Server\80\RS Setup Bootstrap\Log\RSStp_.cab
```

Spending Some Time in Basic Training

You now have Reporting Services installed and ready to go. As mentioned at the end of Chapter 1, we will take time to ensure that you understand the basics of database architecture and querying before we actually begin creating reports. Chapter 3 will give you this database basic training. This basic training won't be as tough as army boot camp, but it will get you ready to attack all those tough data-reporting challenges.

Chapter 3 will also introduce you to Galactic Delivery Services (GDS), what it does, how it is structured, and what its data processing systems look like. We will use GDS and its business needs for all our sample reports throughout the book.

Report Authoring

DB 101:
Database Basics

IN THIS CHAPTER:

Database Structure
Galactic Delivery Services
Querying Data
On to the Reports

Before you begin creating reports, it is important that you have a good understanding of relational databases. In the first part of this chapter, you will look at the tables, rows, and columns that make up relational databases. You will also learn about concepts such as normalization and relationships. It is these characteristics that make a relational database…, well, relational.

Once you have covered the basics, you will be introduced to Galactic Delivery Services (GDS). The business needs of GDS will serve as the basis for all the sample reports throughout this book. Even though GDS is a very unique company in many respects, you will discover that its reporting needs and its uses of Reporting Services are typical of most companies in this galaxy.

For the remainder of the chapter, you will explore the ins and outs of the SELECT query. This is what you will use to extract data from your data sources for use in your reports. Even though Reporting Services will help you create SELECT queries through a tool called the Query Builder, it is important that you understand how SELECT queries work and how they can be used to obtain the correct data. A report may look absolutely stunning with charts, graphics, special formatting, and snappy colors, but it is completely useless if it contains the wrong data!

Database Structure

Databases are basically giant containers for storing information. They are the electronic crawlspaces and digital attics of the corporate, academic, and governmental worlds. For example, anything that needs to be saved for later use by payroll, inventory management, or the external auditor is placed in a database.

Just like our crawlspaces and attics at home, the information that is placed in a database needs to be organized and classified. Figure 3-1 shows my attic in its

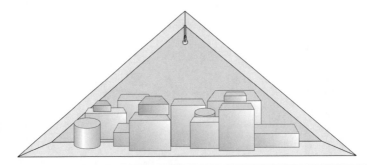

Figure 3-1   *My attic, with no organization*

current state. As you can see, it is going to be pretty hard to find those old kids' clothes for the thrift store clothing drive! I know they are up there somewhere.

Without some type of order placed on it, all the stuff in our home storage spaces becomes impossible to retrieve when we need it. The same is true in the world of electronic storage, as shown in Figure 3-2. Databases, like attics, need structure; otherwise, we won't be able to find anything!

Getting Organized

The first step in getting organized is to have a place for everything and to have everything in its place. In order to achieve this, you need to add structure to the storage space, whether it is a space for box storage like my attic or a space for data storage like a database. In order to maintain this structure, you also need to have discipline of one sort or another as you add items to the storage space.

Tables, Rows, and Columns

To get my attic organized, I need some shelves, a few labels, and some free time so that I can add the much-needed structure to this storage space. To keep my attic organized, I will also need the discipline to pay attention to my new signs each time I put another box into storage. Figure 3-3 shows my attic as it exists in my fantasy world where I have tons of free time and loads of self-discipline.

Structure in the database world comes in the form of tables. Each database is divided up into a number of tables. It is these tables that actually store the information. Each table contains only one type of information. Figure 3-4 shows customer

Figure 3-2   *An unorganized database*

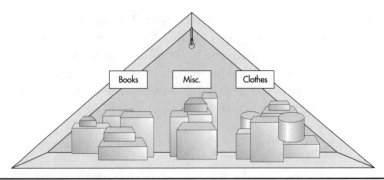

Figure 3-3 *My attic in my fantasy world*

information in one table, payment information in another, and invoice header information in a third.

NOTE

Invoice Header is used as the name of the third table for consistency with the sample database that will be introduced later in this chapter and used throughout the remainder of the book. The Invoice Header name helps to differentiate this table from the Invoice Detail table that stores the detail lines of the invoice. The Invoice Detail table is not discussed here, but it will be present in the sample database.

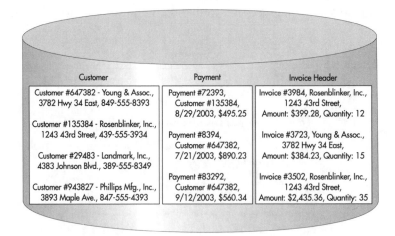

Figure 3-4 *A database organized by tables*

Dividing each table into rows and columns brings additional structure to the database. Figure 3-5 shows the Customer table divided into several rows—one row for each customer whose information is being stored in the table. In addition, the Customer table is divided into a number of columns. Each column is given a name: Customer Number, Customer Name, Address, and Phone. These names tell you what information is being stored in each column.

With a database structured as tables, rows, and columns, you know exactly where to find a certain piece of information. For example, it is pretty obvious that the customer name for customer number 135384 will be found in the Name column of the second row of the Customer table. We are starting to get this data organized, and it was a lot easier than cleaning out the attic!

NOTE

Rows in a database are also called records. *Columns in a database are also called* fields. *Reporting Services uses the terms* rows *and* records *interchangeably. It also uses the terms* columns *and* fields *interchangeably. Don't be confused by this!*

Columns also force some discipline on anyone putting data into the table. Each column has certain characteristics assigned to it. For instance, the Customer Number column in Figure 3-5 may only contain strings of digits (0–9), no letters (A–Z) allowed. It is also limited to a maximum of six characters. In data design lingo, these are known as *constraints*. Given these constraints, it is not possible to store a customer's name in the Customer Number column. The customer's name is likely too long and

Customer

Customer #	Customer Name	Address	Phone
647382	Young & Assoc.	3782 Hwy 34 East	849-555-8393
135384	Rosenblinker, Inc.	1243 43rd Street	439-555-3934
29483	Landmark, Inc.	4383 Johnson Blvd.	389-555-8349
943827	Phillips Mfg., Inc.	3893 Maple Ave.	847-555-4393

Figure 3-5   *A database table organized by rows and columns*

it contains characters that are not legal in the Customer Number column. Constraints provide the discipline to force organization within a database.

Typically, when you design a database, you create tables for each of the things you want to keep track of. In Figure 3-4, the database designer knew that her company needed to track information for customers, payments, and invoices. Database designers call these things *entities*. The database designer created tables for the customer, payment, and invoice header entities. These tables are named Customer, Payment, and Invoice Header.

Once the entities have been identified, the database designer determines what information needs to be known about each entity. In Figure 3-5, the designer identified the customer number, customer name, address, and phone number as the things that need to be known for each customer. These are *attributes* of the customer entity. The database designer creates a column in the Customer table for each of these attributes.

Primary Key

As entities and attributes are being defined, the database designer needs to identify a special attribute for each entity in the database. This special attribute is known as the *primary key*. The purpose of the primary key is to be able to uniquely identify a single entity, or in the case of a database table, a single row in the table.

There are two simple rules for primary keys. First, every entity must have a primary key value. Second, no two rows in an entity can have the same primary key value. In Figure 3-5, the Customer Number column can serve as the primary key. Every customer is assigned a customer number and no two customers can be assigned the same customer number.

For most entities, the primary key is a single attribute. However, in some cases, two attributes must be combined to create a unique primary key. This is known as a *composite primary key*. For instance, if you were defining an entity based on Presidents of the United States, first name would not be a valid primary key. John Adams, John Quincy Adams, and John Kennedy all have the same first name. You would need to create a composite key combining first name, middle name, and last name to have a valid primary key.

Normalization

As the database designer continues to work on identifying entities and attributes, she will notice that two different entities have some of the same attributes. For example, in Figure 3-6 both the customer entity and the invoice header entity have attributes of Customer Name and Address. This duplication of information seems rather wasteful.

Customer

Customer #	Customer Name	Address	Phone
647382	Young & Assoc.	3782 Hwy 34 East	849-555-8393
135384	Rosenblinker, Inc.	1243 43rd Street	439-555-3934
29483	Landmark, Inc.	4383 Johnson Blvd.	389-555-8349
943827	Phillips Mfg., Inc.	3893 Maple Ave.	847-555-4393

Invoice Header

Invoice #	Customer Name	Address	Amount	Quantity
3984	Rosenblinker, Inc.	1243 43rd Street	$399.28	12
3723	Young & Assoc.	3782 Hwy 34 East	$384.23	15
3502	Rosenblinker, Inc.	1243 43rd Street	$2,435.36	35

Figure 3-6   *Database tables with duplicate data*

Not only is the customer's name and address duplicated between the Customer and Invoice Header tables, but they are also duplicated in several rows in the Invoice Header table itself.

The duplicate data also leads to another problem. Suppose that Rosenblinker, Inc. changes its name to RB, Inc. Then, Ann in the data processing department changes the name in the Customer table because this is where we store information about the customer entity. However, the customer name has not been changed in the Invoice Header table. Because the customer name in the Invoice Header table no longer matches the customer name in the Customer table, it is no longer possible to determine how many invoices are outstanding for RB, Inc. Believe me, the accounting department will think that this is a bad situation.

In order to avoid these types of problems, database tables are normalized. *Normalization* is a set of rules for defining database tables so that each table contains attributes from only one entity. The rules for creating normalized database tables can be quite complex. You can hear database designers endlessly debating whether a proper database should be in third normal form, fourth normal form, or one hundred and twenty-seventh normal form. Let the database designers debate all they want. All you really need to remember is this: A normalized database avoids data duplication.

Relations

A *relation* is a tool that the database designer uses to avoid data duplication when creating a normalized database. It is simply a way to put the duplicated data in one place and then point to it from all the other places in the database where it would otherwise occur. The table that contains the data is called the *parent* table. The table that contains a pointer to the data in the parent table is called the *child* table. Just like parents and children of the human variety, the parent table and the child table are said to be *related*.

In our example, the customer name and address are stored in the Customer table. This is the parent table. A pointer is placed in the Invoice Header table in place of the duplicate customer names and addresses it had contained. The Invoice Header table is the child table.

As was mentioned previously, each customer is uniquely identified by their customer number. Therefore, the Customer Number column serves as the primary key for the Customer table. In the Invoice Header table, we need a way to point to a particular customer. It makes sense to use the primary key in the parent table, in this case the Customer Number column, as that pointer. This is illustrated in Figure 3-7.

Each row in the Invoice Header table now contains a copy of the primary key of a row in the Customer table. The Customer Number column in the Invoice Header table is called the *foreign key*. It is called a foreign key because it is not one of the native attributes of the invoice header entity. The customer number is a native attribute of the customer entity. The only reason the Customer Number column exists in the Invoice Header table is to create the relationship.

Let's look back at the name change problem, this time using our new database structure that includes the parent-child relationship. When Rosenblinker, Inc. changes its name to RB, Inc., Ann changes the name in the Customer table as before. In our new structure, however, the customer name is not stored in any other location. Instead, the Invoice Header table rows for RB, Inc. point back to the Customer table row that has the correct name. The accounting department stays happy because it can still figure out how many invoices are still outstanding for RB, Inc.

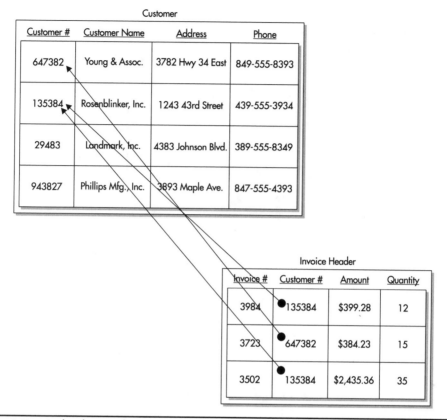

Figure 3-7   *A database relation*

Cardinality of Relations

Database relations can be classified by the number of records that can exist on each side of the relationship. This is known as the *cardinality* of the relation. For example, the relation in Figure 3-7 is a *one-to-many relation.* In other words, one parent record can have many children. More specifically, one customer can have many invoices.

It is also possible to have a *one-to-one relation.* In this case, one parent record can have only one child. For example, let's say that our company rewards customers with a customer loyalty discount. Because only a few customers will receive this loyalty discount, we do not want to set aside space in every row in the Customer table to store the loyalty discount information. Instead, we create a new table to store this information. The new table is related to the Customer table, as shown in Figure 3-8. Our company's business rule says that a given customer can only receive one loyalty

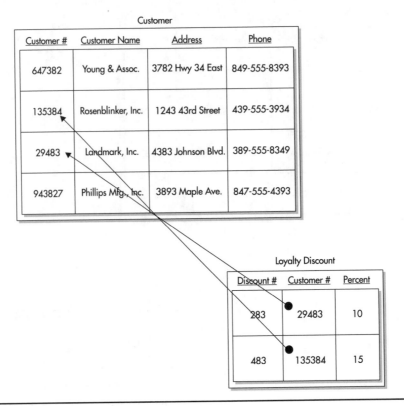

Figure 3-8   *A one-to-one relation*

discount. Because the Loyalty Discount table has only one Customer Number column, each row can link to just one customer. The combination of the business rule and the table design make this a one-to-one relation.

It is also possible to have a *many-to-many relation*. This relation no longer fits our parent/child analogy. It is better thought of as a brother/sister relationship. One brother can have many sisters, and one sister can have many brothers.

Suppose that we need to keep track of the type of business that is engaged in by each of our customers. We can add a Business Type table to our database with columns for the business type code and the business type description. We can add a column for the business type code to the Customer table. We now have a one-to-many relation, where one business type can be related to many customers. This is shown in Figure 3-9.

The problem with this structure becomes apparent when we have a customer that does multiple things. If Landmark, Inc. only produces paper products, there isn't a problem. We can put the business type code for "Paper Products" in the Customer

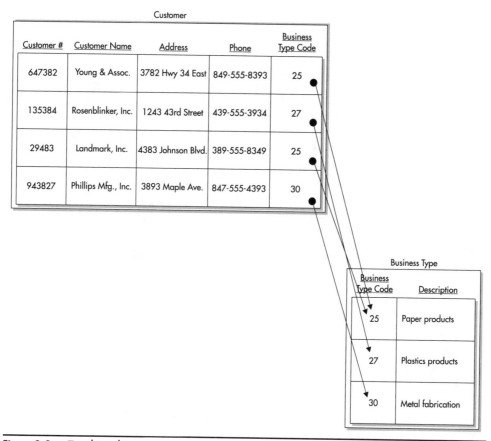

Figure 3-9   *Tracking business type using a one-to-many relation*

table row for Landmark, Inc. We run into a bit of a snag, however, if Landmark, Inc. also produces plastics. We could add a second business type code column to the Customer table, but this still limits a customer to a maximum of two business types. In today's world of national conglomerates, this is not going to work.

The answer is to add a third table to the mix to create a many-to-many relationship. This additional table is known as a *linking table.* Its only purpose is to link two other tables together in a many-to-many relation. To use a linking table, you create the Business Type table just as before. This time, instead of creating a new column in the Customer table, we'll create a new table called Customer To Business Type Link. The new table has columns for the customer number and the business type code. Figure 3-10 shows how this linking table relates the Customer table to the Business Type table.

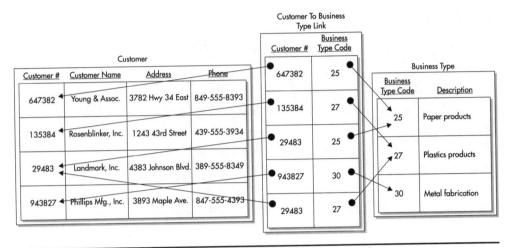

Figure 3-10 *Tracking the business type using a many-to-many relation*

By using the linking table, we can relate one customer to many business types. In addition, we can relate one business type to many customers.

Retrieving Data

We now have all the tools we need to store our data in an efficient manner. With our data structure set, it is time to figure out how we can access that data to use it in our reports. Data that was split up into multiple tables must be recombined for reporting. This is done using a database tool called a *join*. In most cases, we will also want the data in the report to appear in a certain order. This is accomplished using a sort.

Inner Joins

Suppose we need to know the name and address of the customer associated with each invoice. This is certainly a reasonable desire, especially if we want to send invoices to these clients and actually have those invoices paid. Checking the Invoice Header table, you will see that it contains the customer number, but not the name and address. The name and address is stored in the Customer table.

To print our invoices, we will need to join the data in the Customer table with the data in the Invoice Header table. This join is done by matching the customer number in each record of the Invoice Header table with the customer number in the Customer table. In the language of database designers, we are joining the Customer table to the Invoice Header table on the Customer Number column.

The result of the join is a new table that contains information from both the Customer table and the Invoice Header table in each row. This new table is known as a *result set*. The result set from the Customer table–to–Invoice Header table join is shown in Figure 3-11. You will note that the result set table contains nearly the same information that was in the Invoice Header table before it was normalized. The result set is a *denormalized* form of the data in the database.

It may seem like we are going in circles, first normalizing the data and then denormalizing it. There is, however, one very important difference between the denormalized form of the Invoice Header table that we started with in Figure 3-6 and the result set in Figure 3-11. The denormalized result set is a temporary table. It exists only as long as it is needed; then it is automatically deleted. The result set is re-created each time we execute the join; therefore, the result set is always up-to-date.

Let's go back one more time to Ann, our faithful employee in Data Processing. We will again consider the situation where Rosenblinker, Inc. changes its name to RB, Inc. Ann makes the change in the Customer table, as in the previous example. The next time we execute the join, this change is reflected in the result set. The result set has the new company name because our join gets a new copy of the customer information from the Customer table each time it is executed. The join finds the information in the Customer table based on the primary key, the customer number, which has not changed. Our invoices are linked to the proper companies, so Accounting can determine how many invoices are outstanding for RB, Inc., and everyone is happy!

Customer/Invoice Header Join Result Set

Customer #	Customer Name	Address	Phone	Invoice #	Customer #	Amount	Quantity
135384	Rosenblinker, Inc.	1243 43rd Street	439-555-3934	3984	135384	$399.28	12
647382	Young & Assoc.	3782 Hwy 34 East	849-555-8393	3723	647382	$384.23	15
135384	Rosenblinker, Inc.	1243 43rd Street	439-555-3934	3502	135384	$2,435.36	35

Data from the Customer table   Data from the Invoice Header table

Figure 3-11   *The result set from the Customer table–to–Invoice Header table join*

Outer Joins

In the previous section, we looked at a type of join known as an *inner join*. When you do an inner join, your result set includes only those records that have a representative on both sides of the join. In Figure 3-11, Landmark, Inc. and Phillips Mfg., Inc. are not represented in the result set, because they do not have any Invoice Header table rows linked to them.

Figure 3-12 shows another way to think about joins. Here, the two tables are shown as sets of customer numbers. The left-hand circle represents the set of customer numbers in the Customer table. It contains one occurrence of each and every customer number that is present in the Customer table. The right-hand circle represents the set of customer numbers in the Invoice Header table. It contains one occurrence of each and every customer number that is present in the Invoice Header table. The center region, where the two sets intersect, contains one occurrence of each and every customer number that is present in both the Customer table and the Invoice Header table. Looking at Figure 3-12, you can quickly tell that there are no customer numbers that are present in the Invoice Header table, but not in the Customer table. This is as it should be. We should not have any invoice headers that are assigned to a customer that does not exist in the Customer table.

Figure 3-13 shows a graphical representation of the inner join in Figure 3-11. Only records with customer numbers that appear in the shaded section will be included in the result set. Remember that there are two rows in the Invoice Header table that contain customer number 135384. For this reason, the result set contains

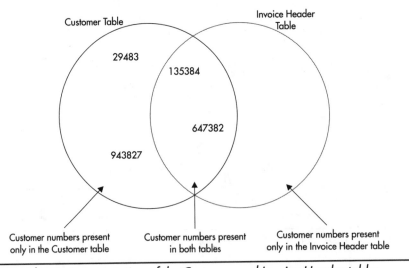

Figure 3-12   *The set representation of the Customer and Invoice Header tables*

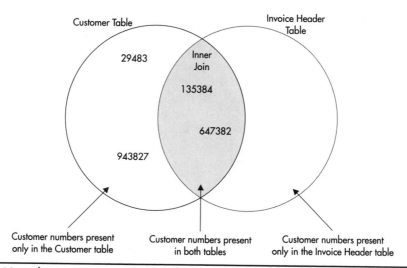

Figure 3-13   *The set representation of the inner join of the Customer table and the Invoice Header table*

three rows—two rows for customer number 135384 and one row for customer number 647382.

The result set in Figure 3-11 allows us to print invoice headers that contain the correct customer name and address. Now let's look at customers and invoice headers from a slightly different angle. Suppose we have been asked for a report showing all customers and the invoice headers that have been sent to them. If we were to print this customers/invoice headers report from the result set in Figure 3-11, it would exclude Landmark, Inc. and Phillips Mfg., Inc. because they do not have any invoices and, therefore, would not fulfill the requirements.

What we need is a result set that includes all the customers in the Customer table. This is illustrated graphically in Figure 3-14. This type of join is known as a *left outer join.* The name comes from the fact that this join is not limited to the values in the intersection of both circles. It also includes the values that are to the left of the inner, overlapping sections of the circles.

We can also perform a *right outer join* on two tables. In our example, a right outer join would return the same number of rows as the inner join. This is due to the fact that there are no customer numbers to the right of the intersection.

The result set produced by a left outer join of the Customer table and the Invoice Header table is shown in Figure 3-15. Notice the fact that the columns populated by data from the Invoice Header table are empty in rows for Landmark, Inc. and Phillips

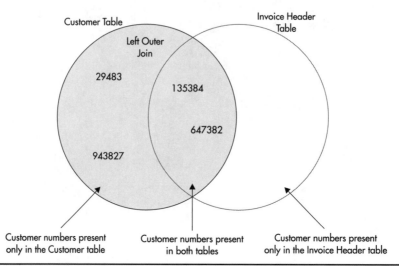

Figure 3-14 *The set representation of the left outer join of the Customer table and the Invoice Header table*

Mfg., Inc. The columns are empty because these two customers do not have any Invoice Header rows to provide data on the right side of the join.

Customer/Invoice Header Left Outer Join Result Set

Customer #	Customer Name	Address	Phone	Invoice #	Customer #	Amount	Quantity
135384	Rosenblinker, Inc.	1243 43rd Street	439-555-3934	3984	135384	$399.28	12
647382	Young & Assoc.	3782 Hwy 34 East	849-555-8393	3723	647382	$384.23	15
135384	Rosenblinker, Inc.	1243 43rd Street	439-555-3934	3502	135384	$2,435.36	35
29483	Landmark, Inc.	4383 Johnson Blvd.	389-555-8349				
943827	Phillips Mfg., Inc.	3893 Maple Ave.	847-555-4393				

Data from the Customer table   Data from the Invoice Header table

Figure 3-15 *The result set from the left outer join of the Customer table and the Invoice Header table*

Joining Multiple Tables

Joins, whether inner or outer, always involve two tables. However, in Figure 3-10, you were introduced to a many-to-many relation that involved three tables. How do you retrieve data from this type of relation? The answer is to chain together two different joins, each involving two tables.

Figure 3-16 illustrates the joins that are required to reassemble the data from Figure 3-10. Here, the Customer table is joined to the Customer To Business Type Link table using the Customer Number column common to both tables. The Customer To Business Type Link table is then joined to the Business Type table using the Business Type Code column that is present in both tables. The final result set contains the data from all three tables.

Self-Joins

In our previous example, we needed to join three tables to get the required information. Other joins may only require a single table. For instance, we may have a customer that is a subsidiary of another one of our customers. In some cases, we'll want to treat these two separately, so both appear in our result set. This requires us to keep the two customers as separate rows in our Customer table. In other cases, we may

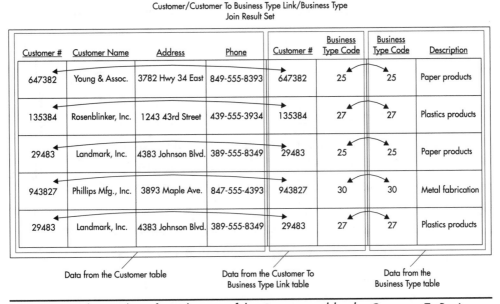

Figure 3-16   *The result set from the join of the Customer table, the Customer To Business Type Link table, and the Business Type table*

want to combine information from the parent company and the subsidiary into one record. To do this, our database structure must include a mechanism to tie the subsidiary to its parent.

To track a customer's connection to its parent, we need to create a relationship between the customer's row in the Customer table and its parent's row in the Customer table. To do this, we add a Parent Customer Number column to the Customer table, as shown in Figure 3-17. In the customer's row, the Parent Customer Number column will contain the customer number of the row for the parent. In the row for the parent, and in all the rows for customers that do not have a parent, the Parent Customer Number column is empty.

When we want to report from this parent/subsidiary relation, we need to do a join. This may seem like a problem at first because a join requires two tables, and we only have one. The answer is to use the Customer table on one side of the join and a "copy" of the Customer table on the other side of the join. The second occurrence of the Customer table is given a nickname, called an *alias*, so we can tell the two apart. This type of join, which uses the same table on both sides, is known as a *self-join*. Figure 3-18 shows the results of the self-join on the Customer table.

Sorting

In most cases, one final step is required before our result sets can be used for reporting. Let's go back to the result set produced in Figure 3-15 for the customers/invoice

Customer

Customer #	Customer Name	Address	Phone	Parent Customer #
647382	Young & Assoc.	3782 Hwy 34 East	849-555-8393	
135384	Rosenblinker, Inc.	1243 43rd Street	439-555-3934	
29483	Landmark, Inc.	4383 Johnson Blvd.	389-555-8349	135384
943827	Phillips Mfg., Inc.	3893 Maple Ave.	847-555-4393	647382

Figure 3-17   *The Customer/Parent Customer relation*

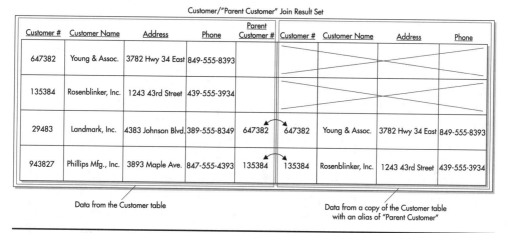

Figure 3-18   *The result set from the Customer table self-join*

headers report. Looking back at this result set, you will notice that the customers do not appear to be in any particular order. In most cases, users do not appreciate reports with information presented in this unsorted manner. This is especially true when two rows for the same customer do not appear consecutively, as is the case here.

We need to sort the result set as it is being created in order to avoid this situation. This is done by specifying the columns that should be used for the sort. Sorting by Customer Name probably makes the most sense for the customers/invoice headers report. Columns can be sorted either in ascending order, smallest to largest (A–Z), or descending order, largest to smallest (Z–A). An ascending sort on Customer Name would be most appropriate.

We still have a situation where the order of the rows is left to chance. Because there are two rows with the same customer name, we do not know which of these two rows will appear first and which will appear second. A second sort field is necessary to break this "tie." All the data copied into the result set from the Customer table will be the same in both of these rows. We need to look at the data copied from the Invoice Header table for a second sort column. In this case, an ascending sort on Invoice Number would be a good choice. Figure 3-19 shows the result set sorted by Customer Name, ascending, and then Invoice Number, ascending.

Customer/Invoice Header Left Outer Join Result Set

Customer #	Customer Name	Address	Phone	Invoice #	Customer #	Amount	Quantity
29483	Landmark, Inc.	4383 Johnson Blvd.	389-555-8349				
943827	Phillips Mfg., Inc.	3893 Maple Ave.	847-555-4393				
135384	Rosenblinker, Inc.	1243 43rd Street	439-555-3934	3502	135384	$2,435.36	35
135384	Rosenblinker, Inc.	1243 43rd Street	439-555-3934	3984	135384	$399.28	12
647382	Young & Assoc.	3782 Hwy 34 East	849-555-8393	3723	647382	$384.23	15

Data from the Customer table   Data from the Invoice Header table

Figure 3-19   *The sorted result set from the left outer join of the Customer table and the Invoice Header table*

Galactic Delivery Services

Throughout the remainder of this book, you will get to know Reporting Services by exploring a number of sample reports. These reports will be based on the business needs of a company called Galactic Delivery Services (GDS). To better understand these sample reports, here is some background on GDS.

Company Background

GDS provides package-delivery service between several planetary systems in the near galactic region. It specializes in rapid delivery featuring same-day, next-day, and previous-day delivery. The latter is made possible by its new Photon III transports, which travel faster than the speed of light. This faster than light capability allows GDS to exploit the properties of general relativity and actually deliver a package on the day before it was sent.

Package Tracking

Despite GDS's unique delivery offerings, it has the same data-processing needs as any more conventional package-delivery service. It tracks packages as they are moved from one interplanetary hub to another. This is important not only for the smooth operation of the delivery service, but also to allow customers to check on the status of their delivery at any time.

In order to remain accountable to its clients and to prevent fraud, GDS investigates every package that is lost en route. These investigations help to find and eliminate problems throughout the entire delivery system. One such investigation discovered that a leaking antimatter valve on one of the Photon III transports was vaporizing two or three packages on each flight.

GDS stores its data in a database called Galactic. Figure 3-20 shows the portion of the Galactic database that stores the information used for package tracking. The tables and their column names are shown. A key symbol in the gray square next to a column name indicates that this column is the primary key for that table. The lines connecting the tables show the relations that have been created between these tables in the database. The key symbol at the end of the line points to the primary key column used to create the relation. The infinity sign, at the opposite end of the line to the key symbol, points to the foreign key column used to complete the relation. (The infinity sign looks like two circles or a sideways *8*.)

Each relation shown in Figure 3-20 is a one-to-many relation. The side of the relation indicated by the key is the "one" side of the relation. The side indicated by the infinity sign is the many side of the relation. For example, if you look at the line between the Customer table and the Delivery table, you can see that one customer may have many deliveries.

You may wish to refer back to these diagrams as we create sample reports from the Galactic database. Don't worry if the diagrams seem a bit complicated right now. They will make more sense as we consider the business practices and reporting needs at GDS. Also, our first report examples will contain only a few tables and the corresponding relations, so we will start simple and work our way up.

Personnel

Every business needs a personnel department to look after its employees. GDS is no different. The GDS personnel department is responsible for the hiring and firing of

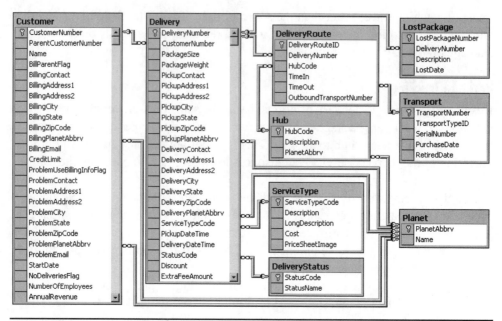

Figure 3-20   *The package tracking tables from the Galactic database*

all the robots employed by GDS. This department is also responsible for tracking the hours put in by the robotic laborers and paying them accordingly. (Yes, robots get paid at GDS. After all, GDS is an equal-opportunity employer.)

The personnel department is also responsible for conducting annual reviews of each employee. At the annual review, goals are set for the employee to attain over the coming year. After a year has passed, several of the employee's co-workers are asked to rate the employee on how well they did in reaching those goals. The employee's manager then uses the ratings to write an overall performance evaluation for the employee and establish new goals for the following year.

Figure 3-21 shows the tables in the Galactic database used by the personnel department. Notice that the Rating table has key symbols next to both the EvaluationID column name and the GoalID column name. This means that the Rating table uses a composite primary key that combines the EvaluationID column and the GoalID column.

Accounting

The GDS accounting department is responsible for seeing that the company is paid for each package that it delivers. GDS invoices its customers for each delivery

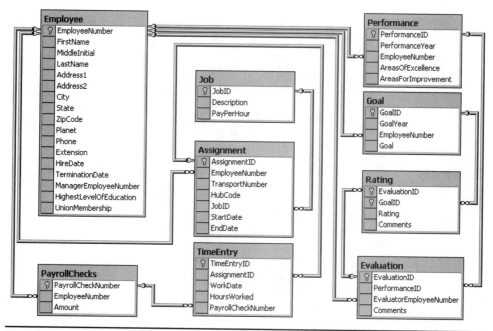

Figure 3-21 *The personnel department tables from the Galactic database*

completed. The invoices are sent to the customer and payment is requested within 30 days.

Even though GDS delivers its customers' packages at the speed of light, those same customers pay GDS at a much slower speed. "Molasses at the northern pole of Antares Prime," was the analogy used by the current Chief Financial Droid. Therefore, GDS must track when invoices are paid, how much was paid, and how much is still outstanding.

Figure 3-22 shows the tables in the Galactic database used by the accounting department. You will notice that the Customer table appears in both Figure 3-20 and Figure 3-22. This is the same table in both diagrams. It is shown in both, because it is a major part of both the package tracking and accounting business processes.

Transport Maintenance

In addition to all of this, GDS must maintain a fleet of transports. Careful records are kept on the repair and preventative maintenance work done on each transport. There is also a record of each flight that a transport makes and of any accidents and mishaps involved.

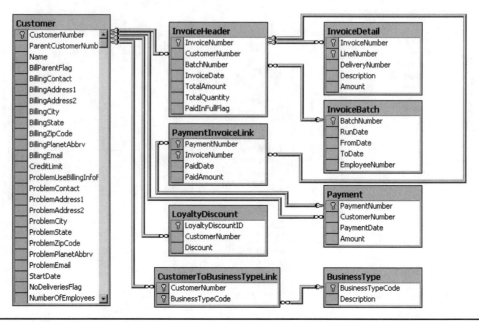

Figure 3-22   *The accounting department tables from the Galactic database*

Maintenance records are extremely important, not only to GDS itself, but also to the Federation Space Flight Administration (FSFA). Without proper maintenance records on all its transports, GDS would be shut down by the FSFA in a nanosecond. You may think this is an exaggeration, but the bureaucratic androids at the FSFA have extremely high clock rates.

Figure 3-23 shows the transport maintenance tables in the Galactic database.

Querying Data

You have now looked at the database concepts of normalization, relations, and joins. You have also been introduced to the Galactic database. We will use this relational database throughout the remainder of this book for our examples. Now it is time to look more specifically at how you retrieve the data from the database into a format that you can use for reporting. This is done through the database query.

A *query* is a request for some action on the data in one or more tables. An *INSERT query* adds one or more rows to a database table. An *UPDATE query* modifies the data in one or more existing rows of a table. A *DELETE query* removes one or more

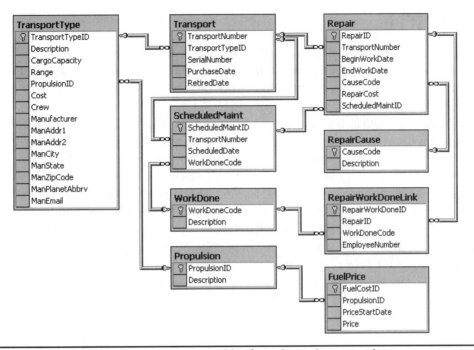

Figure 3-23   *The transport maintenance tables from the Galactic Database*

rows from a table. Because we are primarily interested in retrieving data for reporting, the query that we are going to concern ourselves with is the *SELECT query,* which reads data from one or more tables (it does not add, update, or delete data).

We will look at the various parts of the SELECT query. This is to help you become familiar with this important aspect of reporting. The good news is that Reporting Services provides a tool to guide you through the creation of queries including the SELECT query. That tool is the Query Builder.

If you are familiar with SELECT queries and are more comfortable typing your queries from scratch, you can bypass the Query Builder and type in your queries directly. If SELECT queries are new to you, the following section will help you become familiar with the SELECT query and what it can do for you. Rest assured, the Query Builder will allow you to take advantage of all the features of the SELECT query without having to memorize syntax or type a lot of code.

NOTE

If you have another query-creation tool you like to use instead of the Query Builder, you can create your queries with that tool and then copy them into the appropriate locations in the report definition.

The SELECT Query

The SELECT query is used to retrieve data from tables in the database. When a SELECT query is run, it returns a result set containing the data that has been selected. With very few exceptions, your reports will be built on result sets that are created by SELECT queries.

The SELECT query is often referred to as a *SELECT statement.* One reason for this is that it can be read very much like an English sentence or statement. As with a sentence in English, it is made up of clauses that modify the meaning of the statement.

The various parts, or clauses, of the SELECT statement allow you to control the data that is contained in the result set. Use the *FROM clause* to specify which table the data will be selected from. The *FIELD LIST* permits you to choose the columns that will appear in the result set. The *JOIN clause* allows you to specify additional tables that will be joined with the table in the FROM clause to contribute data to the result set. The *WHERE clause* enables you to set conditions that determine which rows will be included in the result set. Finally, you can use the *ORDER BY clause* to sort the result set, and the *GROUP BY clause* and the *HAVING clause* to combine detail rows into summary rows.

The FROM Clause

The SELECT statement in its simplest form includes only a FROM clause. Here is a SELECT statement that retrieves all rows and all columns from the Customer table:

```
SELECT *
FROM dbo.Customer
```

The word "SELECT" is required to let the database know that this is going to be a SELECT query as opposed to an INSERT, UPDATE, or DELETE query. The asterisk (*) means that all columns will be included in the result set. The remainder of the statement is the FROM clause. It says that the data is to be selected from the Customer table. We will discuss the meaning of "dbo." in a moment.

As was stated earlier, the SELECT statement can be read as if it were a sentence. This SELECT statement is read, "Select all columns from the Customer table." If we run this SELECT statement in the Galactic database, the results would appear similar to Figure 3-24. The SELECT query is being run in the Query Builder window of Visual Studio. Note that the scroll bars on the right and on the bottom of the result set area indicate that not all the rows and columns returned can fit on the screen.

You will note that the table name, Customer, has "dbo." in front of it. The "dbo" is the name of the owner of the table. Usually this is the user who created the table.

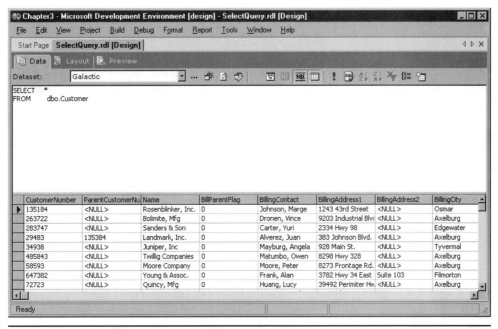

Figure 3-24   *The SELECT statement in its simplest form*

Here, "dbo" stands for "database owner," meaning that the user who owns the database is also the user who owns the table. The dbo abbreviation is also another name for the system administrator login. In many cases, an administrative user, logged into the database, will create the database tables. Because of this, the table owner will more than likely be "dbo."

In the Galactic database, the dbo.Customer table was created by the system administrator. If another user with a database login of "User2" also has rights to create tables in the Galactic database, they could also create a Customer table. This second table would be known as "User2.Customer."

This situation, with two tables of the same name in the same database, does not happen very often and is probably not a great idea. It can quickly lead to confusion and errors. Even though this is a rare occurrence, the Query Builder needs to account for this situation. The Query Builder uses both the name of the table owner and the name of the table itself in the queries it builds and executes for you.

The FIELD LIST

In the previous example, the result set created by the SELECT statement contained all the columns in the table. In most cases, especially when creating reports, you will only need to work with some of the columns of a table in any given result set. Including all the columns in a result set when only a few columns are required wastes computing power and network bandwidth.

A FIELD LIST provides the capability you need to specify which columns to include in the result set. When a FIELD LIST is added to the SELECT statement, it appears similar to the following:

```
SELECT CustomerNumber, Name, BillingCity
FROM dbo.Customer
```

The bold portion of the SELECT statement indicates changes from the previous SELECT statement.

This statement returns only the Customer Number, Name, and Billing City columns from the Customer table. The result set created by this SELECT statement is shown in Figure 3-25.

In addition to the names of the fields to include in the result set, the FIELD LIST can contain a word that influences the number of rows in the result set. Usually, there is one row in the result set for each row in the table from which you are selecting data. However, this can be changed by adding the word "DISTINCT" at the beginning of the FIELD LIST.

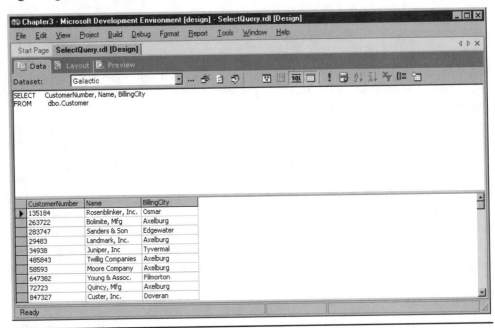

Figure 3-25   *A SELECT statement with a FIELD LIST*

When you use DISTINCT in the FIELD LIST, you are saying that you only want one row in the result set for each distinct set of values. In other words, the result set from a DISTINCT query will not have any two rows that have exactly the same values in every column. Here is an example of a DISTINCT query:

```
SELECT DISTINCT BillingCity
FROM dbo.Customer
```

This query returns a list of all the billing cities in the Customer table. There are a number of customers with the same billing city, but these duplicates have been removed from the result set, as shown in Figure 3-26.

The JOIN Clause

When your database is properly normalized, you are likely to need data from more than one table in order to fulfill your reporting requirements. As we discussed earlier in this chapter, the way to get information from more than one table is to use a join. The JOIN clause in the SELECT statement allows you to include a join of two or more tables in your result set.

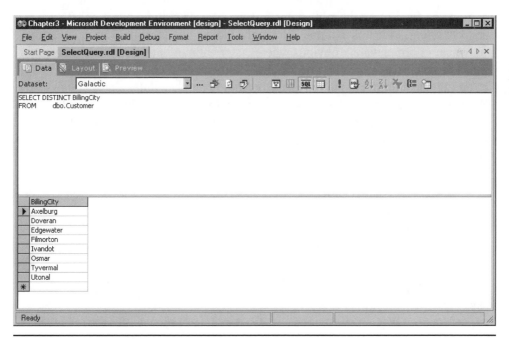

Figure 3-26 *A DISTINCT query*

The first part of the JOIN clause specifies which table is being joined. The second part determines the two columns that are linked to create the join. Joining the Invoice Header table to the Customer table looks like this:

```
SELECT dbo.Customer.CustomerNumber,
    dbo.Customer.Name,
    dbo.Customer.BillingCity,
    dbo.InvoiceHeader.InvoiceNumber,
    dbo.InvoiceHeader.TotalAmount
FROM dbo.Customer
INNER JOIN dbo.InvoiceHeader
 ON dbo.Customer.CustomerNumber = dbo.InvoiceHeader.CustomerNumber
```

With the Customer table and the Invoice Header table joined, you have a situation where some columns in the result set have the same name. For example, there is a Customer Number column in the Customer table and a Customer Number column in the Invoice Header table. When you use the FIELD LIST to tell the database which fields to include in the result set, you need to uniquely identify these fields using both the table name and the column name.

If you do not do this, the query will not run and you will receive an error. Nothing prevents you from using the table name in front of each column name, whether it is a duplicate or not, as in this example. Using the table name in front of each column name makes it immediately obvious where every column in the result set is selected from. The result set created by this SELECT statement is shown in Figure 3-27.

You can add a third table to the query by adding another JOIN clause to the SELECT statement. This additional table can be joined to the table in the FROM clause or to the table in the first JOIN clause. In this statement, we will add the Loyalty Discount table and join it to the Customer table:

```
SELECT dbo.Customer.CustomerNumber,
    dbo.Customer.Name,
    dbo.Customer.BillingCity,
    dbo.InvoiceHeader.InvoiceNumber,
    dbo.InvoiceHeader.TotalAmount,
    dbo.LoyaltyDiscount.Discount
FROM dbo.Customer
INNER JOIN dbo.InvoiceHeader
 ON dbo.Customer.CustomerNumber = dbo.InvoiceHeader.CustomerNumber
INNER JOIN dbo.LoyaltyDiscount
 ON dbo.Customer.CustomerNumber = dbo.LoyaltyDiscount.CustomerNumber
```

The result set from this SELECT statement is shown in Figure 3-28. Notice that the result set is rather small. This is because Landmark, Inc. is the only customer

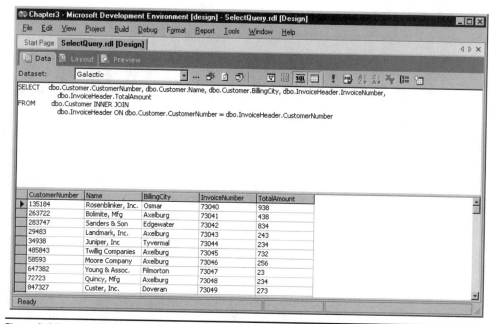

Figure 3-27   *A SELECT statement with a JOIN clause*

currently receiving a loyalty discount. Because an INNER JOIN was used to add the Loyalty Discount table, only customers that have a loyalty discount are included in the result set.

To make our result set a little more interesting, let's try joining the Loyalty Discount table with an OUTER JOIN rather than an INNER JOIN. Here is the same statement, except the Customer table is joined to the Loyalty Discount table with a LEFT OUTER JOIN:

```
SELECT dbo.Customer.CustomerNumber,
    dbo.Customer.Name,
    dbo.Customer.BillingCity,
    dbo.InvoiceHeader.InvoiceNumber,
    dbo.InvoiceHeader.TotalAmount,
    dbo.LoyaltyDiscount.Discount
FROM dbo.Customer
INNER JOIN dbo.InvoiceHeader
 ON dbo.Customer.CustomerNumber = dbo.InvoiceHeader.CustomerNumber
LEFT OUTER JOIN dbo.LoyaltyDiscount
 ON dbo.Customer.CustomerNumber = dbo.LoyaltyDiscount.CustomerNumber
```

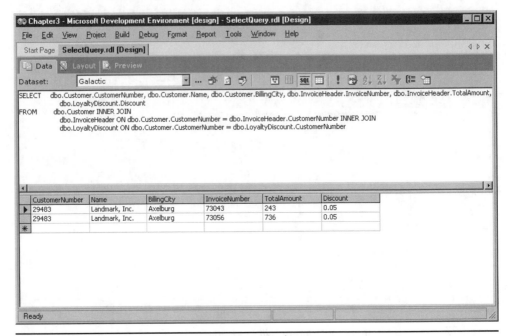

Figure 3-28   *A SELECT statement with two JOIN clauses*

The result set for this SELECT statement is shown in Figure 3-29. Notice that the value for the Discount column is NULL in the rows for all the customers except for Landmark, Inc. This is to be expected because there is no record in the Loyalty Discount table to join with these customers. When there is no value in a column, the result set will contain a NULL value.

The WHERE Clause

Up to this point, the result sets have included all the rows in the table or all the rows that result from the joins. The FIELD LIST limits which columns are being returned in the result set. Nothing, however, placed a limit on the rows.

In order to limit the number of rows in the result set, you need to add a WHERE clause to your SELECT statement. The WHERE clause includes one or more logical expressions that must be true for a row before it can be included in the result set. Here is an example of a SELECT statement with a WHERE clause:

```
SELECT dbo.Customer.CustomerNumber,
    dbo.Customer.Name,
    dbo.Customer.BillingCity,
    dbo.InvoiceHeader.InvoiceNumber,
```

```
        dbo.InvoiceHeader.TotalAmount,
        dbo.LoyaltyDiscount.Discount
FROM dbo.Customer
INNER JOIN dbo.InvoiceHeader
 ON dbo.Customer.CustomerNumber = dbo.InvoiceHeader.CustomerNumber
LEFT OUTER JOIN dbo.LoyaltyDiscount
 ON dbo.Customer.CustomerNumber = dbo.LoyaltyDiscount.CustomerNumber
WHERE (dbo.Customer.BillingCity = 'Axelburg')
```

The word 'Axelburg' (enclosed in single quotes) is a *string constant*. A string
constant, also known as a *string literal,* is an actual text value. The string constant
instructs SQL Server to use the text between the single quotes as a value rather than
the name of a column or a table. In this example, only customers with a value of
Axelburg in their Billing City column will be included in the result set, as shown in
Figure 3-30.

NOTE

*Microsoft SQL Server 2000, in its standard configuration, insists on single quotes around string
constants, such as 'Axelburg' in the previous SELECT statement. SQL Server 2000 assumes that
anything enclosed in double quotes is a field name.*

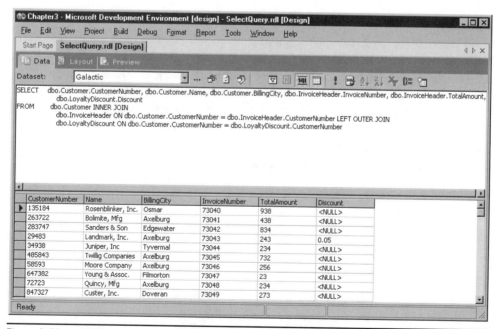

Figure 3-29   *A SELECT statement with an INNER JOIN and an OUTER JOIN*

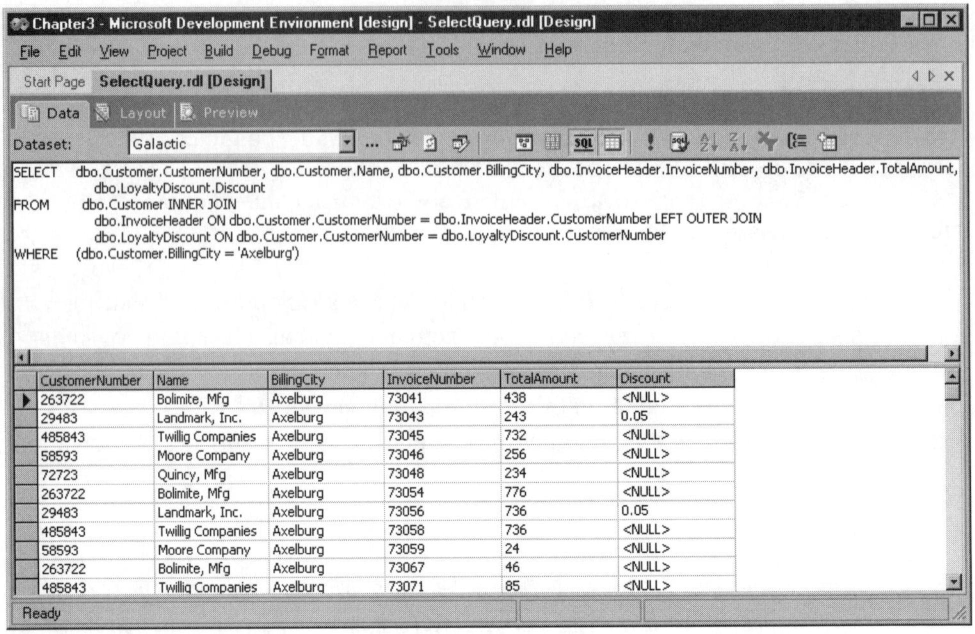

Figure 3-30   *A SELECT statement with a WHERE clause*

To create more complex criteria for your result set, you can have multiple logical expressions in the WHERE clause. The logical expressions are linked together with an AND or an OR. When an AND is used to link logical expressions, the logical expressions on both sides of the AND must be true for a row in order for that row to be included in the result set. When an OR is used to link two logical expressions, either one or both of the logical expressions must be true for a row in order for that row to be included in the result set.

This SELECT statement has two logical expressions:

```
SELECT dbo.Customer.CustomerNumber,
    dbo.Customer.Name,
    dbo.Customer.BillingCity,
    dbo.InvoiceHeader.InvoiceNumber,
    dbo.InvoiceHeader.TotalAmount,
    dbo.LoyaltyDiscount.Discount
FROM dbo.Customer
INNER JOIN dbo.InvoiceHeader
  ON dbo.Customer.CustomerNumber = dbo.InvoiceHeader.CustomerNumber
LEFT OUTER JOIN dbo.LoyaltyDiscount
```

```
ON dbo.Customer.CustomerNumber = dbo.LoyaltyDiscount.CustomerNumber
WHERE (dbo.Customer.BillingCity = 'Axelburg')
AND (dbo.Customer.Name > 'C')
```

Only customers with a value of Axelburg in their Billing City column and with a name that comes after C will be included in the result set. This result set is shown in Figure 3-31.

The ORDER BY Clause

Up to this point, the data in the result sets has shown up in any order that it pleases. As we discussed previously, this will probably not be acceptable for most reports. You can add an ORDER BY clause to your SELECT statement to obtain a sorted result set. This statement includes an ORDER BY clause with multiple columns:

```
SELECT dbo.Customer.CustomerNumber,
    dbo.Customer.Name,
    dbo.Customer.BillingCity,
    dbo.InvoiceHeader.InvoiceNumber,
    dbo.InvoiceHeader.TotalAmount,
    dbo.LoyaltyDiscount.Discount
FROM dbo.Customer
INNER JOIN dbo.InvoiceHeader
 ON dbo.Customer.CustomerNumber = dbo.InvoiceHeader.CustomerNumber
LEFT OUTER JOIN dbo.LoyaltyDiscount
 ON dbo.Customer.CustomerNumber = dbo.LoyaltyDiscount.CustomerNumber
WHERE (dbo.Customer.BillingCity = 'Axelburg')
AND (dbo.Customer.Name > 'C')
ORDER BY dbo.Customer.Name DESC, dbo.InvoiceHeader.InvoiceNumber
```

The result set created by this SELECT statement, shown in Figure 3-32, is first sorted by the contents of the Name column in the Customer table. The "DESC" that follows "dbo.Customer.Name" in the ORDER BY clause specifies the sort order for the customer name sort. DESC means that this sort is done in descending order. In other words, the customer names will be sorted from the end of the alphabet to the beginning.

Several rows have the same customer name. For this reason, a second sort column is specified. This second sort is only applied within each group of identical customer names. For example, Twillig Companies has three rows in the result set. These three rows are sorted by the second sort, which is invoice number. No sort order is specified for the invoice number sort, so this defaults to an ascending sort. In other words, the invoice numbers are sorted from lowest to highest.

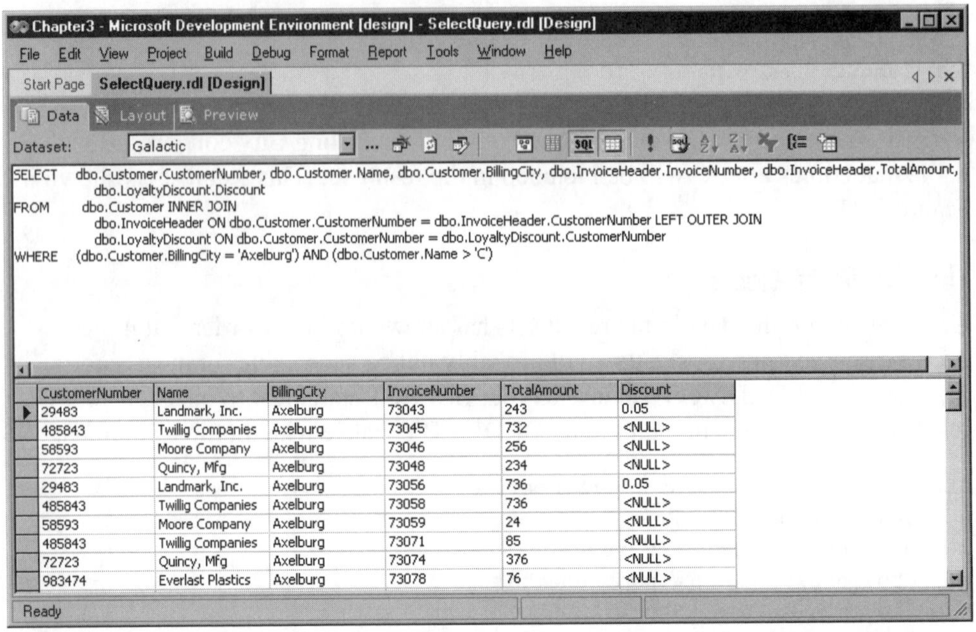

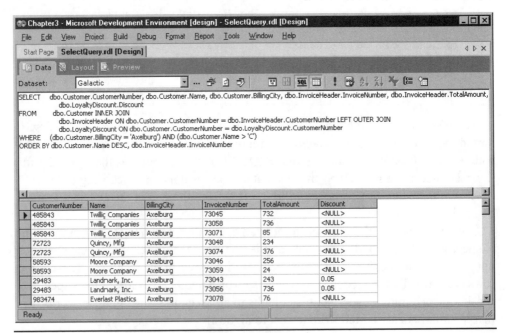

Figure 3-31 *A SELECT statement with two logical expressions in the WHERE clause*

Figure 3-32 *A SELECT statement with an ORDER BY clause*

Constant and Calculated Fields

Our SELECT statement examples thus far have used an asterisk symbol or a FIELD LIST that includes only columns. A FIELD LIST can, in fact, include other things as well. For example, a FIELD LIST can include a constant value, as is shown here:

```
SELECT dbo.Customer.CustomerNumber,
    dbo.Customer.Name,
    dbo.Customer.BillingCity,
    dbo.InvoiceHeader.InvoiceNumber,
    dbo.InvoiceHeader.TotalAmount,
    dbo.LoyaltyDiscount.Discount,
    'AXEL' AS ProcessingCode
FROM dbo.Customer
INNER JOIN dbo.InvoiceHeader
 ON dbo.Customer.CustomerNumber = dbo.InvoiceHeader.CustomerNumber
LEFT OUTER JOIN dbo.LoyaltyDiscount
 ON dbo.Customer.CustomerNumber = dbo.LoyaltyDiscount.CustomerNumber
WHERE (dbo.Customer.BillingCity = 'Axelburg')
AND (dbo.Customer.Name > 'C')
ORDER BY dbo.Customer.Name DESC, dbo.InvoiceHeader.InvoiceNumber
```

The string constant 'AXEL' has been added to the FIELD LIST. This creates a new column in the result set with the value AXEL in each row. By including "AS ProcessingCode" on this line, we give this result set column a column name of ProcessingCode. Constant values of other data types, such as dates or numbers, can also be added to the FIELD LIST. The result set for this SELECT statement is shown in Figure 3-33.

In addition to adding constant values, you can also include calculations in the FIELD LIST. This SELECT statement calculates the discounted invoice amount based on the total amount of the invoice and the loyalty discount:

```
SELECT dbo.Customer.CustomerNumber,
    dbo.Customer.Name,
    dbo.Customer.BillingCity,
    dbo.InvoiceHeader.InvoiceNumber,
    dbo.InvoiceHeader.TotalAmount,
    dbo.LoyaltyDiscount.Discount,
    dbo.InvoiceHeader.TotalAmount -
      (dbo.InvoiceHeader.TotalAmount *
          dbo.LoyaltyDiscount.Discount)
              AS DiscountedTotalAmount
FROM dbo.Customer
```

```
INNER JOIN dbo.InvoiceHeader
  ON dbo.Customer.CustomerNumber = dbo.InvoiceHeader.CustomerNumber
LEFT OUTER JOIN dbo.LoyaltyDiscount
  ON dbo.Customer.CustomerNumber = dbo.LoyaltyDiscount.CustomerNumber
WHERE (dbo.Customer.BillingCity = 'Axelburg')
AND (dbo.Customer.Name > 'C')
ORDER BY dbo.Customer.Name DESC, dbo.InvoiceHeader.InvoiceNumber
```

The result set for this SELECT statement is shown in Figure 3-34. Notice that the value for the calculated column, DiscountedTotalAmount, is NULL for all the rows that are not for Landmark, Inc. This is because we are using the value of the Discount column in our calculation. The Discount column has a value of NULL for every row except for the Landmark, Inc. rows.

A NULL value cannot be used successfully in any calculation. Any time you try to add, subtract, multiply, or divide a number by NULL, the result is NULL. The only way to receive a value in these situations is to give the database a valid value to

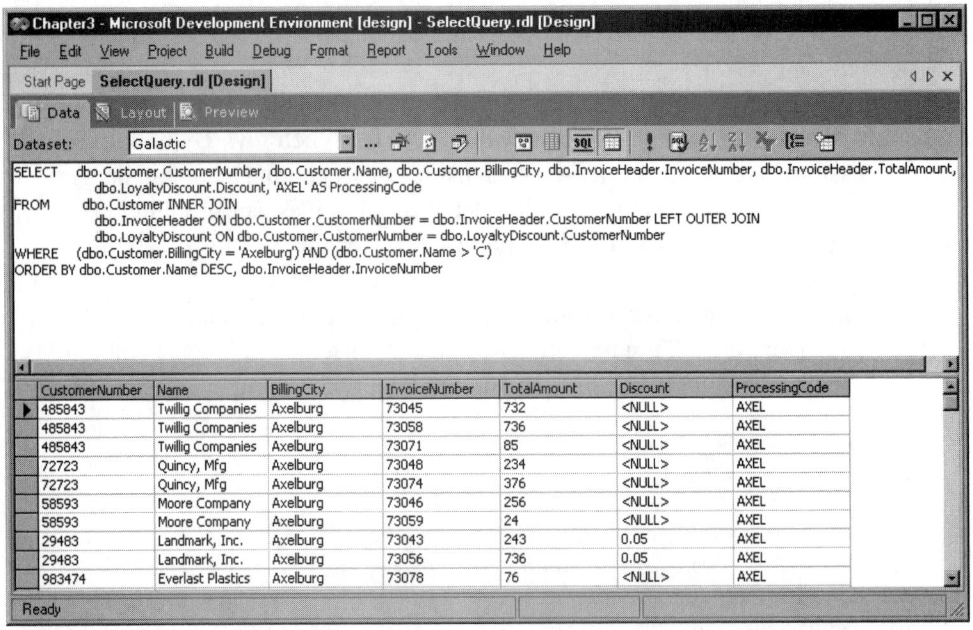

Figure 3-33   *A SELECT statement with a constant in the FIELD LIST*

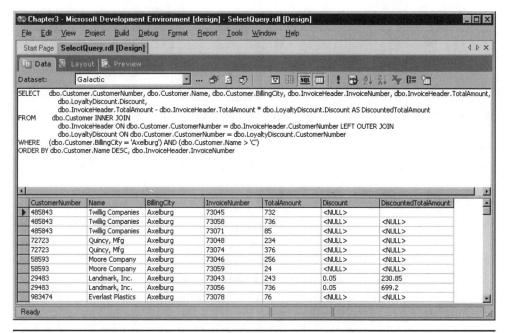

Figure 3-34   *A SELECT statement with a calculated column in the FIELD LIST*

use in place of any NULLs it might encounter. This is done using the ISNULL( ) function, as shown in the following statement:

```
SELECT dbo.Customer.CustomerNumber,
    dbo.Customer.Name,
    dbo.Customer.BillingCity,
    dbo.InvoiceHeader.InvoiceNumber,
    dbo.InvoiceHeader.TotalAmount,
    dbo.LoyaltyDiscount.Discount,
    dbo.InvoiceHeader.TotalAmount -
      (dbo.InvoiceHeader.TotalAmount *
        ISNULL(dbo.LoyaltyDiscount.Discount,0.00))
                AS DiscountedTotalAmount
FROM dbo.Customer
INNER JOIN dbo.InvoiceHeader
 ON dbo.Customer.CustomerNumber = dbo.InvoiceHeader.CustomerNumber
LEFT OUTER JOIN dbo.LoyaltyDiscount
```

```
ON dbo.Customer.CustomerNumber = dbo.LoyaltyDiscount.CustomerNumber
WHERE (dbo.Customer.BillingCity = 'Axelburg')
AND (dbo.Customer.Name > 'C')
ORDER BY dbo.Customer.Name DESC, dbo.InvoiceHeader.InvoiceNumber
```

Now, when the database encounters a NULL value in the Discount column while it is performing the calculation, it substitutes a value of 0.00 and continues on with the calculation. The database only performs this substitution when it encounters a NULL value. If any other value is in the Discount column, it uses that value. The result set from this SELECT statement is shown in Figure 3-35.

The GROUP BY Clause

Our sample SELECT statement appears to resemble a run-on sentence. You have seen, however, that each of these clauses is necessary to change the meaning of the statement and provide the result set that is desired. We will add just two more clauses to the sample SELECT statement before we are done.

There are times, as you are analyzing data, that you only want to see information at a summary level rather than viewing all the detail. In other words, you want the result set to group together the information from several rows to form a summary

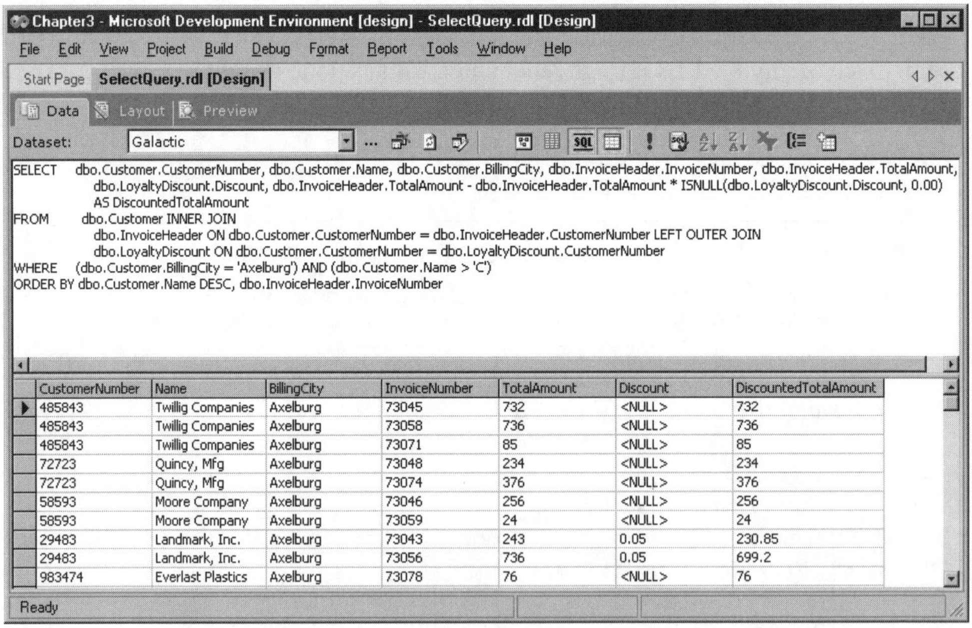

Figure 3-35   *A SELECT statement using the ISNULL( ) function*

row. Additional instructions must be added to our SELECT statement in two places in order for this to happen.

First of all, you need to specify which columns are going to be used to determine when a summary row will be created. These columns are placed in the GROUP BY clause. Consider the following SELECT statement:

```
SELECT dbo.Customer.CustomerNumber,
    dbo.Customer.Name,
    dbo.Customer.BillingCity,
    COUNT(dbo.InvoiceHeader.InvoiceNumber) AS NumberOfInvoices,
    SUM(dbo.InvoiceHeader.TotalAmount) AS TotalAmount,
    dbo.LoyaltyDiscount.Discount,
    SUM(dbo.InvoiceHeader.TotalAmount -
      (dbo.InvoiceHeader.TotalAmount *
        ISNULL(dbo.LoyaltyDiscount.Discount,0.00)))
                    AS DiscountedTotalAmount
FROM dbo.Customer
INNER JOIN dbo.InvoiceHeader
 ON dbo.Customer.CustomerNumber = dbo.InvoiceHeader.CustomerNumber
LEFT OUTER JOIN dbo.LoyaltyDiscount
 ON dbo.Customer.CustomerNumber = dbo.LoyaltyDiscount.CustomerNumber
WHERE (dbo.Customer.BillingCity = 'Axelburg')
AND (dbo.Customer.Name > 'C')
GROUP BY dbo.Customer.CustomerNumber, dbo.Customer.Name,
    dbo.Customer.BillingCity, dbo.LoyaltyDiscount.Discount
ORDER BY dbo.Customer.Name DESC
```

The Customer Number, Name, Billing City, and Discount columns are included in the GROUP BY clause. When this query is run, each unique set of values from these four columns will result in a row in the result set.

Second, you need to specify how the columns in the FIELD LIST that are not included in the GROUP BY clause are to be handled. In the sample SELECT statement, the Invoice Number and Total Amount columns are in the FIELD LIST but are not part of the GROUP BY clause. The calculated column, Discounted Total Amount, is also in the FIELD LIST but is not present in the GROUP BY clause. In the sample SELECT statement, these three columns are the non-group-by columns.

The SELECT statement is asking for the values from several rows to be combined into one summary row. The SELECT statement needs to provide a way for this combining to take place. This is done by enclosing each non-group-by column in a special function called an *aggregate function,* which performs a mathematical operation on values from a number of rows and returns a single result. Aggregate functions include:

- ▶ **SUM( )**   Returns the sum of the values
- ▶ **AVG( )**   Returns the average of the values
- ▶ **COUNT( )**   Returns a count of the values
- ▶ **MAX( )**   Returns the largest value
- ▶ **MIN( )**   Returns the smallest value

The SELECT statement in our group by example uses the SUM( ) aggregate function to return the sum of the invoice amount and the sum of the discounted amount for each customer. It also uses the COUNT( ) aggregate function to return the number of invoices for each customer. The result set from this SELECT statement is shown in Figure 3-36. Note that when an aggregate function is placed around a column name in the FIELD LIST, the SELECT statement can no longer determine what name to use for that column in the result set. You need to supply a column name to use in the result set, as shown in this SELECT statement.

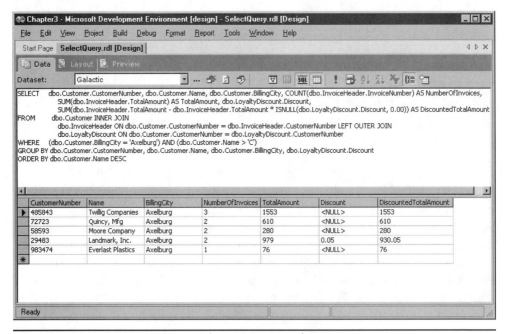

Figure 3-36   *A SELECT statement with a GROUP BY clause*

NOTE

When you're using a GROUP BY clause, all columns in the FIELD LIST must either be included in the GROUP BY clause or be enclosed in an aggregate function. In the sample SELECT statement, the Customer Number column is all that is necessary in the GROUP BY clause to provide the desired grouping. However, because the Name, Billing City, and Discount columns do not lend themselves to being aggregated, they are included in the GROUP BY clause along with the Customer Number column.

The HAVING Clause

The GROUP BY clause has a special clause that can be used with it to determine which grouped rows will be included in the result set. This is the *HAVING* clause. The HAVING clause functions similar to the WHERE clause. The WHERE clause limits the rows in the result set by checking conditions at the row level. The HAVING clause limits the rows in the result set by checking conditions at the group level.

Consider the following SELECT statement:

```
SELECT dbo.Customer.CustomerNumber,
    dbo.Customer.Name,
    dbo.Customer.BillingCity,
    COUNT(dbo.InvoiceHeader.InvoiceNumber) AS NumberOfInvoices,
    SUM(dbo.InvoiceHeader.TotalAmount) AS TotalAmount,
    dbo.LoyaltyDiscount.Discount,
    SUM(dbo.InvoiceHeader.TotalAmount -
      (dbo.InvoiceHeader.TotalAmount *
        ISNULL(dbo.LoyaltyDiscount.Discount,0.00)))
                  AS DiscountedTotalAmount
FROM dbo.Customer
INNER JOIN dbo.InvoiceHeader
 ON dbo.Customer.CustomerNumber = dbo.InvoiceHeader.CustomerNumber
LEFT OUTER JOIN dbo.LoyaltyDiscount
 ON dbo.Customer.CustomerNumber = dbo.LoyaltyDiscount.CustomerNumber
WHERE (dbo.Customer.BillingCity = 'Axelburg')
AND (dbo.Customer.Name > 'C')
GROUP BY dbo.Customer.CustomerNumber, dbo.Customer.Name,
    dbo.Customer.BillingCity, dbo.LoyaltyDiscount.Discount
HAVING COUNT(dbo.InvoiceHeader.InvoiceNumber) >= 2
ORDER BY dbo.Customer.Name DESC
```

The WHERE clause says that a row must have a Billing City column with a value of Axelburg and a Name column with a value greater than C before it can be included in the group. The HAVING clause says that a group must contain at least two invoices before it can be included in the result set. The result set for this SELECT statement is shown in Figure 3-37.

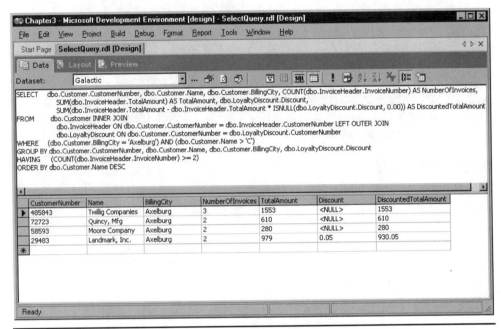

Figure 3-37   *A SELECT statement with a HAVING clause*

On to the Reports

Good reporting depends more on getting the right data out of the database than it does on creating a clean report design and delivering the report in a timely manner. If you are feeling a little overwhelmed by the workings of relational databases and SELECT queries, don't worry. Refer back to this chapter from time to time if you need to.

Also, keep in mind that Reporting Services provides you with the Query Builder tool to assist with the query-creation process. You don't need to remember the exact syntax for the LEFT OUTER JOIN or a GROUP BY clause. What you do need to know is the capabilities of the SELECT statement so that you know what to instruct the Query Builder to create.

Finally, when you are creating your queries, use the same method that was used here; in other words, build them one step at a time. Join together the tables that you will need for your report, determine what columns are required, then come up with a WHERE clause that gets you just the rows you are looking for. After that, you can add in the sorting and grouping. Assemble one clause, and then another and another, and pretty soon you will have a slam-bang query that will give you exactly the data you need!

Now, on to the reports…

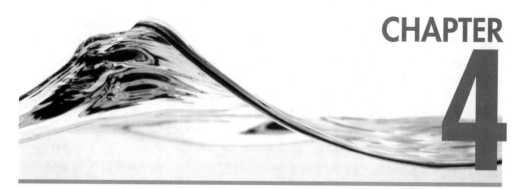

A Visit to Emerald City: The Report Wizard

I f the relational database concepts of Chapter 3 were new to you, you may feel like you have been through a twister and are not in Kansas anymore. You can take heart in the fact that we have completed the preliminaries and are now ready to start building reports. So, with no further ado, strap on your ruby slippers and follow the yellow-brick road, because you are off to see the wizard!

That wizard is, of course, the Report Wizard found in Visual Studio .NET 2003. Like the ruler of Emerald City, the Report Wizard is not all powerful. For example, the Report Wizard will not allow you to make use of all the features available in Reporting Services. The wizard is, however, a great place to get a feel for the way reports are constructed.

NOTE

Beginning with this chapter, we will be creating sample reports using the Galactic database. If you have not done so already, go to http://www.osborne.com, locate the book's page using the ISBN 0072232161, and follow the instructions to download and install the Galactic database.

Your First Report

You are now ready to build your first Reporting Services report. Of course, few people build reports just for the fun of it. Usually there is some business reason for this endeavor. In this book, as was stated in the previous chapter, we will use the business needs of Galactic Delivery Services (GDS) as the basis for our sample reports.

Each of the sample reports used in this book will be presented in a manner similar to what you see in this section. The report will be introduced with a list of the Reporting Services features which it highlights. This will be followed by the business need of our sample company, Galactic Delivery Services, that this report is meant to fill. Next is an overview of the tasks that must be accomplished to create the report.

Finally, we will walk through each task, step by step. In addition to the step-by-step description, each task will include a few notes to provide additional information on the steps you just completed. Follow the step-by-step instructions to complete the task, then read through the task notes to gain additional understanding of the process you have just completed.

The Customer List Report

Here is our first attempt at creating a report, the Customer List Report.

Features Highlighted

▶ Creating a data source

▶ Using the Query Builder to create a dataset

▶ Using the Report Wizard to create a table report

Business Need   The accounting department at Galactic Delivery Services would like an e-mail directory containing all the billing contacts for its customers. The directory should be an alphabetical list of all the GDS customers. It must include the customer name along with a billing contact and a billing e-mail address for each one.

Task Overview

1. Begin a New Project in Visual Studio

2. Create a Data Source

3. Create a Dataset

4. Choose the Report Layout

Customer List Report, Task 1: Begin a New Project in Visual Studio

1. Run Visual Studio .NET 2003. Visual Studio's Start page will appear, as shown here.

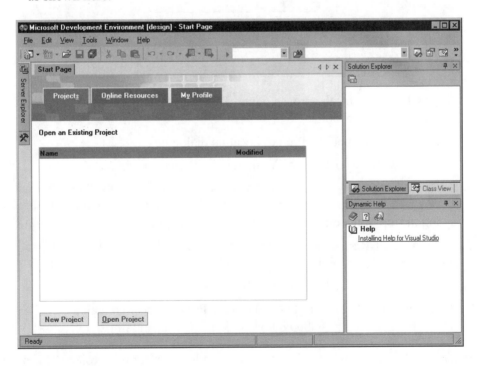

NOTE

The first illustration shows the default configuration of Visual Studio. Your screen may vary if this configuration has been changed.

2. Click the New Project button to create a new project. This will display the New Project dialog box, as shown in the following illustration. (You can create a new project three different ways: Select File | New | Project from the main menu, click the New Project toolbar button, or click New Project on the Start page.)

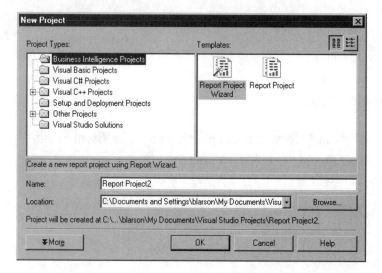

3. Type **Chapter04** for the project name. This project will contain all the reports you create in this chapter.

4. Click Browse to open the Project Location dialog box.

5. Click My Projects to go to the Visual Studio Projects folder.

6. Click the Create New Folder button in the toolbar at the top of the Project Location dialog box. If you have trouble finding the Create New Folder button, look along the top of the dialog box for a picture of a folder with a yellow sparkle.

7. Enter **MSSQLRS** for the name of the new folder. This folder will contain all the projects you create for this book.

8. Click OK in the New Folder dialog box.

9. Click Open in the lower-right corner of the Project Location dialog box. The New Project dialog box should now look like the second illustration.

Task Notes   We have now established a name and location for this project. This must be done for every project you create. Because Visual Studio uses the project name to create a folder for all the project files, the project name must be a valid Windows folder name. You can use the Browse button to browse to the appropriate location, as we did here, or you can type the path in the Location text box.

NOTE

Valid folder names can contain any character except for the following:

$$/ ? : \& \backslash * " < > | \# \%$$

In addition, a folder cannot be named "." or "..".

The project name is appended to the end of the location path to create the full path for the folder that will contain the new project. The full path is shown just above the OK and Cancel buttons near the bottom of the dialog box in the second illustration. In our example, Visual Studio will create a folder called Chapter04 inside the folder MSSQLRS. All the files created as part of the Chapter04 project will be placed in this folder.

Customer List Report, Task 2: Create a Data Source

1. Click OK in the New Project dialog box to start the Report Wizard. The Welcome to the Report Wizard page will appear, as shown here.

2. Click Next. The Select the Data Source page will appear.

3. Type **Galactic** for the data source name.

4. Select Microsoft SQL Server from the Type drop-down list, if it is not already selected.

5. Click Edit. The Data Link Properties dialog box will appear.

6. Type the name of the Microsoft SQL Server database server that is hosting the Galactic database. If the Galactic database is hosted by the computer you are currently working on, you may type **(local)** for the server name.

7. Click the Use a Specific User Name and Password radio button.

8. Type **GalacticReporting** for the user name.

9. Type **gds** for the password.

10. Click the Allow Saving Password check box.

11. Select Galactic from the Select the Database on the Server drop-down list. The Data Link Properties dialog box should now look like this:

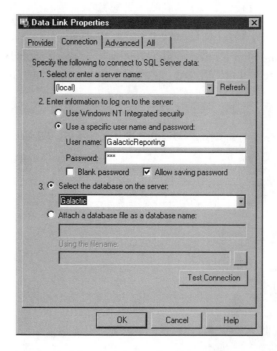

12. Click the Test Connection button. If the message "Test connection succeeded." appears, click OK. If an error message appears, make sure that the name of your database server, the user name, the password, and the name of your database have been entered properly. If your test connection still does not succeed, make sure you have correctly installed the Galactic database.

13. Click OK to return to the Select the Data Source page of the Report Wizard.

14. Click the Make This a Shared Data Source check box so that it is checked. This page should now look like this:

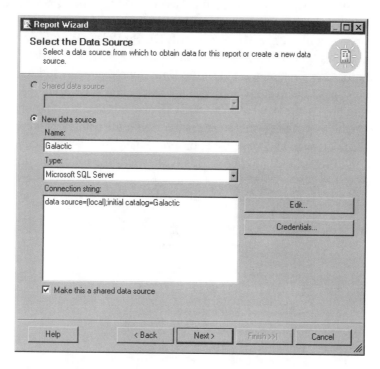

Task Notes   As we discussed in Chapter 1, the data source is actually a set of instructions for connecting to the database server or data file that will provide the information for your report. This set of instructions is also known as a *connection string*. In this sample report, we used the Data Link Properties dialog box to build the connection string. Those of you who memorize connection strings can type the appropriate string on the Select the Data Source page without using the Data Link Properties dialog box at all. The rest of us will continue to use the Data Link Properties dialog box when building future reports to have the connection string created for us.

CAUTION

If you do type in your own connection string, do not include the login and password information. The connection string is stored as plain text in the report definition file, so a password stored as part of the connection string is easy to discover. Instead, use the Credentials button on the Select the Data Source page to enter the login and password so they will be stored in a more secure fashion.

Reporting Services can utilize data from a number of different databases and data files; however, you need to tell the wizard what type of database or data file the report will be using. You did this using the Type drop-down list in step 4 of the previous task. This selection tells Reporting Services which *data provider* to use when accessing the database or data file. When you select Microsoft SQL Server, Reporting Services will use the Microsoft OLE DB Provider for SQL Server. This data provider knows how to retrieve information from a SQL Server database.

The Type drop-down list on the Select the Data Source page includes only a few of the possible types of data sources. If you are using data from a Microsoft SQL Server database, an Oracle database, or ODBC, you can select the appropriate data source type on the Select the Data Source page. If you are using any other type of data source, you will need to choose the appropriate data provider on the Provider tab of the Data Link Properties dialog box. This is shown in the following illustration.

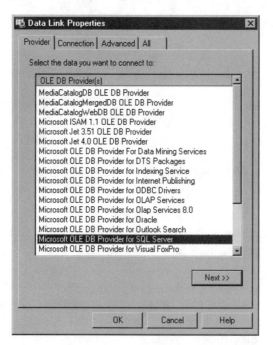

If you are using a data source type other than SQL Server, Oracle, or ODBC, you'll need to insert the following steps into the preceding task:

5a. Click the Provider tab of the Data Link Properties dialog box.

5b. Select the appropriate data provider.

5c. Click Next.

Each data provider requires slightly different bits of information in order to create the connection string. The Connection tab of the Data Link Properties dialog box will change to suit the selected data provider. This means that steps 6 through 11 will vary when you use a data source type other than Microsoft SQL Server. Simply provide the information that is requested on the Connection tab. Be sure to use Test Connection to make sure everything has been entered properly before leaving the Data Link Properties dialog box.

Checking the Allow Saving Password check box on the Select the Data Source page allows Visual Studio to save the data source *credentials* with the data source definition. The data source credentials are the user name and password information required to access that data source. The login credentials are encrypted before they are saved to help protect them. If you are not comfortable having the credentials stored in this manner, leave both the user name and password blank. Visual Studio will prompt you for the credentials every time you execute the report or modify the dataset.

NOTE

If you leave the data source credentials blank and your selected data source requires a login, you will be prompted for database credentials when you click Next on the Select the Data Source page. The credentials you enter here are used to create a connection to the data source for the Design the Query page and for the Query Builder. These credentials are not stored with the data source.

A data source can be used by a single report, or it can be shared by several reports in the same project. Checking the Make This a Shared Data Source check box allows this data source to be used by many reports. Shared data sources are stored separately from the reports that use them. Non-shared data sources are stored right in the report definition. If you have a number of reports in the same project that utilize data from the same database or the same data files, you will save time by using a shared data source.

CAUTION

Even though the data source credentials are encrypted, it is never a good idea to use the system administrator account or any other database login with system administrator privileges to access data for reporting. Always create a database login that has only the privileges required for reporting operations and use this login as the reporting credentials.

Some companies require that reports use data from a development database server while they are being developed and a production database server when the reports are completed. Using a shared data source in this type of an environment makes it easier to switch a number of reports from the development database server to the production database server. The change is made once to the shared data source, and all the reports are ready to go.

Customer List Report, Task 3: Create a Dataset

1. Click Next. The Design the Query page of the Report Wizard will appear.
2. Click Edit. The Query Builder will appear.

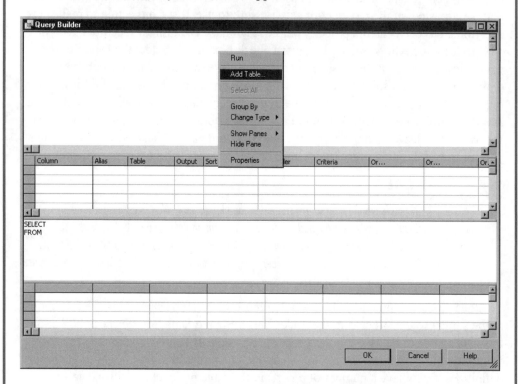

3. The Query Builder is divided into four horizontal sections. The top section is called the *diagram pane*. Right-click in the diagram pane. You will see the context menu as shown above.

4. Select the Add Table command from the context menu. This will display the Add Table dialog box shown to the right. This dialog box contains a list of all the tables in the data source.

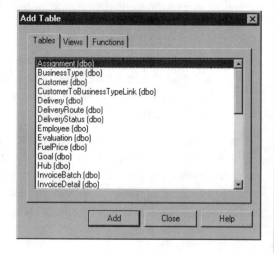

5. Double-click "Customer (dbo)" in the list of tables. The Customer table is added to the query.

6. Click Close to exit the Add Table dialog box.

7. A list of the fields in the Customer table is displayed. Click the check box next to the Name field.

8. Scroll down the list of fields and check the BillingContact and BillingEmail fields as well.

9. The section of the Query Builder directly below the diagram pane is called the *grid pane*. In the grid pane, type **1** in the Sort Order column across from the Name field. Alternatively, you can click in the Sort Order column across from the Name field and select "1" from the drop-down list.

10. The section of the Query Builder directly below the grid pane is the *SQL pane*. Right-click in the SQL pane. You will see the context menu shown here.

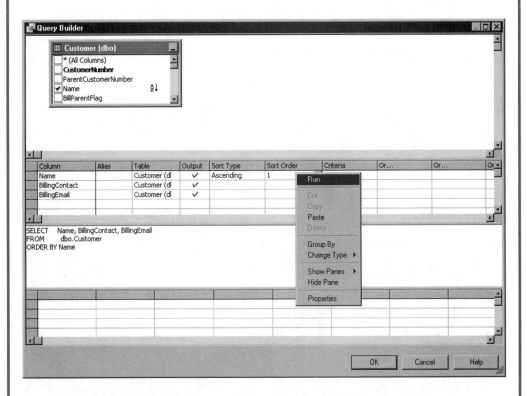

11. Select the Run command from the context menu. This will run the query and display the results in the bottom section of the Query Builder. This

bottom section is called the *results pane*. The Query Builder should now look like this:

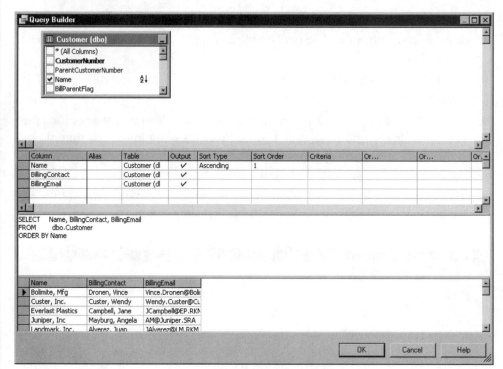

12. Right-click in the Results Pane. Select "Clear Results" from the context menu.

13. Click OK to return to the Design the Query page of the Report Wizard. This page should now look like the illustration here.

Task Notes The dataset represents the information that will be retrieved from the data source and used in your report. The dataset actually consists of two parts. The first part is the database command used to retrieve data. This is the SELECT statement you created using the Query Builder. This database command is called the *query string*.

The second part is the list of the columns in the result set created by executing the query string. This list of columns is called the *structure* or *schema* of the result set. Visual Studio determines the field list by executing the query string in a special manner so that it returns the structure of the result set, but does not return any rows in the result set.

Those of you who are familiar with your data source and are also familiar with the SELECT statement can type your SELECT statement in the Query String text box on the Design the Query page. This is especially appropriate when you are executing a *stored procedure* to retrieve data rather than using a SELECT statement. A stored procedure is a program saved inside the database itself that can be used to modify or retrieve data. We will talk more about using stored procedures in a query string in Chapter 7.

It is a good idea to run the query yourself before exiting the Query Builder. We did this in steps 10 and 11 of this task. This ensures that there are no errors in the SQL statement the Query Builder created for you. It also allows you to look at the result set in the results pane and make sure you are getting the information you expected.

In order to display the result set in the results pane, Visual Studio must first load the result set in memory. Keeping result sets in memory can take up valuable resources that might be needed by other programs. This memory is not automatically cleared when you exit the Query Builder. For this reason, you should always clear the result set yourself, as we did in step 12 of this task. If you do not clear the result set yourself, Visual Studio will eventually display a dialog box reminding you that you have a result set open and asking whether you plan on making any further use of it. If this happens, click No to tell Visual Studio that you do not need the result set any longer.

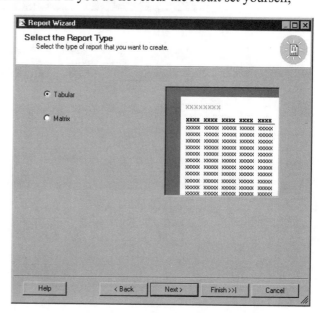

Customer List Report, Task 4: Choose the Report Layout

1. Click Next. The Select the Report Type page of the Report Wizard will appear.

2. Make sure that the Tabular radio button is selected and click Next. The Design the Table page of the Report Wizard will appear.

3. With the Name field highlighted in the Available Fields list, click Details. The Name field will be moved to the Displayed Fields list.

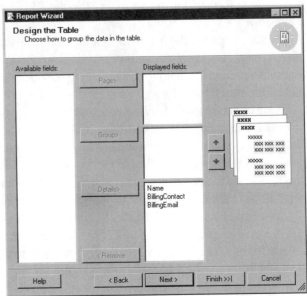

4. Do the same thing with the BillingContact and BillingEmail fields. The Design the Table page should now look like the illustration here.

5. Click Next. The Choose the Table Style page of the Report Wizard will appear, as shown here.

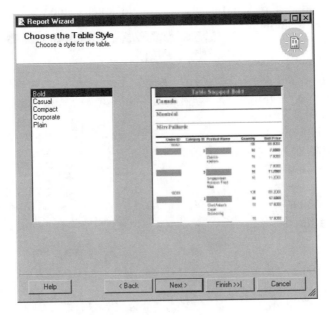

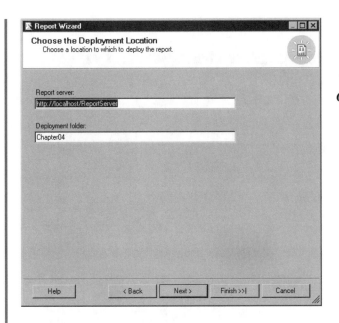

6. Make sure that Bold is selected in the style list and click Next. The Choose the Deployment Location page of the Report Wizard will appear.

7. Click Next. The Completing the Report Wizard page will appear.

8. Type **Customer List** for the report name.

9. Click Finish. The Visual Studio window will appear.

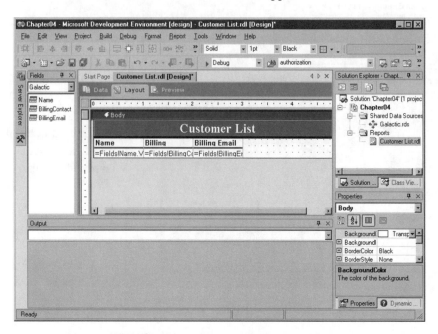

10. Click the Preview tab located near the middle of the screen just above the report layout. A preview of your report will appear.

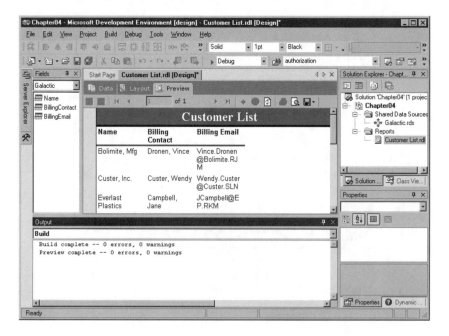

11. Click the Layout tab.

12. The Report Wizard created columns in our report that seem a bit too narrow. We will improve the report by widening the columns. Click the Name heading ("Name" in bold).

13. Place your mouse pointer on the line separating the gray box above the Name heading and the gray box above the Billing Contact heading. Your mouse pointer will change to a double-headed arrow, as shown here.

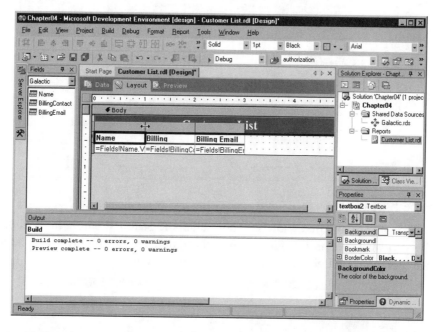

14. Hold down the left mouse button and move the mouse pointer to the right. This will make the Name column wider.

15. Follow the technique described in step 14 of this task to widen the Billing Contact and Billing Email columns as well.

16. Click the Preview tab. Your report should appear as shown here.

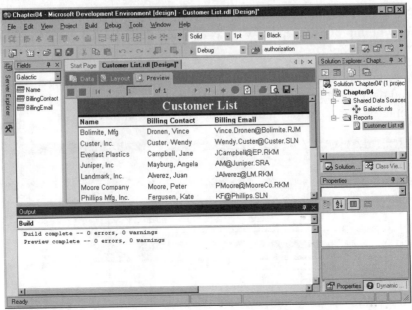

17. Repeat steps 11 through 16 until you are satisfied with the appearance of the report.

18. When you are satisfied with the report, click the Save All button in the toolbar. This will save the project, the shared data source, and the report files. The Save All button is highlighted in the following illustration.

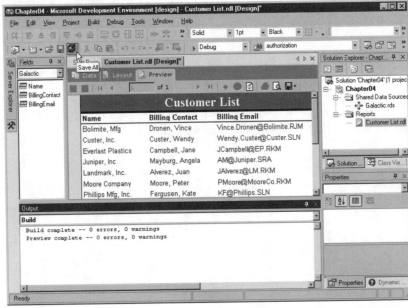

Task Notes   As you may have noticed, the Choose the Table Style page offers several table style choices (refer to the illustration in step 5). You can try these different table styles as you complete the other sample reports in this chapter and as you create your own reports using the Report Wizard. For ease of comparison between sample reports, the figures in this book will continue to use the Bold style.

The report server and deployment folder items on the Choose the Deployment Location page (refer to the illustration in step 6) are used when the report is moved from the development environment to a report server. These items are saved with the project, not with an individual report. For this reason, the Deployment Location page is only displayed by the Report Wizard for the first report created in a project. We will discuss report deployment in Chapter 10.

You probably had to repeat steps 11 through 16 of this task several times to get the report just the way you wanted it to look. This is not a problem. Most reports that you create will require multiple trips between the Layout and the Preview tabs before everything is laid out as it should be. The fact that you can move between layout and preview with such ease is a real plus for the report-authoring environment provided by Visual Studio.

Congratulations! You have now completed your first report.

An Interactive Table Report

Now that you have a taste of how the Report Wizard works and what it can do, let's try something a bit more complex. We will create a table report that implements an interactive feature called *drilldown*. With the drilldown type of report, only the high-level, summary information is initially presented to the viewers. They can then click a special area of the report (in our case, that area is designated by a plus sign) to reveal part of the lower-level, detail information. The viewers drill down through the summary to get to the detail.

The Customer-Invoice Report

Features Highlighted

▶ Using a shared data source

▶ Linking tables in the Query Builder

▶ Assigning columns for page breaks and grouping

▶ Enabling subtotals and drilldown

Business Need   The accounting department would like a report listing all the Galactic Delivery Services (GDS) customers. The customers need to be grouped by Billing City, with each city beginning on a new page. The report will allow a viewer to drill down from the customer level to see the invoices for that customer.

Task Overview

1. Reopen the Chapter04 Project
2. Create a New Report in the Chapter04 Project, Select the Shared Data Source, and Create a Dataset
3. Choose the Report Layout

Customer-Invoice Report, Task 1: Reopen the Chapter04 Project

If you have not closed the Chapter04 project since working on the previous section of this chapter, skip to step 8. Otherwise, follow these steps, starting with step 1:

1. Run Visual Studio .NET 2003.
2. If a link to the Chapter04 project is visible on the Start Page, click this link and the Chapter04 project will open. Proceed to step 8. If a link to the Chapter04 project is not visible on the Start Page, continue with step 3.
3. Select File | Open Solution.
4. Click My Projects.
5. Double-click MSSQLRS.
6. Double-click Chapter04.
7. Double-click Chapter04.sln. (This is the file that contains the solution for Chapter04.)
8. If the CustomerList1 report is displayed in the center of the screen, click the X button in the upper-right corner of the center section of the screen to close this report.

Task Notes   Opening the Chapter04 solution (Chapter04.sln) and opening the Chapter04 project (Chapter04.rptproj) actually produce the same end result, so you can do either. There is only one project in the Chapter04 solution, so that project is automatically opened when the solution is opened. When the Chapter04 project is opened, the last report you worked on will be displayed in the center of the screen. In this case, it is probably the Customer List report.

You do not need to close one report before working on another report. In fact, you can have multiple reports open at one time and use the tabs containing the report names to move between them. In most cases, however, I find that a philosophy of "the less clutter the better" works well when creating reports. For this reason, I recommend that you close all unneeded reports as you move from one report to the next.

Customer-Invoice Report, Task 2: Create a New Report in the Chapter04 Project, Select the Shared Data Source, and Create a Dataset

1. In the Solution Explorer on the right side of the screen, right-click the Reports folder. You will see the context menu shown here.

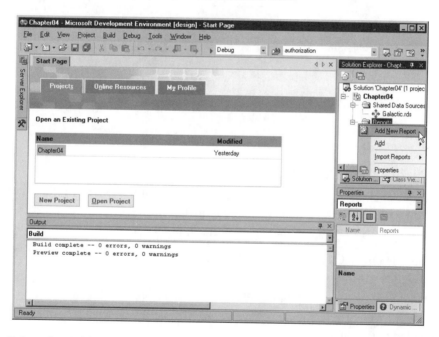

2. Select the Add New Report command from the context menu. This will start the Report Wizard, allowing you to create another report in the current project.

3. Click Next. The Select the Data Source page will appear.

4. Make sure the Shared Data Source radio button is selected and the Galactic data source is selected in the drop-down list, as shown here. Click Next. The Design the Query page will appear.

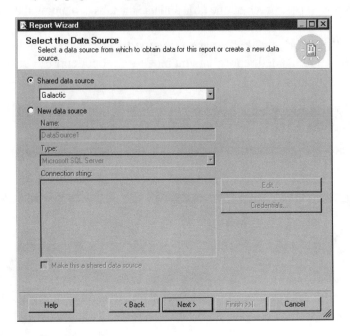

5. Click Edit. The Query Builder will appear.

6. Right-click in the diagram pane (the upper area) of the Query Builder screen. You will see the diagram pane context menu.

7. Select the Add Table command from the context menu.

8. Double-click "Customer (dbo)" in the list of tables. The Customer table is added to the query.

9. Double-click "InvoiceHeader (dbo)" in the list of tables. Make sure you select InvoiceHeader and *not* InvoiceDetail. The InvoiceHeader table is added to the query.

10. Click Close to exit the Add Table dialog box. Notice that the Query Builder automatically created the INNER JOIN between the Customer and the InvoiceHeader tables, as shown in the following illustration.

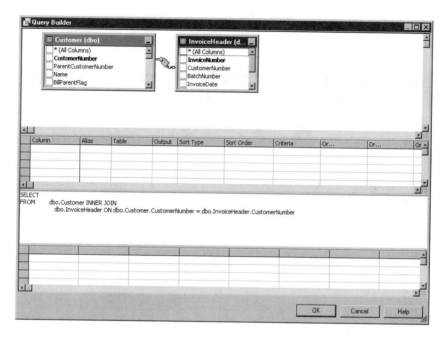

11. Right-click the gray diamond in the middle of the link joining the Customer and the InvoiceHeader tables. The join context menu will be displayed, as shown in the following illustration.

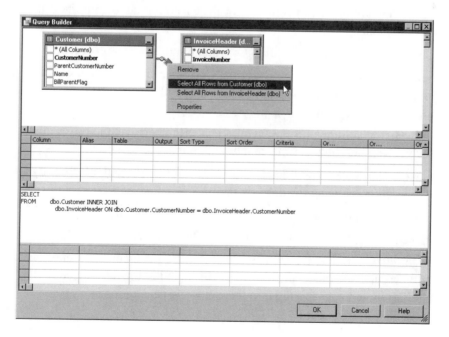

12. Select the Select All Rows from Customer (dbo) option from the context menu. The diamond symbol changes, as shown here.

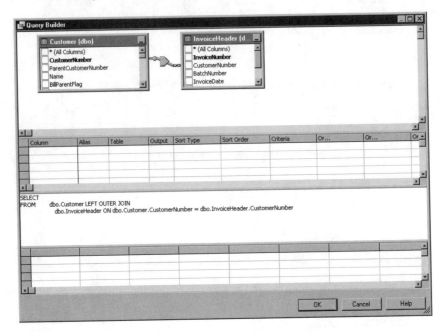

13. Scroll down in the list of columns for the Customer table until the BillingCity column name is visible.

14. Check the box next to the BillingCity column in the Customer table.

15. Scroll up in the list of columns for the Customer table and check the box next to the Name column. This places the Name field after the BillingCity field in the resulting SQL query.

16. In the list of columns for the InvoiceHeader table, check the boxes next to the InvoiceNumber, InvoiceDate, and TotalAmount columns.

17. Place a "1" in the Sort Order column for the BillingCity field either by typing in the cell or by using the drop-down list.

18. Place a "2" in the Sort Order column for the Name field.

19. Place a "3" in the Sort Order column for the InvoiceNumber field.

20. Right-click in the SQL pane and select Run from the context menu. The query will execute, and the result set will be displayed in the results pane. The Query Builder should appear similar to the following illustration.

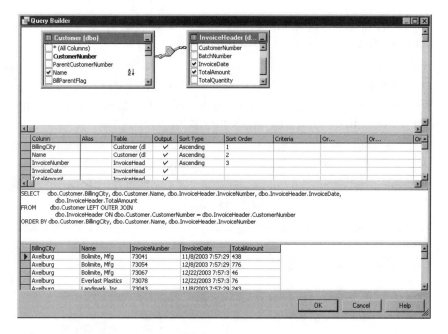

21. Right-click in the Results Pane. Select "Clear Results" from the context menu.

22. Click OK. This will return you to the Design the Query page.

Task Notes   The Galactic data source that you created in the first report is a shared data source. As such, the wizard defaults to using this shared data source on the Select the Data Source page any time a new report is created.

In the Query Builder, when a second table is added to the query, the column names from each table are compared. If the Query Builder finds two columns with the same name and data type, it will create a JOIN based on those columns. You saw this in steps 8 and 9 in this task.

The business need for this report states that the report should include all GDS customers. As you saw in Chapter 3, some customers may not have invoices. Therefore, in order to include all the customers in the report, we need to use a LEFT OUTER JOIN between the Customer table and the InvoiceHeader table. This is accomplished by selecting "Select All Rows from Customer (dbo)," as was done in step 12 of this task.

Customer-Invoice Report, Task 3: Choose the Report Layout

1. Click Next. The Select the Report Type page of the Report Wizard will appear.

2. Make sure that the Tabular radio button is selected and click Next. The Design the Table page of the Report Wizard will appear.

3. With the BillingCity field highlighted in the Available Fields list, click Page. The BillingCity field will be moved to the Displayed Fields list.

4. With the Name field highlighted in the Available Fields list, click Group. The Name field will be moved to the Displayed Fields list.

5. With the InvoiceNumber field highlighted in the Available Fields list, click Details. The InvoiceNumber field will be moved to the Displayed Fields list.

6. With the InvoiceDate field highlighted in the Available Fields list, click Details. The InvoiceDate field will be moved to the Displayed Fields list.

7. With the TotalAmount field highlighted in the Available Fields list, click Details. The TotalAmount field will be moved to the Displayed Fields list. The Design the Table page will appear.

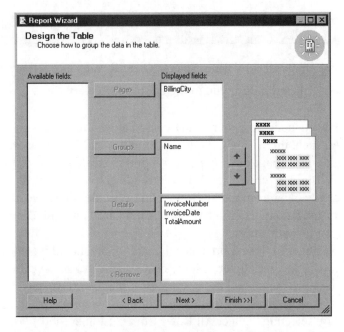

8. Click Next. The Choose the Table Layout page of the Report Wizard will appear. This page appears in the Report Wizard because we put fields in the Grouping area on the Design the Table page.

9. Check the Include Subtotals check box.

10. Check the Enable Drilldown check box. The Choose the Table Layout page will appear.

11. Click Next. The Choose the Table Style page of the Report Wizard will appear.

12. Make sure that Bold is selected in the style list and click Next. The Completing the Report Wizard page will appear.

13. Type **Customer-Invoice Report** for the report name.

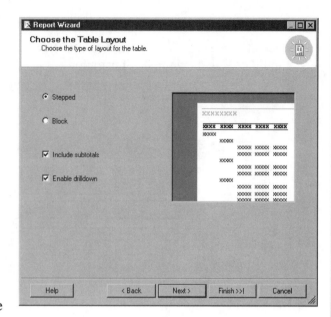

14. Click Finish. The Visual Studio window will appear.

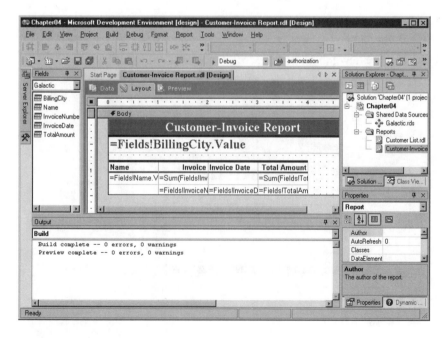

15. Widen the Name column as you did with the previous report.

16. Click the table cell directly under the Invoice heading. This cell will be highlighted, as shown in the illustration.

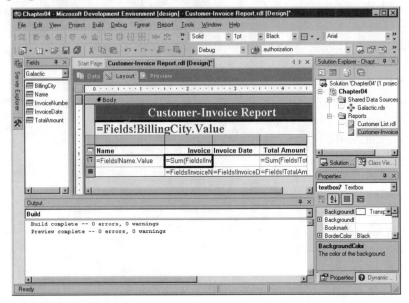

17. Press DELETE on your keyboard to remove the nonsensical totaling of the invoice numbers.

18. Click the Preview tab. A preview of your report will appear.

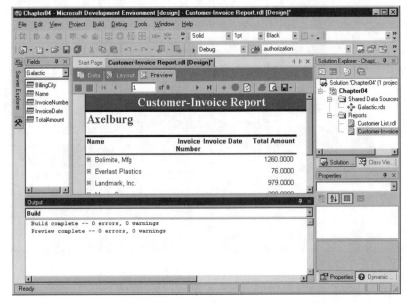

19. Click the plus sign across from "Bolimite, Mfg" to view the invoices for this company, as shown here.

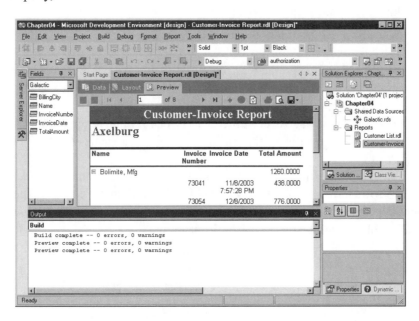

20. Click the blue triangle just below the Preview tab to advance to the next page of the report. The blue triangle is highlighted in the following illustration.

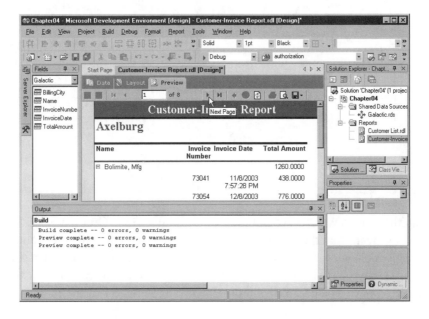

21. You can continue to work with the report preview to get a feel for the way report navigation and drilldown works. (For instance, you may want to try clicking the minus sign.)

22. Click the Save All button in the toolbar.

Task Notes   When we created the Customer List report, we put all the columns from the dataset into the detail line of the report. This time, we put the BillingCity column in the Page area of the table layout. Because of this, the Report Wizard created a report that begins a new page every time there is a new value in the BillingCity column. In addition, the value of the BillingCity column appears at the top of each report page.

The following illustration shows the dataset used in the Customer-Invoice report. The first 13 rows have a value of "Axelburg" for the BillingCity column. Therefore, Axelburg appears at the top of page 1 of the report. All the rows with Axelburg in the BillingCity column will be on page 1 of the report.

Groupings on the Customer-Invoice Report

Using the Report Wizard, we put the Name column in the Group area of the table layout. This means that the report will create a new group each time the value of the Name column changes. Again, looking at the preceding illustration, you can see that the first three rows have a value of "Bolimite, Mfg" in the Name column. Therefore, these three rows will be combined in the first group on page 1 of the report.

By checking the Enable Drilldown checkbox, you told the Report Wizard to create a report where the detail lines for each grouping are initially hidden. The detail lines for a group become visible when the plus sign for that group is clicked. By checking the Include Subtotals check box, you told the Report Wizard to total any numeric columns in the detail and to show those totals in the group header for each group.

Let's look again at the first few rows of the dataset shown in the preceding illustration. The first three rows have a value of "Bolimite, Mfg" in the Name column. Because of this, these three rows are grouped together for the report shown after step 18 in Task 3. In this report, the number 1260.0000 appears across from Bolimite, Mfg. This is the total of all the invoices in the detail rows for Bolimite, Mfg.

Because the Report Wizard tried to add up any and all numeric columns, it also created an entry in the grouping for a total of the invoice numbers. Adding up the invoice numbers does not result in a meaningful value. Therefore, we deleted this grouping entry in steps 16 and 17 of this task.

Creating Matrix Reports

You have now seen much of what the Report Wizard can do for you when it comes to tabular reports. It is now time to look at the other report type that the Report Wizard will produce for you. Prepare yourself; we are going to enter the matrix.

What Reporting Services calls a matrix report is referred to as a *crosstab* or a *pivot table report* elsewhere. In a tabular report, we have columns from a result set across the top and rows from a result set going down the page. In a matrix report, we have row values going across the top and down the page. Matrix reports are much easier to grasp once you have seen one in action, so let's give it a try.

The Invoice-Batch Number Report

Features Highlighted

▶   Using the matrix report type

Business Need   The accounting department processes invoices in batches. Once a week, the accounting department creates invoices to send to their customers for the deliveries that were made over the previous week. A batch number is assigned to each invoice as it is created. All the invoices created on the same day are given the same batch number.

The new report requested by the accounting department will show the total amount of the invoices created in each batch. The report will also allow batches to be broken down by billing city and by customer. In order to allow this type of analysis, you will need to use a matrix report.

Task Overview

1. Reopen the Chapter04 Project, Create a New Report in the Chapter04 Project, Select the Shared Data Source, and Create a Dataset

2. Choose the Report Layout

Invoice-Batch Number Report, Task 1: Reopen the Chapter04 Project, Create a New Report in the Chapter04 Project, Select the Shared Data Source, and Create a Dataset

1. If you have closed the Chapter04 project, reopen it. (If you need assistance with this, see Task 1 of the previous report.)

2. In the Solution Explorer on the right side of the screen, right-click the Reports folder.

3. Select the Add New Report command from the context menu. This will start the Report Wizard, allowing you to create an additional report in the current project.

4. Click Next. The Select the Data Source page will appear.

5. Make sure the Shared Data Source radio button is selected and the Galactic data source is selected in the drop-down list. Click Next.

6. Click Edit. The Query Builder will appear.

7. Right-click in the diagram pane (the upper area) of the Query Builder screen. You will see the diagram pane context menu.

8. Select the Add Table command from the context menu.

9. Add the following tables to the query:
   Customer (dbo)
   InvoiceHeader (dbo)

10. Click Close to exit the Add Table dialog box.

11. Check the following columns in the Customer table in the order shown here:
    BillingCity
    Name

12. Check the following columns in the InvoiceHeader table in the order shown here:
     BatchNumber
     InvoiceNumber
     TotalAmount

13. Right-click in the SQL pane and select Run from the context menu. The query will execute, and the result set will be displayed in the results pane. The Query Builder should appear similar to the illustration.

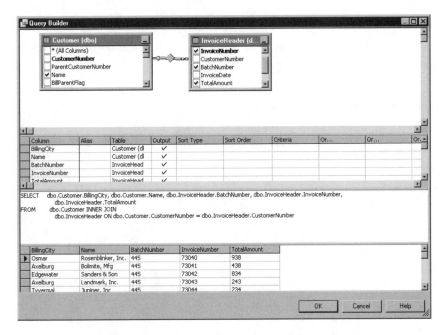

14. Right-click in the Results Pane. Select "Clear Results" from the context menu.

15. Click OK. You will return to the Design the Query page.

Task Notes   Your dataset contains the columns we need to create the matrix report. You will note that we did not specify any sort order for the dataset. The matrix itself will take care of sorting the dataset and displaying things in the correct order. It will present the data in the rows and in the columns in ascending order.

Invoice-Batch Number Report, Task 2: Choose the Report Layout

1. Click Next. The Select the Report Type page of the Report Wizard will appear.

2. Select the Matrix radio button.

3. Click Next. The Design the Matrix page of the Report Wizard will appear.

4. Use the Columns button to place the following fields in the Displayed Fields list:
   BillingCity
   Name

5. Use the Rows button to place the following fields in the Displayed Fields list:
   BatchNumber
   InvoiceNumber

6. Use the Details button to place the following field in the Displayed Fields list:
   TotalAmount

7. Check the Enable Drilldown check box at the bottom of the page. The Design the Matrix page should appear as shown.

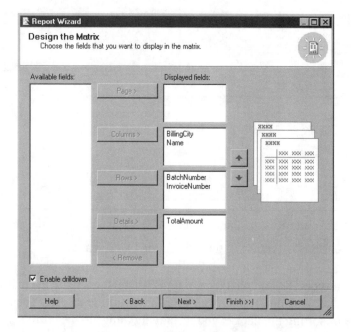

8. Click Next. The Choose the Matrix Style page of the Report Wizard will appear.

9. Make sure that Bold is selected in the style list and click Next. The Completing the Report Wizard page will appear.

10. Type **Invoice-Batch Number Report** for the report name.

11.   Click Finish. The Visual Studio window will appear.

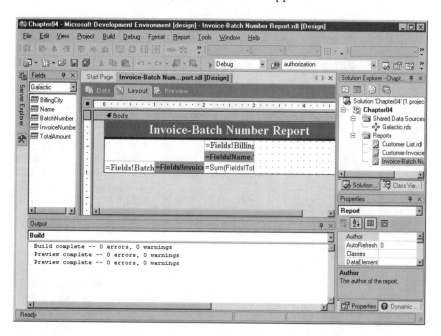

12.   Widen the column on the far right of the matrix, as shown in the illustration.

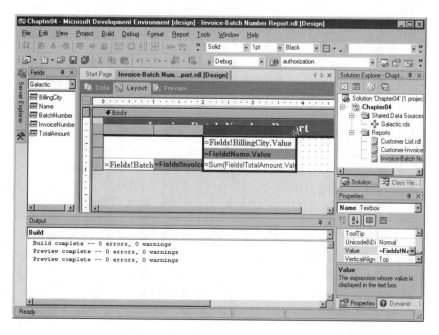

13.   Click the Preview tab. A preview of your report will appear.

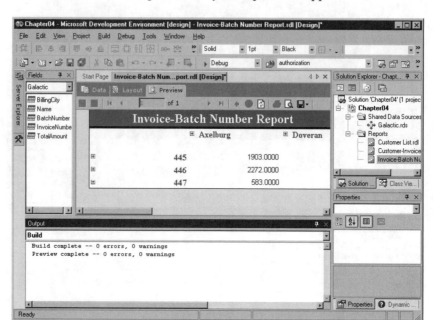

14.   Click the Save All button in the toolbar.

Task Notes   The Invoice-Batch Number report contains a column for each billing city and a row for each batch number. You will need to scroll to the right to see all the columns in the report. The numbers in the matrix are the totals for each batch number in each billing city. For example, $1,903 was invoiced to companies in Axelburg in batch number 445.

The column headings are left justified, whereas the numeric values are right justified. This makes the report a bit hard to read. We will discuss how to correct these types of formatting issues in Chapter 5.

Clicking the plus sign next to a batch number shows you all the invoices in that batch. If you expand batch number 445, you can see that invoice number 73040 included $938 for companies in Osmar and invoice number 73041 included $438 for companies in Axelburg.

Clicking the plus sign next to a billing city shows you all the customers in that city. If you expand Axelburg, you can see that invoice number 73041 included $438 for Bolimite, Mfg. If you click the minus sign next to batch number 445, you can see that batch number 446 included $776 for Bolimite, Mfg.

Report Parameters

From the users' standpoint, all our sample reports up to this point have been "what you see is what you get." These reports each ran a predetermined query to create the dataset. No user input was requested.

In the real world, this is not the way things work. Most reports require the user to specify some criteria that will help determine what information is ultimately in the report. The user may need to enter a start and an end date, or they may need to select the department or sales region that will be included in the report. Users like to have control over their reports so they receive exactly the information they are looking for. Our next report demonstrates how Reporting Services allows you to get user input by using *report parameters*.

The Parameterized Invoice-Batch Number Report

Features Highlighted

▶   Using report parameters

Business Need   The accounting department is very pleased with the Invoice-Batch Number report. Like most users, when they are happy with something, they want to change it. No software or report is ever really completed. It only reaches a resting point until users think of another enhancement.

The accounting department would like to be able to view the Invoice-Batch Number report for one city at a time. They would like to pick the city from a list of all the cities where they have customers. They would also like to specify a start date and an end date and only view batches that were run between those dates.

We will modify the Invoice-Batch Number report to include these features. We will add a WHERE clause to the SELECT statement that creates the dataset. Then we will send the user's selections for city, start date, and end date to the WHERE clause using report parameters.

Task Overview

1. Reopen the Chapter04 Project, Open the Invoice-Batch Number Report, and Add Parameters to the Query in the Original Dataset

2. Create a Second Dataset Containing a List of Cities

3. Customize the Report Parameters

Parameterized Invoice-Batch Number Report, Task 1: Reopen the Chapter04 Project, Open the Invoice-Batch Number Report and Add Parameters to the Query in the Original Dataset

1. If you have closed the Chapter04 project, reopen it. (If you need assistance with this, see Task 1 of the Customer-Invoice report.)

2. If the Invoice-Batch Number report is open, you are ready to go. If it is not open, double-click the entry for the Invoice-Batch Number report in the Solution Explorer on the right side of the screen.

3. Click the Data tab. You will see the Query Builder screen with the query that was built for this report while running the Report Wizard.

NOTE

You can change the size of the Solution Explorer window, the Fields window and the other windows around the outside of the Visual Studio window in order to make more room in the center to create your report. Just click on the separator between the windows and drag in the desired direction.

4. Right-click in the diagram pane and select Add Table from the context menu.

5. The accounting department wants to specify a date range based on the date that each batch was run. This date is stored in the InvoiceBatch table. We will need to join this table with the InvoiceHeader table. Double-click "InvoiceBatch (dbo)" in the list of tables. The Query Builder automatically creates the JOIN for us.

6. Click Close to exit the Add Table dialog box.

7. In the InvoiceBatch table, click the check box next to the RunDate field. This will add RunDate to the grid pane.

8. Now we will create the portion of the WHERE clause involving the billing city. In the grid pane, click the cell across from BillingCity and under Criteria. The cursor will move to that cell. Type **=@City** and press ENTER. The Query Builder portion of the screen will appear, as shown in the following illustration. Notice that the SQL statement in the SQL pane now includes a WHERE clause.

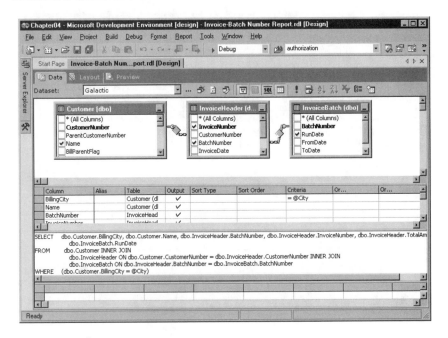

NOTE

Your screen may not look exactly like the illustration. Some of the Visual Studio windows have been closed in the screen in order to make room for the Query Builder.

9. Next, we will create the portion of the WHERE clause involving the RunDate. Scroll down in the grid pane until RunDate is visible. Click the cell across from RunDate and under Criteria. Type **>= @StartDate AND < @EndDate + 1** and press ENTER. The Query Builder portion of the screen will appear as shown in the following illustration. Notice the addition to the WHERE clause in the SQL pane. We will discuss why we are using "@EndDate + 1" in the task notes.

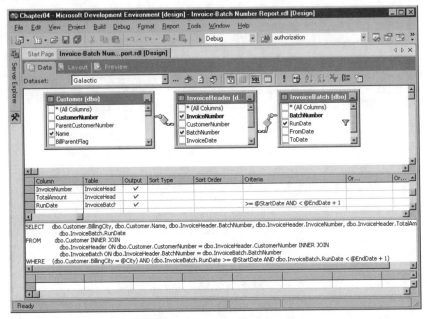

10. We needed to include RunDate in the WHERE clause, but we do not need to include it in the FIELD LIST of the SELECT statement. Click in the cell across from RunDate and under Output to remove the check mark. The RunDate field is no longer in the FIELD LIST for the SELECT statement in the SQL pane.

11. Right-click in the SQL pane and select Run from the context menu.

12. The Query Builder requires values for the three parameters you just created in order to run the query. You will see the Define Query Parameters dialog box. Type **Axelburg** for @City, **12/01/2003** for @StartDate, and **12/31/2003** for @EndDate. Click OK.

13. After viewing the result set, right-click in the results pane and select Clear Results from the context menu.

Task Notes   You have now added three parameters to the WHERE clause of the SELECT statement. Only rows where the City column has a value equal to the value of @City will be displayed in the result set. When you ran the query in the Query

Builder just now, you gave the @City parameter a value of "Axelburg." Therefore, only rows with Axelburg in the City column were included in the result set.

One of the trickiest things about working with dates in SQL Server is remembering that they consist of both a date and a time. SQL Server does not have columns that are just a date, as in 12/31/2003. SQL Server only has a *datetime* data type, which consists of a date and a time together.

When the invoice batches are run at GDS, the invoicing program assigns both the date and the time that the batch was run. For instance, batch 447 was run on 12/31/2003 at 7:54:49 P.M. It has a value of "12/31/2003 7:54:49 PM" stored in its RunDate column by the invoicing program.

When a user is asked to enter a date, most of the time they enter the date without a time. When you were asked for a value for @EndDate, you entered "12/31/2003" without any time specified. Because SQL Server only deals with dates and times together, it adds on a time value for you. The default value that it uses is "00:00:00 AM" or midnight. Keep in mind that midnight is the start of the new day. This means that when you're comparing datetime values, midnight is less than any other time occurring on the same day.

Let's think about the comparison we created in the WHERE clause involving @EndDate. Assume for a moment that instead of using "RunDate < @EndDate + 1," we used the more obvious "RunDate <= @EndDate." When the user enters "12/31/2003" for the end date, they expect the result set will include batches run on 12/31/2003. However, when SQL Server compares the value of RunDate (12/31/2003 7:54:49 PM) with the value of @EndDate (12/31/2003 00:00:00 AM), it finds that RunDate is not less than or equal to @EndDate. This is because 7:54:49 PM, the time portion of RunDate, is greater than 00:00:00 AM, the time portion of @EndDate. Batch 447 would not be included in this result set.

In order to include batches that occur on the day specified by @EndDate, we need to use "RunDate < @EndDate + 1." What this expression does is add one day to the value of @EndDate and checks to see if RunDate is less than this calculated value. Let's look at our example with batch 447. This time, SQL Server compares the value of RunDate (12/31/2003 7:54:49 PM) with the calculated value (12/31/2003 00:00:00 AM + 1 day = 1/1/2004 00:00:00 AM). Now it is true that RunDate is less than our calculated value, so batch 447 is included in the result set.

Parameterized Invoice-Batch Number Report, Task 2: Create a Second Dataset Containing a List of Cities

1. The accounting department wants to be able to select a value for the @City parameter from a list of billing cities. We need to create a second dataset in their report that will provide that list for the users. Start by

selecting "<New Dataset…>" from the Dataset drop-down list, as shown in the following illustration. The Dataset dialog box will appear.

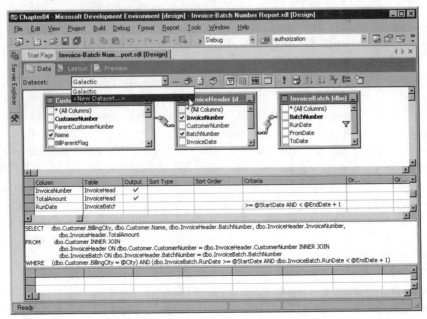

2. Type **BillingCities** for the name. The Galactic data source is already selected for you in the Data Source drop-down list, so this does not need to be changed.

NOTE

Make sure you type "BillingCities" without a space between the two words. Spaces are not allowed in dataset names.

3. Based on what you learned in Chapter 3, we'll compose the query for this dataset without the Query Builder. We want a list of all the billing cities for GDS customers. It also makes sense that each city name should only show up once in the list. Click in the Query String text box and enter the following SQL statement:

```
SELECT DISTINCT BillingCity FROM Customer
```

4. Click OK. You will see the Generic Query Designer with the new BillingCities dataset loaded. The Generic Query Designer is a simplified version of the Query Builder. The Generic Query Designer does not include all of the helpful features that are found in the Query Builder. Queries created in the Report Wizard use the Query Builder by default. Queries created outside of the Report Wizard use the Generic Query Designer. In Chapter 5, we will learn how to switch back and forth between the Generic Query Designer and the Query Builder.

Task Notes   Remember that the word DISTINCT means that we want SQL Server to remove duplicates for us. In order to do this, SQL Server will automatically sort the result set. For this reason, we don't need to specify an ORDER BY clause for the SELECT statement.

Parameterized Invoice-Batch Number Report, Task 3: Customize the Report Parameters

1. From the menu, select Report | Report Parameters. The Report Parameters dialog box will appear.

2. Type **Select a City** in the Prompt field. This is the prompt the user will see when running the report.

3. Make sure the Allow Null Value check box is unchecked. The user must select a city; it cannot be left empty (or "null" in database-speak).

4. For Available Values, select the From query radio button. This will allow us to use our BillingCities dataset to create a drop-down list.

5. From the Dataset drop-down list, select BillingCities. We will discuss the Value Field and the Label Field drop-down lists later in this book.

6. For Default Values, select the Non-queried radio button.

7. Type **Axelburg** in the text box below Default Values. This will serve as the default value for the City parameter. The Report Parameters dialog box should now look like this:

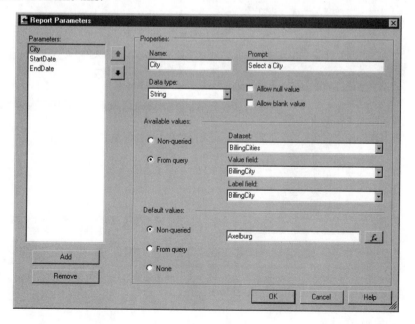

8. Click StartDate in the Parameters list.

9. Type **Enter a Start Date** in the Prompt field.

10. Select DateTime from the Data Type drop-down list.

11. Make sure the Allow Null Value check box is unchecked.

12. Click EndDate in the Parameters list.

13. Type **Enter an End Date** in the Prompt field.

14. Select DateTime from the Data Type drop-down list.

15. Make sure the Allow Null Value check box is unchecked.

16. Click OK. You will return to the Generic Query Designer.

17. Click the Preview tab.

18. The prompts for the three report parameters appear at the top of the preview area. No report will be displayed until a value is entered for each parameter.

19. Select Axelburg from the Select a City drop-down list. Type **12/01/2003** for Enter a Start Date. Type **12/31/2003** for Enter an End Date.

20. Click View Report. The report, based on the parameter values you entered, now appears. The report, with all the rows and columns expanded, is shown here.

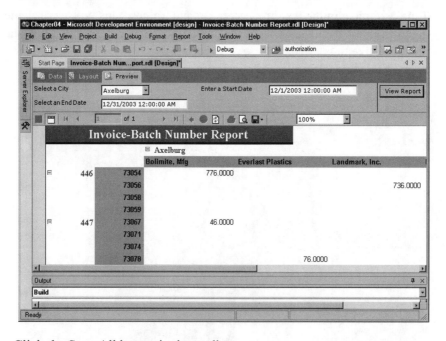

21. Click the Save All button in the toolbar.

Task Notes   Each time you added a parameter to the query in the dataset, Visual Studio created a corresponding report parameter for you. When the report is viewed, the values that are entered for the report parameters are automatically passed on to the query parameters before the query is executed. In this way, the user can enter information and have it used in the WHERE clause of the SELECT statement to affect the contents of the report.

The Report Parameters dialog box allows you to control the user's interaction with the report parameters. You can change the prompts that the user sees. You can specify the data type of a parameter. You can even determine the default value for a parameter.

One of the most powerful features of the Report Parameters dialog box is the ability to create a drop-down list from which the user can select a value for a parameter. In many cases, the user will not know values such as department codes, part numbers, and so forth, without looking them up. This ability to allow the user to select valid values from a list makes the reports much more user friendly.

Flying Solo

You have now seen what the Report Wizard can do for you. It can provide you with a great starting place for a number of reports. However, it does have its limitations, and in most cases, you will need to make additions to the reports that it generates before they are ready for the end user. In the next chapter, you will begin learning how to make those enhancements. In addition, you will learn how to create reports without the aid of the wizard.

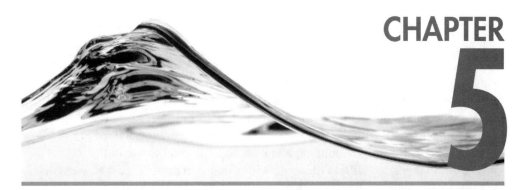

CHAPTER

5

Removing the Training Wheels: Building Basic Reports

IN THIS CHAPTER:

Riding Down Familiar Roads
Data Regions
New Territory
Getting Graphical

I n Chapter 4, you built your first reports using the Report Wizard. This is like learning to ride your first two-wheeler with the training wheels on. Now it is time for the training wheels to come off so you can see what this baby will really do! We are going to begin building reports from scratch. Hopefully, these next few chapters will provide the handholding you need so you can learn to ride *sans* training wheels without getting skinned knees.

First, we will work with the two types of reports you were introduced to in Chapter 4. We will begin by building a table report without the use of the Report Wizard. From there, we will do the same with a matrix report. After that, we will look at two new report types—the chart report and the list report. We will end the chapter by working with some of the basic report items that make up each report— namely, the line control, the text box control, and the rectangle control. Along the way, you will learn more about the Visual Studio .NET 2003 environment that serves as our development platform.

So, the training wheels are off and the wrenches have been put away. Don your helmets; it's time to ride!

Riding Down Familiar Roads

We will cover some familiar territory as we begin building reports without the Report Wizard. In Chapter 4, we used the Report Wizard to create table reports (the Customer List report and the Customer-Invoice report) and matrix reports (the Invoice-Batch Number Matrix report). We will create these types of reports once more, but this time without the aid of the wizard.

Again, we will look at the business needs of Galactic Delivery Services (GDS) and create reports to satisfy those business needs.

The Transport List Report

Features Highlighted

▶ Building a GROUP BY clause using the Query Builder

▶ Creating a table report from scratch

Business Need   The Transport Maintenance Department at Galactic Delivery Services needs a list of all the transports currently in service. They would like this list to be grouped by transport type. The list will include the serial number, purchase date, and the date that the transport was last in for repairs. The list will also include the cargo capacity and range of each transport type.

Task Overview

1. Create the Chapter05 Project, Create a Shared Data Source, and Create a New Report in the Chapter05 Project

2. Create a Dataset

3. Place a Table Item on the Report and Populate It

4. Add Table Grouping and Other Report Formatting

Transport List Report, Task 1: Create the Chapter05 Project, Create a Shared Data Source, and Create a New Report in the Chapter05 Project

1. Run Visual Studio .NET 2003. The Visual Studio Start page will be displayed (or select File | Close Solution from the menu if a solution is already open).

2. Click New Project to create a new project. This will display the New Project dialog box. (Remember, you can create a new project three different ways: Select File | New | Project from the main menu, click the New Project toolbar button, or click New Project on the Start page. All these actions achieve the same result.)

3. Click the Report Project icon in the Templates area of the New Project dialog box. (Be sure to click the Report Project icon and *not* the Report Project Wizard icon.)

4. Type **Chapter05** for the project name. This project will contain all the reports you create in this chapter.

5. Click Browse to open the Project Location dialog box.

6. Click My Projects to go to the Visual Studio Projects folder.

7. In the list of folders, double-click the MSSQLRS folder.

8. Click Open in the lower-right corner of the Project Location dialog box. The New Project dialog box should now look like this:

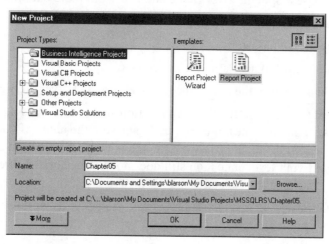

9. Click OK in the New Project dialog box. Visual Studio will create a new project.

10. In the Solution Explorer on the right side of the screen, right-click the Shared Data Sources folder. Select Add New Data Source from the context menu, as shown here.

11. Type the name of the Microsoft SQL Server database server that is hosting the Galactic database or select it from the drop-down list. If the Galactic database is hosted by the computer you are currently working on, you may type **(local)** for the server name.

12. Click the Use a Specific User Name and Password radio button.

13. Type **GalacticReporting** for the user name.

14. Type **gds** for the password.

15. Click the Allow Saving Password check box.

16. Select Galactic from the Select the Database on the Server drop-down list.

17. Click Test Connection. If a "Test connection succeeded." message appears, click OK. If an error message appears, make sure the name of your database server, the user name, the password, and the database have been entered properly. If your test connection still does not succeed, make sure you have correctly installed the Galactic database.

18. Click OK. A new shared data source called Galactic.rds will be created in the Chapter05 project.

19. In the Solution Explorer, right-click the Reports folder.

20. Put your mouse pointer over Add in the context menu and wait for the submenu to appear. Select the Add New Item command from the context menu, as shown here.

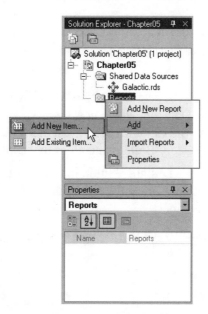

21. Make sure that the Report icon is selected in the Templates area. Enter **TransportList** for the name. The Add New Item - Chapter05 dialog box will appear.

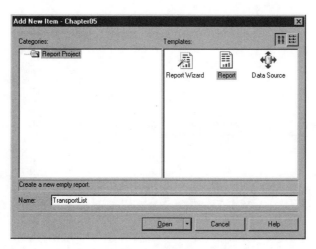

22. Click Open. A new report called TransportList.rdl will be created in the Chapter05 project. You will be taken to the Data tab of this new report.

23. Select <New Dataset...> from the Dataset drop-down list. The Dataset dialog box will appear.

24. Enter **TransportList** for the dataset's name in the Dataset dialog box.

NOTE

The dataset name must not contain any spaces.

25. "Galactic (shared)" will be selected as the data source by default. Click OK. You will return to the Data tab, which now displays the Generic Query Designer. We will use the Generic Query Designer in Chapter 6. For now, we will switch to the Query Builder and all of the helpful tools it provides.

26. Click the Generic Query Designer button in the Data tab toolbar as shown in the following illustration. This will unselect the Generic Query Designer and switch to the Query Builder.

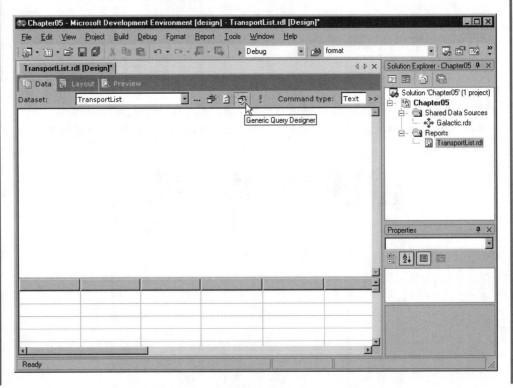

Task Notes   Because we will be creating several reports in the Chapter05 project, all of which will select data from the Galactic database, we started out by creating a shared data source. This will save us time as we create each of the reports. We will continue this practice throughout the remaining chapters.

In steps 19 and 20, we are adding a report to the project. In Chapter 4, you saw that selecting Add New Report from the context menu causes the new report to be created with the Report Wizard. In this chapter, we are looking to build our reports from scratch. That is why we used Add New Item in step 20.

Transport List Report, Task 2: Create a Dataset

1. Right-click in the diagram pane (the upper area) of the Query Builder screen. Select Add Table from the context menu.

2. Add the following tables to the query:
   Transport (dbo)
   TransportType (dbo)
   Repair (dbo)

3. Click Close to exit the Add Table dialog box.

4. Right-click the diamond on the connection between the Transport table and the Repair table. Select the All Rows from Transport (dbo) item from the context menu. You may need to rearrange the TransportType table, the Transport table, and the Repair table in order to see this diamond.

5. Check the following columns in the TransportType table:
   Description
   CargoCapacity
   Range

6. Check the following columns in the Transport table:
   SerialNumber
   PurchaseDate
   RetiredDate

7. Check the following column in the Repair table:
   BeginWorkDate

8. In the grid pane (the second area from the top), type **1** in the Sort Order column across from the Description field and type **2** in the Sort Order column across from the SerialNumber field.

9. The business need for this report states that it is to include only active transports. That means we only want to include transports that do not have a

retired date. Type **IS NULL** in the Criteria column across from the RetiredDate field. Remove the check mark under the Output column across from the RetiredDate field.

10. Right-click in the SQL pane (the third area from the top) and select Run from the context menu. In the results pane (the bottom area), notice that several records appear for serial number P-348-23-4532-22A.

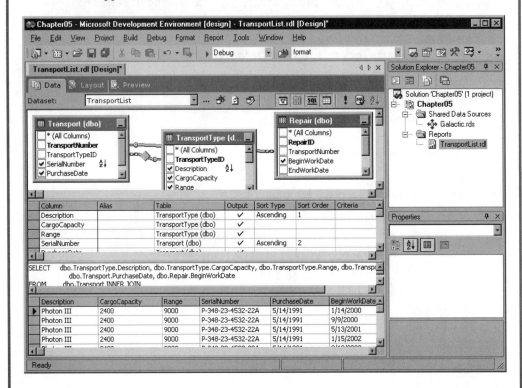

NOTE

You can also run the query by clicking the Run button (the one with a red exclamation point) in the Query Builder toolbar. The Query Builder toolbar is directly below the Data, Layout, and Preview tabs.

11. Right-click in the diagram pane of the Query Builder screen. Select Group By from the context menu. A new column called Group By is added to the grid pane.

12. In the grid pane, click in the Group By column across from the BeginWorkDate row.

13. Use the drop-down list in this cell to select Max, as shown here.

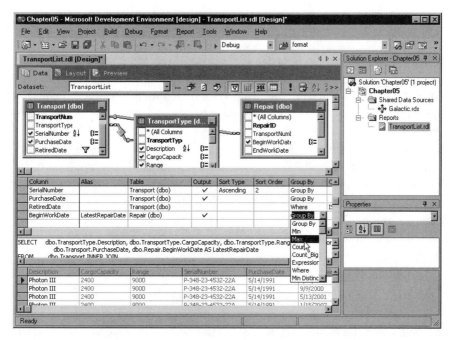

14. Replace "Expr1" with "LatestRepairDate" in the Alias column across from the BeginWorkDate row.

15. Right-click in the SQL pane and select Run from the context menu. Notice that now only one record appears for serial number P-348-23-4532-22A.

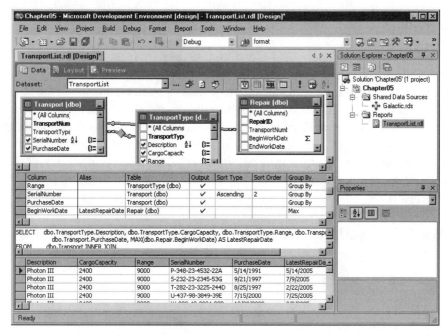

16. Right-click in the results pane and select Clear Results from the context menu.

Task Notes   The relationship between the Transport table and the Repair table is a one-to-many relationship. One transport may have many repairs. When we join these two tables, we get one record in the result set for each match between records in the Transport table and the Repair table. Because transport P-348-23-4532-22A has been in for repairs ten times, it generates ten records in the result set.

This is not exactly what the business requirements call for. Instead, we want to have one record for transport P-348-23-4532-22A with the latest repair date. To accomplish this, we use the GROUP BY clause. In step 11, we instruct the Query Builder to group together records in the result set that have the same value.

When we use the GROUP BY clause, all the fields in the FIELD LIST must fit into one of the following two categories:

▶ The field must be included in the GROUP BY clause.

▶ The field must be enclosed in an aggregate function.

Any fields with the words "Group By" in the Group By column are included in the GROUP BY clause. These fields also have a special group by symbol next to them in the diagram pane. By selecting Max under the Group By column, as we did in step 13, we enclose BeginWorkDate in the MAX() aggregate function. This will return the maximum BeginWorkDate (in other words, the latest repair date) for each transport. Note that there is also a special symbol, the Greek letter sigma, next to the BeginWorkDate field in the diagram pane to signify that it is enclosed in an aggregate function.

When the BeginWorkDate field is enclosed in the MAX() aggregate function, it becomes a calculated field. It is not simply the value of the BeginWorkDate field that is returned as a column in the result set. Instead, it is a calculation using the value of the BeginWorkDate field that makes up this column of the result set. The Query Builder needs a name for this calculated column. This is known as the *alias* for the column. By default, the Query Builder will assign a calculated column an alias of Expr1 or something similar. In order to better remember what is in this result set column when the time comes to use it in a report, we changed the alias to LatestRepairDate.

Transport List Report, Task 3: Place a Table Item on the Report and Populate It

1. Click the Layout tab to begin working on the report layout.

NOTE

Your installation of Visual Studio may be using a feature called Auto-Hide with the Toolbox. Auto-Hide is used to provide more screen space for your report layout. When Auto-Hide is active for the Toolbox, the Toolbox is only represented on the screen by a rectangle containing a tool icon and the word "Toolbox" at the extreme left of the Visual Studio window. To view the actual Toolbox, place your mouse pointer on top of this rectangle. After a second or two, the Toolbox will appear. Once your mouse pointer moves off of the Toolbox, it will be automatically hidden again.

2. Click the Table report item in the Toolbox. The mouse pointer will change to a table icon and crosshairs when you move your mouse pointer over the report layout area, as shown here.

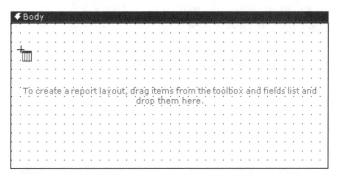

3. Click and drag the mouse over the lower three-quarters of the report layout area, as shown in the following illustration. Note that when you begin dragging, the mouse pointer changes back to the usual arrow icon.

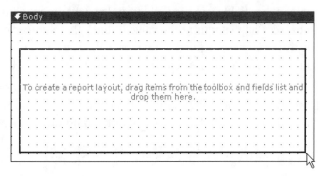

4. When you release the mouse button, after dragging, a table will be created to occupy the area you just defined. By default, every cell in the table is occupied by an empty text box. Click in each cell of the table and note the name and type of report item shown at the top of the Properties window.

5. We will take a few moments to go over the methods for selecting various parts of the table. You have already seen how to select individual cells. The gray border on top of and to the left of the table item provides handles for selecting other parts of the table. Click any of the gray rectangles in the border above the table item. This action selects the corresponding column, as shown here.

6. Click any of the gray rectangles in the border to the left of the table item. This action selects a row, as shown here.

7. Click the gray square in the upper-left corner of the border. This action selects the entire table. When the entire table is selected, the gray border is replaced by the sizing handles (the small white squares) for the table. You must select the entire table before you can move and size the table item.

8. Drag the SerialNumber field from the Fields window and drop it on the middle-left table cell. An expression that returns the value of the SerialNumber field is placed in the text box that occupies the middle-left table cell. The name of the field is used to create a column heading. This is placed in the upper-left table cell.

9. Drag the PurchaseDate field from the Fields window and drop it on the center table cell. Drag the LatestRepairDate field from the Fields window and drop it on the middle-right table cell. The report layout should now appear.

Serial Number	Purchase Date	Latest Repair Date
=Fields! SerialNumber.Value	=Fields! PurchaseDate.Value	=Fields! LatestRepairDate.Value
	Footer	

10. Select the header row (the top row) by clicking the gray rectangle in the border to the left of the row.

11. Make the following changes in the Properties window:

Property	New Value
FontWeight (expand the Font property to find the Font Weight property)	Bold
TextDecoration	Underline

12. Click the line in the gray border between the header row and the detail row. Drag it to reduce the height of the header row.

13. Click the line in the gray border between the detail row and the footer row. Drag it to reduce the height of the detail row.

14. Click the center cell in the table. Hold down SHIFT and click the middle-right cell in the table. Both of these cells are now selected. Make the following changes in the Properties window:

Property	New Value
Format	MM/dd/yyyy
TextAlign	Left

NOTE

Make sure you use uppercase M's in the Format property. "MM" is the placeholder for month in a format string, whereas "mm" is the placeholder for milliseconds.

15. Click the Preview tab to preview the report. The report should appear as shown here.

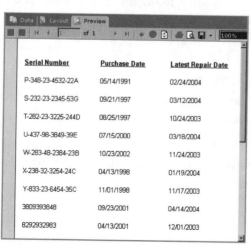

Task Notes In the Properties window are several instances where a group of related properties are combined under a summary property. For instance, the FontStyle, FontFamily, FontSize, and FontWeight properties are combined under the Font property. The Font property serves as a summary of the other four.

Initially, only the summary property is visible in the Properties window. A plus sign to the left of a property tells you that it is a summary property and has several detail properties beneath it. The summary property has a value that concatenates the values of all the detail properties underneath it.

For example, suppose the FontStyle, FontFamily, FontSize, and FontWeight properties have the following values:

FontStyle:	Normal
FontFamily:	Arial
FontSize:	10pt
FontWeight:	Bold

In that case, the Font property has this value:

Font:	Normal, Arial, 10pt, Bold

You can change the value of a detail property by editing the concatenated values in the summary property, or you can expand the summary property and edit the detail properties directly.

Transport List Report, Task 4: Add Table Grouping and Other Report Formatting

1. Click the Layout tab.
2. Right-click the gray border to the left of the table. You may need to click on the table to get the borders to appear. Select Insert Group from the context menu. The Grouping and Sorting Properties dialog box will appear.
3. Enter **TransportType** for the name (no spaces are allowed in the Name field).
4. Select "=Fields!Description.Value" from the drop-down in the first row under Expression. You have to click in this cell to get the drop-down to appear.
5. Uncheck the Include Group Footer check box.
6. Click OK. A new blank row will be added to the table below the header row. This is the grouping row.

7. Click the leftmost cell in the grouping row. Hold down SHIFT and click the center and the rightmost cells in the grouping row. Right-click in any of the selected cells and select Merge Cells from the context menu, as shown here.

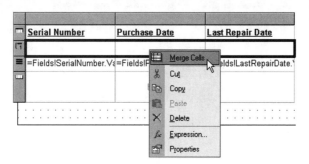

8. Right-click in the newly merged field and select Expression from the context menu. The Edit Expression dialog box appears.

9. Type the following after the equals sign (=), including the quotation marks and the space before the first quotation mark, in the Expression area:

```
"Transport Type: " &
```

10. Click the plus sign to expand the Fields node in the Fields area. You will see all the fields in the TransportList dataset.

11. Click the Description field. Click the Append button to append the Description field to the expression in the Expression area.

CAUTION

If you type the field expression, rather than selecting it from the Fields area, it must be typed in the exact case shown in the Fields area. Fields, as well as the other items shown in the Fields area are case sensitive.

12. Type the following at the end of the expression in the Expression area:

```
& vbcrlf & "       Cargo Capacity: " &
```

There must be a space before and after each ampersand (&) character.

13. Click the CargoCapacity field. Click the Append button to append the CargoCapacity field to the expression in the Expression area.

14. Type the following at the end of the expression in the Expression area:

```
& "   Range: " &
```

There must be a space before and after each ampersand (&) character.

15. Click the Range field. Click the Append button to append the Range field to the expression in the Expression area. The Edit Expression dialog box should appear.

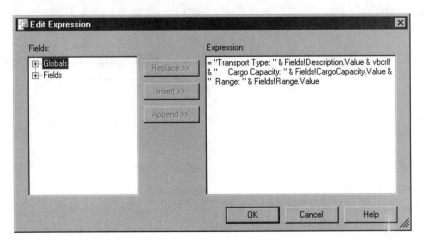

16. Click OK.

17. With the merged field still selected, make the following changes in the Properties window:

Property	New Value
BorderStyle/Bottom (expand the BorderStyle property to find the Bottom property)	Solid
FontWeight	Bold

18. Click the Textbox report item in the Toolbox. The mouse pointer will change to a text box icon and crosshairs when you move your mouse pointer over the report layout area.

19. Click and drag the mouse over the entire area above the table on the report layout area. Note that when you begin dragging, the mouse pointer changes back to the usual arrow icon.

20. When you release the mouse button, after dragging, a text box will be created to occupy the area you just defined. Click the text box and type the following:

    ```
    Transport List
    ```

21. With the text box still selected, make the following changes in the Properties window:

Property	New Value
FontSize	16pt
FontWeight	Bold
TextAlign	Center

22. Click the Preview tab. The report should appear as shown here.

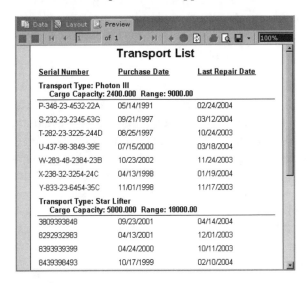

23. Click Save All in the toolbar.

Task Notes   When we added the grouping, we specified an expression in step 4.
This group expression determines when a new group header is placed in the report.
In the Transport List report, we used the Description field from the TransportType
table in the group expression. Because our first sort in the dataset was on the
TransportType.Description column, all the Photon III transports came first in the
dataset, followed by the Starlifter transports, and finally the Warp Hauler transports.
Each time the value of the group expression changes, a new group header will be
added to the report.

Be sure that you do not confuse the grouping in the report with the GROUP BY
clause we have used in SQL SELECT statements. The SQL GROUP BY clause
takes a number of records and combines them into a single record in the result set.
The grouping in the report takes a number of records in the dataset and surrounds
them with a group header and/or group footer when they are output in the report.

In steps 9–15, we combined all the fields that need to be in the group header into one expression. This was done so we could create a multiline group header and also to concatenate or combine the labels ("Transport Type:", "Cargo Capacity:", and "Range:") and the contents of the three fields (Description, CargoCapacity, and Range) into one string. The three columns of the group header were merged together to create room for the resulting expression. The Visual Basic concatenation operator (&) is used to combine the values into one long string. The Visual Basic constant vbcrlf is used to put a carriage return and linefeed in the middle of the string. This causes everything following the carriage return and linefeed to be placed on the next line down, giving us a two-line group header.

Remember that table cells are always occupied by a report item. If no other report item has been placed in a cell, the cell is occupied by a text box. When multiple cells are merged, the report item in the leftmost cell expands to fill the merged table cell. The report items in the other cells involved in the merge are automatically deleted.

We created a border on the bottom of the text box in the merged cells in order to underline our group heading. This is easier and more efficient than adding a Line report item to the report to get the same result. This is especially true when you are trying to underline something in the middle of a table, such as our group header.

When you typed the text in step 20, it looked like you were entering the text directly into the text box. What you were actually doing was changing the Value property of the text box. You can change the Value property of a text box by typing directly into the text box in the report layout area or by using the Properties window.

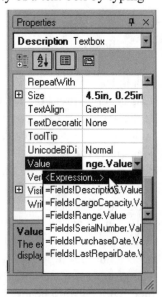

In addition, the Edit Expression dialog box can be used to change the Value property of a text box as well as many other report item properties. In step 8, we used the context menu to bring up the Edit Expression dialog box. The Edit Expression dialog box can also be accessed through a drop-down list in the Properties window, as shown in this illustration. In addition to the Value property of the text box, the Edit Expression dialog box can be used to change a number of properties of various report items. We will discuss this in more detail later in this chapter.

Data Regions

The table item is one of four special report items designed specifically for working with datasets. These special report items are called *data regions*. The other data regions are the matrix, the list, and the chart.

Data regions are able to work with multiple records from a dataset. The data region reads a record from the dataset, creates a portion of the report using the data found in that record, and then moves on to the next record. It does this until all the records from the dataset have been processed.

In the report you just completed, you saw how the table data region creates a detail row for each record in the dataset. The matrix data region creates both rows and columns based on the contents of the dataset. You will see this demonstrated in our next report. The list data region is not limited to rows and columns. It creates a whole section, perhaps a whole page, for each record in the dataset. We will create a report using a list data region later in this chapter. The chart data region creates elements on a graph for each record in a dataset. We will create a report using a chart data region in Chapter 6.

Each data region item has a property called DataSetName. This property contains the name of the dataset used by the data region. In the Transport List report you just created, the DataSetName property of the table has the value TransportList (see the following illustration). Visual Basic automatically set this property for you when you placed the first field, the SerialNumber field, in the table. Because the SerialNumber field is from the TransportList dataset and because the table's DataSetName property was empty, Visual Basic put the value TransportList into the DataSetName property.

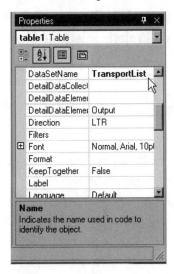

Now let's move down the road a little further and create a matrix report without the wizard.

The Repair Count By Type Report

Features Highlighted

▶ Creating a matrix report from scratch

▶ Using a specialized property dialog box

Business Need   GDS needs to purchase several new transports to update their delivery fleet. The company must decide which type of transport to purchase. One factor in the decision is the amount of time the new transports will spend in the maintenance hanger for repairs and preventative maintenance.

Upper management has asked the GDS maintenance department to provide a report showing the number of each type of repair that has been required by each type of transport. The report should include statistics from all transports, both active and retired. Also, the report should group the repairs by their cause.

Task Overview

1. Reopen the Chapter05 Project, Create a New Report in the Chapter05 Project, Select the Shared Data Source, and Create a Dataset

2. Place a Matrix Item on the Report and Populate It

3. Add Column Grouping and Other Report Formatting

Repair Count By Type Report, Task 1: Reopen the Chapter05 Project, Create a New Report in the Chapter05 Project, Select the Shared Data Source, and Create a Dataset

1. If you have closed the Chapter05 project, reopen it.

2. In the Solution Explorer on the right side of the screen, right-click the Reports folder.

3. Put your mouse pointer over Add in the context menu and wait for the submenu to appear. Select Add New Item from the context menu. This will display the Add New Item - Chapter05 dialog box.

4. Make sure that the Report icon is selected in the Template area. Enter **RepairCountByType** for the name.

5. Click Open. A new report called RepairCountByType.rdl will be created in the Chapter05 project. You will be taken to the Data tab of this new report.

6. Select "<New Dataset…>" from the Dataset drop-down list. The Dataset dialog box will appear.

7. Enter **RepairsByType** for the name in the Dataset dialog box.

8. "Galactic (shared)" will be selected for the data source by default. Click OK. You will return to the Data tab, which now displays the Generic Query Designer.

9. Click the Generic Query Designer button to switch to the Query Builder.

10. Right-click in the diagram pane of the Query Builder screen. Select Add Table from the context menu.

11. Add the following tables to the query:
Repair (dbo)
Transport (dbo)
TransportType (dbo)
RepairWorkDoneLink (dbo)
WorkDone (dbo)
RepairCause (dbo)

12. Click Close to exit the Add Table dialog box.

13. Check the following column in the Repair table:
RepairID

14. Check the following column in the TransportType table:
Description

15. In the grid pane, type **TypeOfTransport** in the Alias column in the Description row.

16. Check the following column in the WorkDone table:
Description

17. In the grid pane, type **TypeOfWork** in the Alias column in the Description row for the WorkDone (dbo) table.

18. Check the following column in the RepairCause table:
Description

19. In the grid pane, type **RepairCause** in the Alias column in the Description row for the RepairCause (dbo) table.

20. Type **1** in the Sort Order column for RepairCause. Type **2** in the Sort Order column for TypeOfWork.

21. Right-click in the SQL pane and select Run from the context menu. The Query Builder should appear similar to this:

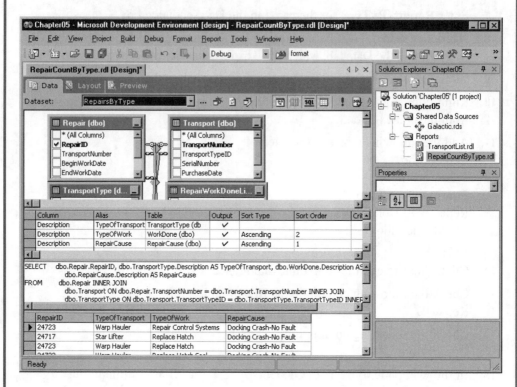

22. Right-click in the results pane and select Clear Results from the context menu.

Task Notes Although this report is a pretty straightforward request, we need to link together a number of tables to collect the necessary data. What we are interested in is repairs, so we start with the Repair table. However, none of the fields we need in the result set are actually in the Repair table. To find the type of transport being repaired, we need to join the Transport table with the Repair table and then join the TransportType table to the Transport table. To find the type of work done, we need to join the RepairWorkDoneLink table to the Repair table and then join the WorkDone table to the RepairWorkDoneLink table. Finally, to group by the cause of the repair, we need to join the RepairCause table to the Repair table. If you get confused by all of this, refer back to Figure 3-23 in Chapter 3.

Repair Count By Type Report, Task 2: Place a Matrix Item on the Report and Populate It

1. Click the Layout tab to begin working on the report layout.

2. Click the Matrix report item in the Toolbox. The mouse pointer will change to a matrix icon and crosshairs when you move your mouse pointer over the report layout area.

3. Click and drag the mouse over the lower three-quarters of the report layout.

4. When you release the mouse button, after dragging, a matrix will be created to occupy the area you just defined. By default, every cell in the matrix is occupied by an empty text box.

5. Drag the TypeOfTransport field from the Fields window and drop it on the cell containing the word "Columns." The values in this column in the dataset will determine the columns in the matrix report.

6. Drag the TypeOfWork field from the Fields window and drop it on the cell containing the word "Rows." The values in this column in the dataset will determine the rows in the matrix report.

7. Drag the RepairID field from the Fields window and drop it on the cell containing the word "Data."

8. In the cell where you just dropped the RepairID field, change "Sum" to "Count" so that the contents of the cell appear as follows:

```
=Count(Fields!RepairID.Value)
```

9. With this cell still selected, change the following property:

Property	New Value
TextAlign	Center

10. Reduce the width and height of the columns in the matrix. When you are finished, your report design should look similar to this:

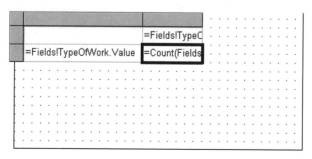

11. Click the Preview tab. Your report should look similar to the following illustration. The rows and columns in your report may appear in a different order from those shown here.

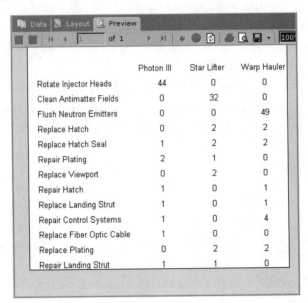

Task Notes   Because the matrix report always groups a number of records from the dataset to create the entries in the matrix, the field which supplies the data for the matrix must be enclosed in some type of aggregate function. If the field placed in the data cell is a number, Visual Studio will enclose the field in the SUM() aggregate function.

The RepairID field, which we placed in the data cell in step 7, is a number. However, it does not make sense to add up the RepairIDs. Instead, we want to count the number of RepairIDs. For this reason, we changed the SUM() aggregate function to the COUNT() aggregate function.

Repair Count By Type Report, Task 3: Add Column Grouping and Other Report Formatting

1. Click the Layout tab to return to the report layout.

2. Click the cell in the upper-right corner of the matrix and change the following properties:

Property	New Value
FontWeight	Bold
TextDecoration	Underline

3. Click the square in the upper-left corner of the gray border to select the matrix item.

4. In the Properties window, click the Property Pages button shown in the following illustration. The Matrix Properties dialog box appears.

5. Click the Groups tab.

6. In the Rows area, click Add. The Grouping and Sorting Properties dialog box appears.

7. Next you will set up your matrix for drill-down. Replace "matrix1_RowGroup2" with "matrix1_RepairCause" for the name. Select Fields!RepairCause.Value from the drop-down list in the first row under Expression. Click OK.

8. In the Rows area, click Up to move matrix1_RepairCause to the top of the list. Click the matrix1_TypeOfWork entry. Click Edit in the Rows area. The Grouping and Sorting Properties dialog box appears.

9. Click the Visibility tab. Set the Initial Visibility to Hidden. Click the "Visibility can be toggled by another report item" check box. Select textbox2 from the Report Item drop-down list. (If textbox2 is not in the drop-down list, type **textbox2** for the Report Item value.)

10. Click OK in the Grouping and Sorting Properties dialog box. Click OK in the Matrix Properties dialog box.

11. Click the cell in the upper-left corner of the matrix and change the following properties:

Property	New Value
FontWeight	Bold
TextDecoration	Underline
Value	Cause/Type of Repair Work

12. Click the Textbox report item in the Toolbox. Click and drag the mouse over the area above the matrix on the report layout area. When you release the mouse button, after dragging, a text box will be created to occupy the area you just defined. Click the text box and type the following:

```
Repair Count By Type Report
```

13. With the text box still selected, make the following changes in the Properties window:

Property	New Value
FontSize	16pt
FontWeight	Bold
TextAlign	Center

Your report layout should appear similar to the illustration.

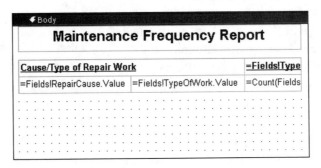

14. Click the Preview tab. The report should appear.

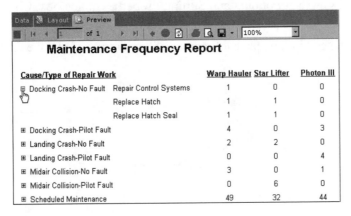

15. Click Save All in the toolbar.

Task Notes   The Property Pages button in the Properties window provides an alternative way to change the properties of a report item. This button displays a dialog box that deals specifically with the properties of the selected report item. These specialized property dialog boxes can make it much easier to modify the properties of a report item. You can also access the specialized property dialog boxes by right-clicking a report item and selecting Properties from the context menu.

New Territory

Now that you have created the table and matrix reports without the aid of the Report Wizard, it is time to venture into new territory. As mentioned previously, the list item is the third type of data region. Just as the table item makes up the main portion of a table report and the matrix item makes up the main portion of a matrix report, the list item is the main part of a list report.

List reports are used when you need to repeat a large area of content—perhaps even an entire page—for each record in the dataset. They are often used to create forms. List reports function similarly to a mail merge in a word processing program such as Microsoft Word.

The Transport Information Sheet

Features Highlighted

► Creating a list report

Business Need   The GDS maintenance department needs an efficient way to look up general information about a particular transport that comes in for repair. The user should be able to select the serial number from a drop-down list and see all the basic information about the transport. This transport information sheet should also include the date of the next scheduled maintenance appointment for this transport.

Task Overview

1. Reopen the Chapter05 Project, Create a New Report in the Chapter05 Project, Select the Shared Data Source, and Create the TransportSNs Dataset
2. Create the TransportInfo Dataset
3. Place a List Item on the Report and Populate It

Transport Information Sheet, Task 1: Reopen the Chapter05 Project, Create a New Report in the Chapter05 Project, Select the Shared Data Source, and Create the TransportSNs Dataset

1. If you have closed the Chapter05 project, reopen it.

2. In the Solution Explorer on the right side of the screen, right-click the Reports folder. Select Add | Add New Item. This will display the Add New Item - Chapter05 dialog box.

3. Make sure the Report icon is selected in the Template area. Enter **TransportInfoSheet** for the name. Click Open.

4. Select <New Dataset...> from the Dataset drop-down list. The Dataset dialog box will appear.

5. Enter **TransportSNs** for the name in the Dataset dialog box.

6. The data source should be "Galactic (shared)."

7. Enter the following for the query string:

```
SELECT SerialNumber FROM Transport WHERE RetiredDate IS NULL ORDER
BY SerialNumber
```

8. Click OK.

9. Click the Generic Query Designer button to switch to the Query Builder.

10. Right-click in the SQL pane and select Run from the context menu. The Query Builder should appear similar to the illustration.

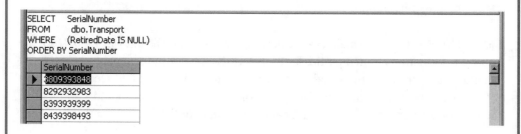

11. Right-click in the results pane and select Clear Results from the context menu.

Task Notes   The TransportSNs dataset provides a list of the serial numbers for all the active transports at GDS. This dataset is used to populate the drop-down list from which the user will select which transport the Transport Information Sheet will be printed for. Because the query for this dataset is relatively straightforward, it is faster to type the query string by hand rather than build it using the Query Builder.

This is not the case with the query string for the second dataset required by this report, as you shall see in the next task.

Transport Information Sheet, Task 2: Create the TransportInfo Dataset

1. Select <New Dateset...> from the Dataset drop-down list. The Dataset dialog box will appear.

2. Enter **TransportInfo** for the name in the Dataset dialog box. The data source should be Galactic. Click OK.

3. Click the Generic Query Designer button to switch to the Query Builder.

4. Right-click in the diagram pane of the Query Builder screen. Select Add Table from the context menu. Add the following tables to the query:
   Transport (dbo)
   TransportType (dbo)
   ScheduledMaint (dbo)
   Repair (dbo)

5. Click Close to exit the Add Table dialog box.

6. Right-click the link between the Transport and the Repair tables and select Remove from the context menu. (You may have to rearrange the tables in the diagram pane to make this visible.)

7. In the Repair table, scroll down until you can see the ScheduledMaintID field. Click this field and drag it to the ScheduledMaintID field in the ScheduledMaint table.

8. Right-click the diamond in the middle of the link that was created in the previous step. Select the command Select All Rows from ScheduledMaint (dbo) in the context menu.

9. Find the diamond in the middle of the link between the Transport and ScheduledMaint tables. (You may have to rearrange the tables in the diagram pane to make this visible.) Right-click this diamond and select Select All Rows

from Transport (dbo) from the context menu. With a bit of rearranging, your screen should look similar to the illustration.

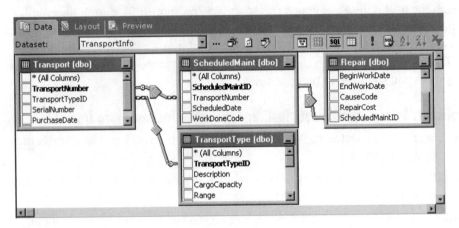

10. Check the following columns in the Transport table:
SerialNumber
PurchaseDate

11. Check the following columns in the TransportType table:
Description
CargoCapacity
Range
Cost
Crew
Manufacturer
ManAddr1
ManAddr2
ManCity
ManState
ManZipCode
ManPlanetAbbrv
ManEmail

12. Check the following column in the ScheduledMaint table:
ScheduledDate

13. Check the following column in the Repair table:
RepairID

14. In the grid pane, type the following in the Criteria column for SerialNumber:

```
= @SerialNumber
```

15. In the Criteria column for RepairID, type this:

```
IS NULL
```

16. Right-click in the diagram pane and select Group By from the context menu.

17. In the grid pane, in the Group By column for ScheduledDate, select Min from the drop-down list.

18. In the Alias column for ScheduledDate, change "Expr1" to "NextMaintDate."

19. Right-click in the SQL pane and select Run from the context menu. Enter **3809393848** for the @SerialNumber parameter and click OK. The Query Builder should appear similar to the illustration.

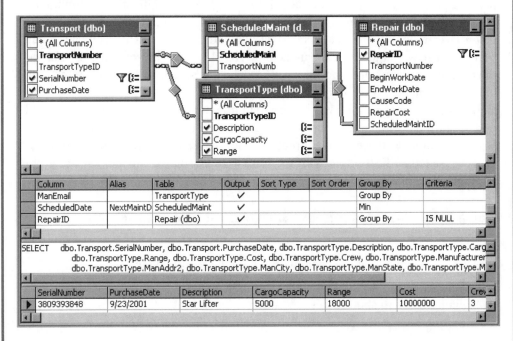

20. Right-click in the results pane and select Clear Results from the context menu.

Task Notes   The TransportInfo dataset must include all the information about a selected transport. This is not complicated except for the last item noted in the business need for this report: the date of the next scheduled maintenance for this transport. You will need a little background on the way that the Galactic database functions with respect to scheduled maintenance in order to understand this query.

Records are added to the ScheduledMaint table for each time a transport needs to come into a maintenance facility for preventative maintenance. These are considered appointments for preventative maintenance. They are scheduled for dates in the future.

Transports may have more than one pending preventative maintenance appointment. The ScheduledMaint table records are linked to a transport by the TransportNumber field.

When a transport comes in for preventative maintenance, a record is added to the Repair table. This indicates that an appointment for preventative maintenance has been fulfilled. The record in the Repair table is linked to the record in the ScheduledMaint table by the ScheduledMaintID field. If a scheduled appointment is missed, the appointment is rescheduled by changing the value in the ScheduledMaint.ScheduleDate field to a value in the future.

Given these business rules, records in the ScheduledMaint table for a given transport that do not have corresponding records in the Repair table represent pending preventative maintenance appointments. The record that has the minimum value in the ScheduledDate field represents the next appointment. To find this record, we are joining the ScheduledMaint table to the Repair table using a left outer join. Because we require the RepairID to be NULL, our result set will only include the pending appointments (that is, the records in the ScheduledMaint table that do not have a matching record in the Repair table).

Because a transport may have more than one pending appointment, we could end up with more than one record for a given transport. We need to use GROUP BY to consolidate these into one record. The MIN() aggregate function is used to find the ScheduledDate field with the lowest value (that is, the next scheduled appointment).

Transport Information Sheet, Task 3: Place a List Item on the Report and Populate It

1. Click the Layout tab to begin working on the report layout.

2. Select Report | Report Parameters from the menu. The Report Parameters dialog box will appear.

3. For the Prompt value, change "SerialNumber" to "Serial Number."

4. Uncheck Allow Null Value.

5. Select From Query for Available Values.

6. Select TransportSNs from the Dataset drop-down list.

7. Click OK.

8. Move your mouse pointer to the bottom of the white report layout area so that it changes from the regular mouse pointer to the double-headed arrow, as shown in the following illustration. The white report layout area is actually the body of the report.

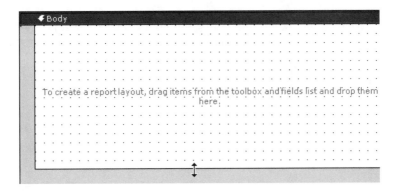

9. Drag the bottom of the report body down to create more room to lay out the list report.

10. Click the List report item in the Toolbox. The mouse pointer will change to a list icon and crosshairs when you move your mouse pointer over the report layout area.

11. Click and drag the mouse over the entire report body.

12. When you release the mouse button, after dragging, a list will be created to occupy the area you just defined.

13. Place a text box across the top of the list. This will be the title. Set its properties as follows:

Property	Value
FontSize	16pt
FontWeight	Bold
Name	Title
TextAlign	Center
Value	Transport Information Sheet

14. Select Textbox from the Toolbox and place a text box under the existing title as a second title. Type **Serial Number:** in this text box. Size the text box so that it just fits this text. This will serve as the label for the Serial Number field.

15. Make sure that TransportInfo is selected in the drop-down list at the top of the Fields window. When TransportInfo is selected, the Fields window will display a list of fields in the TransportInfo dataset.

16. Drag the SerialNumber field from the Fields window and place it to the right of the text box that was added in step 14. Click the white square to the right-center

of the SerialNumber text box and drag it until the text box is approximately twice its original size. Your report layout should appear similar to the illustration.

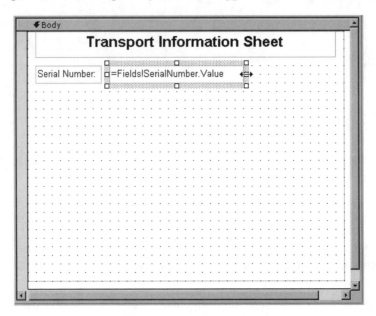

17. Repeat this operation with each of the following fields, creating a label for the field and then placing the field to the right of the label:

Label	Field
Purchase Date:	PurchaseDate
Transport Type:	Description
Cargo Capacity:	CargoCapacity
Range:	Range
Cost:	Cost
Crew:	Crew
Next Maint:	NextMaintDate

18. Set the properties for these fields as follows:

Field	Property	Value
PurchaseDate	Format	MM/dd/yyyy
PurchaseDate	TextAlign	Left
CargoCapacity	TextAlign	Left

Field	Property	Value
Range	TextAlign	Left
Cost	Format	###,###,###.00
Cost	TextAlign	Left
Crew	TextAlign	Left
NextMaintDate	Format	MM/dd/yyyy
NextMaintDate	TextAlign	Left

19. Select Line from the Toolbox and drag a line across the report layout at the bottom of the Serial Number label and Serial Number field. If you drag too far to the right while you are creating the line, Visual Studio will automatically increase the size of the List item and the body of the report. If this happens, simply reduce the size of the line, then reduce the width of the List item, and finally reduce the width of the body of the report.

20. Select Rectangle from the Toolbox and drag a rectangle around the unoccupied portion of the report body below the NextMaint fields. Set the properties of the rectangle as follows:

Property	Value
BorderStyle	Solid

21. Select Textbox from the Toolbox and place a text box in the upper-left corner of the rectangle. Type **Manufacturer:** in this text box. This is the manufacturer label.

22. Drag the Manufacturer field from the Fields window and place it inside the rectangle to the right of the manufacturer label. Size this field until it goes all the way to the right side of the rectangle.

23. Place the ManAddr1 and ManAddr2 fields inside the rectangle, below the Manufacturer field. Make these new fields the same size as the Manufacturer field.

24. Place a text box directly inside the rectangle, below the ManAddr2 field.

25. Right-click in the text box added in step 24 and select Expression from the context menu.

26. Click the plus sign to expand the Fields(TransportInfo) node in the Fields area.

27. Select the ManCity field and click Append.

28. In the Expression area, type the following after Fields!ManCity.Value:

```
& ", " &
```

29. Select the ManState field and click Append.

30. In the Expression area, type the following, including a space before and after each ampersand (&) character after Fields!ManState.Value:

```
& " " &
```

31. Select the ManZipCode field and click Append.

32. In the Expression area, type the following:

```
& " " &
```

33. Select the ManPlanetAbbrv field and click Append. Click OK.

34. Drag the ManEmail field from the Fields window and place it inside the rectangle under the text box added in step 24. Enlarge this text box. Your report layout should appear similar to this:

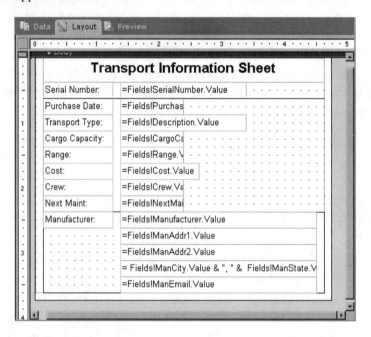

35. Click the Preview tab.

36. Select the first serial number from the Serial Number drop-down list and click View Report. Your report should appear similar to the illustration.

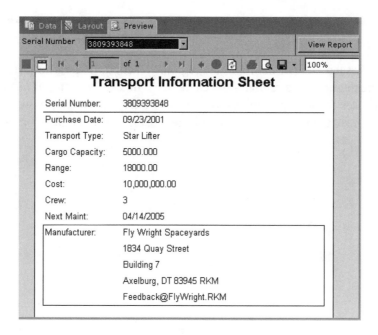

37. Click the Save All button in the toolbar.

Task Notes   As you saw in the Transport Information Sheet report, the List item allows you to place information anywhere. Text boxes, lines, and rectangles can be placed anywhere within the List item to create complex forms. This type of report is good for presenting a large amount of information about a single entity, as we did in this report.

As stated earlier, the contents of the List item are repeated for each record in the dataset. The TransportInfo dataset selects only a single record based on the user's selection of a serial number. Therefore, our report only has one page.

The Line report item is used simply to help format the report. It helps separate information on the report to make it easier for the user to understand. When working with the Table report item, we could use the borders of the text boxes in the table cells to create underlines. In the more freeform layout of the List report, the Line report item often works better than using cell borders.

The Rectangle report item serves two purposes. When its border is set to something other than None, it becomes a visible part of the report. Therefore, it can serve to help separate information on the report in the same manner as the Line report item. This is how we are using the Rectangle report item in this report.

The Rectangle report item can also be used to keep together other items in the report. We will examine this use of rectangles in Chapter 7.

Getting Graphical

You have now seen three of the four data regions in action. In the next chapter, we will examine the final data region—the chart. We will also look at the Image report item and its uses for adding graphics to a report. Finally, in Chapter 6, we will look at ways to control the properties of a report item using Visual Basic expressions.

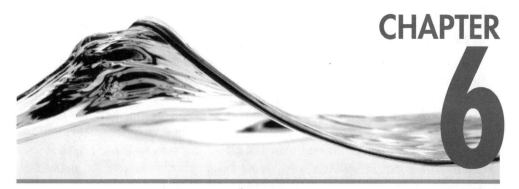

Graphic Expression: Using Charts and Images in Reports

IN THIS CHAPTER:

Chart Your Course

Image Is Everything

Building Higher

W e live in a world today where image is everything. Color and graphics are used to add interest and convey meaning. This is true, not only for TV, newspapers, and magazines, but also for some of the reports you create. Reports that are going to managers or executives need to provide the quick, concise communication of charts and graphs. Reports that are shared with customers need the polish provided by a well-placed image or two. Reporting Services has the tools you need to effectively communicate and impress in each of these situations.

In this chapter, we will explore the final data region, the chart, and how it can be used to summarize and express data. We will also use the image report item to add graphics to our reports. Next, we will investigate the possibilities for and restrictions on adding ActiveX controls to reports. Finally, we will end this chapter by looking at properties that can be used to format the report output and creative ways to control those properties.

Chart Your Course

In many cases, the best way to convey business intelligence is through business graphics. Bar charts, pie charts, and line graphs are very useful tools for giving meaning to endless volumes of data. They can quickly reveal trends and patterns to aid in data analysis. They compress lines upon lines of numbers into a format that can be understood in a moment.

In addition, charts can increase the reader's interest in your information. A splash of color excites the reader. Whereas endless lines of black on white lull people to sleep, bars of red and blue and pie wedges of purple and green wake people up.

You create charts in Reporting Services using the chart report item. The chart report item is a data region like the table, matrix, and list report items. This means that the chart can process multiple records from a dataset. The table, matrix, and list report items allow you to place other report items in a row, a column, or a list area that is repeated for every record in the dataset. The chart, on the other hand, uses the records in a dataset to create bars, lines, or pie wedges. You cannot place other report items inside of a chart item.

In the next sections of this chapter, we will explore the many charting possibilities provided by the chart report item.

The Fuel Price Chart

Features Highlighted

▶   Creating a report using the chart report item

▶   Refining the look of the chart to best present the information

Business Need   Galactic Delivery Services needs to analyze the fluctuations in the price of neutron fuel from month to month. The best way to perform this analysis is by creating a chart of the price over time. The user needs to be able to select the year from a drop-down list.

Task Overview

1. Create the Chapter06 Project, a Shared Data Source, a New Report, and Two Datasets

2. Place a Chart Item on the Report and Populate It

3. Refine the Chart

Fuel Price Chart, Task 1: Create the Chapter06 Project, a Shared Data Source, a New Report, and Two Datasets

1. Create a new Reporting Services project called Chapter06 in the MSSQLRS folder. (If you need help with this task, see the section "The Transport List Report" in Chapter 5.)

2. Create a shared data source called Galactic for the Galactic database. (Again, if you need help with this task, see the section "The Transport List Report" in Chapter 5.)

3. Add a blank report called FuelPriceChart to the Chapter06 project. (Do not use the Report Wizard.)

4. Select <New Dateset…> from the Dataset drop-down list. The Dataset dialog box will appear.

5. Enter **FuelPrices** for the name in the Dataset dialog box.

6. Galactic will be selected for the data source by default. Click OK. You will return to the Data tab, which now displays the Generic Query Designer.

7. Type the following in the SQL pane:

```
SELECT Description AS FuelType,
     PriceStartDate,
     Price
FROM FuelPrice
INNER JOIN Propulsion
     ON FuelPrice.PropulsionID = Propulsion.PropulsionID
WHERE (YEAR(PriceStartDate) = @Year)
AND (Description = 'Neutron')
ORDER BY FuelType, PriceStartDate
```

8. Click the Run button in the Generic Query Designer toolbar to run the query and make sure there are no errors. Correct any typos that may be detected. When the query is correct, the Define Query Parameters dialog box will appear. Enter **2003** for the @Year parameter and click OK.

9. The business needs for the report specified that the user should select the year from a drop-down list. We will need to define a second dataset to populate this drop-down list. Select <New Dateset...> from the Dataset drop-down list. The Dataset dialog box will appear.

10. Enter **Years** for the name in the Dataset dialog box.

11. Galactic will be selected for the data source by default. Type the following in the Query String area of the dialog box:

```
SELECT DISTINCT YEAR(PriceStartDate) AS Year FROM FuelPrice
```

12. Click OK. The Generic Query Designer will now display the Year dataset. Run the query to make sure it is correct. You will see a list of the distinct years that are in the FuelPrice table.

Task Notes   We created two datasets in the FuelPriceChart report—one to populate the Year drop-down list and the other to provide data for the chart. Only one of these two datasets can be displayed on the Data tab at a time. You use the Dataset drop-down list to switch between the two datasets on the Data tab. In the same manner, the Fields window only shows the fields from one dataset at a time. You use the drop-down list at the top of the Fields window to change which dataset's fields are being displayed.

You have undoubtedly noticed that both the datasets for this report were created by typing a query, either into the SQL pane of the Generic Query Designer or into the Query String area of the Dataset dialog box. The graphical tools of the Query Builder are very helpful if you are still learning the syntax of SELECT queries or if you are unfamiliar with the database you are querying. However, it is more efficient to simply type the query into the SQL pane or the Dataset dialog box. In addition, some complex queries must be typed in because they cannot be created through the Query Builder.

Throughout the remainder of this book, we will type our SELECT statements rather than create them using the Query Builder. This allows us to quickly create the necessary datasets and then concentrate on the aspects of report creation that are new and different in each report. As you create your own reports, use the interface—Query Builder or Generic Query Designer—with which you are most comfortable.

Fuel Price Chart, Task 2: Place a Chart Item on the Report and Populate It

1. Switch to the Layout tab.

2. Select Report | Report Parameters from the menu. The Report Parameters dialog box will appear.

3. A report parameter called Year has been created to correspond to the @Year parameter from the FuelPrices dataset. Make sure the check box Allow Null Values is not checked.

4. Select Available Values: From Query.

5. In the Dataset drop-down list, select Years. Click OK to exit the Report Parameters dialog box.

6. Click and drag the edges of the report layout area so that the layout area fills the available space on the screen.

7. Place a chart report item on the report layout. The chart should cover almost the entire report layout because it will be the only item on the report. (If the report items are not showing to the left of the report layout, select View | Toolbox from the top menu.)

8. The chart has three areas where you can drop fields: Drop Data Fields Here, Drop Series Fields Here, and Drop Category Fields Here. If these areas are not visible, double-click the center of the chart to display them. You may also need to scroll the layout window to see each of the drop areas.

NOTE

If you need to move the chart after you have placed it in the report layout, click the report layout so that the chart is not selected and then click the chart item so that it is selected but the three "Drop Fields Here" areas are not visible. Now you can click the edge of the chart item to drag it to the appropriate location. Click the chart item one more time to get the three "Drop Fields Here" areas to reappear.

9. Select FuelPrices from the drop-down list in the Fields window, if it is not already selected. Drag the FuelType field and drop it on Drop Series Fields Here.

10. Drag the PriceStartDate field and drop it on Drop Category Fields Here.

11. Drag the Price field and drop it on Drop Data Fields Here.

12. Right-click the chart and select Chart Type | Line | Simple Line from the context menu. The report layout should appear similar to the following illustration.

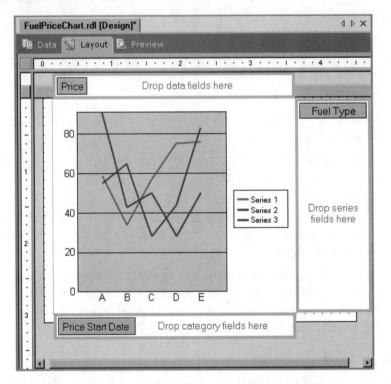

13. Select the Preview tab. Select 2003 from the Year drop-down list and then click View Report. Your report will appear similar to this:

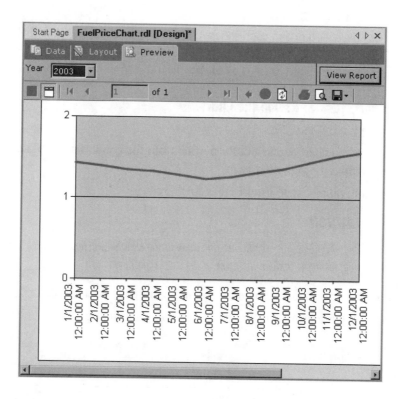

Task Notes   You have now seen how easy it is to create a chart using the chart report item. Simply drag and drop the fields from your dataset onto the appropriate locations, select the type of chart you would like, and you have a functioning chart. In the next sections, we will explore ways to manipulate the properties of the chart to create more complex results.

The field you dropped in the Data Fields area (the Price field in this report) provides the values for the data points. The field you dropped in the Category Fields area (the PriceStartDate field in this report) provides the labels for the x-axis of the chart. This category field also groups the rows from the dataset into multiple categories. One entry is created on the x-axis for each category. In our Fuel Price Chart, we used the PriceStartDate field to create our categories. Because we are looking at data for a single year and because there is one record for each month, we get 12 distinct values for PriceStartDate in our dataset and 12 categories along the x-axis of our chart (one category for each month in the year we are charting).

One series of categories is created for each distinct value in the field you dropped in the Data Series area. Each series is usually charted in its own color; one series in green, one series in blue, and so on. The legend, located to the right in this chart, tells the reader which color has been assigned to each series. Our dataset contains only one fuel type, Neutron. Therefore, we get only one series of data points on our chart.

Now let's use some of the properties of the chart to refine our results.

Fuel Price Chart, Task 3: Refine the Chart

1. Select the Layout tab.

2. Right-click the chart and select Properties from the context menu. The Chart Properties dialog box will appear.

3. On the General tab, type **Fuel Prices** for the title.

CAUTION

Do not confuse Title with Name. Title contains the text that will appear above the report, whereas Name contains the name of the chart report item itself.

4. Click the Style button (the paint brush and paint pail) next to Title.

5. Set the following properties on the Style Properties dialog box:

Property	Value
Size	14pt
Weight	Bold
Decoration	Underline

6. Click OK.

7. Select the Data tab.

8. Click Edit (next to Values). The Edit Chart Value dialog box will appear.

9. Select the Appearance tab. Check the Show Markers check box and then select Diamond to place a diamond shape at each data point.

10. Click OK to return to the Chart Properties dialog box.

11. Select the X Axis tab. Set the following properties:

Property	Value
Title	=Parameters!Year.Value
Format Code	MMM
Numeric or Time-Scale Values	(checked)

12. Select the Y Axis tab. Set the following properties:

Property	Value
Title	Price in Dollars
Scale, Minimum	0
Scale, Maximum	6

13. Click OK.

14. Select the Preview tab. Select 2003 from the Year drop-down list and then click View Report. Your report will appear similar to the illustration.

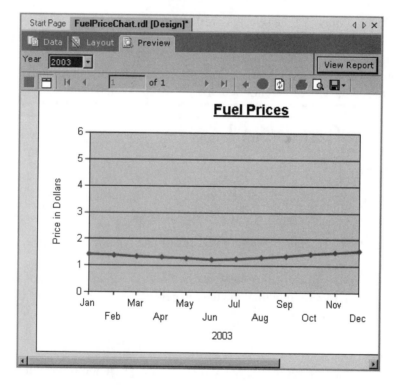

15. Click Save All in the toolbar.

Task Notes   As you have seen, the Chart Properties dialog box provides a great deal of control over the appearance and function of the chart. It is divided into seven different tabs, as shown in the following table, each controlling a different aspect of the chart.

Tab	Charting Aspect Controlled
General	Name of the report item, title, chart type, and color palette. (Chart Type can also be selected from the chart item context menu.)
Data	Dataset fields used to control the data values, categories, and series.
X Axis	Title and scale of the x-axis.
Y Axis	Title and scale of the y-axis.
Legend	If and where a legend containing information on the chart series is included.
3-D Effect	Whether the chart appears as a two-dimensional or three-dimensional object.
Filters	Filtering conditions applied to the data.

We will look at more of the settings available on the Chart Properties dialog box as we create additional charts in this chapter. You can also experiment with these settings to get exactly the chart format you need.

The format code "MMM" is a date formatting code. It causes the chart to use only the first three characters of the month name for the x-axis labels.

The Fuel Price Chart, Version 2

Features Highlighted

▶ Creating a report using the chart report item with multiple series

▶ Using the union operator in a SELECT statement

▶ Using a WHERE clause to return records of one type or of all types

Business Need   GDS now needs to analyze the fluctuations in the price of all fuel types from month to month. Allow the user to select a single fuel type or all fuel types from a drop-down list.

Task Overview

1. Create a New Dataset for the Second Drop-down List and Revise the FuelPrices Dataset to Allow for Multiple Fuel Types

Fuel Price Chart, Version 2, Task 1: Create a New Dataset for the Second Drop-down List and Revise the FuelPrices Dataset to Allow for Multiple Fuel Types

1. Reopen the Chapter06 project if it has been closed. Double-click the FuelPriceChart report in the Solution Explorer, if it does not open automatically.

2. Select the Data tab.

3. Choose <New Dataset…> from the Dataset drop-down list. The Dataset dialog box will appear.

4. Enter **FuelTypes** for name in the Dataset dialog box.

5. Galactic will be selected for the data source by default. Click OK. You will return to Generic Query Designer in the Data tab.

6. Type the following in the SQL pane:

```
SELECT '_All_' AS FuelType
UNION
SELECT Description FROM Propulsion ORDER BY FuelType
```

7. Run the query to make sure it is correct. You will see a list of the distinct fuel types in the FuelPrice table. There will also be a record with a value of "_All_".

8. Choose FuelPrices from the DATASET drop-down list.

9. Change the SELECT statement to the following (the only change is in the second half of the WHERE clause):

```
SELECT Description AS FuelType,
       PriceStartDate,
       Price
FROM FuelPrice
INNER JOIN Propulsion
     ON FuelPrice.PropulsionID = Propulsion.PropulsionID
WHERE (YEAR(PriceStartDate) = @Year)
     AND ((Description = @PropulsionType)
      OR (@PropulsionType = '_All_'))
ORDER BY FuelType, PriceStartDate
```

10. Run the query to make sure it is correct. The Define Query parameters dialog box will appear. Enter **2003** for the @Year parameter, **_All_** for the @PropulsionType parameter, and click OK. Clear the query results.

11. Select the Layout tab. (A report parameter is not created for PropulsionType until you leave the Data tab.)

12. Select Report | Report Parameters from the main menu. The Report Parameters dialog box appears.

13. A report parameter called PropulsionType has been created to correspond to the @PropulsionType parameter from the FuelPrices dataset. Select this parameter in the Parameters list box.

14. Select Available Values: From Query.

15. In the Dataset drop-down list, select FuelTypes. Click OK to exit the Report Parameters dialog box.

16. Select the Preview tab. Select 2003 from the Year drop-down list, select _All_ from the PropulsionType drop-down list, and then click View Report. Your report will appear similar to the illustration.

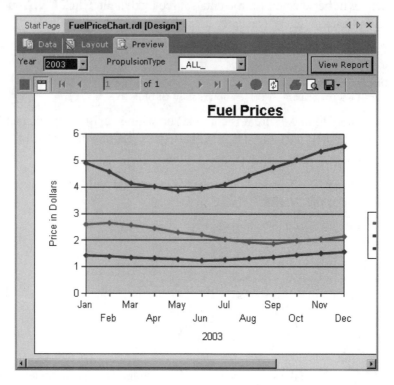

17. Click Save All in the toolbar.

Task Notes   The query that creates the FuelTypes dataset is actually two SELECT statements combined to produce one result set. The first SELECT statement returns a single row with the constant value "_All_" in the FuelType column. The underscores are placed around the word "All" to make sure it sorts to the top of the list. The second SELECT statement returns a row for each record in the Propulsion table. Each row has a single column called Description. The two result sets are unified into a single result set by the UNION operator in between the two SELECT statements.

When result sets are "unioned," the names of the columns in the result set are taken from the first SELECT statement in the union. That is why the FuelTypes dataset has a single column called FuelType rather than Description. When SELECT statements are unioned, only the last SELECT statement can have an ORDER BY clause. This ORDER BY clause is used to sort the entire result set after it has been unified into a single result set.

The UNION operator can be used with any two SELECT statements as long as the following is true:

▶   The result set from each SELECT statement has the same number of columns.

▶   The corresponding columns in each result set have the same data type.

In fact, the UNION can be used to combine any number of SELECT statements into a unified result set as long as these two conditions hold true for all the SELECT statements in the UNION.

The field we chose for our series field, FuelType, will have three distinct values in the dataset when the "_All_" option is chosen for the PropulsionType report parameter. When this option is selected, the chart will contain three series of data points. The legend tells the reader that the green series represents the data for antimatter, the blue series represents the data for fusion, and the purple series represents the data for neutron. Each series contains 12 categories. Three series multiplied by 12 categories means that we have 36 data points on our chart.

It is important that you understand categories and series as we get into more complex charting. If you are a bit fuzzy on this, review the first part of this chapter before moving on.

The Business Type Distribution Chart

Features Highlighted

▶   Creating a report using a pie chart

▶   Using the Data Label property

▶   Changing the chart palette

▶   Using the 3-D effect

Business Need   The Galactic Delivery Services marketing department needs to analyze what types of businesses are using GDS for their delivery services. This information should be presented as a pie chart.

Task Overview

1. Create a New Report and a Dataset
2. Place a Chart Item on the Report and Populate It

Business Type Distribution Chart, Task I: Create a New Report and a Dataset

1. Reopen the Chapter06 project if it has been closed. Close the FuelPriceChart report.
2. Add a blank report called BusinessTypeDistribution to the Chapter06 project. (Do not use the Report Wizard.)
3. Select <New Dateset...> from the Dataset drop-down list. The Dataset dialog box will appear.
4. Enter **CustomerBusinessTypes** for the name in the Dataset dialog box.
5. "Galactic (shared)" will be selected for the data source by default. Click OK. You will return to the Data tab, which now displays the Generic Query Designer.
6. Type the following in the SQL pane:

```
SELECT Name AS CustomerName,
     Description AS BusinessType
FROM Customer
INNER JOIN CustomerToBusinessTypeLink
     ON Customer.CustomerNumber
          = CustomerToBusinessTypeLink.CustomerNumber
INNER JOIN BusinessType
     ON CustomerToBusinessTypeLink.BusinessTypeCode
          = BusinessType.BusinessTypeCode
```

7. Run the query to make sure there are no errors. Correct any typos that may be detected.

Task Notes   The CustomerBusinessTypes dataset simply contains a list of customer names and their corresponding business type. Remember that some customers are linked to more than one business type. That means that some of the customers will appear in the list more than once.

This dataset will be used to populate a pie chart in the next task. The BusinessType field will be used to create the categories for the pie chart. The items in the CustomerName field will be counted to determine how many customers are in each category.

Business Type Distribution Chart, Task 2: Place a Chart Item on the Report and Populate It

1. Switch to the Layout tab then click and drag the edges of the report layout area so that the layout area fills the available space on the screen.

2. Place a chart report item on the report layout. The chart should cover almost the entire report layout because it will be the only item on the report.

3. Right-click the chart and select Chart Type | Pie | Simple Pie from the context menu.

4. Drag the CustomerName field from the Fields window and drop it on Drop Data Fields Here.

5. Drag the BusinessType field and drop it on Drop Category Fields Here.

6. Right-click the chart and select Properties from the context menu. The Chart Properties dialog box will appear.

7. On the General tab, type **Customer Business Types** for the title.

8. Click the Style button (next to the Title). The Style Properties dialog box appears.

9. Set the following properties on the Style Properties dialog box:

Property	Value
Size	14pt
Weight	Bold
Decoration	Underline

10. Click OK to exit the Style Properties dialog box.

11. Select Semi-Transparent from the Palette drop-down list.

12. Select the Data tab.

13. Click Edit (next to Values). The Edit Chart Value dialog box will appear.

14. Select the Point Labels tab. Check the Show Point Labels check box.

15. Click the Expression button (the button with *fx* on it) next to the Data Label entry area. The Edit Expression dialog box will appear.

16. Type the following in the Expression area:

```
=Fields!BusinessType.Value & vbcrlf &
     "(" & CSTR(Count(Fields!CustomerName.Value)) & ")"
```

17. Click OK to exit the Edit Expression dialog box.

18. Click Label Style. The Style Properties dialog box will appear.

19. Select Bold from the Weight drop-down list.

20. Click OK to exit the Style Properties dialog box.

21. Click OK to exit the Edit Chart Value dialog box.

22. Select the Legend tab.

23. Uncheck Show Legend.

24. Select the 3-D Effect tab.

25. Check Display Chart with 3-D Visual Effect.

26. Click OK to exit the Chart Properties dialog box.

27. Select the Preview tab. Your report will appear similar to the illustration.

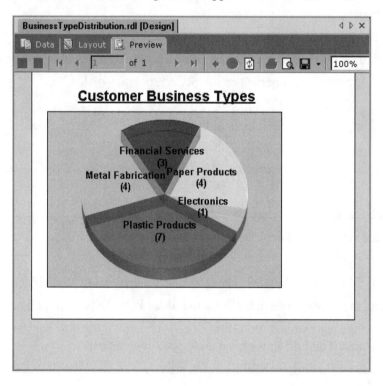

28. Click Save All in the toolbar.

Task Notes   By default, the pie chart uses a legend to the side of the chart to provide labels for each wedge in the pie. In the Business Type Distribution chart, we changed this default behavior. We used the Show Legend check box on the Legend tab to turn off the legend. We used the Data Label entry area on the Point Label tab to put a label for each wedge right on the pie chart itself.

We are actually using the data label to do double duty for us. It is displaying both the business type for each pie wedge and the number of companies of that business type. This provides the reader with both a graphical representation of the data, in the form of the pie wedge, and the underlying numbers for additional reference. The expression in the Data Label area concatenates the business type and the count of the number of customers with a carriage return/linefeed (vbcrlf) in between. The carriage return/linefeed causes the business type and the count to each appear on its own line.

In this chart, we are also using the 3-D effect. The 3-D effect can help to add interest to a chart by taking a flat graphic and lifting it off the page.

Now we will try one more chart before looking at incorporating images in reports.

The Days in Maintenance Chart

Features Highlighted

▶   Creating a report using a 3-D, stacked, column chart

Business Need   The Galactic Delivery Services transport maintenance department is looking to compare the total maintenance downtime for each year. They would also like to know how that maintenance time is distributed among the different transport types. They would like a graph showing the number of days that each type of transport spent "in for repairs." This information should be presented as a 3-D, stacked column chart. The underlying data should be displayed as a label on each column in the chart.

Task Overview

1.   Create a New Report, Create a Dataset, Place a Chart Item on the Report, and Populate It

Days in Maintenance Chart, Task 1: Create a New Report, Create a Dataset, Place a Chart Item on the Report, and Populate It

1.   Reopen the Chapter06 project if it has been closed. Close the BusinessTypeDistribution report.

2. Add a blank report called DaysInMaint to the Chapter06 project. (Do not use the Report Wizard.)

3. Select <New Dataset...> from the Dataset drop-down list. The Dataset dialog box will appear.

4. Enter **DaysInMaint** for the name in the Dataset dialog box.

5. "Galactic (shared)" will be selected for the data source by default. Click OK. You will return to the Data tab, which now displays the Generic Query Designer.

6. Type the following in the SQL pane:

```
SELECT Description AS PropulsionType,
    YEAR(BeginWorkDate) AS Year,
    DATEDIFF(dd, BeginWorkDate, EndWorkDate) AS DaysInMaint
FROM Repair
INNER JOIN Transport
    ON Repair.TransportNumber = Transport.TransportNumber
INNER JOIN TransportType
    ON Transport.TransportTypeID = TransportType.TransportTypeID
ORDER BY PropulsionType, Year
```

7. Run the query to make sure there are no errors. Correct any typos that may be detected.

8. Switch to the Layout tab.

9. Set the following properties of the Body:

Property	Value
Width	7.5in
Height	4.375in

10. Place a chart report item on the report layout. The chart should cover almost the entire report layout because it will be the only item on the report.

11. Drag the PropulsionType field from the Fields window and drop it on Drop Series Fields Here.

12. Drag the Year field and drop it on Drop Category Fields Here.

13. Drag the DaysInMaint field from the Fields window and drop it on Drop Data Fields Here.

NOTE

The following uses a more abbreviated format for specifying which items need to be changed for the chart. A table will be provided for each dialog box or for each tab within a dialog box. Simply navigate to the appropriate dialog box or tab and change the items specified. Navigation hints are provided with some of the tables for certain dialog boxes and tabs that are a little harder to find.

14. Right-click the chart and select Properties from the context menu. The Chart Properties dialog box will appear. Set the chart properties, as follows, in the General tab:

Property	Value
Title	Days in Maintenance
Chart sub-type	Stacked column chart

Click the Style button (paintbrush and bucket) next to the Title on the General tab to access the Style Properties dialog box. Then set the following properties for Report Title:

Property	Value
Size	14pt
Weight	Bold
Decoration	Underline

Click the Edit button next to the Values list on the Data tab to access the Edit Chart Value dialog box. Set the following property on the Values tab:

Property	Value
Series Label	=Sum(Fields!DaysInMaint.Value)

Click the Point Labels tab in the Edit Chart Value dialog box and set these properties:

Property	Value
Show point labels	(checked)
Data label	=Sum(Fields!DaysInMaint.Value)

Click the Edit button next to the Category Groups list on the Data tab to access the Grouping and Sorting Properties dialog box. Set the following property for Category Groups:

Property	Value
Label	= "Total Maint. Hours - " & Sum(Fields!DaysInMaint.Value) & vbcrlf & vbcrlf & Fields!Year.Value

Click the Edit button next to the Series Groups list on the Data tab to access the Grouping and Sorting Properties dialog box. Set the following property for Series Groups:

Property	Value
Label	= Fields!PropulsionType.Value & " Total Maint. Hours (All Years)"

Click the X Axis tab and set the following property:

Property	Value
Title	Year

Click the Style button (paintbrush and bucket) next to Title on the X Axis tab to access the Style Properties dialog box. Set the following properties for X-Axis Title:

Property	Value
Size	12pt
Weight	Bold

Click the Y Axis tab and set the following property:

Property	Value
Title	="Days in" & vbcrlf & "Maintenance" & vbcrlf & "Hanger"

Click the Style button (paintbrush and bucket) next to Title on the Y Axis tab to access the Style Properties dialog box. Set the following properties for Y-Axis Title:

Property	Value
Size	12pt
Weight	Bold

Click the Legend tab and set the following property:

Property	Value
Position	(Select the square in the center of the bottom row of the Position selector.)

15. After you have made all these modifications, click OK to exit the Chart Properties dialog box.

16. Select the Preview tab. Your report will appear similar to this:

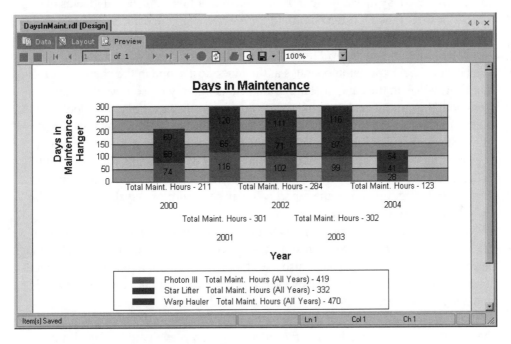

17. Click Save All in the toolbar.

Task Notes   The stacked column chart is a very good choice to fulfill the business needs for this report, because it can graphically illustrate two different pieces of information at the same time. Each colored section of the graph shows the number of maintenance days for a given propulsion type. In addition, the combined height of the three sections of the column shows the fluctuations in the total maintenance days from year to year.

Above and beyond the graphical information that is provided in the chart, several additional pieces of information are provided numerically on the chart. This includes the category labels along the x-axis, the legend at the bottom of the graph, and the detail data displayed right on the column sections themselves. The values on the columns are the result of the expression entered for the data label on the Point labels tab.

TIP

If the legend does not display completely, you may need to make the chart area wider on the Layout tab.

The expression entered for the data label uses the SUM() function to add up the values from the DaysInMaint field. It may seem that this sum should give us the total values from the DaysInMaint field for every row in the dataset. The reason this does not occur is because of the *scope* in which this expression is evaluated. The scope sets boundaries on which rows from the dataset are used with a given expression.

The data label expression operates at the innermost scope in the chart. That means that expressions in the data label are evaluated using only those rows that come from both the current category and the current series. For example, let's look at the column section for Star Lifters for the year 2000. This column section is part of the Star Lifter series. It is also part of the year 2000 category. When the report is evaluating the data label expression to put a label on the "Star Lifter/year 2000" column section, it uses only those rows in the result set for the Star Lifters in the year 2000. Using this scope, the report calculates the sum of DaysInMaint for Star Lifters in the year 2000 as 68 days.

Next, let's consider the summary data that appears in the column labels along the x-axis. These entries are the result of the expression entered for the label in the category groups. This expression also uses the SUM() function to add up the values from the DaysInMaint column. However, it calculates different totals because it is operating in a different scope.

In this case, the calculations are being done in the category scope, which means that the expression for the label in the category group is evaluated using all the records from the current category. For example, let's look at the column label for the year 2000 column. This column is part of the year 2000 category. When the report is evaluating the label expression to put a label below this column, it uses all the rows in the result set for the year 2000. The propulsion type of each row does not make a difference, because it is not part of this scope. Using the year 2000 category scope, the report calculates the sum of DaysInMaint for the year 2000 as 211 days.

Finally, we come to the summary data that appears in the legend below the chart. These entries are the result of two expressions that are concatenated when the report is created. The first expression comes from the label in the series groups. The second expression comes from the Series label on the Values tab. If you leave the label in the series group empty, a generic series label (Series 1, Series 2, and so on) will be created by default. If the Series label on the Values tab is left blank, it is ignored. When both the label in the series group and the Series label on the Values tab contain expressions, the results of the two expressions are concatenated with a dash in between.

The expression in the Series label on the Values tab of our current chart also uses the SUM() function to add up the values from the DaysInMaint column. Once again, it is working in a different scope, so it comes up with different results. Here, the calculations are being done in the series scope. That means that the expressions for both the Series label on the Values tab and the label in the series group are evaluated using all the records from the current series. For example, let's look at the entry in the legend for the Star Lifter series. When the report is evaluating the Series label expression from the Values tab and the label expression from the series group to put a label in the legend, it uses all the rows in the result set for Star Lifters. The year of each row does not make a difference, because it is not part of this scope. Using the Star Lifter series scope, the report calculates the sum of DaysInMaint for the Star Lifters as 332 days.

In a number of the expressions used in this chart, we are concatenating together several strings to create the labels we need. This is being done using the Visual Basic string concatenation operator (&). You may notice that several of the fields being concatenated are numeric rather than string fields. The reason these concatenations work is that the & operator will automatically convert numeric values to strings. In this way, we can take "Total Maint. Hours - " and concatenate it with 211 to get the first line of the year 2000 column label. The 211 is actually converted to "211" and then concatenated with the rest of the string.

The final noteworthy item on this report is the expression used to create the label on the y-axis. In order to have this label fit nicely along the y-axis, we used our old friend the carriage return/linefeed to split the label onto three lines. Since the text is rotated 90 degrees, the first line of the label is farthest from the y-axis, the next line is to the right of the first line, and the last line is to the right of the other two.

Image Is Everything

Now that we have charted up a storm, it is time to turn our attention to two other methods for adding color to a report. One way is through the use of borders and background colors. Almost all the report items have properties you can use to specify borders and background colors.

The other way to add color to your reports is through the use of images. Images can be placed on a report using the image report object. They can serve as a background for other report objects. They can even serve as the background to the main body of the report itself.

In addition to determining where an image will be placed on the report, you also have to determine where the image will come from. Images can be external to the report, embedded in the report, or pulled from a binary field in a database. Each image location has its own benefits and drawbacks.

Images that are external to the report are saved as separate files. They are not stored as part of the report definition. This means that when the report is rendered, the renderer must find each of these image files in order to render the report correctly.

External images are easier to update if they have to be changed in the future. You can simply modify the image file because it is not embedded in a report definition file. External images can also be shared among several reports. However, because the report and its required images exist as separate files, some care has to be taken to ensure that the renderer can always locate the images when it is rendering the report.

Embedded images are stored right in the report definition file. With embedded images, only one file is required for rendering the report. There is no risk of the renderer not being able to find a required image. The downside of embedded images is that it is more difficult to update an image. In order to change an embedded image, you need to modify the source image, re-embed the modified image, and redeploy the report. Also, it is not possible to share an embedded image. It can only be used by the report in which it is embedded.

Images stored in a database file can be shared among reports and are easy to track down when a report is rendered. In addition, when images are stored with the data in the database, it is possible to use a different image in your report for each row in the dataset. This is very difficult to do with external or embedded images.

Images in the database do pose a couple of concerns. First of all, retrieving images from the database will put an additional load on your database server. Care must be taken to make sure your server can handle this additional load without degradation in response time. In addition, managing large binary objects, such as images, in database records is not always a trivial task.

As a rule of thumb, images, such as company logos, that will be shared among many reports should be kept external. These shared images should be put in one central location so they can be accessed by the reports when they are needed. Images that have a strong association with data in a particular record in a database table should be stored in the database itself. For example, a picture of a particular employee has a strong association with that employee's record in the Employee table. We will only be interested in displaying the picture of a particular employee when the row in the dataset for that employee is being processed. Any images that do not fall into these two categories should be embedded in the report.

Conference Nametags

Features Highlighted

▶ Using background colors on report objects

▶ Using borders on report objects

▶ Placing an image on a report

Business Need   Galactic Delivery Services is preparing for its annual customer conference. The billing contact for each customer has been invited to the conference. As part of the preparations for the conference, the GDS art department must create nametags for the conference attendees. Because the names of all the billing contacts are available in the Galactic database, and this database can easily be accessed from Reporting Services, the art department has decided to use Reporting Services to create the nametags.

The conference nametags should include the name of the attendee and also the name of the company they work for. The art department would like the nametags to be bright and colorful. They should include the GDS logo.

Task Overview

1. Create a New Report, Create a Dataset, Place the Report Items on the Report

Conference Nametags, Task 1: Create a New Report, Create a Dataset, Place the Report Items on the Report

1. Reopen the Chapter06 project if it has been closed. Close the DaysInMaint report.

2. Add a blank report called Nametags to the Chapter06 project. (Do not use the Report Wizard.)

3. Select <New Dataset...> from the Dataset drop-down list. The Dataset dialog box will appear.

4. Enter **BillingContacts** for the name in the Dataset dialog box.

5. "Galactic (shared)" will be selected for the data source by default. Click OK. You will return to the Data tab, which now displays the Generic Query Designer.

6. Type the following in the SQL pane:

```
SELECT BillingContact, Name
FROM Customer
ORDER BY BillingContact
```

7. Run the query to make sure there are no errors. Correct any typos that may be detected.

8. Switch to the Layout tab.

9. Drag a list from the Toolbox and drop it onto the report layout. Modify the following properties of the list:

Property	Value
BackgroundColor	DarkOrange
Location: Left	0.125in
Location: Top	0.125in
Size: Width	4.75in
Size: Height	2.125in

We are using a list here because this report will have a freeform layout rather than the rows and columns of a table or matrix.

10. Drag the BillingContact field from the Fields window and drop it onto the list. Modify the following properties of the text box that results:

Property	Value
BackgroundColor	Gold
BorderColor	DarkBlue
BorderStyle	Solid
BorderWidth	4pt
Color	DarkBlue
Font: FontSize	20pt
Font: FontWeight	Bold
Location: Left	0.125in
Location: Top	0.125in
Size: Width	4.5in
Size: Height	0.5in
TextAlign	Center
VerticalAlign	Middle

11. Drag the Name field from the Fields window and drop it onto the list. Modify the following properties of the text box that results:

Property	Value
BackgroundColor	Gold
BorderColor	DarkBlue
BorderStyle	Solid
BorderWidth	4pt
Color	DarkBlue
Font: FontSize	16pt
Font: FontWeight	Bold
Location: Left	0.125in
Location: Top	0.875in
Size: Width	4.5in
Size: Height	0.375in
TextAlign	Center
VerticalAlign	Middle

12. Drag a text box from the Toolbox and drop it onto the list. Modify the following properties of this text box:

Property	Value
Font: FontSize	25pt
Location: Left	1in
Location: Top	1.375in
Size: Width	3.625in
Size: Height	0.625in
TextAlign	Center
Value	GDS Conference 2004
VerticalAlign	Middle

13. Drag a line from the Toolbox and drop it onto the list. Modify the following properties of the line:

Property	Value
EndPoint: Horizontal	4.75in
EndPoint: Vertical	2.125in
LineColor	DarkBlue
LineWidth	10pt
Location: Left	0in
Location: Top	2.125in

14. Drag an image report item from the Toolbox and drop it onto the list. The Image Wizard will appear. Click Next.

15. Click the Project radio button. This will be an external image. The Image Wizard will place it in the Chapter06 project for us. Click Next.

16. Click New Image. The Import Image dialog box will appear.

17. Navigate to the GDS.gif image file and select it. Click Open.

NOTE

The image files used in the reports in this chapter are available on the website for this book. If you have not done so already, go to http://www.osborne.com, locate the book's page using the ISBN 0072232161, and follow the instructions to download the image files.

18. Click Next and then click Finish.

19. Modify the following properties of the image in the Properties window:

Property	Value
Location: Left	0.125in
Location: Top	1.375in
Sizing	AutoSize

20. Check to make sure that the list is still the correct size. Change the dimensions to match the following, if necessary:

Property	Value
Size: Width	4.75in
Size: Height	2.125in

21. Click in the report layout area. This will cause the report body to be selected in the Properties window. Modify the following properties of the report body:

Property	Value
BackgroundColor	DarkBlue
Size: Width	5in
Size: Height	2.25in

22. Click the Preview tab. The nametags are ready to be printed, cut apart and placed in nametag holders, as shown here.

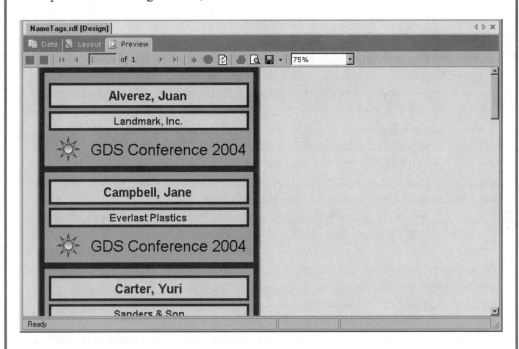

23. Click Save All in the toolbar.

Task Notes   We used several properties of the report objects in our Conference Nametags report to add color. The BackgroundColor property controls the color in the background of the report item. This defaults to Transparent, meaning that whatever is behind the item shows through. When the BackgroundColor property is set to a color rather than Transparent, that color fills in and covers up everything that is behind the item.

The BorderColor property controls the color of the border around the outside of the report item. BorderColor works in cooperation with two other properties: BorderStyle and BorderWidth. The BorderStyle property defaults to None. When BorderStyle is None, the border is not visible. No matter what color you set for BorderColor, it will not show up when the BorderStyle is set to None.

In order to have a visible border around an object, you must change the BorderSyle property to a solid line (Solid), a dotted line (Dotted), a dashed line (Dashed), a double line (Double), or one of the other settings in the BorderStyle drop-down list. Once you have selected one of these visible settings for the BorderStyle property, you can set the color of the border using the BorderColor property and the thickness of the border using the BorderWidth property.

The border settings for each side of a report item can be controlled separately or altogether. If you expand any of the three border properties, you will see that they have separate entries for Default, Left, Right, Top, and Bottom. The Default property is, just as it says, the default value for all four sides of the report item. When the Left, Right, Top, or Bottom property is blank, the setting for that particular side is taken from the Default property. For example, if the BorderStyle: Default property is set to None, and BorderStyle: Left, BorderStyle: Right, BorderStyle: Top, and BorderStyle: Bottom are all blank, there will be no border around the report item. If the BorderStyle: Bottom property is set to Double, this will override the default setting and a double line will appear across the bottom of the item. The border on the other three sides of the item (left, right, and top) will continue to use the default setting.

The Color property controls the color of the text that is created by a report item. You will find the Color property on a text box, which is expected, because the main purpose of a text box is to create text. You will also find the Color property on each of the data regions, tables, matrixes, lists, and charts. A data region can create a text message when there are no rows in the dataset attached to it. The Color property specifies the color of the text in this special "no rows" message when it is displayed. (We will talk more about the "no rows" message in Chapter 7.)

The final color property we used in the Conference Nametags report is the LineColor property. This property exists only for line report items. It should come as no surprise that this property controls the color of the line.

One thing you will quickly notice when you begin using background colors is that a report item with a BackgroundColor property set to Transparent is only transparent when the report is rendered. The report item is not transparent on the Layout tab. Report items that have a BackgroundColor property set to Transparent will have a white background on the Layout tab. This makes it easier to select a report item as you are moving things around or changing properties in the report layout.

We have used the TextAlign property to adjust the way text is placed horizontally inside a text box (left, center, or right). In this report, we also used the VerticalAlign property to adjust the way text is placed vertically inside a text box (top, middle, or bottom). The vertical alignment of text in a text box is not usually an issue unless the border of the text box is visible and you can see where the text is being placed relative to the top and bottom of the text box.

Conference Place Cards

Features Highlighted

▶ Using background images on report objects

▶ Using embedded images

▶ Using the WritingMode property of a text box

Business Need   Galactic Delivery Services is continuing its preparations for the annual customer conference. In addition to the nametags, the GDS art department must also create place cards for the conference attendees. The place cards will be put on the table in front of each attendee during roundtable discussions. As with the nametags, place cards should be created for all the billing contacts.

The conference place cards should include the name of the attendee and also the name of the company they work for. The art department would like the place cards to continue the color scheme set by the nametags, but with a more intricate pattern. They should include the GDS logo.

Task Overview

1. Create a New Report, Create a Dataset, Place the Report Items on the Report

Conference Place Cards, Task 1: Create a New Report, Create a Dataset, Place the Report Items on the Report

1. Reopen the Chapter06 project if it has been closed. Close the Nametags report.

2. Add a blank report called PlaceCards to the Chapter06 project. (Do not use the Report Wizard.)

3. Select <New Dateset...> from the Dataset drop-down list. The Dataset dialog box will appear.

4. Enter **BillingContacts** for the name in the Dataset dialog box.

5. "Galactic (shared)" will be selected for the data source by default. Click OK. You will return to the Data tab, which now displays the Generic Query Designer.

6. Type the following in the SQL pane:

```
SELECT BillingContact, Name
FROM Customer
ORDER BY BillingContact
```

7. Run the query to make sure there are no errors. Correct any typos that may be detected.

8. Switch to the Layout tab.

9. Select Report | Embedded Images from the main menu. The Embedded Images dialog box will appear.

10. Click New Image. The Import Image dialog box will appear.

11. Navigate to the GDSBackRect.gif image file and select it. Click Open.

12. Click New Image. The Import Image dialog box will appear.

13. Navigate to the GDSBackOval.gif image file and select it. Click Open.

14. Click New Image. The Import Image dialog box will appear.

15. Navigate to the GDSBig.gif image file and select it. Click Open.

16. Click OK to exit the Embedded Images dialog box.

17. Click in the report layout area. This will cause the report body to be selected in the Properties window. Modify the following properties of the report body:

Property	Value
BackgroundColor	DarkOrange
BackgroundImage: Source	Embedded
BackgroundImage: Value	gdsbackrect (The drop-down list will show all the images embedded in the report.)
Size: Width	8.875in
Size: Height	3.2in

18. Drag a list from the Toolbox and drop it onto the report layout. Modify the following properties of the list:

Property	Value
Location: Left	0in
Location: Right	0in

Property	Value
Size: Width	8.75in
Size: Height	3.2in

19. Drag the BillingContact field from the Fields window and drop it onto the list. Modify the following properties of the text box that results:

Property	Value
BackgroundImage: Source	Embedded
BackgroundImage: Value	Gdsbackoval
Font: FontSize	30pt
Font: FontWeight	Bold
Location: Left	2.5in
Location: Top	1.75in
Size: Width	6.125in
Size: Height	0.625in
TextAlign	Center
VerticalAlign	Middle

20. Drag the Name field from the Fields window and drop it onto the list. Modify the following properties of the text box that results:

Property	Value
BackgroundImage: Source	Embedded
BackgroundImage: Value	Gdsbackoval
Color	DarkBlue
Font: FontSize	30pt
Font: FontWeight	Bold
Location: Left	2.5in
Location: Top	2.5in
Size: Width	6.125in
Size: Height	0.625in
TextAlign	Center
VerticalAlign	Middle

21. Drag an image report item from the Toolbox and drop it onto the list. The Image Wizard will appear.

22. Click Next.

23. Make sure that Embedded is selected. Click Next.

24. Select the gdsbig image. Click Next.

25. Click Finish to exit the Image Wizard.

26. Modify the following properties of the image:

Property	Value
BorderStyle	Double
BorderWidth	3pt
Location: Left	0.3in
Location: Top	1.715in
Size: Width	1.625in
Size: Height	1.375in
Sizing	Fit

27. Drag a text box from the Toolbox and drop it onto the list. Modify the following properties of this text box:

Property	Value
Font: FontSize	9pt
Font: FontWeight	Bold
Location: Left	0.05in
Location: Top	1.715in
Size: Width	0.25in
Size: Height	1.375in
TextAlign	Center
Value	GDS Conference 2004
WritingMode	tb-rl

This textbox will look very strange on the Layout tab. Have faith; it will look fine in the Preview tab.

28. Drag a text box from the Toolbox and drop it onto the list. Modify the following properties of this text box:

Property	Value
Font: FontSize	9pt
Font: FontWeight	Bold
Location: Left	1.925in
Location: Top	1.715in
Size: Width	0.25in
Size: Height	1.375in
TextAlign	Center
Value	GDS Conference 2004
VerticalAlign	Bottom
WritingMode	tb-rl

This text box will also look very strange on the Layout tab.

29. Click the Preview tab. The place cards are ready to be printed, cut apart, folded, and placed on the tables, as shown here.

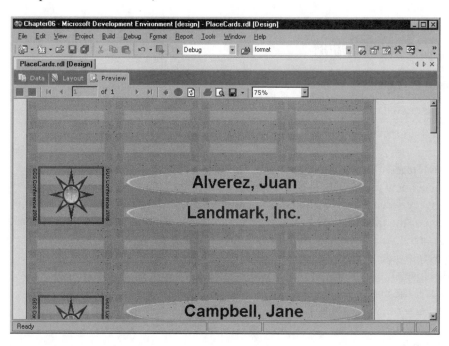

30. Click Save All in the toolbar.

Task Notes In this report, we used embedded images instead of using external images as we did in the previous report. Remember, the method of storing the image has nothing to do with the way the image is used in the report. External images can be used as background images. Embedded images can be used in image report items.

The Embedded Images dialog box allows you to manage the images embedded in the report. It is important to remember that an embedded image remains in the report even if there is no report item referencing it. The only way to remove an embedded image from a report is to use the Delete button in the Embedded Images dialog box. Always remove embedded images from the report if they are not being used. This way, the report definition does not become any larger than it needs to be.

Also in this report, we used the WritingMode property to rotate the contents of two text boxes by 90 degrees. The normal writing mode for English text in a text box is left-to-right, top-to-bottom (lr-tb). We changed this default writing mode and told these two text boxes to output our text top-to-bottom, right-to-left (tb-rl). The WritingMode property was implemented to allow Reporting Services to work with languages that are written from top to bottom and right to left. However, that does not prevent us from using the WritingMode property to produce a fancy effect with our English text.

The Rate Sheet Report

Features Highlighted

▶ Using database images

▶ Using rectangle report items within table cells

Business Need The Galactic Delivery Services marketing department needs to produce a new rate sheet. The rate sheet needs to include a description of each type of delivery service provided by GDS. Each type has its own image to help customers remember the three types of service. The rate sheet also includes the name of each service type with a longer description below it and the cost of each service type off to the right side of the page.

Because all the information on the three types of service is available in the database, the marketing department would like to produce the rate sheet from a report rather than creating or updating a document each time the rates change.

Task Overview

1. Create a New Report, Create a Dataset, Place the Report Items on the Report

2. Refine the Report Layout

Rate Sheet Report, Task 1: Create a New Report, Create a Dataset, Place the Report Items on the Report

1. Reopen the Chapter06 project if it has been closed. Close the PlaceCards report.

2. Add a blank report called RateSheet to the Chapter06 project. (Do not use the Report Wizard.)

3. Select <New Dateset…> from the Dataset drop-down list. The Dataset dialog box will appear.

4. Enter **ServiceTypes** for the name in the Dataset dialog box.

5. "Galactic (shared)" will be selected for the Data source by default. Click OK. You will return to the Data tab, which now displays the Generic Query Designer.

6. Type the following in the SQL pane:

```
SELECT Description, LongDescription, Cost, PriceSheetImage
FROM ServiceType
ORDER BY Cost
```

7. Run the query to make sure there are no errors. Correct any typos that may be detected.

8. Switch to the Layout tab.

9. Drag an image report item from the Toolbox and drop it onto the report layout. The Image Wizard will appear.

10. Click Next.

11. Select Project and then click Next.

12. Select the GDS image and then click Next.

13. Click Finish to exit the Image Wizard.

14. Modify the following properties of the image:

Property	Value
Location: Left	0in
Location: Top	0in

15. Drag a text box from the Toolbox and drop it onto the report layout. Modify the following properties of this text box:

Property	Value
Color	DarkBlue
Font: FontSize	30pt

Property	Value
Font: FontWeight	Bold
Location: Left	0.875in
Location: Top	0in
Size: Width	6in
Size: Height	0.625in
Value	Galactic Delivery Services
VerticalAlign	Middle

16. Drag a text box from the Toolbox and drop it onto the report layout. Modify the following properties of this text box:

Property	Value
Color	DarkOrange
Font: FontSize	25pt
Font: FontWeight	Bold
Location: Left	0.875in
Location: Top	0.625in
Size: Width	6in
Size: Height	0.5in
Value	Types of Service
VerticalAlign	Middle

17. Drag a text box from the Toolbox and drop it onto the report layout. Modify the following properties of this text box:

Property	Value
Color	Gold
Font: FontSize	20pt
Font: FontWeight	Bold
Format	MMMM d,yyyy
Location: Left	0.875in
Location: Top	1.125in
Size: Width	6in

Property	Value
Size: Height	0.5in
TextAlign	Left
VerticalAlign	Middle

18. Right-click the last text box added to the report and select Expression from the context menu. The Edit Expression dialog box will appear.

19. Expand "Globals" in the Fields area.

20. Click ExecutionTime. Click Append.

21. Click OK to exit the Edit Expression dialog box.

22. Drag a table from the Toolbox and place it on the report layout.

23. Right-click in the gray rectangle to the left of the header row. Select Table Header to unselect it on the context menu. This will remove the header row.

24. Right-click in the gray rectangle to the left of the footer row. Select Table Footer to unselect it on the context menu. This will remove the footer row.

25. Click the gray square in the upper-left corner of the table. This will select the table. Modify the following properties of the table:

Property	Value
DataSetName	ServiceTypes
Location: Left	0.875in
Location: Top	1.75in
Size: Width	6.25in
Size: Height	2.125in

26. Drag an image report item from the Toolbox and drop it onto the leftmost table cell. The Image Wizard will appear.

27. Click Next.

28. Select Database. Click Next.

29. Select PriceSheetImage from the Image field drop-down list.

30. Select "image/gif" from the MIME Type drop-down list.

31. Click Next.

32. Click Finish to exit the Image Wizard.

33. Click the center table cell. Click the gray rectangle above the center table cell. Modify the following property of the table column:

Property	Value
Width	2.45in

34. Drag the Description field from the Fields window and drop it onto the center table cell. Modify the following properties of the text box that results:

Property	Values
Color	DarkBlue
Font: FontSize	14pt
Font: FontWeight	Bold

35. Drag the Cost field from the Fields window and drop it onto the rightmost table cell. Modify the following properties of the text box that results:

Property	Values
Font: FontSize	14pt
Format	$###,###.00
VerticalAlign	Middle

36. Click the Preview tab. Your report will appear similar to the illustration.

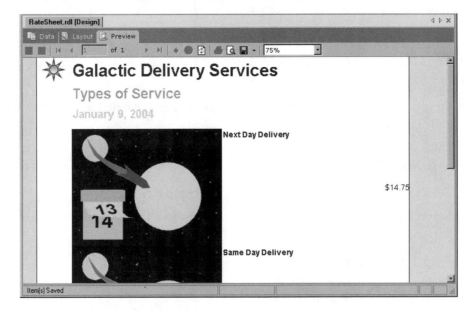

Task Notes   In the Rate Sheet Report, we used image data that is stored in a database table. As we discussed earlier in the chapter, this allows the report to have a different image for each row in the table report object. The Next Day Delivery row, the Same Day Delivery row, and the Previous Day Delivery row each have its own unique image on the report.

Although the image data appears correctly on the report, the formatting leaves something to be desired. The images are all run together. The bottom of one image touches the top of the next. Also, the business needs specified that the long description of the service type should come below the name of that service type.

Let's reformat our report a bit to see if we can improve the look of the images and include the long description in the report.

Rate Sheet Report, Task 2: Refine the Report Layout

1. Click on the Layout tab.

2. Click the leftmost table cell containing the image. This will select the image report item.

3. Press DELETE (the Delete key) to remove the image report item. The image report item has been removed from the table cell and, by default, a text box is created and put there in its place.

4. Drag a rectangle from the Toolbox and drop it on the leftmost table cell. There is now a rectangle report item in the leftmost table cell.

5. Drag an image from the Toolbox and drop it on the rectangle you just created. The Image Wizard will appear.

6. Click Next.

7. Select Database and then click Next.

8. Select PriceSheetImage from the Image Field drop-down list.

9. Select "image/gif" from the MIME Type drop-down list.

10. Click Next.

11. Click Finish to exit the Image Wizard.

12. Modify the following properties of the image:

Property	Value
BorderColor	DarkBlue
BorderStyle	Double
BorderWidth	4pt

Property	Value
Location: Left	0.125in
Location: Top	0.125in
Size: Width	1.75in
Size: Height	1.375in
Sizing	Fit

13. Click the center table cell. This will select the text box in the cell.

14. Press DELETE to remove the text box.

15. Drag a rectangle from the Toolbox and drop it on the center table cell. There is now a rectangle report item in the center table cell.

16. Drag the Description field from the Fields window and drop it on the rectangle you just created.

17. Modify the following properties of the text box that results:

Property	Value
Color	DarkBlue
Font: FontSize	14pt
Font: FontWeight	Bold
Location: Left	0.125in
Location: Top	0.125in
Size: Width	2.3in
Size: Height	0.375in

18. Drag the LongDescription field from the Fields window and drop it onto the same rectangle that contains the text box for the Description field. Modify the following properties of the text box that results:

Property	Value
Location: Left	0.125in
Location: Top	0.625in
Size: Width	2.3in
Size: Height	0.875in

19. Click the Preview tab. Your report will appear similar to the illustration.

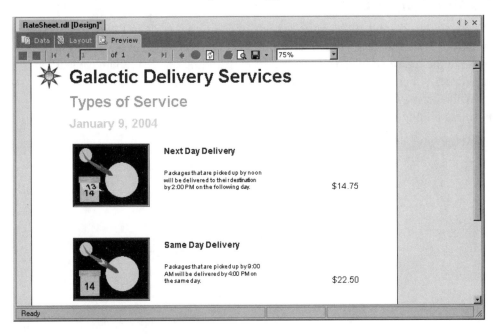

20. Click Save All in the toolbar

Task Notes   Looking at our second attempt, we can see that the rectangle saved the day. It solved both of our formatting problems. Having a rectangle in the leftmost cell allowed us to size the image so that it did not fill the entire cell. We were able to adjust the size of the image because the Sizing property of the image was set to Fit. This, in turn, created some white space between the images, making them look much nicer. We even took advantage of that white space by adding a border to the image object.

The rectangle solved our second problem as well. The business needs specified that the long description of the service type should appear below the name of the service type. We were able to accomplish this by putting a rectangle in the center table cell and then putting two text boxes inside the rectangle.

The Rate Sheet Report is ready to go.

Building Higher

We have now covered all the basic aspects of creating reports in Reporting Services. In the next two chapters, we will continue to look at report creation, but we will move to the intermediate and advanced level. Building on what you have learned so far, we will create more complex reports with more interactivity.

With each new feature you encounter, you gain new tools for turning data into business intelligence.

Kicking It Up a Notch: Intermediate Reporting

IN THIS CHAPTER:
Never Having to Say "I'm Sorry"
Handling Errors in Reports
Under the Hood
Practicing Safe Source
Advance, Never Retreat

Basic training is at an end. Boot camp is over. You now know the basics of building reports in Reporting Services. You should be able to create reports both with the Report Wizard and from scratch. When needed, you can spice up your reports with color, images, and charts.

In the last chapter, you learned how to add punch to your reports with color and graphics. In this chapter, you will learn how to add value to your reports through summarizing and totaling, and added interactivity. All this enhances the users' experience and allows them to more readily turn information into business intelligence.

We will begin the chapter, however, by looking for a way to enhance your experience as a report developer. In the first section, we will create a report template that can be used to standardize the look of your reports. The report template can also take care of some of the basic formatting tasks so that they do not need to be repeated for each report.

Never Having to Say "I'm Sorry"

Users can be very particular about the way their reports are laid out. In many cases, you will be creating new reports to replace existing ones. It may be that the user was getting a report from a legacy system, from an Access report or a spreadsheet, or from a ledger book. Whatever the case, the user is used to seeing the data presented in a certain way with everything arranged just so.

Now you come along with Microsoft SQL Server 2000 Reporting Services, telling the user that the new reporting system is infinitely better than the old way—more efficient, more timely, with more delivery options. That is all well and good with the user, but invariably the question will arise, "Can you make the report look the same as what I have now?" No matter how antiquated or inefficient the current reporting system might be, it is familiar, perhaps even comforting to your users. Change is difficult. The irony of the human race is that on a large scale we like change, but on an individual level, we mainly want things to stay the same.

Even if Reporting Services is well established and you are not converting reports from an existing system, users will still have preconceived notions. They will have a vision for the way a new report should be laid out. These visions need to be respected. After all, the report developer is not the one who has to look at the report every day, week, or month—the user is! The user is the one who probably knows how to best turn the data into something useful.

What the users don't want to hear is, "I'm sorry, but we can't do it that way in Reporting Services." You will be miles ahead if you spend your time fulfilling your users' vision rather than convincing them that Reporting Services is a great tool, despite the fact that it cannot do what they want it to do. The techniques in this section, and also in parts of Chapter 8, will help you to make Reporting Services reports do exactly what your users want them to do. After all, if your users ain't happy, ain't nobody happy!

Successful report development means never having to say, "I'm sorry."

The Report Template

Features Highlighted

▶ Creating a reusable template for reports

▶ Using values from the Globals collection

Business Need   Galactic Delivery Services is looking to increase the efficiency of its report developers. GDS would like a template that can be used for each new report created. The report template will include the GDS logo and the company name in a header across the top of each page. The template will also include a footer across the bottom of each page showing the date and time the report was printed, who printed the report, the current page number, and the total number of pages in the report.

Task Overview

1. Create the Template Project and the Template Report with a Page Header

2. Create the Page Footer on the Template Report

3. Copy the Template to the Report Project Directory

Report Template, Task 1: Create the Template Project and the Template Report with a Page Header

1. Create a new Reporting Services project called Template in the MSSQLRS folder. (If you need help with this task, see the section "The Transport List Report" in Chapter 5.)

2. Add a blank report called GDSReport to the Template project. (Do not use the Report Wizard.)

3. Select the Layout tab.

4. From the main menu, select Report | Page Header. A space for the page header layout will appear above the layout area for the body of the report. (If Report is not showing on the main menu, click anywhere on the report layout. The Format and Report menu choices will appear.) Drag the gray bar separating the page header and the body down so that the page header area is larger.

5. From the Toolbox, place an image item in the layout area for the page header. The Image Wizard will appear.

6. Click Next.

7. The Embedded choice should be selected. Click Next.

8. Click New Image. Browse to the GDS.gif image file and select it. Click Open.

9. Click Next.

10. Click Finish to exit the Image Wizard. The image will be placed in the page header.

11. Modify the following properties of the image:

Property	Value
Location: Left	0in
Location: Top	0in
Name	tmpl_Logo

12. Place a text box in the layout area for the page header. Modify the following properties of the text box:

Property	Value
Color	DarkBlue
Font: FontSize	30pt
Font: FontWeight	Bold
Location: Left	0.75in
Location: Top	0in
Name	tmpl_Name
Size: Width	5.25in
Size: Height	0.625in
Value	Galactic Delivery Services
VerticalAlign	Middle

TIP

You can use the toolbar buttons on the Formatting toolbar to set the contents of a text box to be bold, italicized or underlined. You can also use this toolbar to change color, background color, and text alignment. If you do not see the Formatting toolbar in Visual Studio, select View | Toolbars | Formatting from the main menu.

13. Click in the page header layout area outside of the text box and image. Page Header is selected in the drop-down list at the top of the Properties window.

14. Modify the following property for the page header:

Property	Value
Size: Height	0.75in

Task Notes   Reporting Services reports have a page header layout area that can be used to create a page heading for the report. The page header has properties so that it can be turned off on the first page or the last page of the report. Aside from these options, if the page header is turned on in the Report menu, it will appear on each report page.

The page header can be populated with images, text boxes, lines, and rectangles. You cannot, however, place any data regions, tables, matrixes, lists, or charts in a page header. In fact, you cannot directly reference fields from a dataset in the page header.

Each report item placed in the report layout is given a name. Up to this point, we have been letting Visual Studio provide a default name for each item (textbox1, image2, and so on). In most cases, these default names will work just fine. The only time you need to provide a more meaningful name is when you need to reference one report item from another, such as when one item toggles the visibility of another, or when you are creating a template.

The reason we need to provide nondefault names for our report template is to avoid any naming collisions when we create reports using our template. When you add the first text box to a report created with our template, it will automatically be called textbox1. This will cause a problem if we already have a text box called textbox1 that came from our template.

In order to avoid these naming collisions, we need to provide names for the report items in our template that are not likely to be duplicated in a report. For this reason, we put the prefix "tmpl_" in front of the name of each item. These names should be unique enough to prevent naming collisions when we put our template to use.

Report Template, Task 2: Create the Page Footer on the Template Report

1. Click in the report layout area.

2. From the main menu, select Report | Page Footer. A space for the page footer layout will appear below the layout area for the body of the report.

3. Page Footer will be selected. Modify the following property for the page footer:

Property	Value
Size: Height	0.375in

4. Place a text box in the layout area for the page footer. Modify the following properties of the text box:

Property	Value
Font: FontSize	8pt
Location: Left	0in
Location: Top	0.125in
Name	tmpl_ReportName
Size: Width	2.25in
Size: Height	0.25in

5. Right-click the text box and select Expression from the context menu, or select <Expression...> from the drop-down list for the Value property in the Property window. Select Expression from the context menu. The Edit Expression dialog box will appear.

6. Expand "Globals" under Fields.

7. Highlight "ReportName" under Fields. Click Insert. The expression to return ReportName from the Globals collection is placed in the Expression area.

8. Click OK to exit the Edit Expression dialog box.

9. Place a second text box in the layout area for the page footer. Modify the following properties of the text box:

Property	Value
Font: FontSize	8pt
Location: Left	2.75in
Location: Top	0.125in

Property	Value
Name	tmpl_PageNumber
Size: Width	1in
Size: Height	0.25in

10. Right-click this text box and select Expression from the context menu. The Edit Expression dialog box will appear.

11. Type the following in the Expression area after the equals sign:

```
"Page " &
```

There should be a space both before and after the ampersand character (&).

12. Expand "Globals" under Fields.

13. Highlight "PageNumber" under Fields. Click Append. The expression to return PageNumber from the Globals collection is added to the Expression area.

14. After the PageNumber expression, type the following:

```
& " of " &
```

There should be a space both before and after each ampersand.

15. Highlight "TotalPages" under Fields. Click Append. The expression to return TotalPages from the Globals collection is added to the Expression area.

16. Click OK to exit the Edit Expression dialog box.

17. Place a third text box in the layout area for the page footer. Modify the following properties of the text box:

Property	Value
Font: FontSize	8pt
Location: Left	4.25in
Location: Top	0.125in
Name	tmpl_DateTime
Size: Width	2.25in
Size: Height	0.25in
TextAlign	Right

18. Right-click this text box and select Expression from the context menu. The Edit Expression dialog box will appear.

19. Expand "Globals" under Fields.

20. Highlight "ExecutionTime" under Fields. Click Insert. The expression to return ExecutionTime from the Globals collection is added to the Expression area.

21. Click OK to exit the Edit Expression dialog box. Your report layout should appear similar to Figure 7-1.

22. Select the Preview tab. Your report should appear similar to Figure 7-2.

23. For a better look at what the header and footer will look like on a printed report, click the Print Preview button, as shown in Figure 7-3.

24. Let's put the page header closer to the top of the page and the page footer closer to the bottom of the page. Select the Layout tab.

25. In the main menu, select Report | Report Properties. The Report Properties dialog box will appear.

26. Select the Layout tab in the Report Properties dialog box.

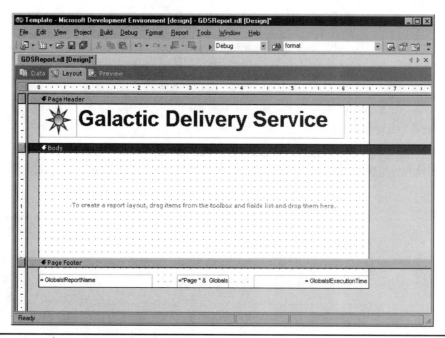

Figure 7-1 *The report template layout*

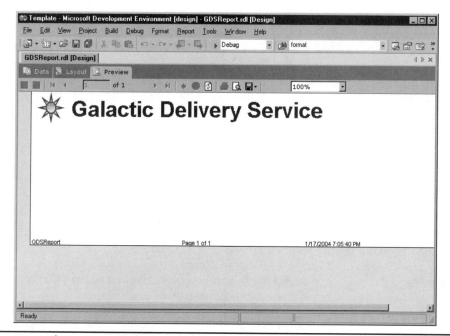

Figure 7-2 *The report template on the Preview tab*

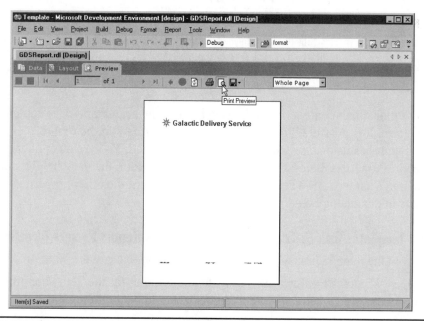

Figure 7-3 *The report template in Print Preview mode*

27. Modify the following values:

Property	Value
Top margin	0.5in
Bottom margin	0.5in

28. Click OK.
29. Select the Preview tab.
30. Click the Print Preview button.
31. Click Save All in the toolbar.

Task Notes   Reporting Services provides a number of global values you can use in your reports, including the following:

ExecutionTime	The date and time the report was executed. (This is not the time it takes for the report to run but rather the time at which the report was run.)
Language	The language the report is output in.
Page Number	The current page number within the report.
ReportFolder	The folder that the report resides in.
ReportName	The name of the report.
ReportServerURL	The URL of the Internet server hosting the report.
TotalPages	The total number of pages in the report.
UserID	The network user name of the person executing the report.

These global values are commonly used in the page header and page footer areas of the report. It is possible, however, to use them anywhere in the report.

The report has its own properties that can be modified. You are most likely to use the Report Properties dialog box to modify the page width, the page height, and the margins. In Chapter 8, however, we will explore some of the other properties available in this dialog box.

Report Template, Task 3: Copy the Template to the Report Project Directory

1. From the main menu, select File | Close Solution to close the solution.
2. Open Windows Explorer and navigate to the folder for the Template project. From the My Documents folder, the path should be the following:

```
Visual Studio Project\MSSQLRS\Template
```

3. In the Template folder, highlight the file GDSReport.rdl. This is the template report we just created.

4. Press CTRL-C to copy this file.

5. Navigate to the directory where Reporting Services stores its templates. In a default installation of SQL Server 2000 and Reporting Services, this path will be this:

```
C:\Program Files\Microsoft SQL Server\80\Tools\Report Designer\
        ProjectItems\ReportProject
```

6. Select the ReportProject folder.

7. Press CTRL-V to paste the copied file in this directory.

8. Close Windows Explorer.

Task Notes   When we add a new item to a report project, Visual Studio looks in the ProjectItems\ReportProjects folder. Any report files (.rdl) it finds in this folder are included in the Templates area of the Add New Item dialog box. This is shown in Figure 7-4.

In the remainder of this chapter, we will use our new template to create reports.

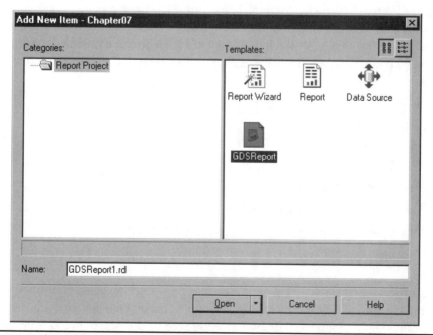

Figure 7-4   *The Add New Item dialog box with custom templates*

Handling Errors in Reports

As you create more complex reports and use more intricate expressions in those reports, you increase the chance of introducing errors. Visual Studio lets you know you have an error when you try to preview a report. You will receive a message in the Preview tab saying, "There are compilation errors. See Task List for details."

Fortunately, Visual Studio also provides tools for dealing with errors. A list of detailed error messages is displayed in both the Build section of the Output Window and in the Task List Window. In most cases, these error messages provide a pretty good description of the problem. In many cases, the problem is a syntax error in an expression you constructed in a property of a report item.

If you double-click an error entry in the Task List Window, you return to the Layout tab (if you are not already there) and the report item that contains the offending expression is selected. You can then use the error message to determine which property contains the error and fix the problem. In some cases, if you open the Properties dialog box for the report item, the property containing the error has an exclamation mark surrounded by a red circle placed next to it.

Once you have made changes to remedy each error listed in the Task List Window, you can click the Preview tab to run the report. If all of the errors have been corrected, the Build section of the Output Window shows "0 errors" and all of the entries are cleared out of the Task List Window. If you still have errors, continue the debugging process by double-clicking on a Task List Window entry and try again to correct the error.

The Employee Time Report

Features Highlighted

- ▶ Using a report template
- ▶ Putting totals in headers and footers
- ▶ Using the scope parameter in an aggregate function
- ▶ Toggling visibility

Business Need The Galactic Delivery Services personnel department needs a report showing the amount of time entered by its employees on their weekly timesheets. The report should group the time by job, employee, and week, with totals presented for each grouping. The groups should be collapsed initially, and the user should be able to drill down into the desired group. Group totals should be visible even when the group is collapsed.

Task Overview

1. Create the Chapter07 Project, a Shared Data Source, a New Report, and a Dataset
2. Populate the Report Layout
3. Add Drilldown Capability
4. Add Totaling

Employee Time Report, Task 1: Create the Chapter07 Project, a Shared Data Source, a New Report, and a Dataset

1. Create a new Reporting Services project called Chapter07 in the MSSQLRS folder. (If you need help with this task, see the section "The Transport List Report" in Chapter 5.)

2. Create a shared data source called Galactic for the Galactic database. (Again, if you need help with this task, see the section "The Transport List Report" in Chapter 5.)

3. Right-click Reports in the Solution Explorer. Select Add | Add New Item from the context menu. The Add New Item dialog box will appear.

4. Single-click GDSReport in the Templates area to select it. Change the Name to EmployeeTime and click Open.

5. Select <New Dateset...> from the Dataset drop-down list. The Dataset dialog box will appear.

6. Enter **EmployeeTime** for the name in the Dataset dialog box.

7. Galactic will be selected for the data source by default. Click OK. You will return to the Data tab, which now displays the Generic Query Designer.

8. Type the following in the SQL pane:

```
SELECT Description AS Job,
    Employee.EmployeeNumber,
    FirstName,
    LastName,
    CONVERT(char(4),DATEPART(yy, WorkDate))+'-'+
        CONVERT(char(2),DATEPART(wk, WorkDate)) AS Week,
    WorkDate,
    HoursWorked
FROM TimeEntry
INNER JOIN Assignment
    ON TimeEntry.AssignmentID = Assignment.AssignmentID
```

```
INNER JOIN Employee
     ON Assignment.EmployeeNumber = Employee.EmployeeNumber
INNER JOIN Job
     ON Assignment.JobID = Job.JobID
ORDER BY Job, Employee.EmployeeNumber, Week, WorkDate
```

9. Run the query to make sure there are no errors.

10. Select the Layout tab.

Task Notes If you need to, refer back to the database diagram for the personnel department in Chapter 3 to see how the TimeEntry, Assignment, Employee, and Job tables are related. Our query joins these four tables together to determine what work hours were entered for each employee and what job they held.

We are using a combination of the CONVERT() and DATEPART() functions to create a string containing the year and the week number for each time entry. This allows us to group the time into work weeks. Note that the year comes first in this string so that it will sort correctly across years.

When you selected the Layout tab, there was already content in the page header and page footer of the report. This, of course, is due to the fact that we used our new GDSReport template to create the report. By using our report template, we will have a consistent header and footer on our reports without having to work at it.

Employee Time Report, Task 2: Populate the Report Layout

1. Place a text box onto the body of the report. Modify the following properties of this text box:

Property	Value
Font: FontSize	25pt
Font: FontWeight	Bold
Location: Left	0in
Location: Top	0in
Size: Width	2.875in
Size: Height	0.5in
Value	Employee Time

2. Place a table onto the body of the report immediately below the text box you just added.

3. Drag the WorkDate field into the detail row in the center column of the table.

4. Drag the HoursWorked field into the detail row in the right-hand column of the table.

5. Select the entire header row in the table. Modify the following property:

Property	Value
TextDecoration	Underline

6. Right-click in the gray square to the upper-left of the table. Select Properties from the context menu. The Table Properties dialog box will appear. Select the Groups tab.

7. Click Add. The Grouping and Sorting Properties dialog box will appear.

8. Type **JobGroup** for the name. (No spaces are allowed in group names.)

9. In the Expression area, select "=Fields!Job.Value" from the drop-down list.

10. Click OK to exit the Grouping and Sorting Properties dialog box.

11. Click Add again. The Grouping and Sorting Properties dialog box will appear.

12. Type **EmpNumGroup** for the name.

13. In the Expression area, select "=Fields!EmployeeNumber.Value" from the drop-down list.

14. Click OK to exit the Grouping and Sorting Properties dialog box.

15. Click Add a third time. The Grouping and Sorting Properties dialog box will appear.

16. Type **WeekGroup** for the name.

17. In the Expression area, select "=Fields!Week.Value" from the drop-down list.

18. Click OK to exit the Grouping and Sorting Properties dialog box.

19. Click OK to exit the Table Properties dialog box.

20. Click in any cell in the table. Notice how three group header rows and three group footer rows have been added to the table. The gray boxes to the left of the table identify the group rows as 1, 2, and 3. Drag the Job field into the leftmost cell in the group 1 header row.

21. Right-click the gray rectangle above the leftmost column in the table. Select Insert Column to the Right from the context menu.

22. Drag the EmployeeNumber field into the cell in the column you just created and in the Group 2 header row.

23. Drag the width of the leftmost column in the table until the column is just wide enough for the word "Job" in the table header cell.

24. Select the two leftmost cells in the row for the Group 1 header, right-click them, and select Merge Cells from the context menu. (Click and drag or hold down SHIFT while clicking to select multiple cells at the same time.)

25. Right-click the gray rectangle above the second-from-the-left column in the table. Select Insert Column to the Right from the context menu.

26. Drag the Week field into the cell in the column you just created in the Group 3 header row.

27. Drag the width of the second column from the left until it is just wide enough for the words "Employee Number" in the table header cell.

28. Drag the width of the third column from the left until it is just wide enough for the "=Fields!Week.Value" expression in the Group 3 header cell.

29. Select the three group header rows at the same time. Modify the following property in the Property window:

Property	Value
Font: FontWeight	Bold

30. Select the three cells in the center of the Group 2 header row, right-click them, and select Merge Cells from the context menu.

31. Modify the following properties for the merged cell that results from step 30:

Property	Value
TextAlign	Left
Value (Select <Expression...> from the drop-down list to make editing easier. You can select the field expressions from the Fields area and use Append to add them to the Expression area. Remember, the Globals, Parameters, and Fields expressions are case sensitive!)	=Fields!EmployeeNumber.Value & "-" & Fields!FirstName.Value & " " & Fields!LastName.Value

Your report layout should appear similar to Figure 7-5.

32. Select the Preview tab. Your report should appear similar to Figure 7-6.

Task Notes We have placed a table on our report to contain the employee time information. We have created three groups within the table to contain the groups required by the business needs for this report. The detail information is grouped into

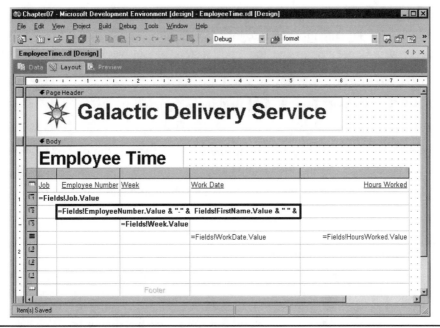

Figure 7-5   *Employee Time Report layout after Task 2*

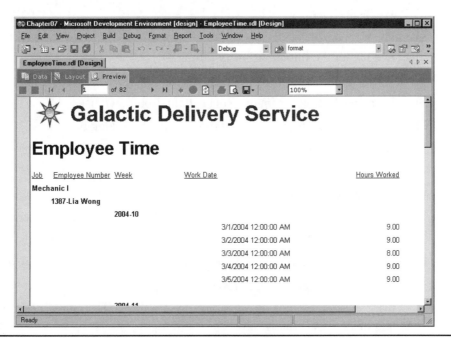

Figure 7-6   *Employee Time Report preview after Task 2*

weeks (WeekGroup). The week groups are grouped into employees (EmpNumGroup). The employee groups are grouped into jobs (JobGroup). By merging cells in the grouping rows, we are able to give the report a stepped look yet keep the width of our steps small so there is enough room for the detail information.

Employee Time Report, Task 3: Add Drilldown Capability

1. Select the Layout tab.
2. Select the entire table and bring up the Table Properties dialog box as we did in step 6 of Task 2. Select the Groups tab.
3. Select EmpNumGroup and click Edit. The Grouping and Sorting Properties dialog box will appear.
4. Select the Visibility tab.
5. Select Hidden for the Initial Visibility setting.
6. Check the box labeled Visibility Can Be Toggled By Another Report Item.
7. Select Job from the Report Item drop-down list.
8. Click OK to exit the Grouping and Sorting Properties dialog box.
9. Select WeekGroup and click Edit. The Grouping and Sorting Properties dialog box will appear.
10. Select the Visibility tab.
11. Select Hidden for the Initial Visibility setting.
12. Check the box labeled Visibility Can Be Toggled By Another Report Item.
13. Select EmployeeNumber from the Report Item drop-down list.
14. Click OK to exit the Grouping and Sorting Properties dialog box.
15. Click Details Grouping. The Details Grouping dialog box will appear.
16. Select the Visibility tab.
17. Select Hidden for the Initial Visibility setting.
18. Check the box labeled Visibility Can Be Toggled By Another Report Item.
19. Select Week from the Report Item drop-down list. (It is at the bottom of the list.)
20. Click OK to exit the Details Grouping dialog box.
21. Click OK to exit the Table Properties dialog box.
22. Select the Preview tab. Your report should appear similar to Figure 7-7 after expanding the top few groups.

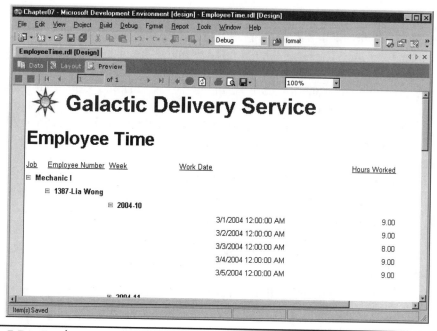

Figure 7-7   *Employee Time Report preview after Task 3*

Task Notes   We now have the drilldown capability working as required for this report. This was done by using the visibility and toggling properties of the groupings in the table. The visibility of each group is set to be toggled by a report item that is in the group above it. Therefore, EmpNumGroup is set to be toggled by the Job report item in JobGroup, and WeekGroup is set to be toggled by the EmployeeNumber report item in EmpNumGroup.

For the purposes of visibility, the detail row of the table is treated as a group. It is called the details grouping. The details grouping is set to be toggled by the Week report item, which is part of WeekGroup.

EmpNumGroup, WeekGroup, and the details grouping all have their initial visibility set to Hidden. This means that when you run the report in the Preview tab, you do not see any of these groups. Only the top group, JobGroup, is visible.

Remember that in data regions, the items are repeated according to the rows in the dataset. Therefore, the report contains a number of JobGroup rows, one for each distinct job contained in the dataset. Each JobGroup contains sets of EmpNumGroup rows, WeekGroup rows, and the details grouping rows.

The first JobGroup contains a Job report item (text box) with a value of "Mechanic I". There is a small plus sign in front of "Mechanic I" because it controls the visibility of the EmpNumGroup rows in the "Mechanic I" JobGroup. Clicking the plus sign changes the visibility of all the EmpNumGroup rows in the "Mechanic I" JobGroup from hidden to visible. The EmpNumGroup rows in the "Mechanic I" JobGroup now show up on the report.

When the EmpNumGroup rows are visible in the "Mechanic I" JobGroup, the plus sign next to "Mechanic I" changes to a minus sign. Clicking the minus sign will again change the visibility of all the EmpNumGroup rows in the "Mechanic I" JobGroup, this time from visible to hidden. The EmpNumGroup rows in the "Mechanic I" JobGroup now disappear from the report.

Click the plus and minus signs to change the visibility of various groups and detail rows in the report. Make sure you have a good understanding of how visibility and toggling are working in the report. We will make it a bit more complicated in Task 4.

Employee Time Report, Task 4: Add Totaling

1. Select the Layout tab.
2. Right-click the rightmost cell in the Group 1 header row and select Properties from the context menu. The Textbox Properties dialog box will appear.
3. Type the following for Value:

    ```
    =Sum(Fields!HoursWorked.Value)
    ```

NOTE

To save some typing, you can select "=Fields!HoursWorked.Value" from the Value drop-down list and then add in the additional text.

4. Click Advanced. The Advanced Textbox Properties dialog box will replace the Textbox Properties dialog box.
5. Select the Visibility tab.
6. Check the box labeled Visibility Can Be Toggled By Another Report Item.
7. Select Job from the Report Item drop-down list. (We are leaving Initial Visibility set to Visible.)
8. Click OK to exit the Advanced Textbox Properties dialog box.
9. Right-click the rightmost cell in the Group 2 header row and select Properties from the context menu. The Textbox Properties dialog box will appear.
10. Type the following for Value:

    ```
    =Sum(Fields!HoursWorked.Value)
    ```

11. Click Advanced. The Advanced Textbox Properties dialog box will replace the Textbox Properties dialog box.

12. Select the Visibility tab.

13. Check the box labeled Visibility Can Be Toggled By Another Report Item.

14. Select EmployeeNumber from the Report Item drop-down list. (We are leaving Initial Visibility set to Visible.)

15. Click OK to exit the Advanced Textbox Properties dialog box.

16. Right-click the rightmost cell in the Group 3 header row and select Properties from the context menu. The Textbox Properties dialog box will appear.

17. Type the following for Value:

```
=Sum(Fields!HoursWorked.Value)
```

18. Click Advanced. The Advanced Textbox Properties dialog box will replace the Textbox Properties dialog box.

19. Select the Visibility tab.

20. Check the box labeled Visibility Can Be Toggled By Another Report Item.

21. Select Week from the Report Item drop-down list. (We are leaving Initial Visibility set to Visible.)

22. Click OK to exit the Advanced Textbox Properties dialog box.

23. Click the gray square for the Group 1 footer row. Modify the following properties for this footer row using the Properties window (the drop-down list at the top of the Properties window will call this TableRow8):

Property	Value
Visibility: Hidden	True
Visibility: ToggleItem	Job

24. Click the gray square for the Group 2 footer row. Modify the following properties for this footer row using the Properties window:

Property	Value
Visibility: Hidden	True
Visibility: ToggleItem	EmployeeNumber

25. Click the gray square for the Group 3 footer row. Modify the following properties for this footer row using the Properties window:

Property	Value
Visibility: Hidden	True
Visibility: ToggleItem	Week

26. Select the rightmost cell in the Group 3 footer row. Modify the following properties for this text box using the Properties window:

Property	Value
BorderStyle: Top	Solid
Font: FontWeight	Bold
Value (Select <Expression...> from the drop-down list to make it easier to enter this value.)	=Sum(Fields!HoursWorked.Value)

NOTE

You can accomplish steps 27 and 28 by copying the text box whose properties you modified in step 26 and pasting it into the cells specified in steps 27 and 28. Make sure that you have the text box selected without the flashing text edit cursor inside of it, before you try to copy it.

27. Repeat step 26 for the rightmost cell in the Group 2 footer row.

28. Repeat step 26 for the rightmost cell in the Group 1 footer row.

29. Select the rightmost cell in the table footer row. Modify the following properties for this text box using the Properties window:

Property	Value
BorderStyle: Top	Double
BorderWidth: Top	3pt
Font: FontWeight	Bold
Value (Select <Expression...> from the drop-down list to make it easier to enter this value.)	=Sum(Fields!HoursWorked.Value)

Your report layout should appear similar to Figure 7-8.

30. Select the Preview tab. Your report should appear similar to Figure 7-9 when the top few groups are expanded.

31. Click Save All in the toolbar.

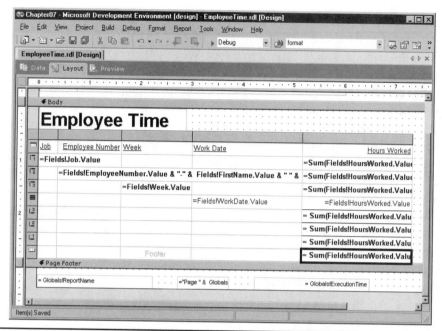

Figure 7-8 *The Employee Time Report layout after Task 4*

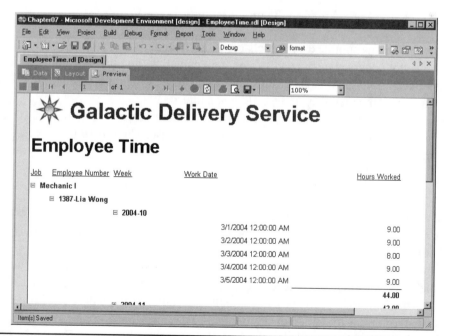

Figure 7-9 *The Employee Time Report preview after Task 4*

Task Notes   Now we not only have a report with group totals, we have a report that keeps its group totals where they ought to be. When the group is collapsed, the group total is on the same line with the group header. When the group is expanded, the group total moves from the group header to the group footer.

When you think about it, this is how you would expect things to work. When the group is collapsed, we expect it to collapse down to one line. Therefore, the group total should be on the line with the group header. When the group is expanded, there is a column of numbers in the group. We would naturally expect the total for that column of numbers to be below it. Therefore, the group total should move to the group footer.

We achieved this functionality by using our toggle items to control the visibility of three other items at the same time. In the previous section, we discussed the fact that "Mechanic I" controls the visibility of the EmpNumGroup rows in the "Mechanic I" JobGroup. Now, "Mechanic I" also controls the visibility of the Hours Worked total in the group header and the Hours Worked total in the group footer. The Hours Worked total in the group header is initially set to Visible. The Hours Worked total in the group footer is initially set to Hidden.

When the plus sign next to "Mechanic I" is clicked, three things occur:

▶   The EmpNumGroup rows are set to Visible.

▶   The Hours Worked total in the group header is set to Hidden.

▶   The Hours Worked total in the group footer is set to Visible.

When the minus sign next to "Mechanic I" is clicked, the reverse takes place. This same behavior occurs at each level. Again, you can click the plus and minus signs to change the visibility of various groups and detail rows in the report. Make sure you understand how the visibility and toggle items interrelate.

The other feature of note used in this task is the Sum() aggregate function. If you were paying attention, you will have noticed that we used the following expression in a number of different locations:

```
= Sum(Fields!HoursWorked.Value)
```

If you were paying close attention, you would have also noticed that this expression yields a number of different results. How does this happen? It happens through the magic of *scope*.

Scope is the data grouping in which the aggregate function has been placed. For example, the Sum() function placed in the JobGroup header row (the Group 1 header row) uses the current JobGroup as its scope. It sums hours worked only for those records in the current JobGroup data grouping. The Sum() function placed in the EmpNumGroup header row (the Group 2 header row) uses the current EmpNumGroup as its scope. It sums the hours worked only for those records in the current EmpNumGroup data grouping. The Sum() function placed in the table footer row is not within any data grouping, so it sums the hours worked in the entire dataset.

As you have seen in this report, it does not make a difference whether the aggregate function is placed in the group header or the group footer. Either way, the aggregate function acts on all the values in the current data grouping. At first, this may seem a bit counterintuitive. It is easy to think of the report being processed sequentially from the top of the page to the bottom. In this scenario, the total for a group would only be available in the group footer after the contents of that group had been processed. Fortunately, this is not the way Reporting Services works. The calculation of aggregates is separate from the rendering of the report. Therefore, aggregates can be placed anywhere in the report.

Finally, it is very important not to confuse the aggregate functions within Reporting Services with the aggregate functions that exist within the environs of SQL Server. Many of the Reporting Services aggregate functions have the same names as SQL Server aggregate functions. Despite this fact, Reporting Services aggregate functions and SQL Server aggregate functions work in different locations.

SQL Server aggregate functions work within a SQL Server query. They are executed by SQL Server as the dataset is being created by the database server. SQL Server aggregate functions do not have a concept of scope. They simply act on all the data that satisfies the WHERE clause of the query. As we just discussed, Reporting Services aggregate functions are executed, after the dataset is created, as the report is executing and are very dependent on scope.

The Employee List Report

Features Highlighted

▶ Implementing user-selectable grouping

▶ Implementing user-selectable sorting

▶ Using explicit page breaks

Business Need   The Galactic Delivery Services personnel department would like a flexible report for listing employee information. Rather than having a number of reports for each of their separate grouping and sorting needs, they would like a single report where they can choose the grouping and sort order each time the report is run. The report should be able to group on job, hub, or city of residence. The report should be able to sort by employee number, last name, or hire date. Also, each new group should start on a new page.

Task Overview

1. Create a New Report and a Dataset
2. Create the Report Layout

Employee List Report, Task 1: Create a New Report and a Dataset

1. Reopen the Chapter07 project if it has been closed. Close the Employee Time Report if it is still open.

2. Right-click Reports in the Solution Explorer and select Add | Add New Item from the context menu. The Add New Item dialog box will appear.

3. Single-click GDSReport in the Templates area to select it. Change the name to EmployeeList and click Open.

4. Choose <New Dataset...> from the Dataset drop-down list. The Dataset dialog box will appear.

5. Enter **Employees** for the name in the Dataset dialog box.

6. Galactic will be selected for the data source by default. Click OK. You will return to the Generic Query Designer in the Data tab.

7. Type the following in the SQL pane:

```
SELECT Job.Description AS Job,
      Hub.Description AS Hub,
      Employee.EmployeeNumber,
      FirstName,
      LastName,
      Address1,
      City,
      State,
      ZipCode,
      HireDate,
      HighestLevelOfEducation,
      UnionMembership
FROM Employee
INNER JOIN Assignment
    ON Employee.EmployeeNumber = Assignment.EmployeeNumber
INNER JOIN Job
    ON Assignment.JobID = Job.JobID
INNER JOIN Hub
    ON Assignment.HubCode = Hub.HubCode
```

8. Run the query to make sure it is correct.

Task Notes   You will notice that there is no ORDER BY clause in our SELECT statement. In most cases, this would cause a problem. Users like to have their information show up in something other than a random sort order. In this case it is fine, because we will be sorting the data within the report itself according to what the user selects as report parameters.

Employee List Report, Task 2: Create the Report Layout

1. Select the Layout tab.
2. Place a text box onto the body of the report. Modify the following properties of this text box:

Property	Value
Font: FontSize	25pt
Font: FontWeight	Bold
Location: Left	0in
Location: Top	0in
Size: Width	2.875in
Size: Height	0.5in
Value	Employee List

3. Place a table onto the body of the report immediately below the text box you just added.
4. Drag the EmployeeNumber field into the leftmost cell in the detail row of the table.
5. Drag the FirstName field into the middle cell in the detail row of the table.
6. Drag the LastName field into the rightmost cell in the detail row of the table.
7. Right-click the gray rectangle above the rightmost column in the table and select Insert Column to the Right from the context menu.
8. Drag the Address1 field into the detail row of the newly created column.
9. Repeat steps 7 and 8 for the City, State, ZipCode, HireDate, HighestLevelOfEducation, and UnionMembership fields.
10. Select the cell in the detail row containing the HireDate expression. Modify the following property:

Property	Value
Format	MM/dd/yyyy

NOTE

The value for the Format property is case sensitive.

11. Size each column appropriately. Use the Preview tab to check your work. Continue switching between the Layout tab and the Preview tab until you have the table columns sized appropriately.

12. Drag the right edge of the report body layout area until it is just touching the right side of the table.

13. Click the gray square for the table header row. Modify the following property:

Property	Value
TextDecoration	Underline

14. Click in the report layout area. From the main menu, select Report | Report Parameters. The Report Parameters dialog box will appear.

15. Click Add.

16. Type **GroupOrder** for Name and **Group By** for Prompt.

17. Uncheck the Allow Blank Value option.

18. Fill in the Available Values table as follows:

Label	Value
Job	Job
Hub	Hub
City	City

19. Select Non-queried for Default Values.

20. Type **Job** in the text box for Default Values.

21. Click Add to add a second report parameter.

22. Type **SortOrder** for Name and **Sort By** for Prompt.

23. Uncheck the Allow Blank Value option.

24. Fill in the Available Values table as follows:

Label	Value
Emp Num	Emp Num
Last Name	Last Name
Hire Date	Hire Date

25. Select Non-queried for Default Values.

26. Type **Emp Num** in the text box for Default Values.

27. Click OK to exit the Report Parameters dialog box.

28. Select the entire table and bring up the Table Properties dialog box.

29. Check the box labeled Repeat Header Rows on Each Page.

30. Select the Groups tab.

31. Click Add. The Grouping and Sorting Properties dialog box will appear.

32. Select <Expression...> from the Expression drop-down list. The Edit Expression dialog box will appear.

33. Type the following in the Expression area:

```
= IIF( Parameters!GroupOrder.Value = "Job", Fields!Job.Value,
        IIF(Parameters!GroupOrder.Value = "Hub", Fields!Hub.Value,
            Fields!City.Value))
```

NOTE

Use the Parameters and Fields entries on the left side of the Edit Expression dialog box to help build expressions such as the one above. Click on the desired parameter or field to highlight it, then click the Append button to add it to the end of the expression you are building.

34. Highlight the entire expression you just entered and press CTRL-C to copy this text.

35. Click OK to exit the Edit Expression dialog box.

36. Check the box labeled Page Break at End.

37. Uncheck the box labeled Include Group Footer.

38. Select the Sorting tab.

39. Select <Expression...> from the Expression drop-down list. The Edit Expression dialog box will appear.

40. Delete the equals sign from the Expression area and press CTRL-V to paste the expression into the Expression area. This should be the same expression you entered in step 33.

41. Click OK to exit the Edit Expression dialog box.

42. Leave the sort direction as Ascending. Click OK to exit the Grouping and Sorting Properties dialog box.

43. Select the Sorting tab.

44. Select <Expression…> from the Expression drop-down list. The Edit Expression dialog box will appear.

45. Type the following in the Expression area:

```
= IIF( Parameters!SortOrder.Value = "Emp Num", Fields!EmployeeNumber.Value,
       IIF(Parameters!SortOrder.Value = "Last Name", Fields!LastName.Value,
           Fields!HireDate.Value))
```

46. Click OK to exit the Edit Expression dialog box.

47. Leave the sort direction as Ascending. Click OK to exit the Table Properties dialog box.

48. Select the three leftmost cells in the Group 1 header row. Right-click these cells and select Merge Cells from the context menu.

49. Right-click these cells again and select Expression from the context menu.

50. Delete the equals sign from the Expression area and press CTRL-V to paste the expression into the Expression area. This should be the same expression you entered in step 33.

51. Click OK to exit the Edit Expression dialog box.

52. Modify the following property of the merged cells:

Property	Value
Font: Weight	Bold

Your report layout should appear similar to Figure 7-10.

53. Select the Preview tab. Select a grouping and a sort order, then click View Report. Your report should appear similar to Figure 7-11. Experiment with changing the grouping and sort order. Remember to click View Report each time you want the report to refresh.

54. Click Save All in the toolbar.

Task Notes   In this report, the report parameters are used to control properties within the report rather than as parameters to a SQL query. Because of this, we needed to create

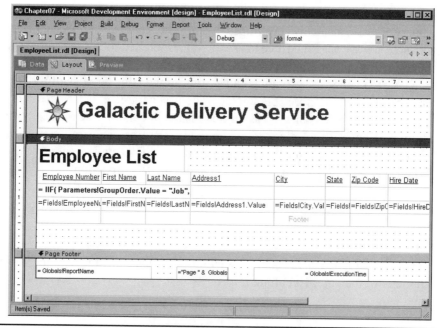

Figure 7-10   *The Employee List Report layout*

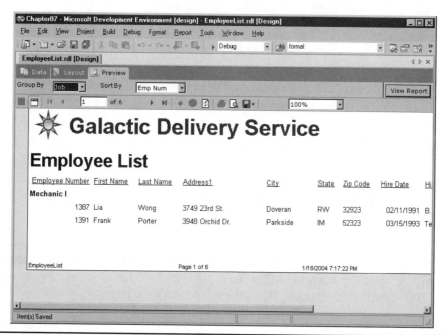

Figure 7-11   *The Employee List Report preview*

these report parameters manually rather than having them created automatically from the dataset query. We also manually constructed lists of valid values and provided a default value for each one. We were then able to use the values selected for those parameters to change the grouping and sorting of the table in the report.

We are able to change the grouping and sorting of the table because of the IIF() function. This function has three parameters. The first parameter is a Boolean expression (in other words, an expression that results in either a true or false value). The second parameter is the value that is returned if the Boolean expression is true. The third parameter is the value that is returned if the Boolean expression is false.

Let's take a look at one of our expressions using the IIF() function:

```
= IIF( Parameters!GroupOrder.Value = "Job", Fields!Job.Value,
        IIF(Parameters!GroupOrder.Value = "Hub", Fields!Hub.Value,
            Fields!City.Value))
```

This expression actually uses two IIF() functions, one nested inside the other. The first parameter of the outer IIF() function is

```
Parameters!GroupOrder.Value = "Job"
```

If "Job" is selected for the grouping, the value of the second parameter is returned by the function. In this case, the second parameter is

```
Fields!Job.Value
```

Therefore, if "Job" is selected for the grouping, the value of the Job field is used.

If "Job" is not selected for the grouping, the value of the third parameter is returned. The value of this third parameter is another complete IIF() function:

```
IIF(Parameters!GroupOrder.Value = "Hub", Fields!Hub.Value,
            Fields!City.Value)
```

In this second IIF() function, if "Hub" is selected for the grouping, the second parameter of this IIF() function is returned. Here, the second parameter is

```
Fields!Hub.Value
```

Therefore, if "Hub" is selected for the grouping, the value of the Hub field is used.

Finally, if "Hub" is not selected for the grouping, the value of the third parameter of this IIF() function is returned. Here, the third parameter is

```
Fields!City.Value
```

Therefore, if "Hub" is not selected for the grouping, the value of the City field is used.

We used sorting in different places to make sure that the report comes out the way we expect. We first specified a sort expression in the table grouping. This will sort the groups themselves so they come out in the proper order. We also used the Sorting tab in the Table Properties dialog box. This sorts the contents within each group, so they come out in the order specified by the user. If "Job" is selected for the grouping and "Emp Num" is selected for the sort order, the groups are first sorted by the Job field. Then, within each group, the rows are sorted by the Employee Number field.

In many cases, a report needs to start each new group on a new page. We used the Page Break at End option in the grouping properties to force the report to start a new page after each grouping. Page break options can be set before or after new groupings. Page breaks can also be set before or after a report item. For instance, you can force a page break before the beginning of a table or after the end of a table.

The Overtime Report

Features Highlighted

▶ Implementing cascading parameters

▶ Using SQL stored procedures

▶ Using table filters

▶ Using the NoRows property

Business Need The Galactic Delivery Services personnel department needs to monitor the amount of overtime put in at each of its repair and distribution hubs to determine when additional personnel must be hired. The personnel department needs a report that will list the employees with over 45 hours worked in a given week at a given hub. The report should have two sections. The first section should list employees with more than 45 hours and less than 55 hours worked for the selected week. The second section should list employees with more than 55 hours worked for the selected week.

The user should be able to select a work week from a drop-down list and then see a second drop-down list showing the hubs that have one or more employees with more than 45 hours for the selected week. The user will select a hub from this second list and then see the report for that hub.

Two stored procedures in the Galactic database should be used for retrieving data. The stp_HubsOver45 stored procedure will return a list of hubs with one or more employees who have over 45 hours worked for the selected week. The stp_EmployeesOver45 stored procedure will return a list of employees who have over 45 hours worked for the selected week at the selected hub. We will discuss stored procedures in the task notes.

Task Overview

1. Create a New Report and Three Datasets
2. Create the Report Layout

Overtime Report, Task 1: Create a New Report and Three Datasets

1. Reopen the Chapter07 project if it has been closed. Close the Employee List Report if it is open.

2. Right-click Reports in the Solution Explorer and select Add | Add New Item from the context menu. The Add New Item dialog box will appear.

3. Single-click GDSReport in the Templates area to select it. Change the name to **Overtime** and click Open.

4. Choose <New Dataset...> from the Dataset drop-down list. The Dataset dialog box will appear.

5. Enter **Weeks** for the name in the Dataset dialog box.

6. Galactic will be selected for the data source by default. Click OK. You will return to the Generic Query Designer in the Data tab.

7. Type the following in the SQL pane:

```
SELECT DISTINCT CONVERT(char(4), DATEPART(yy,WorkDate))+'-'+
                CONVERT(char(2), DATEPART(wk,WorkDate)) as Week
FROM TimeEntry
ORDER BY Week
```

8. Run the query to make sure it is correct.

9. Choose <New Dataset...> from the Dataset drop-down list. The Dataset dialog box will appear.

10. Enter **HubsOver45** for the name in the Dataset dialog box.

11. Galactic will be selected for the data source by default.

12. Select StoredProcedure from the Command Type drop-down list.

13. Click OK. You will return to the Generic Query Builder in the Data tab.

14. Select **stp_HubsOver45** from the Stored procedure drop-down list in the Data tab toolbar.

15. Run the stored procedure to make sure it is functioning properly. When you run the stored procedure, Visual Studio will determine what parameters are required. Type **2004-15** for the @Week parameter in the Define Query Parameters dialog box and click OK.

16. Choose <New Dataset...> from the Dataset drop-down list. The Dataset dialog box will appear.

17. Enter **EmployeesOver45** for the name in the Dataset dialog box.

18. Galactic will be selected for the data source by default.

19. Select StoredProcedure from the Command Type drop-down list.

20. Type **stp_EmployeesOver45** for the query string.

NOTE

You can select the stored procedure from the Stored procedure drop-down list in the Data tab toolbar or you can type in the name of the stored procedure yourself; whichever is most convenient at the time.

21. Click OK. You will return to the stored procedure version of the Generic Query Designer in the Data tab.

22. Run the stored procedure to make sure it is functioning properly. Type **2004-15** for the @Week parameter and **BLNR** for the @HubCode parameter in the Define Query Parameters dialog box and then click OK.

Task Notes   For two of our three datasets, we used stored procedures rather than queries. A stored procedure is a query or a set of queries that is given a name and stored in the database itself. You can think of a stored procedure as a data-manipulation program that is created and kept right inside the database.

Stored procedures have several advantages over queries:

▶ **Speed**   A certain amount of preprocessing must be done on any query before it can be run in the database. Stored procedures are preprocessed when they are created, and this preprocessing information is saved with them. This means that when you execute a stored procedure, you do not need to wait for the preprocessing. The result is faster execution time.

▶ **Simplicity**   A developer or database administrator can create a stored procedure that uses a number of intricate queries. When you execute the stored procedure, you do not need to understand, or even see, this complexity. All you need to do is execute the stored procedure to get the result set you need.

▶ **Security**   When you query a set of tables, you must be given rights to see any and all data in each of the tables. However, when a stored procedure is used, you only need rights to execute the stored procedure. You do not need rights to any of the tables being queried by the stored procedure. The stored procedure can then control which rows and which columns can be seen by each user.

▶ **Reusability**   A single stored procedure can be used by a number of reports. Therefore, complex queries do not have to be created over and over again when a number of reports need to use the same data.

▶ **Maintainability**   When changes are made to the database structure, the developer or database administrator can make the corresponding changes in the stored procedure, so the stored procedure continues to return the same result set. Without stored procedures, a change in the database structure could result in a number of reports needing to be edited.

For these reasons, it is often advantageous to use stored procedures rather than queries for your datasets.

NOTE

Querying against database views has a number of the same benefits as stored procedures and is also a very good choice as the source for your datasets. Because querying views is much the same as querying tables (they present fields to the Query Builder just as tables do), we will not spend time discussing views.

When you are using a stored procedure for your dataset, all you need to do is set Command Type to StoredProcedure and enter the name of the stored procedure. Visual Studio will figure out the parameters required by the stored procedure and add them to the report. Can't get much simpler than that.

Overtime Report, Task 2: Create the Report Layout

1. Select the Layout tab.

2. From the main menu, select Report | Report Parameters. The Report Parameters dialog box will appear.

3. With "Week" selected in the Parameters list, change Available Values to From Query. The Dataset drop-down list should be set to Weeks.

4. Select HubCode from the Parameters list.

5. Change Prompt to Hub.

6. Change Available Values to From Query.

7. Select HubsOver45 from the Dataset drop-down list. Select HubCode from the Value field drop-down list. The Label field drop-down list should be set to Hub.

8. Click OK to exit the Report Parameters dialog box.

9. Place a text box onto the body of the report. Modify the following properties of this text box:

Property	Value
Font: FontSize	25pt
Font: FontWeight	Bold
Location: Left	0in
Location: Top	0in
Size: Width	2in
Size: Height	0.5in
Value	Overtime

10. Place a second text box onto the body of the report. Modify the following properties of this text box:

Property	Value
Font: FontSize	16pt
Location: Left	0in
Location: Top	0.5in
Size: Width	5.25in
Size: Height	0.375in

11. Right-click this text box and select Expression from the context menu.

12. Type the following in the Expression area:

```
= "Week: " &  Parameters!Week.Value &
"       Hub: " &  Parameters!HubCode.Value
```

13. Click OK to exit the Edit Expression dialog box.

14. Place a third text box onto the body of the report. Modify the following properties of this text box:

Property	Value
Font: FontSize	16pt
Font: FontWeight	Bold
Location: Left	0in
Location: Top	1.125in
Size: Width	5.25in
Size: Height	0.375in
Value	Employees with 45 to 55 hours for this week

15. Place a table onto the body of the report immediately below the third text box.

16. Select EmployeesOver45 from the drop-down box at the top of the Fields window.

17. Drag the EmployeeNumber field into the leftmost cell in the detail row of the table.

18. Drag the FirstName field into the center cell in the detail row of the table.

19. Drag the LastName field into the rightmost cell in the detail row of the table.

20. Right-click the gray bar above the rightmost column and select Insert Column to the Right from the context menu.

21. Drag the HoursWorked field into the cell in the detail row in the column you just added.

22. Right-click the gray square to the left of the footer row. Select Table Footer from the context menu to toggle off the table footer.

23. Select the table header row. Modify the following property:

Property	Value
TextDecoration	Underline

24. Select the leftmost table column. Modify the following property:

Property	Value
TextAlign	Left

25. Select the entire table and bring up the Table Properties dialog box.

26. Select the Filters tab.

27. Type **=CStr(Fields!HoursWorked.Value)** for the expression.

28. From the Operat... drop-down list, select "<=".

29. Type **55.00** for the value.

30. Click OK to exit the Table Properties dialog box.

31. Modify the following property for the table using the Properties window:

Property	Value
NoRows	No Employees

32. Select both the table and the text box with the string "Employees with 45 to 55 hours for this week." Press CTRL-C to copy these two report items.

33. Drag the bar between the report body and the page footer so that the report body is larger.

34. Press CTRL-V to paste a copy of the two report items. Drag the two new items so that they are below the originals.

35. Select the new text box. Change the value of the text box to "Employees with over 55 hours for this week." (You can edit it right in the text box itself.)

36. Select the new table and bring up the Table Properties dialog box.

37. Select the Filters tab.

38. From the Operat... drop-down list, select ">".

39. Click OK to exit the Table Properties dialog box. Your report layout should appear similar to Figure 7-12.

40. Select the Preview tab.

41. Notice that the Week drop-down list is enabled, but the Hub drop-down list is disabled. Select 2004-15 from the Week drop-down list.

42. Once a week has been selected, the Hub drop-down list is enabled. Select Borlaron Repair Base from the Hub drop-down list. Click the View Report button. Your report should appear similar to Figure 7-13.

43. Select 2004-10 from the Week drop-down list. Borlaron Repair Base will still be selected in the Hub drop-down list. Click the View Report button. Note the text under the "Employees with over 55 hours for this week" heading.

44. Click Save All in the toolbar.

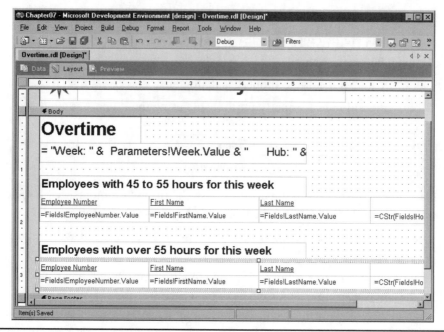

Figure 7-12   *The Overtime Report layout*

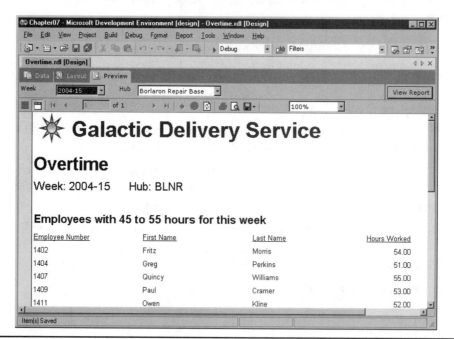

Figure 7-13   *The Overtime Report preview*

Task Notes   In this report, we used the same dataset to populate two tables. We got different information in the two tables by applying different filters on each table. The filter for the upper table on the report says that we only want records in this table where the hours worked is less than or equal to 55. The filter for the lower table on the report says that we only want records in this table where the hours worked is greater than 55. In this way, we were able to divide up the data in the dataset to fulfill the business requirements of the report.

You may have noted that we used the Visual Basic function CStr() to convert the hours worked to a string data type in our filter expressions. This is due to a quirk (some might call it a bug) in the operation of the filter expressions. Because of this quirk, filters deal much better with strings than they do with other data types. To get around this, we simply convert our numbers to strings, and everything works fine.

In addition to what you saw here, filters can be applied to data in other locations as well. A dataset can have a filter applied to it after it has been selected from the database. Individual groups within a table, matrix, or chart can also utilize filters.

Filters work well in situations like the one in this report where we want to use one dataset to provide a slightly different set of records to multiple data regions. They can also be useful for taking data from a stored procedure that provides almost, but not quite, the result set you need. It is usually best, however, to have your filtering done by your select query or stored procedure, rather than by the report. The reason is, in most cases, it is considerably faster and more efficient if the database does the filtering as it executes the query or stored procedure. It does not make sense to have your query select 1,000 records from the database if your report is going to filter out all but 10 of these records. Filters are a good tool to have; just remember to use them wisely.

In the Overtime Report, we used two drop-down lists to allow the user to select the parameters for our report. The Week drop-down list allows the user to select the week of the year for which the report should be run. This drop-down list is populated by the Week dataset. The Hub drop-down list allows the user to select the hub for which the report should be run. This drop-down list is populated by the HubsOver45 dataset. The HubsOver45 dataset requires a value from the Week drop-down list before it can return a list of the hubs with employees working over 45 hours for that week. In this way, the data that populates the Hub drop-down list is dependent on the value selected in the Week drop-down list.

Reporting Services is smart enough to recognize this dependency and act accordingly. If there is no value selected in the Week drop-down list, the Hub drop-down list cannot be populated, so it is disabled. Every time the selected value in the Week drop-down list changes, the Hub drop-down list is repopulated.

Finally, in this report we used the NoRows property of each of the tables. This property allows you to define a string that is output when there are no rows to populate the table. When the filter on the lower table in the report filters out all the rows in the dataset, the contents of the NoRows property are displayed. This is more helpful to the user than simply having a blank space where a table ought to be. The NoRows property is available on any of the data region report items.

Under the Hood

We talked early on in this book about the fact that the report definitions are stored using the Report Definition Language (RDL). RDL was created by Microsoft specifically for Reporting Services. Two things set this file structure apart from other Microsoft file structures, such as a Word document or an Excel spreadsheet. First, RDL is a published standard. Second, RDL is an Extensible Markup Language (XML) document.

Microsoft has gone public with the specifications for RDL. Third parties can create their own authoring environments for creating report definitions. If the RDL from these third-party tools conforms to the RDL standard, the reports created by these tools can be managed and distributed by Reporting Services.

The fact that RDL is an XML document means that you can actually look at a report definition in its raw form. If you try that with a Word document or an Excel spreadsheet, you will see nothing but gibberish. If you were so inclined, you could use Notepad to open an RDL file and look at its contents. In fact, you don't even need Notepad. You can look at the contents of an RDL file right in Visual Studio.

Viewing the RDL

Right-click the entry for Overtime.rdl in the Solution Explorer and then select View Code from the context menu. You will see a new tab in the layout area called "Overtime.rdl [XML]." This tab contains the actual RDL of the report, as shown in Figure 7-14.

XML Structure

Because the RDL is an XML document, it is made up of pairs of tags. There is a begin tag at the beginning of an item and an end tag at the end of the item. A begin tag is simply a string of text, the tag name, with "<" at the front and ">" at the back. An end tag is the same string of text with "</" at the front and ">" at the back. This pair of tags creates an XML element. The information in between the two tags is the value for that element. In the following example, the Height element has a value of 0.625in:

```
<Height>0.625in</Height>
```

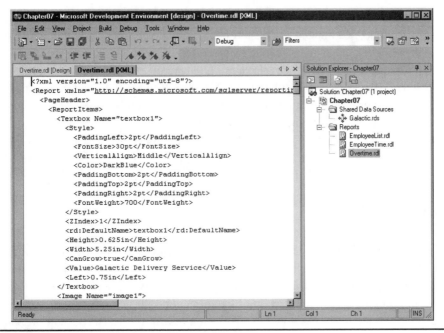

Figure 7-14   *The RDL for the Overtime Report*

There can never be a begin tag without an end tag, and vice versa. In fact, it can be said that XML is the Noah's Ark of data structures, because everything must go two by two.

In addition to simple strings of text, XML elements can contain other elements. In fact, a number of elements can nest one inside the other to form complex structures. Here's an example:

```
<Textbox>
  <Style>
    <Color>DarkBlue</Color>
  </Style>
</Textbox>
```

In some cases, begin tags contain additional information in the form of attributes. An attribute comes in the form of an attribute name, immediately following the tag name, followed by an equal sign (=) and the value of the attribute. In this example, the Textbox element has an attribute called Name with a value of "tmpl_Name":

```
<Textbox Name="tmpl_Name">...</Textbox>
```

The RDL contains several sections: the page header, the body, the data sources, the datasets, the embedded images, the page footer, and the report parameters. Each section starts with a begin tag and is terminated by an end tag. For example, the page header section of the RDL starts with <PageHeader> and is terminated by </PageHeader>.

In Figure 7-14, you can see the entire XML structure for the text box we placed in the page header. The begin tag of the text box includes a Name attribute. This corresponds to the Name property of the text box. In between the begin and end tags of the text box element are additional elements, such as FontSize, Color, and Width. These elements correspond to the other properties of this text box. Only those properties that have been changed from their default values are stored in the RDL.

Editing the RDL

One other interesting thing about viewing the RDL in Visual Studio is the fact that you can make changes to the RDL and have them affect the report design. Find the Color element within the tmpl_Name Textbox element, as shown in Figure 7-15. Replace DarkBlue with Red. Right-click the entry for Overtime.rdl in the Solution Explorer and then select View Designer from the context menu. You will notice that the text in the page header is now red. (It is pretty hard to miss!) You will probably want to change this back to dark blue, although if you like red, you can leave it as is.

If you do find a reason to make modifications directly to the RDL, do so with care. If you break up a begin/end pair or enter an invalid value for a property element (such as puce for a color), you can end up with a report that will not load in the report designer. Save your work immediately before making changes directly to the RDL. In just about every case, however, the designer works better for making changes to a report layout, so do your editing there.

Practicing Safe Source

Visual Studio works with another software tool called Visual SourceSafe (VSS). VSS controls access to source code, such as report definitions. This can prevent two report designers from trying to modify the same report at the same time. Even if you do not have multiple report designers, VSS can provide a consistent location where all your reporting projects can be found. VSS stores all the source code entrusted to its safekeeping in its own library database. If this VSS library database is located on a network, you have a central location where all the source code can be backed up regularly.

VSS has one more, very valuable feature. It keeps multiple versions of your source code. When you check in your source code, VSS does not write over the

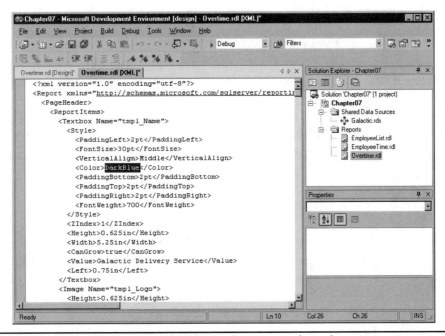

Figure 7-15   *The Color element within the tmpl_Name Textbox element*

previous version. Instead, it keeps both the older version and the new version. You will continue to work with the newest version of the source code unless there is a problem and you ask to go back to an earlier version. This can really be a lifesaver when you make those massive formatting changes to a report and then you or your users decide that it was really better the way it was.

Using Visual SourceSafe

Visual SourceSafe is very tightly integrated with Visual Studio. Once VSS is installed and configured on your PC, you can probably do almost all your interaction with VSS through the Visual Studio menus. We will look at adding a reporting project to VSS control, checking reports into and out of VSS, and reverting back to an older version of a report.

Adding a Reporting Project to Visual SourceSafe Control

Once VSS is set up on your PC, adding a reporting project to VSS control is very simple. Right-click the solution or the project in the Solution Explorer and select

Add Solution to Source Control. You will be prompted to log in to VSS and to specify the VSS database you wish to use. Provide this login information and click OK. You will see the Add to SourceSafe Project dialog box displaying the project folder hierarchy in your VSS database. Modify the project name at the top of the dialog box if desired, then browse to the appropriate location in the project folder hierarchy and click OK.

Check In, Check Out, and Get Latest Version

Once the solution has been added to VSS control, a small lock icon will appear next to each entry in the Solution Explorer. This indicates that each file is checked into VSS. The local copy of each of these files is marked as read-only. It cannot be modified until it has been checked out.

To check out a report definition file, right-click the entry for that report in the Solution Explorer and select Check Out from the context menu. If you wish, you can enter a comment stating why the report is being checked out. The most recent version of the report will then be copied from the VSS database to your PC. It will no longer be read-only but rather will be ready to accept changes. The lock icon will be replaced by a small check mark in the Solution Explorer to indicate that the report is checked out. Only one person may have a report checked out at any given time.

Once you have completed your changes to the report definition, you need to check the report back into VSS. Right-click the entry for the report in the Solution Explorer and select Check In from the context menu. Again, you can enter a comment summarizing the changes you made. This is helpful if you ever have to revert back to an older version of a report.

If you want to get the latest version of a report that someone else is working on, without actually checking out the report, you can use the Get Latest Version feature of VSS. Right-click the entry for the report in the Solution Explorer and then select Get Latest Version from the context menu. A read-only copy of the latest version of the report will be copied to your PC.

Getting a Previous Version

Retrieving an earlier version of a report from VSS is very straightforward. Select the report in the Solution Explorer and then select File | Source Control | History. The History Options dialog box will appear. You can enter a range of dates to see the history of the report within that date range. You can also enter a user to see the versions checked in by that user. To see the entire history of the report, leave everything blank and click OK.

The History Of dialog box will appear. Here, you can scroll through the previous versions of the report. Click Get to retrieve a copy of a previous version. This previous version will then become your current copy of the report. Any previous versions of the report checked in after the version you just retrieved will continue to reside in the VSS database. Click Rollback to retrieve a copy of a previous version and get rid of any versions of the report that were checked in after the version you just retrieved.

Advance, Never Retreat

In this chapter, we continued to unlock additional features of Reporting Services. We're always working toward the goal of giving you the tools you need to meet your reporting needs. You should now be well on your way to being able to say, "Yes, I can do that!"

In the next chapter, we will look at some of the advanced features of Reporting Services. After that, we will take a brief look at the different formats for rendering reports, and then we'll move on to report serving.

Beyond Wow:
Advanced Reporting

In this chapter, we will explore some of the really flashy features of Reporting Services. These are the features that get us techies excited. If you do not say "Wow!" after seeing at least one of these features in the reports created in this chapter, then I and the developers at Microsoft are not doing our jobs. Just to clarify, the "Wow!" does not need to be said out loud. Simply thinking "Wow!" in your head counts just as much.

Getting you to say, or think, "Wow!" is not ultimately the goal of the Microsoft developers who created Reporting Services, or the goal of this author as he writes this chapter. The developers who create games for Microsoft can be satisfied with eliciting a "Wow!" from their clientele and consider it a job well done. The developers who create business intelligence tools for Microsoft have to aim a bit higher.

If you develop business intelligence tools, you need to go beyond the "Wow!" to the "Ah ha!" The "Wow!" comes when you see a feature of a software product and think, "Wow! That is really cool!" The "Ah ha!" comes when you see a feature of a software product and say, "Ah ha! That is how we can make that report work just the way we need it to," or "Ah ha! That is how we can turn that bit of data into meaningful business intelligence." It is only when we hear the "Ah ha!" that we can be satisfied.

So, don't be shy when that moment comes along. When you get to that "Ah ha!" feature you have been searching for, say it nice and loud. I want to hear it, so I can go home happy.

Speaking in Code

One of the features of Reporting Services that gives it a tremendous amount of power and flexibility is its ability to speak in code—Visual Basic .NET code, that is. Valid Visual Basic .NET expressions can be used to control many of the properties of report items. It can even be used to control the query you are using to create your dataset.

For more complex tasks, you can embed whole Visual Basic .NET functions in your report. If that isn't enough, you can access methods from .NET assemblies. These assemblies are not limited to Visual Basic .NET. They can be written in any .NET language, such as C#.

Let's write some

−.−. −−− −... .

and have some

..−. ..− −.

NOTE

For those of you who may not be familiar with it, the previous sentence contains two words in Morse Code. If you want to know what it says, do what I did: Look it up on the Internet.

The Delivery Status Report

Features Highlighted

▶ Using Visual Basic .NET expressions to control properties

▶ Using multiline headers and footers

▶ Specifying scope in aggregate functions

Business Need   The customer service department at Galactic Delivery Services would like a report to check on the status of deliveries for a customer. The customer service representative should be able to select a customer and a year and see all the deliveries for that customer in that year. The hubs each package went through as it was in transit should be listed.

The status for packages that have been delivered should show up in green. The status for packages still en route should be blue. The status for packages that have been lost should be red. In case of a problem, the name and e-mail address of the person to be contacted at that customer site should appear below the entry for each lost package.

Task Overview

1. Create the Chapter08 Project, a Shared Data Source, a New Report, and Two Datasets

2. Set Up the Report Parameters and Place the Titles on the Report Layout

3. Add a Table to the Report

4. Add the Expressions

Delivery Status Report, Task 1: Create the Chapter08 Project, a Shared Data Source, a New Report, and Two Datasets

1. Create a new Reporting Services project called Chapter08 in the MSSQLRS folder.

2. Create a shared data source called Galactic for the Galactic database.

3. Create a new report called DeliveryStatus using the GDSReport template.

4. Create a new dataset called DeliveryStatus that calls the stp_DeliveryStatus stored procedure.

5. Run the stored procedure using **263722** for @CustomerNumber and **2003** for @Year.

6. Create a second dataset called Customers that uses the following query:

```
SELECT CustomerNumber, Name FROM Customer ORDER BY Name
```

Task Notes   You probably noticed that the instructions are a bit sketchy here. Now that you have reached the level of advanced report authoring, you can handle these basic tasks on your own. If you have any trouble with these steps, refer to the previous chapters for a refresher.

Delivery Status Report, Task 2: Set Up the Report Parameters and Place the Titles on the Report Layout

1. Select the Layout tab.

2. Use the main menu to open the Report Parameters dialog box.

3. Configure the report parameters as follows:

Property	Value
For the CustomerNumber parameter:	
Prompt	Customer
Available values	From query
Dataset	Customers
Value field	CustomerNumber
Label field	Name
For the Year parameter:	
Available values	(Enter the values from the following table)
Default values	Non-queried
Default values text area	2003

Set the Available Values property for the Year parameter as follows:

Label	Value
2001	2001
2002	2002
2003	2003

4. Click OK to exit the Report Parameters dialog box.
5. Place a text box onto the body of the report. Modify the following properties of this text box:

Property	Value
Font: FontSize	16pt
Font: FontWeight	Bold
Location: Left	0in
Location: Top	0in
Size: Width	3.5in
Size: Height	0.375in
Value	="Delivery Status for " & Parameters!Year.Value

6. Place a list onto the body of the report immediately below the text box. Modify the following properties of this list:

Property	Value
Location: Left	0in
Location: Top	0.375in
Size: Width	5.25in
Size: Height	0.5in

7. Right-click the list and select Properties from the context menu. The List Properties dialog box will appear.
8. Select the Filters tab.
9. Type **=Fields!CustomerNumber.Value** for Expression.
10. From the Operat... drop-down list, select "=".
11. Type **=Parameters!CustomerNumber.Value** for Value.
12. Click OK to exit the List Properties dialog box.
13. Select the Customers dataset in the Fields window and drag the Name field onto the list. Modify the following properties of the text box that results:

Property	Value
Font: FontSize	16pt
Font: FontWeight	Bold

Property	Value
Location: Left	0in
Location: Top	0in
Size: Width	5.125in
Size: Height	0.375in

Task Notes   We have two parameters for this report. The CustomerNumber parameter is selected from a drop-down list that is created by a dataset. The customer names are displayed in the drop-down list because Name was chosen as the Label field. However, the customer number is the value assigned to this parameter because CustomerNumber is chosen as the Value field. The Year parameter is selected from a drop-down list that is created by a static list of values that we entered. The Label and Value are the same for each entry in this list.

The items we have placed on the report thus far were put there to provide a heading for the report and to indicate which parameters were selected to create the report. This is pretty straightforward for the Year parameter. All we need is a text box that displays the value of this parameter, with a little explanatory text thrown in for good measure.

The CustomerNumber parameter presents a bit of a problem, though. The parameter contains the customer number of the selected customer. However, it will make more sense to the user if the customer's name is displayed at the top of the report. To accomplish this, we placed a list data region at the top of the report. When we drag the Name field from the Customers dataset onto the list, the list is immediately linked to the Customers dataset. (The DataSetName property of the list is set to Customers.)

If nothing else were done, the list would display the names of all the customers in the Customers dataset at the top of the report. Instead, we set the filter property of the list so it will only display the name of the customer whose customer number matches the customer number selected in the CustomerNumber parameter.

This represents a good application of a filter. In this case, we could not have replaced the filter with a WHERE clause in SQL, because we needed all the customers in the dataset to populate the drop-down list. By using the filter, we were able to reuse the Customers dataset to do two things: to populate the drop-down list for the CustomerNumber parameter and provide us with the name that goes with the selected customer number.

Delivery Status Report, Task 3: Add a Table to the Report

1.   Add a table to the body of the report immediately below the list.

NOTE

Be sure the table ends up below the list and not in the list.

2. Select the DeliveryStatus dataset in the Fields window and drag the Hub field onto the leftmost cell in the details row of the table.

3. Drag the TimeIn and TimeOut fields onto each of the two remaining cells in the details row of the table.

4. Right-click the gray square to the left of the details row and select Insert Group from the context menu. The Grouping and Sorting Properties dialog box will appear.

5. Select "=Fields!DeliveryNumber.Value" from the Expression drop-down list. We are now grouping the information in the table by the values in the DeliveryNumber field.

6. Select the Sorting tab.

7. Select "=Fields!DeliveryNumber.Value" from the Expression drop-down list.

8. Click OK to exit the Grouping and Sorting Properties dialog box.

9. We need to move the labels in the table header row to the group header row. Select the text box that contains the word "Hub." Do this by clicking once in this text box. If you can see a text-editing cursor blinking in this cell, you clicked too many times. If you see the blinking cursor, click elsewhere, then try again.

10. Press CTRL-X to cut the text box from this table header cell. Click in the group header cell immediately below it and press CTRL-V to paste the text box there.

11. Repeat this for the text boxes containing "Time In" and "Time Out."

12. Right-click any gray square to the left of the table and select Table Header from the context menu. This will turn off the table header option for this table. The table header row will disappear. Do the same for the table footer.

13. Right-click the gray square to the left of the group header row and select Insert Row Above from the context menu. An additional group header row will appear. This is not a new grouping but rather an additional row for the current grouping.

14. Drag the ServiceType field to the leftmost cell in the new group header row.

15. Drag the StatusName field to the next cell in the new group header row.

16. Right-click the gray square to the left of the new group header row and select Insert Row Above from the context menu. Another new group header row will appear.

17. Right-click the gray rectangle at the top of the first column in the table and select Insert Column to the Left from the context menu. A new column is added to the table.

18. Drag the DeliveryNumber field to the leftmost cell in the new group header row. Modify the following property of the text box in this cell:

Property	Value
TextAlign	Left

19. Double-click the next cell in the new group header row and type **Pickup:**.

20. Drag the PickupPlanet field to the next cell in the new group header row.

21. Drag the PickupDateTime field to the rightmost cell in the new group header row.

22. Double-click in the group footer cell below "=Fields!Hub.Value" and type **Delivery:**.

23. Drag the DeliveryPlanet field to the next cell in the group footer row.

24. Drag the DeliveryDateTime field to the rightmost cell in the group footer row.

25. Right-click the gray square to the left of the group footer row and select Insert Row Below from the context menu. A new group footer row will appear.

26. Double-click in the group footer cell below "Delivery" and type **Problem Contact:**.

27. Drag the ProblemContact field to the next cell in the new group footer row.

28. Drag the ProblemEMail field to the rightmost cell in the new group footer row.

29. Right-click the gray square to the left of the new group footer row and select Insert Row Below from the context menu. A new group footer row will appear. This row will be left blank.

30. Click in the leftmost cell of the top group header row and hold down the mouse button. Drag the mouse to the rightmost cell of the bottom group header row and release the mouse button. You have selected all the cells in the group header.

31. Modify the following property for these cells:

Property	Value
Font: FontWeight	Bold

32. Repeat steps 30 and 31 for all the cells in the group footer. Your report layout should appear similar to Figure 8-1.

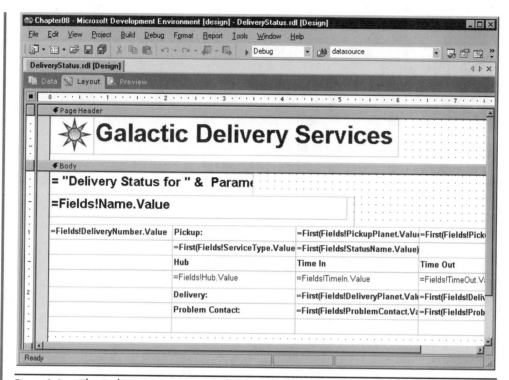

Figure 8-1   *The Delivery Status Report layout after Task 3*

33. Select the Preview tab. Select "Bolimite, Mfg" from the Customer drop-down list. Select "2003" from the Year drop-down list. Click View Report. Your report should appear similar to Figure 8-2.

Task Notes   If you are observant, you will notice that the expressions created for all but one of the fields placed in the group header and footer rows include the First() aggregate function. Only the expression for the DeliveryNumber field does not include this function. This aggregate function must be used because there are many records in each group. Somehow, we need to specify which of these records will be used to supply the values for these fields. By default, the first record in the group is used by including the First() aggregate function with each field expression. However, you could replace the First() aggregate function with any of the other Reporting Services aggregate functions if you desired.

Why is there no aggregate function included in the DeliveryNumber field expression? In step 5, we selected the DeliveryNumber field as the grouping field.

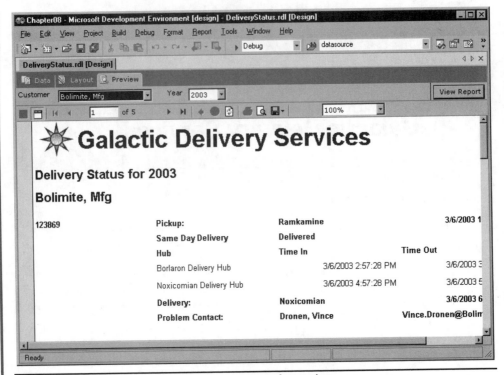

Figure 8-2   *The Delivery Status Report preview after Task 3*

Because the table is grouped on this field, the value of the DeliveryNumber field must be the same for each record in the group. In short, it does not really make a difference which record the DeliveryNumber field comes from because it will be the same value for each record in the group.

NOTE

As it turns out, each of the fields we placed in the group header and footer is directly related to the DeliveryNumber field. Therefore, all these fields have the same value for all the records in the group. Visual Studio cannot determine this at the time you are designing the report, so it puts the aggregate functions in these expressions.

We were able to add rows to both the group header and footer. This allowed us to create more complex group header and footer layouts. In the same fashion, you can add rows to the table header, table footer, or detail line, as needed.

We now have the proper layout for our report, but we do not have the proper behavior of some of the report items. The delivery status is supposed to appear in color. The problem contact information is only supposed to be displayed with lost deliveries. Some additional formatting lines would also make the report more readable. All of this will be accomplished in the next task with the aid of expressions.

Delivery Status Report, Task 4: Add the Expressions

1. Select the Layout tab.

2. Enter the following expression for the Color property of the cell containing the StatusName field:

```
= IIF(Fields!StatusName.Value = "Delivered", "Green",
      IIF(Fields!StatusName.Value = "In Route", "Blue", "Red"))
```

NOTE

When entering each of the expressions, you will probably want to select <Expression...> from the drop-down list and enter this expression in the Edit Expression dialog box. Also, remember that you can get the expressions for fields and parameters from the Fields area on the left side of the Edit Expression dialog box. Remember, expressions involving the Globals, Parameters, and Fields collections are case sensitive.

3. Click the gray square to the left of the top group header row, so the entire row is selected.

4. Enter the following expression for the BorderStyle: Top property:

```
= IIF(Fields!DeliveryNumber.Value =
    FIRST(Fields!DeliveryNumber.Value, "DeliveryStatus")
                              , "Solid", "None")
```

NOTE

"DeliveryStatus" is case sensitive in this expression.

5. Click and hold down the left mouse button in the cell containing the word "Hub." Continue to hold down the left mouse button and drag the cursor through the "Time In" cell to the "Time Out" cell. All three cells should now be selected. Modify the following property for these cells:

Property	Value
BorderStyle: Bottom	Solid

6. Select the following three cells using the same method as in step 5: "Delivery:", "=First(Fields!DeliveryPlanet.Value)", "=First(Fields!DeliveryDateTime.Value)". Modify the following property for these cells:

Property	Value
BorderStyle: Top	Solid

7. Click the gray square to the left of the top group footer row, so the entire row is selected. Enter the following expression for the BorderStyle: Bottom property for this row:

```
= IIF(Fields!StatusName.Value = "Lost", "None", "Solid")
```

8. Click the gray square to the left of the middle group footer row, so the entire row is selected. Enter the following expression for the BorderStyle: Bottom property:

```
= IIF(Fields!StatusName.Value <> "Lost", "Solid", "None")
```

9. Enter the following expression for the Visibility: Hidden property for this same row:

```
= IIF(Fields!StatusName.Value = "Lost", false, true)
```

10. Select the Preview tab. Select "Bolimite, Mfg" from the Customer drop-down list. Select "2003" from the Year drop-down list. Click View Report. Your report should appear similar to Figure 8-3.

11. Select Save All in the toolbar.

Task Notes   If you scroll through the pages of the report, you will see that the report now meets the business needs specified. Let's look at what each expression is doing. The expression entered in step 2 returns green when the status is "Delivered," and blue when the status is "In Route." Otherwise, it returns red.

The expression in step 4 is a bit more complex. It checks whether the current value of the DeliveryNumber field is equal to the first value of the DeliveryNumber field in the DeliveryStatus dataset. As you saw in Chapter 7, aggregate functions act within a scope. By default, the First() aggregate function would return the value for the first record in the current scope. Because this expression is in the group header, by default it would return the value for the first record in each group.

However, in this expression, the First() aggregate function includes a second parameter that specifies the scope it should use. This parameter specifies that the

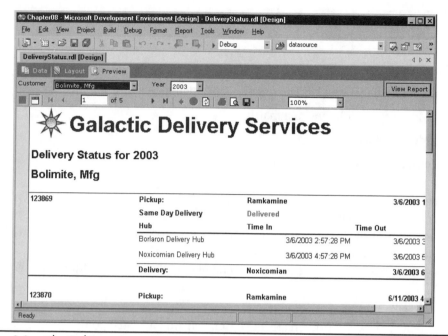

Figure 8-3 *The Delivery Status Report preview after Task 4*

First() aggregate function should use the scope of the entire DeliveryStatus dataset rather than just the current group. Therefore, it returns the first record in the dataset. When the current delivery number is equal to the first delivery number in the dataset, a solid border is created across the top of these text boxes. When the current delivery number is not equal to the first delivery number in the dataset, no border is created.

The expressions in step 7 and step 8 use the value of the StatusName field to control the border across the bottom of each grouping. If the row with the problem contact is displayed, the border should appear across the bottom of this row. However, if the row with the problem contact is not displayed, the border should appear across the bottom of the row above it. The expression in step 9 controls whether the grouping row containing the problem contact is displayed. This is also based on the value of the StatusName field.

As you can see, expressions can be very useful when the formatting or even the visibility of a report item needs to change depending on some condition in the report. Expressions can also be used to calculate the values to appear in a text box, as you will see in the next report.

The Lost Delivery Report

Features Highlighted

▶ Using Visual Basic .NET expressions to calculate values in a text box

▶ Adding static columns to a matrix

▶ Adding totals to a matrix

▶ Formatting total cells in a matrix

Business Need   The quality assurance department at Galactic Delivery Services would like a report to help them analyze the packages lost during delivery. The report should show the number of packages lost each year at each processing hub. It should break down these numbers by the cause for each loss. It should also show the number of losses by cause as a percentage of the total number of packages lost for each hub.

Task Overview

1. Create a New Report, Create a Dataset, and Add a Matrix to the Report

2. Add a Calculated Column to the Matrix

3. Add Totals to the Matrix

Lost Delivery Report, Task 1: Create a New Report, Create a Dataset, and Add a Matrix to the Report

1. Reopen the Chapter08 project if it has been closed.

2. Create a new report called LostDelivery using the GDSReport template.

3. Create a new dataset called LostDelivery that calls the stp_LostDeliveries stored procedure.

4. Place a matrix onto the body of the report. Drag the DeliveryNumber field into the Data cell. Edit the aggregate function in the resulting expression to change it from Sum to Count.

5. Drag the Cause field into the Rows cell. Drag the Hub field into the Columns cell.

6. Open the Matrix Properties dialog box and select the Groups tab.

7. Click Add in the Columns area. The Grouping and Sorting Properties dialog box will appear.

8. Type the following for Expression to group the values by year:

```
=Year(Fields!PickupDateTime.Value)
```

9. Click OK to exit the Grouping and Sorting Properties dialog box.

10. Click Up in the Columns area.

11. Click OK to exit the Matrix Properties dialog box.

12. Modify the following properties of the text box in the upper-left corner of the matrix:

Property	Value
BackgroundColor	Gainsboro (A light gray, near the top of the list)
Font: FontSize	18pt
Font: FontWeight	Bold
Size: Width	2in
Value	Lost Deliveries by Cause

13. Modify the following property of the text box in the lower-left corner of the matrix:

Property	Value
BackgroundColor	Gainsboro

14. Modify the following properties of the text box in the upper-right corner of the matrix:

Property	Value
BackgroundColor	Gainsboro
BorderStyle: Left	Solid
Font: FontSize	14pt
Font: FontWeight	Bold
TextAlign	Center

15. Modify the following properties of the text box in the center of the right-hand column of the matrix:

Property	Value
BackgroundColor	Gainsboro
BorderStyle: Left	Solid
BorderStyle: Bottom	Solid
Font: FontWeight	Bold
TextAlign	Center

16. Modify the following property of the text box in the lower-right corner of the matrix:

Property	Value
BorderStyle: Left	Solid

Task Notes   So far we have a fairly straightforward matrix report. Let's see what happens when we add another column and totals to the matrix.

Lost Delivery Report, Task 2: Add a Calculated Column to the Matrix

1. Right-click the text box in the lower-right corner of the matrix and select Add Column from the context menu. A new column and a new set of column headings appear.

2. Modify the following properties of the new text box in the lower-right corner of the matrix:

Property	Value
BorderStyle: Left	Solid
Format	###.00%
TextAlign	Right
Value	=Count(Fields!DeliveryNumber.Value) / Count(Fields!DeliveryNumber.Value,"matrix1_Hub")

3. Modify the following properties of the text box immediately above the text box modified in step 2:

Property	Value
BackgroundColor	Transparent
BorderStyle: Left	Solid
BorderStyle: Bottom	None
Font: FontWeight	Normal
TextAlign	Right
TextDecoration	Underline
Value	% of Column

4. Modify the following properties of the text box immediately to the left of the text box modified in step 3:

Property	Value
BackgroundColor	Transparent
BorderStyle: Left	Solid
BorderStyle: Bottom	None
Font: FontWeight	Normal
TextAlign	Right
TextDecoration	Underline
Value	# Lost

Your report layout should appear similar to Figure 8-4.

5. Select the Preview tab. Your report should appear similar to Figure 8-5.

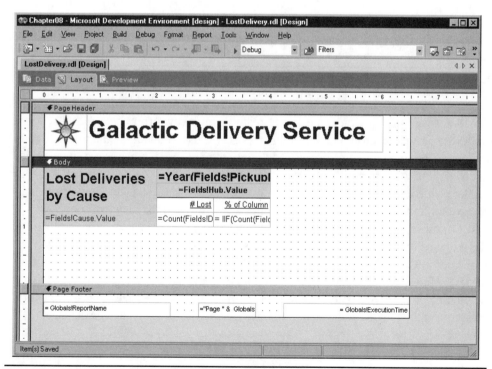

Figure 8-4 *The Lost Delivery Report layout after Task 2*

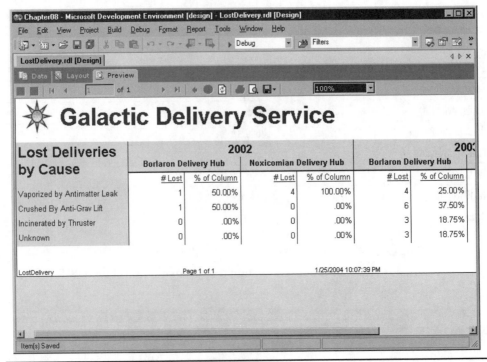

Figure 8-5 *The Lost Delivery Report preview after Task 2*

Task Notes In the previous report, we created a multirow group header and a multirow group footer in a table. In this report, we have now created a multicolumn detail section in a matrix. When we add the second column, a new set of headers is added so that we can identify the contents of each column.

Our new column takes the count from the current row and calculates it as a percentage of the total for the column. This is done, once again, through the magic of scope. The first Count() aggregate function does not have a scope parameter, so it defaults to the scope of the current cell. In other words, it counts the number of lost deliveries in the current cell. The second Count() aggregate function has a scope parameter of matrix1_Hub. This is the name of the column group that creates the column for each hub. Therefore, this aggregate function counts the number of lost deliveries in the entire column. We then divide and use the "##.00%" format string to create a percentage.

Lost Delivery Report, Task 3: Add Totals to the Matrix

1. Select the Layout tab.
2. Right-click the text box in the lower-left corner of the matrix and select Subtotal from the context menu. A "total" cell is added to the bottom of the matrix.

3. Modify the following property of the text box in this new cell:

Property	Value
BorderStyle: Top	Solid

4. Select the Preview tab. Notice that the border we added to the top of the text box only affects the text box with the word "Total" in it. It did not affect any of the text boxes that contain the actual totals.

5. Select the Layout tab.

6. Click the green triangle in the upper-right corner of the text box with the word "Total" in it. It may take a few tries to click the green triangle and not the total cell text box. When you have done it correctly, the drop-down list at the top of the Properties window will change to "Subtotal." Modify the following properties:

Property	Value
BorderStyle: Left	Solid
BorderStyle: Top	Solid

7. Select the Preview tab. We now have the desired format, with the border at the top of each text box that contains a total.

8. Select the Layout tab.

9. Right-click the text box in the upper-right corner of the matrix. Select Subtotal from the context menu. A "total" cell is added to the right of the matrix.

10. Modify the following properties of the text box in this new cell:

Property	Value
BorderStyle: Left	Solid
BorderStyle: Bottom	Solid

Your report layout should appear similar to Figure 8-6.

11. Select the Preview tab. Your report should appear similar to Figure 8-7.

12. Select Save All in the toolbar.

Task Notes   As you just saw, adding subtotals to a row or column in a matrix involves just a couple clicks. However, formatting the text boxes that contain those totals can be a little trickier. When you add a total to a matrix row or column, the text box in

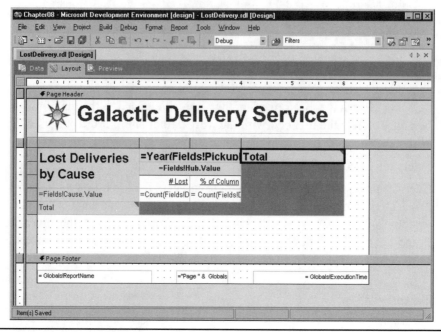

Figure 8-6   *The Lost Delivery Report layout after Task 3*

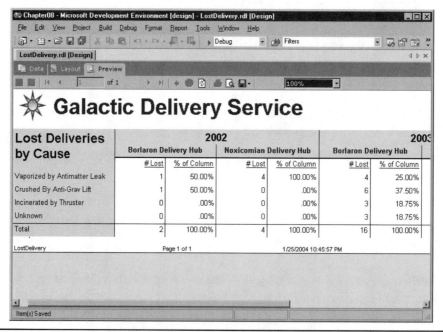

Figure 8-7   *The Lost Delivery Report preview after Task 3*

the new cell is the header for the total row or total column. Changing the properties of this text box only affects the header. You have to click the green triangle to modify the properties for the text boxes that contain the totals.

You have seen how expressions can be used to control properties and to provide the calculated contents of a text box. Now let's look at using an expression in the query definition for a dataset.

The Customer List Report—Revisited

Features Highlighted

▶   Using Visual Basic .NET expressions to specify a dataset query

Business Need   The Customer List Report that you developed for the Galactic Delivery Services accounting department (in Chapter 4) has proved to be very popular. Several other departments would like similar reports to help them track their own lists of e-mail contacts. Rather than create separate reports for each department, which would be hard to maintain, the IT Manager has asked for one report that allows the user to select which type of contact they would like to view.

Task Overview

1.   Copy the Report from the Chapter04 Project and Add It to the Chapter08 Project
2.   Add a Report Parameter and Modify the Dataset to Use the Report Parameter

Customer List Report—Revisited, Task 1: Copy the Report from the Chapter04 Project and Add It to the Chapter08 Project

1.   Use Windows Explorer to copy the report definition file for the Customer List Report (CustomerList1.rdl) from the Chapter04 project folder and paste it in the Chapter08 project folder. Both of these folders should be found under My Documents in the Visual Studio Project\MSSQLRS folder.

2.   In Visual Studio, reopen the Chapter08 project if it has been closed.

3.   Right-click the Reports folder in the Solution Explorer and select Add | Add Existing Item from the context menu. The Add Existing Item – Chapter08 dialog box appears.

4.   Make sure you are looking at the Chapter08 folder in the dialog box and select the CustomerList1.rdl file. Click Open to exit the Add Existing Item – Chapter08 dialog box.

5. Double-click the CustomerList1.rdl entry in the Solution Explorer to open the report definition.

6. Select the Preview tab to show that this report is functioning properly in the Chapter08 project.

Task Notes   Because the entire definition of a report is contained within a single RDL file, it is easy to copy reports to different locations. As you saw here, we can even add them to a project other than the project within which they were originally created. The Customer List Report uses a shared data source called Galactic. We did not need to copy the shared data source because we already have a shared data source with the same name and the same properties in the Chapter08 project. If this was not the case, we could have copied the shared data source file (Galactic.rds) along with the report file and added that to our new project as well.

Customer List Report—Revisited, Task 2: Add a Report Parameter and Modify the Dataset to Use the Report Parameter

1. Select the Data tab.

2. Open the Report Parameters dialog box.

3. Add a new report parameter and modify the properties for this new parameter as follows:

Property	Value
Name	ListType
Prompt	Select a List
Allow blank value	unchecked
Available Values	(See the following table)

Set the Available Values property for the ListType parameter as follows:

Label	Value
Billing Contacts	B
Manufacturer Contacts	M
Problem Contacts	P

4. Click OK to exit the Report Parameters dialog box.

5. Click the Generic Query Designer button in the Query Builder toolbar. The Generic Query Designer, rather than the Query Builder, is displayed on the Data tab.

6. Replace the entire select statement with the following expression:

```
=IIF(Parameters!ListType.Value="B", "EXEC stp_BillingContacts",
    IIF(Parameters!ListType.Value="M",
        "EXEC stp_ManufacturerContacts",
        "EXEC stp_ProblemContacts"))
```

7. Click the ... button in the Generic Query Designer toolbar. The Dataset dialog box will appear.

8. Select the Fields tab.

9. Change the Fields table to match the following:

Field Name	Type	Value
Name	Database Field	Name
Contact	Database Field	Contact
Email	Database Field	Email

10. Click OK to exit the Dataset dialog box.

11. Select the Layout tab.

12. Drag the Contact field and drop it on the text box that currently contains the expression for the BillingContact field.

13. Double-click the table header cell directly above the text box from step 12 and change the text to "Contact."

14. Drag the Email field and drop it on the text box that currently contains the expression for the BillingEmail field.

15. Double-click the table header cell directly above the text box from step 14 and change the text to "E-mail."

16. Select Save All in the toolbar.

17. Select the Preview tab. Try selecting each of the list types. Remember to click View Report.

NOTE

The database does not contain a contact name for each manufacturer, so there are no contact names in the manufacturer list.

Task Notes   Rather than specifying the query in the Query Designer, we used an expression to choose between three possible queries (in this case, three stored procedure calls). This is known as a *dynamic query*. The name comes from the fact that the query that is actually run depends on input from the user at the time the report is run.

Because the contents of the query are not known until run time, Visual Studio cannot "pre-run" the query to determine the fields that will result. Instead, we need to manually specify the fields that will result from our dynamic query. All the possible queries that could be run should return result sets with the same field names in order for your report to work properly.

At this point, you may be ready to suggest two or three alternative approaches to creating this report. It is certainly not unusual to come up with a number of possible ways to meet the business needs of a report. When this happens, use the following criteria to evaluate the possible solutions:

▶ Efficiency of operation

▶ Your comfort with implementing and debugging a given solution in a reasonable amount of time

▶ Maintainability

▶ Your need to illustrate a certain point in a book chapter

Well, maybe that last point won't apply to you, but it was, in fact, the overriding reason for choosing this approach for this particular report.

Payroll Checks

Features Highlighted

▶ Using Visual Basic .NET functions embedded in the report to create reusable code

▶ Using a stored procedure that modifies the data

▶ Grouping in the details row of a data region

▶ Using nested data regions

Business Need The Galactic Delivery Services accounting department needs a report to print payroll checks for its hourly employees. The checks should have the check portion in the top one-third of the page and the check register in the bottom two-thirds of the page. The check register should list the hours worked that are included in this check. The user should be able to select a week for which there is unpaid time entered and receive the payroll checks for that week. The planetary system tax amount (25 percent) and state tax amount (5 percent) must be deducted from the amount being paid.

Task Overview

1. Create a New Report, Create Two Datasets, Add a List to the Report Layout, and Populate It

2. Add a Table to the Report Layout and Populate It

3. Configure the Report Parameter and Add Embedded Code to the Report

Payroll Checks, Task 1: Create a New Report, Create Two Datasets, Add a List to the Report Layout, and Populate It

1. Reopen the Chapter08 project if it has been closed.

2. Create a new report called PayrollChecks. Do *not* use the GDSReport template.

3. Create a new dataset called PayrollChecks that calls the stp_PayrollChecks stored procedure. Do *not* run the stored procedure in the Query Designer. This will mark records as having been paid.

4. Create a new dataset called WeekNumbers that calls the stp_WeekNumbers stored procedure.

5. Select the Layout tab.

6. Place a list onto the body of the report. Modify the following properties of this list in the Properties window:

Property	Value
BackgroundColor	LightGreen
BorderStyle	Solid
DataSetName	PayrollChecks
PageBreakAtStart	True

7. Open the List Properties dialog box. Click Edit Details Group. The Details Grouping dialog box will appear.

8. Select "=Fields!PayrollCheckNumber.Value" from the Expression drop-down list.

9. Click OK to exit the Details Grouping dialog box. Click OK to exit the List Properties dialog box.

10. Add text boxes to the list to get the layout shown in Figure 8-8. You can create text boxes containing fields by dragging the fields from the Fields window. You can create a text box containing a constant string by dragging a text box from the Toolbox and typing the constant string in the new text box.

11. Modify the following property of the text box containing the sum of the LineAmount values:

Property	Value
Format	C

Task Notes   Our payroll check has two separate parts: the check itself and the check register. The check register contains a line showing the amount paid for each day worked during the selected work week. The check is essentially a summary of the information in the check register. The check amount is the sum of the amount to be paid for all the days worked.

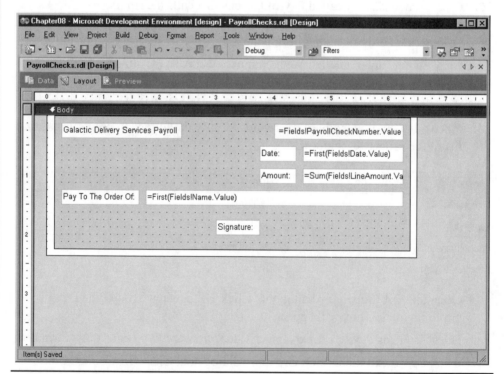

Figure 8-8   *The payroll check layout after Task 1*

We could use two different datasets to provide data to these two areas. However, to be a little more efficient with our database resources, we are going to use a single dataset. The dataset will include all the detail information required by the check register. It will have one row for each date worked. However, we do not want to create a check for each date worked. We only want one check for all the days worked by a given employee in the week.

To accomplish this, we need to group the detail data in order to print the check. We did this by adding the details grouping in steps 7 through 9. Because we want one check per check number, the PayrollCheckNumber field seems an obvious choice for grouping. (The number in the PayrollCheckNumber field is generated by the stored procedure.) With this details grouping, our list will receive one record for each check number; therefore, we will get one check per check number.

Payroll Checks, Task 2: Add a Table to the Report Layout and Populate It

1. Increase the height of the report body and the list.

2. Place a table *inside* the list below the signature text box.

3. Drag the WorkDate, HoursWorked, and LineAmount fields into the cells in the details row of the table.

4. Drag the LineAmount field into the rightmost table footer cell and set the following properties for this new text box:

Property	Value
BorderStyle: Top	Solid
Format	C

5. Set the following property for the text box in the rightmost details row cell:

Property	Value
Format	C

6. Set the following properties for the table:

Property	Value
BackgroundColor	White
NoRows	No Uncut Checks For This Week
PageBreakAtEnd	True

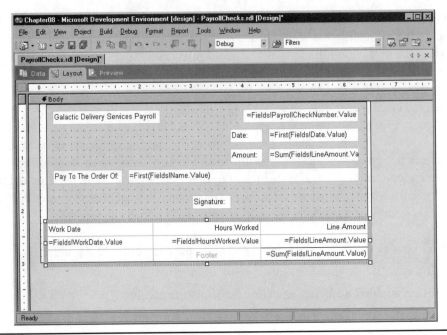

Figure 8-9   *The payroll check layout after Task 2*

7. Drag the bottom of the list and the bottom of the report body up so they are the same as the bottom of the table. Your report layout will appear similar to Figure 8-9.

Task Notes   In Task 1, we created a list with a detail grouping to create the check portion of our payroll checks. In Task 2, we created a table to provide the detail information for the check register. The table data region must be nested inside of the list data region so that we get one set of detail information for each check. If the table was placed below the list, we would get all the checks first and then all the check register information at the end.

The PageBreakAtEnd property was set on the table so that there will be a page break immediately after the table. This keeps our output to one check per page.

Payroll Checks, Task 3: Configure the Report Parameter and Add Embedded Code to the Report

1. Use the main menu to open the Report Parameters dialog box.

2. Modify the following properties for the WeekNumber parameter:

Property	Value
Prompt	WeekNumber
Available values	From query
Dataset	WeekNumber
Value field	WeekNumber
Label field	WeekNumber

3. Click OK to exit the Report Parameters dialog box.

4. Select Report | Report Properties from the main menu. The Report Properties dialog box will appear.

5. Select the Code tab.

6. Enter the following in the Custom code area:

```
' State and Planetary System Tax Deductions
Public Function TaxDeductions(ByVal Amount As Double) As Double
        ' Planetary System Tax = 25%
        ' State Tax = 5%
        TaxDeductions = Amount * .25 + Amount * .05
End Function
```

7. Click OK to exit the Report Properties dialog box.

8. Right-click the text box that is in the list, but not in the table, containing the sum of the LineAmount values and select Expression from the context menu. The Edit Expression dialog box will appear.

9. Replace the contents of the Expression area with the following:

```
=Sum(Fields!LineAmount.Value) -
        Code.TaxDeductions(Sum(Fields!LineAmount.Value))
```

10. Click OK to exit the Edit Expression dialog box.

11. Repeat steps 8 through 10 with the text box in the table containing the sum of the LineAmount values.

12. Right-click the text box in the details row of the table containing the LineAmount value and select Expression from the context menu. The Edit Expression dialog box will appear.

13. Replace the contents of the Expression area with the following:

```
=Fields!LineAmount.Value - Code.TaxDeductions(Fields!LineAmount.Value)
```

14. Click OK to exit the Edit Expression dialog box.

15. Select the Preview tab.

16. Select "10-2004" from the Week Number drop-down list and click View Report. Your report should appear similar to Figure 8-10. Remember, once checks have been run for a given week, you cannot produce checks for that week again. Each time you enter the report, the Week Number drop-down list will only contain entries for weeks that have not been run. (The check number you see on the first page in your preview may be different from the check number shown in the figure. This is normal.)

17. Select Save All from the toolbar.

Task Notes   Tax calculations are more straightforward on the planets where Galactic Delivery Services operates than they are here. Everyone pays 25 percent of their pay to the Planetary System government and 5 percent of their pay to the State government. Even though this is a simple formula, we need to use it in three different places. Using the embedded code feature of Reporting Services, we are able to put this formula in one location and use it in several locations. This also makes things easier to change when one or the other of these tax amounts goes up.

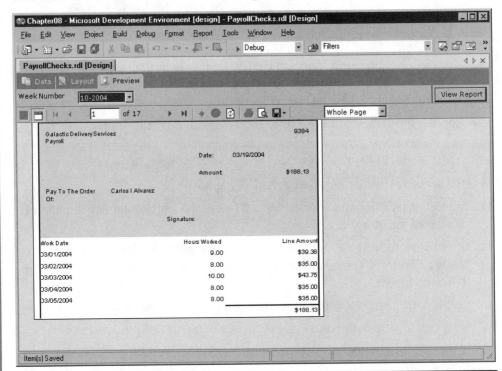

Figure 8-10   *The payroll check preview*

The Weather Report

Features Highlighted

▶   Referencing .NET assemblies in the report

Business Need   The Galactic Delivery Services flight control department needs a way to quickly list the current weather conditions at each of the planets served by GDS. (After all, space transports have to go through the atmosphere to take off and land.) One of the GDS programmers has created a .NET assembly that uses a web service to get the weather from various locations. A call must be made to a method of this .NET assembly for each of the planets and the results incorporated into the report.

Task Overview

1. Copy the .NET Assembly into the Appropriate Location and Create a Reference to the Assembly

2. Create a New Report, Create a Dataset, Add a Table to the Report Layout, and Populate It

Weather Report, Task 1: Copy the .NET Assembly into the Appropriate Location and Create a Reference to the Assembly

1. If you have not already done so, download the WeatherInfo.dll assembly from the website for this book.

2. Copy this file to the Report Designer folder. The default path for the Report Designer folder is

    ```
    C:\Program Files\Microsoft SQL Server\80\Tools\Report Designer
    ```

3. Reopen the Chapter08 project if it has been closed.

4. Create a new report called WeatherReport using the GDSReport template.

5. Select Report | Report Properties from the main menu. The Report Properties dialog box appears. Select the References tab.

6. Click ... next to the References area. The Add Reference dialog box appears.

7. Click Browse. The Select Component dialog box appears. Navigate to the Report Designer folder. (The path to this folder was given previously.) Select WeatherInfo.dll and click Open to select this file and exit the Select Component dialog box.

8. Click OK to exit the Add Reference dialog box. Click OK to exit the Report Properties dialog box.

Task Notes In order for a custom assembly to be used in our reports, the assembly must be in a location where it can be found by Reporting Services. When you are designing reports, the assembly must be either in the Report Designer folder or in the Global Assembly Cache. We placed the WeatherInfo.dll assembly in the Report Designer folder in step 2. Consult your .NET documentation for information on placing an assembly in the Global Assembly Cache.

We are using a class from the WeatherInfo assembly called PlanetaryWeather and a method from that class called GetWeather. The GetWeather method is a shared method. This means that you do not need to create an instance of the PlanetaryWeather class in order to use the GetWeather method.

To use a method that is not a shared method, you need to use the Classes area of the Report Properties dialog box. First, create a reference in the References area, as we did in steps 6 and 7. Then, under Class name, specify the name of the class within that assembly that you wish to instantiate. Finally, provide a name for the instance of that class. Reporting Services will create an instance of the class with the name you provide when the report is run.

Once the assembly is in the correct location and you have created a reference to that assembly, you can use the methods of this assembly in your reports. When referencing a shared method in an assembly, use the following syntax:

```
Namespace.ClassName.MethodName(Parameters…)
```

For the WeatherInfo assembly, the syntax is

```
WeatherInfo.PlanetaryWeather.GetWeather(PlanetAbbrv)
```

To use a nonshared method from a class that you instantiated, use the syntax

```
Code.InstanceName.MethodName(Parameters…)
```

Weather Report, Task 2: Create a New Report, Create a Dataset, Add a Table to the Report Layout, and Populate It

1. Create a new dataset called Planets. Use the following for the query string:

```
SELECT Name, PlanetAbbrv FROM Planet ORDER BY Name
```

2. Select the Layout tab.

3. Place a text box and a table onto the body of the report. Complete your report layout so it is similar to Figure 8-11.

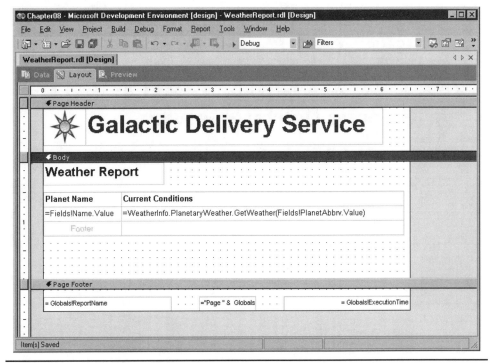

Figure 8-11   *Weather Report layout*

4. Select the Preview tab. Your report should appear similar to Figure 8-12.

NOTE

Keep in mind that the GetWeather method is actually going out to the Internet and retrieving weather conditions when you run the report. Because of this, you must be connected to the Internet when you run this report. Also, the weather conditions you see in your report will vary from those shown in the report preview. Finally, some locations may show "null" for a certain condition if that condition has not been reported in the past hour.

5. Select Save All from the toolbar.

Task Notes   Remember that the WeatherInfo assembly happens to use a web service to gather its weather information. Therefore, a connection to the Internet is required when previewing this report. The preview will take a minute or so to complete because the report needs to access the web service for each planet.

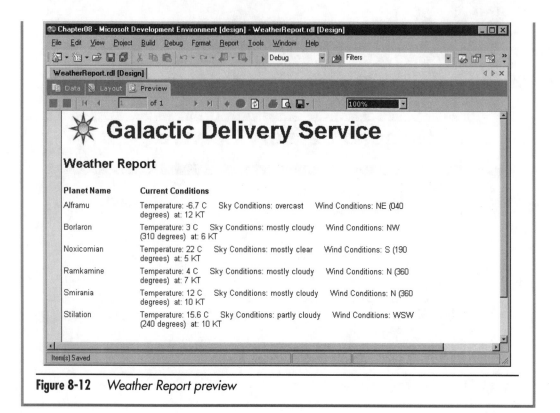

Figure 8-12   *Weather Report preview*

Reports Within Reports

Thus far, we have placed report items within report items, and data regions within data regions. In this section, we will look at putting whole reports inside one another. This is done using the subreport report item; the only item in the Toolbox that we have not yet used.

The subreport item is simply a placeholder in a report. It sits in the parent report and shows the space that will be occupied by another report when the parent report is run. There is nothing special about a report that is placed in a subreport item. Any report can be used as a subreport.

The report placed in the subreport can even contain parameters. These parameter values can be passed from the parent report to the subreport. Any field value, parameter value, or expression in the parent report can be used as a parameter in the subreport.

Subreports are used for many reasons. They can provide an easy way to reuse a complex report layout within a parent report. They can also be used to implement a more complex form of drilldown.

The following subreports are anything but subpar!

The Employee Evaluation Report

Features Highlighted

▶ Using a subreport as reusable code

▶ Using the page width and page height properties for a landscape report

▶ Using a rectangle for grouping

Business Need   The Galactic Delivery Services personnel department has created an application for employees to conduct peer reviews as a part of each employee's annual review process. They are also collecting a review and comments from each employee's manager. They need a report that can be used to present the results of the peer review at the employee's meeting with their supervisor.

The manager's review and comments should be noted as coming from the manager. The peer reviews, however, should be presented anonymously.

Task Overview

1. Create a New Report, Create a Dataset, Add a Table to the Report Layout, and Populate It

2. Create a New Report, Create a Dataset, and Populate the Report Layout

3. Add a Rectangle

Employee Evaluation Report, Task 1: Create a New Report, Create a Dataset, Add a Table to the Report Layout, and Populate It

1. Reopen the Chapter08 project if it has been closed.

2. Create a new report called EvalDetail. Do *not* use the GDSReport template.

3. Create a new dataset called EvalRatings that calls the stp_EvalRatings stored procedure.

4. Select the Layout tab.

5. Place a table onto the body of the report.

6. Place the Goal, Rating, and GoalComment fields in the details row of the table.

7. Add a group to the table using EvaluatorEmployeeNumber as the grouping expression.

8. Complete your report layout so it is similar to Figure 8-13. The top row has the BorderStyle: Top property set to Solid. The bottom row has the BorderStyle: Top property set to Solid and the BorderWidth: Bottom property set to 5pt.

Task Notes   The EvalDetail report will be used in two subreports in our parent report. It will be used in one location to display the peer reviews and in another location to display the manager review. We can create this layout for displaying review information and then use it in multiple places.

Employee Evaluation Report, Task 2: Create a New Report, Create a Dataset, and Populate the Report Layout

1. Create a new report called EmployeeEval using the GDSReport template.

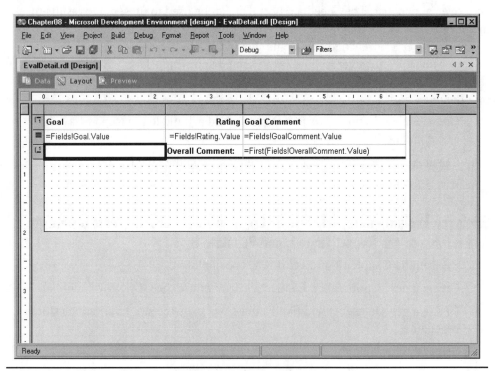

Figure 8-13   *The Employee Evaluation Detail Report layout*

2. Create a new dataset called EvalPerformance that calls the stp_EvalPerformance stored procedure.

3. Select the Layout tab.

4. Modify the following properties of the report:

Property	Value
PageSize: Width	11in
PageSize: Height	8.5in

This will create a landscape page layout rather than a portrait page layout.

5. Drag the right edge of the report body until it is 10 inches wide. Use the ruler at the top of the layout area as a guide.

6. Drag the EmployeeName field onto the report body. Modify the following properties of the text box that results:

Property	Value
Font: FontSize	20pt
Font: FontWeight	Bold
Location: Left	0in
Location: Top	0in
Size: Width	6.875in
Size: Height	0.5in

7. Place a text box onto the report body. Modify the following properties of this text box:

Property	Value
Font: FontSize	20pt
Font: FontWeight	Bold
Location: Left	8.25in
Location: Top	0in
Size: Width	1.625in
Size: Height	0.5in
Value	=Parameters!Year.Value

8. Place a text box onto the report body. Modify the following properties of this text box:

Property	Value
Font: FontSize	16pt
Font: FontWeight	Bold
Location: Left	0in
Location: Top	0.625in
Size: Width	2in
Size: Height	0.375in
Value	Peer Evaluations

9. Place a subreport onto the report body immediately below the text box. Modify the following properties of this subreport:

Property	Value
Location: Left	0in
Location: Top	1in
Size: Width	6.875in
Size: Height	1.125in

10. Right-click the subreport and select Properties from the context menu. The Subreport Properties dialog box will appear.

11. Select EvalDetail from the Subreport drop-down list.

12. Select the Parameters tab.

13. Configure the parameters as shown here:

Parameter Name	Parameter Value
EmpNum	=Parameter!EmpNum.Value
Year	=Parameter!Year.Value
MgrFlag	=0

Remember to use the Edit Expression dialog box to select the parameter values.

14. Click OK to exit the Subreport Properties dialog box.

15. Select the Peer Evaluations text box and the subreport. Press CTRL-C to copy these two items. Press CTRL-V to paste a copy of these items on the report body. Drag the two copied items so that they are immediately below the original subreport.

16. Modify the new text box to read "Manager Evaluation." Adjust the width of the text box as needed.

17. Open the Subreport Properties dialog box for the new subreport and select the Parameters tab.

18. Change the parameter value for MgrFlag from "=0" to "=1". This will cause the second subreport to contain the manager's evaluation rather than the peer evaluations.

19. Click OK to exit the Subreport Properties dialog box.

20. Place a text box onto the report body. Modify the following properties of this text box:

Property	Value
Font: FontWeight	Bold
Location: Left	7.125in
Location: Top	1in
Size: Width	2in
Size: Height	0.25in
Value	Areas of Excellence

21. Drag the AreasOfExcellence field onto the report body. Modify the following properties of the text box that results:

Property	Value
Location: Left	7.125in
Location: Top	1.375in
Size: Width	2.75in
Size: Height	0.25in

22. Place a text box onto the report body. Modify the following properties of this text box:

Property	Value
Font: FontWeight	Bold
Location: Left	7.125in
Location: Top	1.875in
Size: Width	2in

Property	Value
Size: Height	0.25in
Value	Areas for Improvement

23. Drag the AreasForImprovement field onto the report body. Modify the following properties of the text box that results:

Property	Value
Location: Left	7.125in
Location: Top	2.25in
Size: Width	2.75in
Size: Height	0.25in

24. Select the Preview tab. Enter **1394** for EmpNum and **2003** for Year and then click View Report. Your report should appear similar to Figure 8-14.

Task Notes   Two steps are required to get each subreport item ready to use. First, we have to specify which report is going to be used within the subreport. Once this is

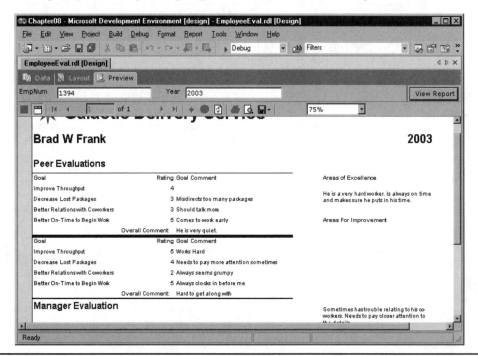

Figure 8-14   *The Employee Evaluation Report preview after Task 2*

done, we need to specify a value for each of the parameters in the selected report. With these two tasks completed, our subreports are ready to go.

In this report, we are using several fields outside of a data region: the EmployeeName field, the AreasOfExcellence field, and the AreasForImprovement field. Remember, data regions are set up to repeat a portion of their content for each record in the result set. When a field value occurs outside of a data region, it is not repeated, but occurs only once. Therefore, the field value must be put inside of an aggregate function to determine how to get one value from the many records in the result set. The First() aggregate function is chosen by default.

In this particular report, the EvalPerformance dataset has only one record. Of course, Visual Studio does not know at design time how many records the dataset will have at run time. (Even if the dataset has only one record at design time, it could have 100 at run time.) Therefore, Visual Studio insists on the aggregate functions for this field value.

Finally, you may have noticed a little problem with the text box that contains the contents of the AreasForImprovement field. It seems to be sliding down the page. In actuality, it was pushed down the page when the subreport grew.

The text boxes that contain the Areas of Excellence title, the AreasOfExcellence field value, and the Areas for Improvement title are all even with the first subreport. However, the text box containing the value of the AreasForImprovement field starts below the bottom of the first subreport. When the subreport grows due to its contents, the text box is pushed further down the report so that it remains below the bottom of the subreport.

In Task 3, we will look at a way to prevent this problem.

Employee Evaluation Report, Task 3: Add a Rectangle

1. Select the Layout tab.

2. Select the Areas of Excellence text box, the AreasOfExcellence field value text box, the Areas for Improvement text box, and the AreasForImprovement field value text box. Press CTRL-X to cut these four text boxes.

3. Select a rectangle from the Toolbox and place it in the area just vacated by these four text boxes.

4. With the rectangle still selected, press CTRL-V to paste the four text boxes into the rectangle.

5. Arrange the rectangle and the four text boxes as needed. Your layout should appear similar to Figure 8-15.

6. Select the Preview tab. Enter **1394** for EmpNum and **2003** for Year and then click View Report. Your report should appear similar to Figure 8-16.

7. Select Save All from the toolbar.

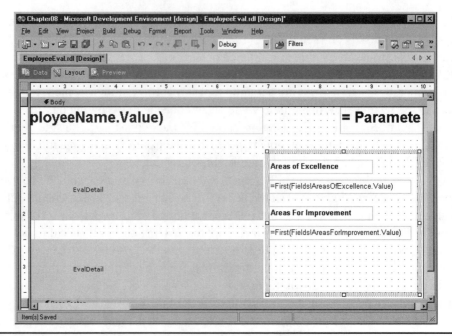

Figure 8-15 *The Employee Evaluation Report layout with a rectangle*

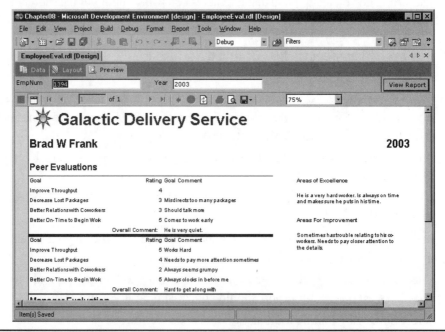

Figure 8-16 *The Employee Evaluation Report preview with a rectangle*

Task Notes   The rectangle report item comes to our rescue here. Once the four text boxes are inside the rectangle, they remain together no matter how much the subreport grows. As your report designs become more complex, rectangles will often be necessary to keep things right where you want them.

The Invoice Report

Features Highlighted

▶   Using a subreport in a table

▶   Using a subreport to facilitate drilldown

Business Need   The Galactic Delivery Services accounting department would like an interactive Invoice Report. The Invoice Report will show the invoice header and invoice detail information. The user will then be able to expand an invoice detail entry to view information on the delivery that created that invoice detail.

Task Overview

1. Create a New Report, Create a Dataset, and Copy the Layout from the DeliveryStatus Report

2. Create a New Report, Create a Dataset, and Populate the Report Layout

Invoice Report, Task 1: Create a New Report, Create a Dataset, and Copy the Layout from the DeliveryStatus Report

1. Reopen the Chapter08 project if it has been closed.

2. Create a new report called DeliveryDetail. Do *not* use the GDSReport template.

3. Create a new dataset called DeliveryStatus that calls the stp_DeliveryDetail stored procedure.

4. Select the Layout tab.

5. Double-click the entry for the DeliveryStatus report in the Solution Explorer to open the DeliveryStatus report.

6. Select the table in the DeliveryStatus report and press CTRL-C to copy it. (Make sure you have the entire table selected, not just a single cell in the table.)

7. Close the DeliveryStatus report and return to the DeliveryDetail report.

8. Press CTRL-V to paste the table into the report body.

9. Move the table to the upper-left corner of the report body. Size the report body so that it exactly contains the table.

Task Notes   Instead of re-creating a layout for the delivery detail, we borrowed a layout we created previously in another report. This works because the stp_DeliveryDetail stored procedure returns the same columns as the stp_DeliveryStatus stored procedure used for the previous report. The other requirement needed to make this cut-and-paste operation successful was to use the same name for the dataset in both reports.

When you have a layout that is nice and clean, it is always a good idea to reuse it whenever possible. It would be even better to modify the DeliveryStatus report to use our new DeliveryDetail report in a subreport. That way, we would only need to maintain this layout in one location.

Consider that an extra credit project.

Invoice Report, Task 2: Create a New Report, Create a Dataset, and Populate the Report Layout

1. Create a new report called Invoice using the GDSReport template.

2. Create a new dataset called InvoiceHeader that calls the stp_InvoiceHeader stored procedure.

3. Create a second dataset called InvoiceDetail that calls the stp_InvoiceDetail stored procedure.

4. Select the Layout tab.

5. Place a list onto the report body.

6. Size the list and add fields and text boxes to create the layout shown in Figure 8-17.

7. Drag the report body to make it larger.

8. Place a table onto the report body immediately below the list.

9. Select InvoiceDetail from the drop-down list at the top of the Fields window.

10. Drag the LineNumber, Description, and Amount fields into the details row of the table.

11. Size the table columns appropriately. Type a "C" for the Format property of the text box containing the Amount field value.

12. Turn off the table header and table footer.

13. Add a second details row below the existing details row.

14. Merge the three cells in this new details row.

15. Place a subreport in the merged cell.

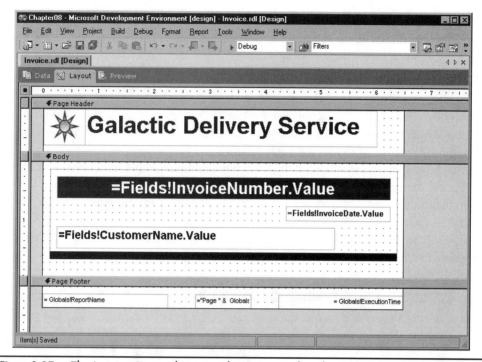

Figure 8-17   *The Invoice Report layout with an invoice header*

16. Open the Subreport Properties dialog box. Set the subreport to DeliveryDetail.
17. Select the Parameters tab and configure it as follows:

Parameter Name	Parameter Value
DeliveryNumber	=Fields!DeliveryNumber.Value

18. Click OK to exit the Subreport Parameters dialog box.
19. Click the gray box to the left of the row containing the subreport. Modify the following properties for this table row:

Property	Value
Visibility: Hidden	True
Visibility: ToggleItem	LineNumber

20. Select the Preview tab. Type **73054** for InvoiceNumber and click View Report.
21. Expand one of the invoice detail entries and observe how the subreport appears.

22. You can widen the report body, list, and table so that the report layout does not expand when the subreport appears. Your report should appear as shown in Figure 8-18.

23. Select Save All from the toolbar.

Task Notes   In the Invoice Report, we placed our subreport right in a table cell. A field from the table's dataset is used as the parameter for the subreport. Because of this, the subreport is different for each details row in the table.

We chose to have the subreport initially hidden in our report. The reason for this is that the subreport contains a large amount of detail information. This detail would overwhelm the users if it were displayed all at once. Instead, the users can selectively drill down to the detail they need.

In our next report, we will look at another way to manage large amounts of detail by using the drill-through feature of Reporting Services.

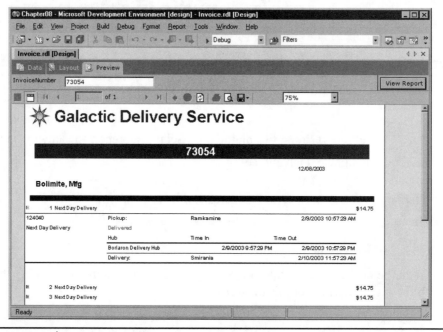

Figure 8-18   *The Invoice Report preview*

Interacting with Reports

In many cases, your reports can be much more effective when users can view them electronically. Reporting Services offers a number of options for allowing the user to interact with the reports when viewed electronically. We have already seen several examples of drill-down interactivity. This type of interactivity hides detail information until it is needed by the user.

In this section, we will look at additional methods for navigating within reports and even moving between reports. We will also look at a way to link a report to other Internet content. Finally, we will look at a way for your report to interact with you by always keeping its data up to date.

So don't be shy; interact!

The Invoice Front End Report

Features Highlighted

▶   Using drill-through navigation to move between reports

▶   Using the document map to navigate within a report

▶   Using bookmarks to navigate within a report

▶   Using links to navigate to Internet content

Business Need   The Galactic Delivery Services accounting department is very pleased with the Invoice Report. They would now like a front end to make the Invoice Report easier to use. The front-end report should list all invoices by customer and allow the user to click an invoice to see the complete Invoice Report. The front end should have each customer start on a new page. In addition, the front end should provide a quick way to navigate to the page for a particular customer, and a way to move from a customer to the page for its parent company. Finally, the front end should include a link to the customer's website for further information on the customer.

Task Overview

1.   Create a New Report, Create a Dataset, and Populate the Report Layout

2.   Add the Navigation

Invoice Front End Report, Task 1: Create a New Report, Create a Dataset, and Populate the Report Layout

1. Reopen the Chapter08 project if it has been closed.
2. Create a new report called FrontEnd using the GDSReport template.
3. Create a new dataset called CustomerInvoices that calls the stp_CustomerInvoices stored procedure.
4. Select the Layout tab.
5. Place a table onto the report body.
6. Drag the InvoiceNumber, InvoiceDate, and TotalAmount fields into the details row of the table.
7. Type a "C" for the Format property for the text box containing the TotalAmount field value.
8. Turn off the table header and table footer.
9. Add a group to the table using the CustomerName as the grouping expression. The group should have a group header, but not a group footer. There should be a page break at the start of each new group.
10. Drag the CustomerName field into the leftmost cell in the group header row. Set the Font Weight property to Bold for this text box.
11. Drag the ParentName field into the center cell in the group header row.

Task Notes   We have the layout for the Invoice Front End Report. However, it is not really a front end because it does not lead anywhere yet. Let's continue on with the good stuff.

Invoice Front End Report, Task 2: Add the Navigation

1. Right-click the leftmost cell in the details row (the cell containing the invoice number) and select Properties from the context menu. The Textbox Properties dialog box will appear.
2. Click Advanced. The Advanced Textbox Properties dialog box replaces the Textbox Properties dialog box.
3. Select the Navigation tab.
4. Select the Jump To Report option for the Hyperlink action.
5. Select Invoice from the Jump To Report drop-down list.

6. Click Parameters. The Parameters dialog box will appear.

7. Select InvoiceNumber from the Parameter Name drop-down list.

8. Select "=Fields!InvoiceNumber.Value" from the Parameter Value drop-down list.

9. Click OK to exit the Parameters dialog box.

10. Click OK to exit the Advanced Textbox Properties dialog box.

11. Right-click the leftmost cell in the group header row (the cell containing the customer name) and select Properties from the context menu. The Textbox Properties dialog box will appear.

12. Click Advanced. The Advanced Textbox Properties dialog box replaces the Textbox Properties dialog box.

13. Select the Navigation tab.

14. Select "=Fields!CustomerName.Value" from the Document Map Label drop-down list.

15. Select "=Fields!CustomerName.Value" from the Bookmark ID drop-down list.

16. Click OK to exit the Advanced Textbox Properties dialog box.

17. Right-click the center cell in the group header row (the cell containing the parent name) and select Properties from the context menu. The Textbox Properties dialog box will appear.

18. Click Advanced. The Advanced Textbox Properties dialog box replaces the Textbox Properties dialog box.

19. Select the Navigation tab.

20. Select the Jump To Bookmark option for the Hyperlink action.

21. Select "=Fields!ParentName.Value" from the Jump To Bookmark drop-down list.

22. Click OK to exit the Advanced Textbox Properties dialog box.

23. Right-click the rightmost cell in the group header row and select Properties from the context menu. The Textbox Properties dialog box will appear.

24. Type **Website Link** for Value.

25. Click Advanced. The Advanced Textbox Properties dialog box replaces the Textbox Properties dialog box.

26. Select the Navigation tab.

27. Select the Jump To URL option for the Hyperlink action.

28. Select "=Fields!CustomerWebsite.Value" from the Jump To URL drop-down list.

29. Click OK to exit the Advanced Textbox Properties dialog box.

30. Select the Preview tab.

31. Select Save All from the toolbar.

Task Notes   When you look at the report preview, you will notice a new feature to the left of the report. This is the *document map,* which functions like a table of contents for your report. We created entries in the document map when we placed an expression in the Document Map Label drop-down list in step 14.

Because you used the customer name as the document map label, when you expand the FrontEnd entry in the document map, you see a list of all the customer names. (FrontEnd is the name of the report. That is why it is the top entry in the document map.) When you click a customer name in the document map, you are taken directly to the page for that customer.

If you are not using the document map, you can hide it by clicking the Document Map button in the report viewer toolbar. The Document Map button is the leftmost button in the toolbar. Clicking this button a second time will cause the document map to return.

In addition to creating document map entries for each customer name, we also created bookmarks for each customer name. This was done in step 15. We are using these bookmarks to link child companies to their parent company. We are creating a Jump To Bookmark using the value of the ParentName field. This was done in steps 20 and 21.

When a customer has a value in the ParentName field, a Jump To Bookmark link is created on that parent name (the center cell in the group header row). The bookmark link jumps to the page for the customer with the matching name. To try this out, use the document map to jump to the page for Everlast Plastics. Everlast's parent company is Young & Assoc. Click the link for Young & Assoc., and you will jump to the page for Young & Assoc.

We also created a Jump To URL link for each customer. This link was placed in the cell that reads "Website Link" and was created in steps 27 and 28. Clicking this cell is supposed to take you to the website for each customer. However, we are not able to connect to the Inter-galactic-net used by GDS and its customers. Instead, clicking this link will open a browser and take you to the Osborne website.

Then, we created a Jump To Report. This was done in steps 4 through 8. Clicking an invoice number will jump you to the Invoice Report and will pass the invoice number as a parameter. This allows you to see the detail information for the invoice. When you are done looking at the invoice, you can return to the Invoice Front End Report by clicking the Back button in the report viewer toolbar.

The Transport Monitor Report

Features Highlighted

► Using the autorefresh report property

Business Need   The Galactic Delivery Services maintenance department needs a report to assist in monitoring transport operations. Each transport feeds real-time sensor data back to the central database. The maintenance department needs a report to display this information for a selected transport. Because the sensor data is updated every 15 seconds, the report should refresh every 15 seconds. Any values that are out of the normal ranges should be displayed in red.

Task Overview

1. Create a New Report, Create a Dataset, Populate the Report Layout, and Set Report Properties

Transport Monitor Report, Task 1: Create a New Report, Create a Dataset, Populate the Report Layout, and Set Report Properties

1. Reopen the Chapter08 project if it has been closed.

2. Create a new report called TransportMonitor. Do *not* use the GDSReport template.

3. Create a new dataset called TransportMonitor that calls the stp_TransportMonitor stored procedure.

4. Create a second dataset called TransportList that calls the stp_TransportList stored procedure.

5. Select the Layout tab.

6. Configure the TransportNumber Report Parameter as follows:

Property	Value
Prompt	Transport
Available values	From query
Dataset	TransportList
Value field	TransportNumber
Label field	TransportNumber

7. Click OK to exit the Report Parameters dialog box.

8. Place a table onto the report body.

9. Drag the Name and Value fields into two of the cells in the details row of the table.

10. Remove the unoccupied column from the table.

11. Modify the following properties for the text box containing the Value field:

Property	Value
BackgroundColor	=IIF(Fields!Status.Value = "OutOfNorm", "Red","Transparent")
Format	###.00
Size: Width	0.875in

12. Resize the report body so that it is the same size as the table.

13. Select Report | Report Properties from the main menu. The Report Properties dialog box will appear.

14. Check Autorefresh and set the autorefresh rate to 15 (seconds).

15. Click OK to exit the Report Properties dialog box.

16. Select the Preview tab.

17. Select a transport number from the drop-down list and click View Report. (Autorefresh is not supported in the report preview.)

18. Select Save All from the toolbar.

Task Notes   We used autorefresh to meet the business requirements of this report. When the Autorefresh property is set, the report will be automatically rerun on the schedule you specify. Unfortunately, autorefresh is only supported in the Report Manager. You can see autorefresh in action if you deploy this report to the Report Manager after reading Chapter 11.

A Conversion Experience

Reporting Services is not the first report-authoring environment to come along. Hundreds of thousands of reports have been created using other tools. If you have legacy reports and are looking to switch to Reporting Services, these legacy reports will need to be re-created—that is, unless your legacy reports were written in Microsoft Access. If that is the case, you are in luck.

The report-authoring environment in Visual Studio includes an import tool for taking Access reports and making them into Reporting Services reports. Not everything in your Access reports will import directly into Reporting Services. Even so, this import tool will give you a leg up on having to rebuild each entire report from scratch.

We will go through a sample report import here to give you an introduction to the import tool. You can consult the Reporting Services Books Online for more information on exactly which features the Access report import will and won't import.

The Paid Invoices Report

Features Highlighted

▶   Importing an Access report

Business Need   The Galactic Delivery Services accounting department has an Access report that lists paid invoices. The accounting department would like to convert this report to Reporting Services and get rid of the InvoiceInfo.mdb file. The MDB file uses linked tables to pull data from the SQL Server database.

NOTE

The Access import can only be done if you have Microsoft Access installed on the PC where you are running Reporting Services.

Task Overview

1.   Import the Access Report and Change the Data Source

Paid Invoices Report, Task 1: Import the Access Report and Change the Data Source

1.   If you have not already done so, download the InvoiceInfo.mdb file from the website for this book.

2.   Create a System ODBC data source called Galactic that points to the Galactic database. Use "GalacticReporting" for the SQL login and "gds" for the password. This ODBC data source is used by the linked tables in InvoiceInfo.mdb to access the Galactic database in SQL Server. This ODBC data source must be in place in order for the conversion to function properly.

CAUTION

This is a Windows ODBC data source, not a Reporting Services data source. Use the ODBC Data Source Administrator under Administrative Tools in the Control Panel to create this data source.

3. Reopen the Chapter08 project if it has been closed.

4. Right-click the Reports folder in the Solution Explorer and select Import Reports | Microsoft Access from the context menu. The Open dialog box will appear.

5. Browse to the InvoiceInfo.mdb file, select it, and click Open.

6. Visual Studio will import any reports it finds in the selected MDB file.

7. When the import is complete, you will have a new report called PaidInvoices.rdl in your Solution Explorer. Double-click this report to open it.

8. Select the Data tab.

9. Click the ... button in the Query Builder toolbar. The Dataset dialog box will appear.

10. Click the ... button next to the Data Source drop-down box. The Data Source dialog box will appear.

11. If you examine the connection string, you will see that the data source is going back to the MDB file to get its data. Because the MDB file was using linked tables and pulling data from the SQL Server database, it makes sense to now go to the SQL Server database directly.

12. Click Cancel to exit the Data Source dialog box.

13. Select "Galactic (shared)" from the Data Source drop-down list.

14. Click OK to exit the Dataset dialog box.

15. Remove the "dbo_" prefix from the table names in the SQL panel.

16. Run the query to verify that it will now work properly with the SQL tables.

17. Clear your query results.

18. Select the Preview tab.

19. Select Save All from the toolbar.

Task Notes   You can see that the column headings from the Access report have been placed in the page header in the Reporting Services report. This looks rather strange, but it is nothing a minute or two of additional formatting couldn't fix. The import does not create a perfect replica of your Access report in Reporting Services. It does, however, save you a lot of time over rebuilding each report from scratch.

What's Next

We have now touched on almost all the report-authoring features for Reporting Services. It is time to move on from report development to report deployment and delivery. We will take a quick look at the various formats available for Reporting Services reports, then move on into the world of the Report Manager.

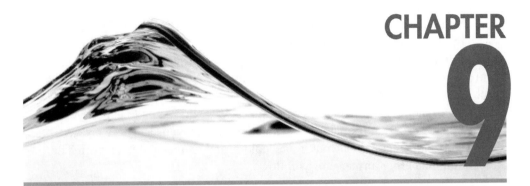

A Leading Exporter: Exporting Reports to Other Rendering Formats

U p to this point, we have been viewing reports in the preview format. The preview format works great during report development for checking out your report layout and interactivity. However, when you want to present your report to users who do not have Visual Studio, you need something other than the preview format to do the job.

In place of the preview format, Reporting Services allows you to export your report to other rendering formats so it can be presented to a user. These *presentation rendering formats* retain the layout, fonts, colors, and graphics of the report. The presentation rendering formats are as follows:

▶   TIFF Image

▶   Adobe PDF

▶   MHTML (web archive)

▶   Excel

▶   Print

▶   HTML

Reporting Services also lets you export your report to two additional formats, which are used primarily for rendering report data into a form that can be used by other computer programs. These *data exchange rendering formats* contain the data portion of the report along with a minimal amount of formatting. Here are the data exchange rendering formats:

▶   Comma-Separated Values (CSV)

▶   XML

Most of these rendering formats can be generated from the Preview tab in Visual Studio using the Export toolbar button. This allows you to render a report to a file or to a printer and manually distribute it to your users. It also allows you to verify what the report will look like when your users choose to receive your report rendered in one of these formats.

In this chapter, we will look at each of these rendering formats, which report features they support, and how they can best be used. To demonstrate each rendering format, we will use a report project that contains a set of reports with many of the layout and interactivity characteristics discussed in the previous chapters. If you wish to "play along at home," you can download the Chapter09 report project from the website for this book and try exporting the report to each rendering format yourself.

A Report in Any Other Format Would Look as Good

If Reporting Services only allowed you to view reports in the preview format when using Visual Studio and in a browser when using the Report Manager, it would be an interesting tool. The fact that reports can be delivered in a number of other presentation formats while maintaining their basic look and feel makes Reporting Services a very powerful tool. Adding the ability to transfer information using a pair of data exchange formats further enhances the flexibility of Reporting Services.

Exporting and Printing a Report

We will look at each of the export formats in detail later in this chapter. First, let's look at how the export process works in Visual Studio. We will try exporting a report and then displaying it with the appropriate viewer. Then, we will print the report from Visual Studio.

Exporting a Report

Follow these steps to export a report.

1. If you have downloaded the Chapter09 project, open this project, double-click the RenderingTest report, and select the Preview tab. If you have not downloaded the Chapter09 project, open your favorite report project from one of the previous chapters, double-click a report, and select the Preview tab. The report will be displayed in the preview format.

2. Expand the Bolimite row and the 2002 column in the matrix.

3. Click the Export button in the toolbar below the Preview tab. You will see a drop-down list showing all the available export formats, as shown in Figure 9-1.

4. Select any of the available formats. (Choose one of the presentation formats to make this a more interesting example.) The Exporting dialog box will appear.

5. After a few moments, the Save As dialog box will appear over the top of the Exporting dialog box. Select the folder where you want the export file to be created. Modify the filename if you desire.

6. The Export dialog box will disappear after the export file is created. The report has now been exported or rendered in the selected format.

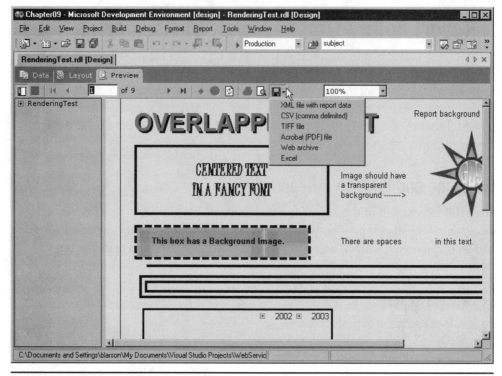

Figure 9-1   *The Export button on the Preview tab*

Viewing the Exported Report

Follow these steps to view the report.

1. To view the export file, open Windows Explorer.
2. Navigate to the folder where the export file was created.
3. Double-click the export file. Windows will open the export file using the appropriate application for viewing this type of file. (We will cover viewer requirements as we discuss each export format later in this chapter.)

Printing a Report

Follow these steps to print the report.

1. Return to the Preview tab in Visual Studio.

2. Click the Print Preview button on the toolbar below the Preview tab. The contents of the Preview tab will be replaced by the print preview, as shown in Figure 9-2.

3. Use the drop-down list in the toolbar below the Preview tab to zoom in or zoom out as needed.

4. Click the Print button just to the left of the Print Preview button. The Print dialog box will appear.

NOTE

You must be in Print Preview mode for the Print button to be active.

5. Select the appropriate printer, set the necessary printer properties, and then click OK. Your report will be printed.

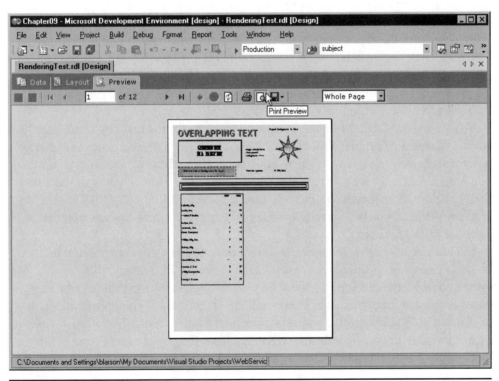

Figure 9-2   *The Print Preview button on the Preview tab*

Presentation Formats

Most of the export or rendering formats provided by Reporting Services are presentation formats. They are intended to reproduce, as faithfully as possible, the format and the interactivity of your report as it appears in the preview format. The degree to which each presentation format can duplicate these things depends, in large part, on the features available in and the limitations of the viewer used by each format. For instance, a TIFF image viewer does not provide any hyperlinks; therefore, the TIFF export does not support the navigation features.

In this section, we will look at the viewer required to display each format. Also, the features that are supported and the features that are not supported by each presentation format are listed. We will also discuss how each presentation format can best be utilized.

We will use the RenderingTest report from the Chapter09 report project to examine some of the features supported by each presentation format. As mentioned earlier, you may download this report project from the website for this book if you wish to perform the exports and make the comparisons yourself. Our standard will be the appearance and behavior of this report in the Preview tab in Visual Studio. The top of the first page of the RenderingTest report in the Preview tab is shown in Figure 9-3. As we look at each presentation format, we will compare it to the way the report looks in this figure.

You should note that I used a font called Juice ITC for the text box containing the words, "Centered Text in a Fancy Font." This was done to demonstrate the behavior of a font that may not be available on other computers. However, because of this, you may not actually see a "fancy font" in this text box. Instead, you will see a font that Visual Studio chooses to substitute for the requested font, which is unavailable. If this is the case, you will have to trust the text and the figures to show you the behavior of this text box.

It should be noted that the preview format does not pay strict attention to the physical page size specified for the report. The preview format will allow a page to grow to be wider than a report page. The preview format does create page breaks based on the length of the page. However, it does this only as an approximation. It does not strictly adhere to the page size specified for the report. Therefore, the page breaks found in the preview format will differ from the page breaks found in formats that exactly follow the size properties of the report.

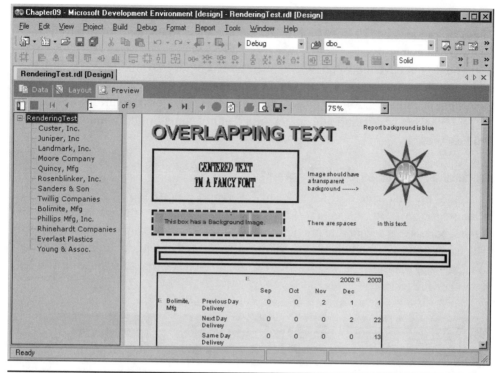

Figure 9-3   *The RenderingTest report in the Preview tab*

TIFF Image Presentation Format

TIFF is an acronym for Tagged Image File Format. It is a file standard for storing images on personal computers, similar to the BMP and PCX formats. Unlike these formats, a TIFF file can store a number of images as multiple pages of a single document. This feature makes TIFF a popular format for storing fax documents.

When a report is rendered to a TIFF file, each page of the report is converted to a bitmap image. When we view the image, we see letters and numbers. However, the TIFF file itself contains only a series of dots. Because the entire report is stored as a bitmap image, TIFF files tend to be rather large.

Viewing TIFF Documents

On most Windows systems, TIFF files can be viewed using the Windows Picture and Fax Viewer. The Windows Picture and Fax Viewer has features for moving between pages, printing, and zooming in and out. This viewer also allows you to add annotations, including highlighting, drawing, text, and "sticky notes," as shown in Figure 9-4. These annotations can be very helpful if reports are distributed electronically while they are being analyzed.

If you do not have the Windows Picture and Fax Viewer available, TIFF viewers are available for just about any personal computer platform. In many cases, a TIFF viewer can be obtained for a minimal charge as shareware or freeware. Note that not all TIFF viewers will include the annotation features found in the Windows Picture and Fax Viewer.

Features Supported by the TIFF Format

The top of the first page of the RenderingTest report exported to a TIFF file is shown in Figure 9-5. As you can see, the TIFF image provides a very faithful representation of the report as it is seen in the preview layout. It will include colors, images (including background images), and charts. It will preserve strings of text, including embedded new lines and multiple spaces in a row. (You will soon see that this causes a problem in another file format.)

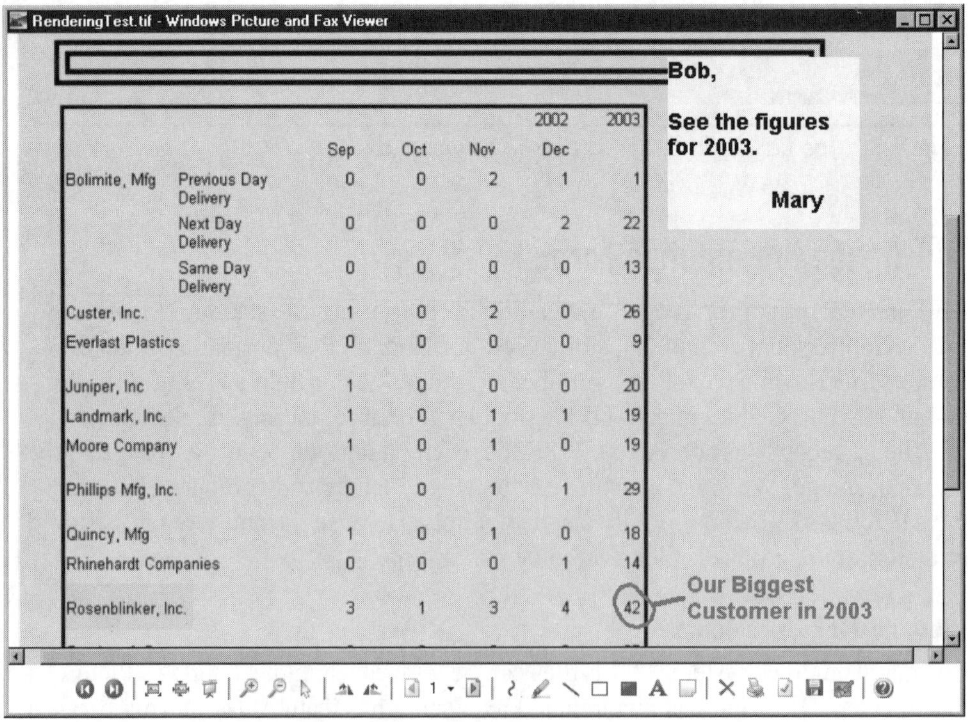

Figure 9-4   *The Windows Picture and Fax Viewer with an annotated report*

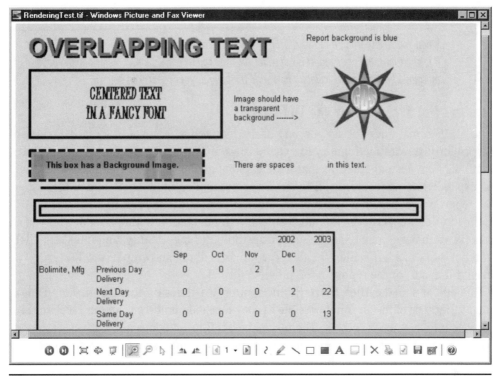

Figure 9-5   *The RenderingTest report exported to a TIFF file*

The TIFF format will preserve the font for all text rendered in the report. This is true even if a font used in the report is not present on the computer being used to view the report. This is the only presentation format that possesses this characteristic. Also, the TIFF format will preserve the exact location of each report item relative to other report items. This is true even if report items overlap one another.

Physical pages are supported by the TIFF format. This means that when a report is exported to a TIFF file, the renderer pays attention to the physical page size specified for the report and does not let a page grow beyond that size. When a report page is taller or wider than the physical page size, the TIFF renderer will split it into multiple pages. Because physical pages are supported, the TIFF format can be printed with the assurance that the printed report will match the report on the screen in both layout and pagination.

NOTE

When you're exporting a report to TIFF or any of the other formats that support physical pages, it is important that your report is not wider than the report page. Be sure to include the page margins when you are calculating how wide the body of your report can be.

Features Not Supported by the TIFF Format

The TIFF format does not support any of the interactive features of a report. You can not use drill-down functionality to expand rows in a table or rows and columns in a matrix. The rows and columns that were expanded when the report was exported will be expanded in the resulting TIFF file. The rows and columns that were hidden when the report was exported will not be included in the resulting TIFF file.

In addition, the TIFF format does not support navigation within a report, between reports, or to a web page. Bookmarks, drill-through functionality, and links to a URL will not work in a TIFF file. The document map will not show up in the TIFF file, even if it is part of the report in the preview format.

Finally, as stated earlier, the TIFF file is simply a series of dots that make up an image. Because of this, it is not possible to copy text and numbers from the TIFF image to paste into another document. Therefore, the TIFF format does not work as a method for passing information to someone who wants to cut and paste it into a spreadsheet and do their own ad hoc analysis.

When to Use the TIFF Format

TIFF format files work well for smaller reports that do not utilize interactive functions. The ability of some TIFF viewers to provide annotation features makes this a good choice for sharing analysis among a number of people. The TIFF format also works well for situations where reports will be viewed both onscreen and in print. However, users cannot copy numbers from the report to paste into another application to perform their own analysis.

Because the entire content of the report is stored as a bitmap image, TIFF files become very large very fast. A report exported to a TIFF file is as much as ten times as large as other export formats. Use the TIFF export with care so as not to create monstrous export files that are unwieldy to deliver and use.

Adobe PDF Presentation Format

PDF is an acronym for Portable Document Format. This document format was developed by Adobe Systems, Inc. It was designed so that a document could be moved from one computer to another—even between computers with different operating systems—and appear exactly the same on both computers.

When a report is rendered to a PDF file, its formatting is stored using a language similar to the PostScript description language. Images that appear in the report are stored right within the PDF file. Text entries in the report remain text; they are not converted to images as they are with the TIFF format.

Viewing PDF Documents

PDF files are viewed using the Adobe Acrobat Reader. The Acrobat Reader is available as a free download from the Adobe website at www.adobe.com. Versions of the Acrobat Reader are available for Windows, Mac, Solaris Sun, Linux, several flavors of UNIX, and even for handheld devices. The Acrobat Reader has features for moving between pages, printing, and zooming in and out.

Features Supported by the PDF Format

The top of the first page of the RenderingTest report exported to a PDF file is shown in Figure 9-6. As with the TIFF format, the PDF format provides a very faithful representation of the report as it is seen in the preview layout. It will include colors, images (including background images), and charts. It also will preserve strings of text, including embedded new lines and multiple spaces in a row. PDF also allows report items to overlap.

Just as in the TIFF format, physical pages are supported by the PDF format. When a report page is taller or wider than the physical page size, the PDF renderer will split it into multiple pages. Because physical pages are supported, the PDF format can be printed with the assurance that the printed report will match the report on the screen in both layout and pagination.

The PDF format supports some of the navigation features available in Reporting Services reports. The report's document map entries become PDF bookmarks. In addition, links to URLs are supported. Also, because the PDF format does retain text and numbers as text and numbers, you can copy these items. Therefore, users can copy and paste information from the PDF format into a spreadsheet and do their own ad hoc analysis.

Features Not Supported by the PDF Format

The PDF format will preserve the font for almost all text rendered in the report. The exception to this is the situation where a font used in the report is not present on the computer being used to view the report. As you can see in Figure 9-6, the text "CENTERED TEXT IN A FANCY FONT" did not appear in a fancy font when viewed on a computer that did not have that font loaded.

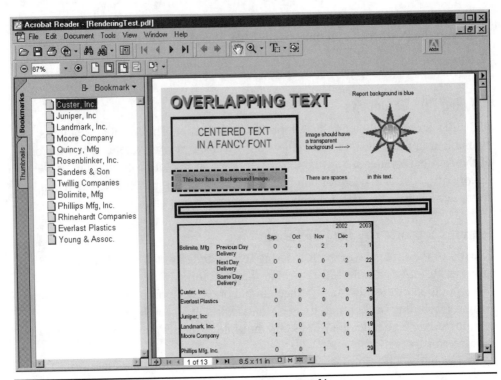

Figure 9-6   *The RenderingTest report exported to a PDF file*

Although the PDF format supports the document map and a link to a URL, it does not support any of the other interactive features of a report. You cannot use drill-down functionality to expand rows in a table or rows and columns in a matrix. The rows and columns that were expanded when the report was exported will be expanded in the resulting PDF file. The rows and columns that were hidden when the report was exported will not be included in the resulting PDF file. The PDF format does not support Reporting Services bookmarks (not to be confused with the PDF bookmarks that act as a document map) and drill-through functionality.

When to Use the PDF Format

The PDF format works well for reports that need to be distributed across a variety of platforms where maintaining the report layout and pagination are required. If an investment is made in Adobe Standard or Adobe Professional, the PDF format can be used when annotation features are required. The PDF format works well for both large and small reports and in situations where reports are viewed both on the screen and in print. The PDF format does allow users to copy numbers from a report and paste them into another application to do ad hoc analysis.

The PDF format does not work for reports where drill-down or drill-through functionality is required. It is also not appropriate for situations where one or more fonts that may not be available on the end user's computer are used in the report and these fonts must be preserved in the report output.

Web Archive Presentation Format

The web archive is a special form of web page. In addition to the HTML formatting code, the web archive file contains all the supporting files required by the page. The supporting files are the images referenced by the HTML. As the name implies, the web archive can be used to gather all the necessary parts of a web page in one place so that it can be easily moved to a different location and archived. This also makes it an excellent candidate for distributing reports in an HTML format.

The extension on web archive files is .mhtml.

Viewing Web Archive Documents

Because web archive documents are actually self-contained web pages, they are viewed using a web browser. Having a web browser available on a computer is usually not an issue these days. Therefore, web archive documents can be distributed across multiple computer platforms. Web archive documents can also be displayed in many e-mail programs that support HTML e-mail messages.

Features Supported by the Web Archive Format

The top of the first page of the RenderingTest report exported to a web archive file is shown in Figure 9-7. The web archive format provides a somewhat faithful representation of the report as it is seen in the preview layout. It will include colors, images (including background images), and charts.

The web archive format retains only one of the navigation features in Reporting Services reports. It allows for links to URLs to be embedded in the report. Also, because the web archive format retains text and numbers as text and numbers, you can copy these items. Therefore, users can copy and paste information from the web format into a spreadsheet and do their own ad hoc analysis.

Features Not Supported by the Web Archive Format

In the web archive format, physical pages are not supported. Instead, the report is presented as one continuous web page. Horizontal lines are added to the report to

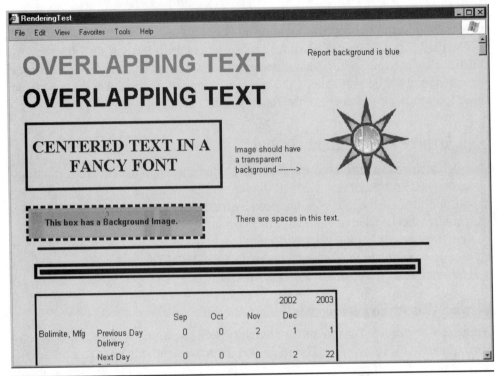

Figure 9-7   *The RenderingTest report exported to a web archive file*

indicate where the page breaks would occur in other formats. Because of this, the web archive format does not work well when printing a report.

You can see in Figure 9-7, the web archive format does not preserve strings of text, including embedded new lines and multiple spaces in a row. (The text "CENTERED TEXT IN A FANCY FONT" should have a new line after the word "TEXT." The sentence "There are spaces in this text," located below the GDS graphic, should have a gap between the word "spaces" and the word "in.") This is a characteristic of HTML rendering that compresses whitespace (such as multiple spaces) and ignores new lines. Another HTML limitation is the inability to support overlapping report items as shown by the top line of the report.

Like the PDF format, the web archive format will preserve the font for almost all text rendered in the report. The exception, again, is the situation where a font used in the report is not present on the computer being used to view the report. In Figure 9-7, the text "CENTERED TEXT IN A FANCY FONT" is no longer in a fancy font.

Although the web archive format supports a link to a URL, it does not support any of the other interactive features of a report. You cannot use drill-down functionality to expand rows in a table or rows and columns in a matrix. The rows and columns that were expanded when the report was exported will be expanded in the resulting web archive file. The rows and columns that were hidden when the report was exported will not be included in the resulting web archive file. The web archive format does not support document maps, bookmarks, or drill-through functionality.

When to Use the Web Archive Format

The web archive format works well for reports that need to be distributed across a variety of platforms, where pagination and printing are not required. It also works well for situations where the content of the report is to be embedded in an e-mail message. The web archive format works well for both large and small reports. The web archive format does allow users to copy numbers from a report and paste them into another application for ad hoc analysis.

The web archive format does not work well in situations where the report's exact formatting must be preserved. Its limitations also make it a bad choice in situations where pagination and printing capabilities are needed. Finally, it will not work when drill-down, drill-through, or other navigation features are required.

Excel Presentation Format

Excel, of course, is Microsoft's spreadsheet application. The Excel presentation format is simply an Excel workbook file. The workbooks created from Reporting Services reports have multiple tabs or spreadsheets to represent the document map and the logical pages in the report.

Viewing Excel Documents

Excel documents are, of course, viewed using Microsoft Excel. Reporting Services requires Excel 2002 (version 10) or Excel 2003 (version 11) to display reports exported in the Excel format. Excel 2002 is part of Microsoft Office XP, whereas Excel 2003 is part of Microsoft Office 2003. Earlier versions of Excel will not work properly with Excel export files.

Features Supported by the Excel Format

The document map portion of the RenderingTest report as it appears in the Excel file is shown in Figure 9-8. The top of the first page of the RenderingTest report as it appears in the Excel file is shown in Figure 9-9. The Excel format provides as faithful a

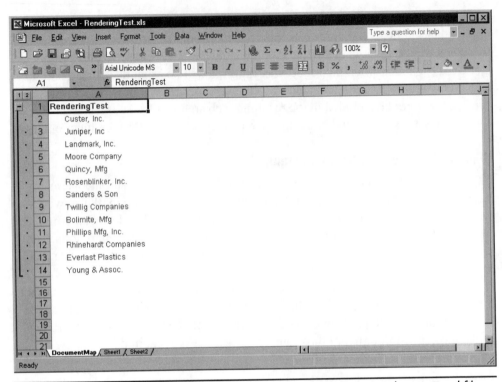

representation of the report as it can within the confines of spreadsheet rows and columns. It will include colors, foreground images, and charts. It should be noted that, if your report contains any charts, they are exported as images by the Excel export. They are not exported as chart objects, so they cannot be modified in Excel.

The Excel format does not create page breaks based on the page size of the report. It does split the report up into separate tabs at locations where your report logic says there should be page breaks. For example, if a grouping on your report has the PageBreakAtStart property set to True, each new instance of this grouping would begin on a new tab in Excel.

The Excel format does include several of the navigation features in Reporting Services reports. It supports the document map as well as bookmarks. It also allows for links to URLs to be embedded in the report. The Excel format does preserve strings of text, including embedded new lines and multiple spaces in a row.

The Excel format is a series of spreadsheets, so naturally it allows for ad hoc analysis to be done on its contents. The contents of most cells are represented as text

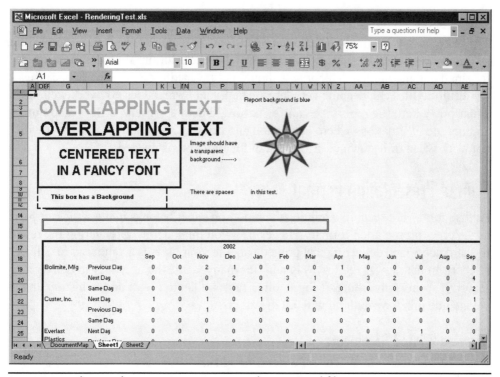

Figure 9-9   *The RenderingTest report exported to an Excel file*

or numeric constants. However, in some cases, the cell may contain a formula. This will result if the value of one report item is a calculation utilizing the value of another report item.

Features Not Supported by the Excel Format

In the Excel format, physical pages are not supported. Only logical page breaks are supported, as mentioned previously. Because of this, the Excel format does not work well when printing a report. As with several of the previous formats, the Excel format will preserve the font, except when a font used in the report is not present on the computer being used to view the report. Even though the Excel format supports foreground images, it does not support background images.

Although the Excel format supports several navigation features, it does not support drill-down functionality. The rows and columns in a table or matrix are completely expanded in the Excel format so that all the rows and columns are included. The Excel format does not support drill-through functionality.

When to Use the Excel Format

The Excel format works well for situations when the end user wants to perform some ad hoc analysis after they receive the report. The Excel format should only be used for small and medium-size reports. It should not be used for large reports because the resulting files can become very large. The Excel format does not work well in situations where the report's exact formatting must be preserved. It is also not appropriate in situations where pagination and printing are required. Finally, it will not work when drill-down or drill-through functionality is needed.

Printed Presentation Format

At first, it may not seem like printing the report on paper belongs in the same category as the other presentation formats. However, if you think about it, rendering the report to "hard copy" and delivering that printed paper to your users is a valid way to deliver a report. In fact, it was the first way and, for many years, the only way to deliver a report. It seems only fitting, if for no other reason than to give a nod to history, that we include this format along with all the others.

Viewing Printed Documents

Printed documents are viewed on paper. Enough said.

Features Supported by the Printed Format

The printed format faithfully captures all the report formatting, along with both physical and logical page breaks.

Features Not Supported by the Printed Format

The only navigation supported by the printed format requires a thumb and forefinger.

When to Use the Printed Format

The printed format should only be used when your end user requires information to be on paper and is not interested in any of the navigation features or ad hoc analysis made available by the other formats.

HTML Presentation Format

HTML is not listed in the export drop-down list in Visual Studio. It is a choice when you are exporting a report from the Report Manager. It is, in fact, the native mode for report viewing in the Report Manager. (We will begin looking at reports in the Report Manager in Chapter 10.)

The HTML format is very similar to the web archive format in the way it handles most formatting. This is not too surprising because both use HTML as their document formatting language. Whereas all the other formats are meant to provide a standalone representation of the report, the HTML format uses the report viewer and the Reporting Services web service to present a connected representation of the report. This connection to Reporting Services allows the HTML format to implement all the navigational features.

Viewing HTML Documents

The HTML format is, of course, viewed using a browser. In order to use features such as document maps, drill-down, and bookmarks, you must have Microsoft Internet Explorer 6.0 with Service Pack 1 or Microsoft Internet Explorer 5.5 with Service Pack 2. In either case, scripting must be enabled in the browser. Drill-through functionality requires Microsoft Internet Explorer 5.01 or above with Service Pack 2 and does not require scripting.

Features Supported by the HTML Format

The HTML format supports almost all the formatting and navigational features of Reporting Services reports. It supports logical page breaks. It also supports physical page breaks, after a fashion. The first page of the RenderingTest report in HTML format is shown in Figure 9-10.

The HTML format does not pay attention to page width. A page can be as wide as it wants. However, the HTML format does create page breaks when a page gets too long. These page breaks do not correspond exactly with the physical size of the page, but rather are only an approximation. If you print the HTML document, the page breaks created by the HTML format will not correspond to the page breaks required by the printer.

Features Not Supported by the HTML Format

The HTML format does not support overlapping report items. It has the same shortcoming with embedded whitespace and new lines as described in the web archive section. Given these exceptions and the quirks with pagination described previously, the HTML format supports all other Reporting Services report features.

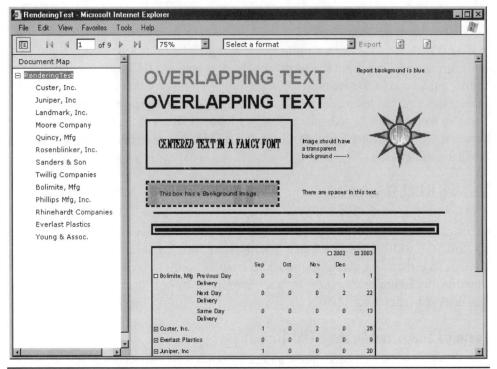

Figure 9-10 *The RenderingTest report exported to an HTML file*

When to Use the HTML Format

The HTML format works well when your user can view the report while connected to the report server. It is the essential format for the occasions when all the navigation features of Reporting Services are required from a single format.

The HTML format does not work well when the report needs to be printed.

Data Exchange Formats

The two remaining export or rendering formats provided by Reporting Services are data exchange formats. They are intended to take the data in a report and put it into a format that can be used by another computer program. In this section, we will look at the basic structure of each of these formats. We will also discuss the customization that can be done with each.

We will continue to use the RenderingTest report from the Chapter09 report project to examine the data that is output by each format.

Comma-Separated Values (CSV) Data Exchange Format

The Comma-Separated Values (CSV) format has been around for a number of years. The CSV format is used to represent tabular data. Each line in the file represents one row in the table. Each value between two commas represents a column in the table. If a column value contains a comma (for example, "Bolimite, Mfg"), the value is enclosed in quotation marks.

CSV exports include the data contained within tables, matrixes, and lists in your report. All the data from the table, matrix, or list is included in the CSV export, even if a column or a row is hidden. CSV exports do not contain values from charts or text boxes that are not within a table, matrix, or list.

Reports that are to be exported using the CSV format should be kept very simple. Only one table, matrix, or list should be placed on the report. When reports with more than one table, matrix, or list are exported using the CSV format, the resulting file can be very complex and confusing.

If you open the CSV file that results from the RenderingTest report in Notepad, it will appear as follows. (A CSV file will open in Excel by default.) This represents the values from the matrix near the top of the report.

```
"Bolimite, Mfg",Previous Day Delivery,0,0,2,1,…
"Bolimite, Mfg",Next Day Delivery,0,0,0,2,…
"Bolimite, Mfg",Same Day Delivery,0,0,0,0,…
"Custer, Inc.",Next Day Delivery,1,0,1,0,…
"Custer, Inc.",Previous Day Delivery,0,0,1,0,…
"Custer, Inc.",Same Day Delivery,0,0,0,0,…
```

XML Data Exchange Format

In Chapter 7, we talked about XML and the fact that reports are stored in an XML format called Report Definition Language (RDL). Here, we are looking at XML as a means of exchanging data between programs. In both cases, the XML files are simply text files with information organized between XML tags.

By default, XML exports include the data contained within tables, matrixes, lists, and charts in your report. All the data from the table, matrix, list, or chart is included in the XML export, even if a column or a row is hidden. XML exports do not contain values from text boxes that are not with a table, matrix, or list.

Because each item in the XML export is labeled with an XML tag, reports that are to be exported using the XML format can be more complex than those exported using the CSV format. Due to this fact, reports that are to be exported using the XML format may have more than one table, matrix, list, or chart.

The following is a section of the XML file that results from the RenderingTest report:

```
<Report xmlns="RenderingTest" …>
<matrix1>
   <matrix1_CustomerName_Collection>
     <matrix1_CustomerName CustomerName="Bolimite, Mfg">
       <matrix1_RowGroup2_Collection>
         <matrix1_RowGroup2 textbox6="Previous Day Delivery">
                <matrix1_Year_Collection>
            <matrix1_Year Year="2002">
                     <matrix1_ColumnGroup2_Collection>
                       <matrix1_ColumnGroup2 textbox5="Sep">
            <Cell DeliveryNumber="0" />
          </matrix1_ColumnGroup2>
                       <matrix1_ColumnGroup2 textbox5="Oct">
            <Cell DeliveryNumber="0" />
          </matrix1_ColumnGroup2>
```

You can quickly see how the XML structure follows the report layout. The Report tag provides information about the report as a whole. After that tag is a series of tags that contain the data in the matrix near the top of the report. Again, note that, by default, the text boxes at the top of the report are not included in the XML export.

Customizing the XML Data Exchange Format

You can customize the XML Export to fit your needs. Let's change the XML export to include the contents of the text box that reads "CENTERED TEXT IN A FANCY FONT." We will also change the "matrix1_RowGroup2_Collection" tag to "DeliveryTypes" and the "matrix1_RowGroup2" tag to "DeliveryType." Finally, we will remove the DeliveryNumber altogether.

If you have downloaded the Chapter09 project, open the project and try this procedure:

1. Open the RenderingTest report.

2. Select the Layout tab.

3. Right-click the text box containing "CENTERED TEXT IN A FANCY FONT." Select Properties from the context menu. The Textbox Properties dialog box will appear.

4. Click the Advanced button. The Advanced Textbox Properties dialog box will replace the Textbox Properties dialog box.

5. Select the Font tab.

6. Look in the Family drop-down list for "Juice ITC." If it is not there, select a font that is present in the list. (You will not be able to save the changes made in this dialog box unless there is a valid font selected.)

7. Select the Data Output tab.

8. Type **FancyFont** for ElementName. (This will specify the name to use for this element.)

9. Select Yes for Output. (This will force this item to be output in the XML.)

10. Select Element for Render As. (This will cause the item to be output as an element rather than as an attribute.)

11. Click OK to exit the Advanced Textbox Properties dialog box.

12. Select "matrix1" from the drop-down list at the top of the Properties window.

13. Click the Property Pages button in the Properties window to display the Matrix Properties dialog box.

14. Select the Groups tab.

15. Select "matrix1_RowGroup2" and click Edit next to the Rows area. The Grouping and Sorting Properties dialog box will appear.

16. Select the Data Output tab.

17. Enter **DeliveryType** for Element name.

18. Enter **DeliveryTypes** for Collection.

19. Click OK to exit the Grouping and Sorting Properties dialog box.

20. Click OK to exit the Matrix Properties dialog box.

21. Right-click the text box in the lower-right corner of the matrix. Select Properties from the context menu. The Textbox Properties dialog box will appear.

22. Click the Advanced button. The Advanced Textbox Properties dialog box will replace the Textbox Properties dialog box.

23. Select the Data Output tab.

24. Select No for Output. (This will cause this item not to be output in the XML.)

25. Click OK to exit the Advanced Textbox Properties dialog box.

26. Click the Preview tab.

27. Select XML File with Report Data from the Export drop-down list.

28. Select a location to store this export, enter a filename, then click Save.

29. Use the Windows Explorer to find the file you just created and then double-click the file to open it.

The first few lines of the XML file will appear similar to the following:

```
<Report xmlns="RenderingTest"... >
  <FancyFont>CENTERED TEXT IN A FANCY FONT</FancyFont>
  <matrix1>
    <matrix1_CustomerName_Collection>
      <matrix1_CustomerName CustomerName="Bolimite, Mfg">
        <DeliveryTypes>
          <DeliveryType textbox6="Previous Day Delivery">
          <matrix1_Year_Collection>
            <matrix1_Year Year="2002">
              <matrix1_ColumnGroup2_Collection>
                <matrix1_ColumnGroup2 textbox5="Sep">
                  <Cell />
                </matrix1_ColumnGroup2>
                <matrix1_ColumnGroup2 textbox5="Oct">
                  <Cell />
                </matrix1_ColumnGroup2>
```

The values on the Data Output tab for each item in your report can be used in this way to completely customize the XML output generated by the report.

Call the Manager

It is now time to move on to the Report Manager. In the next chapters in this book, we will look at ways to put your reports into the Report Manager and ways to administer those reports once they are there.

Report Serving

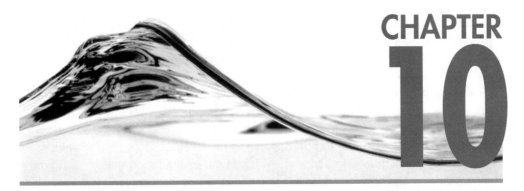

How Did We Ever Manage Without You? The Report Manager

I n Part II of this book, we focused on report authoring. You have learned fancy techniques for creating whiz-bang reports. However, the fact is, even the whiz-bangiest of reports are not much good if you cannot easily share them with end users.

In this chapter, you will learn how to do just that. We will move from authoring to managing reports and delivering them to the end users. This is done through the Report Server and its Report Manager web interface.

We took a brief look at the Report Server and the Report Manager in Chapter 1. Now, we will take a more detailed look. Much of our examination will focus on the Report Manager and how it is used to access and control the Report Server.

The first step is moving your report definitions and supporting files from the development environment to the Report Catalog. Recall that the Report Catalog is the SQL Server 2000 database where the Report Server keeps all its information. This information includes the definitions of the reports it is managing. We will look at several ways to accomplish this report deployment.

Once your reports are available through the Report Server, you'll need to control how they are executed. We will use the Report Server's security features to control who can access each report, and we will use the caching and report history to control how a report is executed each time it is requested by a user. Finally, we will control all these Report Server features using the Report Manager.

In short, in this chapter we will take your reports from a single-user development environment to a secure, managed environment where they can be executed by a number of users.

Folders

Before you deploy reports to the Report Server, you need to have an understanding of the way the Report Server organizes reports in the Report Catalog. In the Report Catalog, reports are arranged into a system of folders similar to the Windows or Mac file system. Folders can contain reports, supporting files such as external images and shared data sources, and even other folders. The easiest way to create, view, and maintain these folders is through the Report Manager.

Although the Report Catalog folders look and act like Windows file system folders, they are not actually file system folders. You will not find them anywhere in the file system on the computer running the Report Server. Report Catalog folders are screen representations of records in the Report Catalog database.

Each folder is assigned a name. Folder names can include just about any character, including spaces. However, folder names cannot include any of the following characters:

```
; ? : @ & , \ * < > | " /
```

In addition to a name, folders can also be assigned a description. The description can contain a long explanation of the contents of the folder. The description can help users determine what type of reports are in a folder without having to actually open that folder and look at the contents. Both the folder name and the description can be searched by a user to help them find a report.

The Report Manager

The Report Manager web application provides a very straightforward method for creating and navigating folders in the Report Catalog. When you initially install Reporting Services, the Home folder is created by default. This is the only folder that exists at first.

Use the following URL to access the Report Manager site on the computer running Reporting Services:

```
http://ComputerName/reports
```

In this case, ComputerName is the name of the computer where Reporting Services was installed. If you are using a secure connection to access the Report Manager site, replace "http:" with "https:". If you are on the same computer where Reporting Services is running, you can use the following URL:

```
http://localhost/reports
```

You can also access the Report Manager by clicking the Start button then selecting All Programs | Microsoft SQL Server | Reporting Services | Report Manager.

No matter how you get there, when you initially access the Report Manager, it will appear similar to Figure 10-1.

You will notice that the URL shown in Figure 10-1 is a bit different from the URLs given previously. This is due to the fact that the Report Manager web application redirects you to the Pages/Folder.aspx web page. The Folder.aspx page is used to display folder contents.

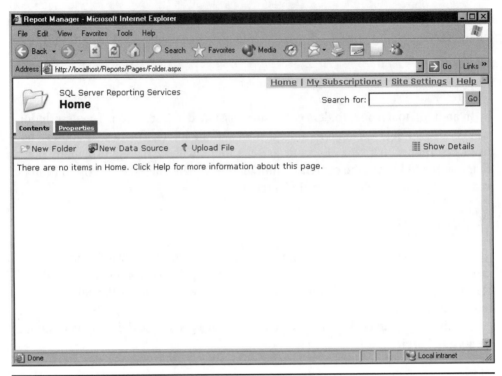

Figure 10-1   *The Report Manager with no folders defined*

NOTE

Figure 10-1 shows the Report Manager as it appears for a user with content manager privileges. If you do not see the New Folder, New Data Source, and Upload File buttons in the toolbar on the Contents tab, you do not have content manager privileges and will not be able to complete the exercises in this section of the chapter. If possible, log out and log in with a Windows login that has local administration privileges on the computer running the Report Server.

In order to use the Report Manager, you must be using Microsoft Internet Explorer 6.0 with Service Pack 1 (SP1) or Internet Explorer 5.5 with Service Pack 2 (SP2). In either case, you must have scripting enabled.

Adding a New Folder using the Report Manager

Let's create a new folder into which we will deploy some of the Galactic Delivery Services reports from the previous chapters. Here are the steps to follow:

NOTE

Examples later in this chapter showing report deployment assume that the Galactic Delivery Services folder is created in the Home folder. If you already have other folders created in your Report Catalog, be sure you are in the Home folder when you complete the following steps.

1. Click the New Folder button in the toolbar on the Content tab. The New Folder page will appear, as shown in Figure 10-2.

2. Type **Galactic Delivery Services** for Name and **Reports created while learning to use Reporting Services** for Description.

3. Click OK to create the new folder and return to the Home folder.

You will see an entry for your new folder with its name and description on the Contents tab of the Home folder. The text "!NEW" next to the folder name will remain there for 48 hours. This helps to notify users of new content added to your Report Server.

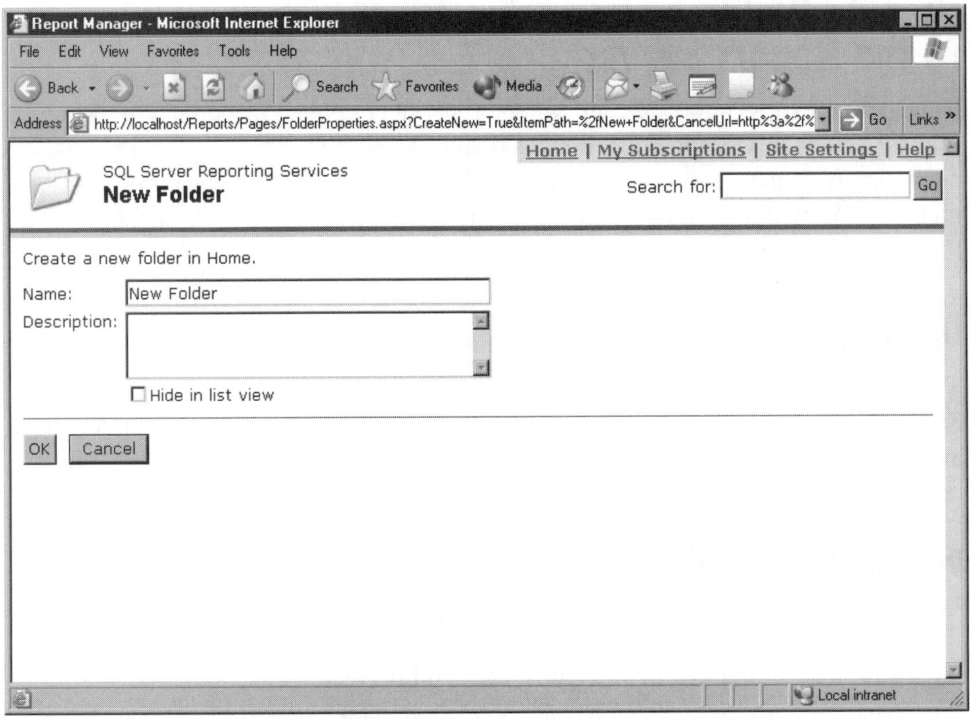

Figure 10-2 *The New Folder page*

If you were observant, you will have noticed one item on the New Folder page we did not use. (If you missed it, look back at Figure 10-2). This is the Hide in List View check box. When the Hide in List View check box is checked, the new folder will not appear on the Contents tab. This is useful when you want to make the reports in a folder available through a custom interface, but not available through the Report Manager. We will discuss this in detail in Chapter 12.

To view the contents of the new folder, click the folder name. The name of the current folder appears in bold text near the top of the page. Immediately above the name of the current folder is the path from the Home folder to the current folder. Because the Galactic Delivery Services folder is in the Home folder, the path only contains "Home >". You can return to any folder in the current path by clicking that folder name in the path shown near the top of the page. You can return to the Home folder by clicking Home at the beginning of the current path or by clicking Home in the blue rectangle at the top of the page.

Moving Reports and Supporting Files to the Report Server

Now that you know how to create folders, it is time to put some content in those folders. You do this by moving reports and their supporting files from the development environment to the Report Server. This can be done using a number of different methods. We will look at two of those methods now: using Visual Studio and using the Report Manager.

Deploying Reports Using Visual Studio

The most common method of moving reports to the Report Server is by using Visual Studio. Once you are satisfied with a report you have developed, you can make it available to your users without leaving the development environment. This ability to create, preview, and deploy a report from a single authoring tool is a real plus.

Deploying Reports in the Chapter09 Project Using Visual Studio

Let's try deploying the report project from Chapter 9. To do so, follow these steps:

1. Start Visual Studio and open the Chapter09 project.
2. Select Project | Chapter09 Properties from the main menu. The Chapter09 Property Pages dialog box will appear.

3. Type **Galactic Delivery Services/Chapter 09** for TargetFolder. This is the folder into which the report will be deployed.

4. Type **http://ComputerName/ReportServer** for TargetServerURL, where ComputerName is the name of the computer where the Report Server is installed. You should replace "http:" with "https:" if you are using a secure connection. You can use "localhost" in place of the computer name if the Report Server is installed on the same computer you are using to run Visual Studio (see Figure 10-3).

5. Click OK to exit the Chapter09 Property Pages dialog box.

6. Right-click the Chapter09 project entry in the Solution Explorer and select Deploy from the context menu.

7. Visual Studio will build all the reports in the project and then deploy all the reports, along with their supporting files, to the Report Server. (During the build process, Visual Studio checks the report for any errors that would prevent it from executing properly on the Report Server.) The results of the build and deploy will be shown in the Visual Studio Output window.

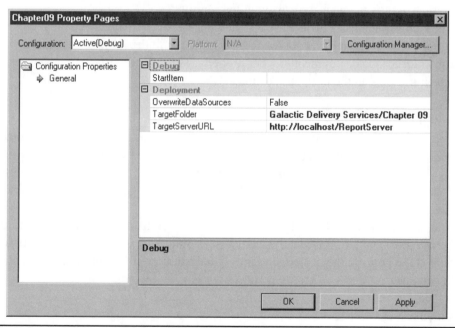

Figure 10-3   *The Chapter09 Property Pages dialog box*

8. Open the Report Manager in your browser. Click the Galactic Delivery Services folder to view its content. You will see that Visual Studio created a new folder in the Galactic Delivery Services folder called Chapter 09.

9. Click the Chapter 09 folder to view its content. All the items in the Chapter09 project—three reports and a shared data source—were deployed.

10. Click the RenderingTest report. You will see the HTML version of the RenderingTest report.

NOTE

You can also deploy the contents of a project by selecting Build | Deploy Solution or Build | Deploy {Project Name} from the main menu.

Working Through the Web Service

When Visual Studio deploys reports, it works through the Reporting Services web service. The Report Manager web application provides a human interface to Reporting Services. The web service provides an interface for other programs to communicate with Reporting Services. Because Visual Studio falls into the latter of these two categories, it uses the web service to deploy reports.

The web service has a different URL than the Report Manager. You must enter the URL for the web service and not the Report Manager in the Properties Pages dialog box in order for the deployment to work properly. The default URL for the web service is shown in step 4 in the previous section.

Creating Folders While Deploying

In steps 2 through 5, you entered information into properties of the Chapter09 project. These values tell Visual Studio where to put the reports and supporting items when the project is deployed. In this case, you instructed Visual Studio to put our reports and shared data source in the Chapter 09 folder within the Galactic Delivery Services folder.

You created the Galactic Delivery Services folder in the previous section. You did not create the Chapter 09 folder. Instead, Visual Studio created that folder for us as it deployed the items in the project. In fact, Visual Studio will create folders for any path you specify.

Deploying a Single Report

In step 6, you used the project's context menu to deploy all the items in the project. Alternatively, you could have right-clicked a report and selected Deploy from the report's context menu. However, this would have deployed only this report, not the entire project.

On some occasions, you will want to deploy a single report rather than the entire project. At times, one report will be completed and ready for deployment while the other reports in the project are still under construction. At other times, one report will be revised after the entire project has already been deployed. In these situations, it is only necessary to redeploy the single revised report.

Deploying Shared Data Sources

Even when a single report is deployed, any shared data sources used by that report are automatically deployed along with it. This only makes sense. A report that requires shared data sources will not do much if those shared data sources are not present.

If you look back at Figure 10-3, you will notice an OverwriteDataSources item in the dialog box. This controls whether a shared data source that has been deployed to the Report Server is overwritten by subsequent deployments. In most cases, shared data sources do not change, so they do not need to be overwritten. For this reason, OverwriteDataSources is set to False, meaning "Do not overwrite existing data sources."

Aside from saving unnecessary effort, not overwriting data sources also helps out in another way. Consider the environment shown in Figure 10-4. In this environment, reports are developed in Visual Studio using a shared data source that points to a development database server. Once the first version of the report is completed, it is deployed to a production Report Server, as shown in Figure 10-5. As soon as the deployment is complete, the shared data source on the production Report Server needs to be changed to point to the production database server. This is shown in Figure 10-6.

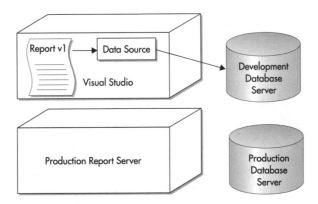

Figure 10-4   *A report and shared data source ready to deploy*

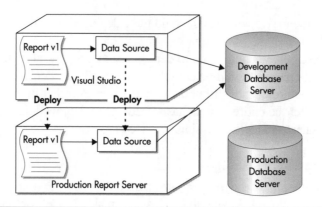

Figure 10-5 *Deploying the report and shared data source*

Now, as time has passed, a new version of the report (version 2) is created in the development environment. This time, when version 2 of the report is deployed to the production Report Server, the shared data source already exists there. If OverwriteDataSources is set to True, the data source from the development environment would overwrite the data source in the production environment, and we would be back to the situation in Figure 10-5. With this setting, we would have to redirect the shared data source each time a report is deployed.

To avoid this, OverwriteDataSources is set to False. Now when version 2 of the report (and subsequent versions) is deployed to the production Report Server, the shared data source is not overwritten. It remains pointing to the production database server. This is shown in Figure 10-7. We have saved a bit of extra effort with each deployment.

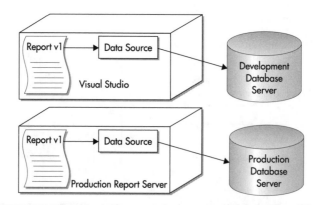

Figure 10-6 *Modifying the shared data source to point to the production database server*

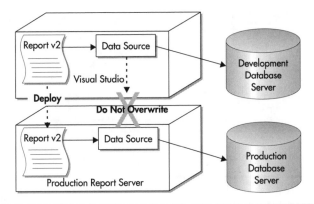

Figure 10-7   *A subsequent deployment with OverwriteDataSources set to False*

Additional Properties in the Property Pages Dialog Box

If you look back at Figure 10-3, you will see a couple additional items in the Property Pages dialog box that we have not discussed. We will take a look at those two items now.

Maintaining Multiple Configurations   At the top of the dialog box is the Configuration drop-down list. This drop-down list allows you to maintain several different deployment configurations for the same project. Each configuration has its own values for TargetFolder, TargetServerURL, and the other settings in the dialog box.

This is useful if you need to deploy the reports in a project to more than one Report Server. Perhaps you have the Report Server loaded on your own PC for your own testing, a development Report Server where the report will undergo quality assurance testing, and a production Report Server where the report will be made available to the end users. You can enter the properties for deploying to the Report Server on your PC in the DebugLocal configuration, the properties for deploying to the development Report Server in the Debug configuration, and the properties for deploying to the production Report Server in the Production configuration.

You can then easily switch between deploying to each of these Report Servers as new versions of your reports go from your own testing to quality assurance testing and are then made available to the users. You can change the configuration you are using for deployment through the Solution Configurations drop-down list in the Visual Studio toolbar, as shown in Figure 10-8.

NOTE

"Active(Debug)" in the Configuration drop-down list simply refers to the Debug configuration that is currently the selected or active configuration.

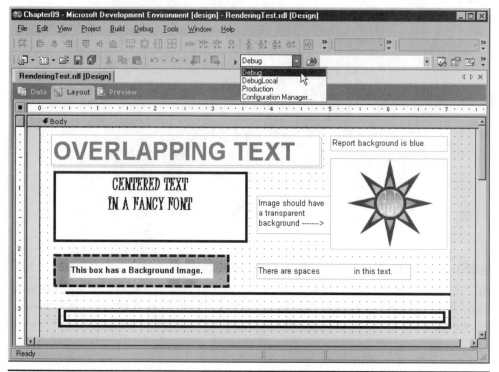

Figure 10-8 *The Solution Configurations drop-down list*

Running a Report Project   The final item we want to look at in the Project Property Pages dialog box is StartItem, which is used when running your report project. Use the StartItem drop-down list to select which report from your project will be executed when you run the project. The report selected as the "start item" will be displayed in a browser window in HTML format.

When you run a report project, you deploy all the reports in the project to the target server and target folder in your active configuration. Once the deployment is complete, the report specified as the start item is executed in a browser window. You can then "debug" this report, making sure it looks correct and functions properly in HTML format. You can run the project by clicking the Start button on the toolbar (to the left of the Solution Configuration drop-down list) or by selecting any of the following items from the Debug menu (or by pressing any of the shortcut keys that correspond to these menu items):

▶   Start

▶   Start Without Debugging

- ▶ Step Into
- ▶ Step Over

There really is no such thing as stepping into or over a report. These menu items simply run the project. The report selected as the start item is executed in a browser window from start to finish.

Uploading Reports Using Report Manager

Another common method of moving a report to the Report Server is by using the Report Manager. This is known as *uploading* the report. Deploying reports from Visual Studio can be thought of as pushing the reports from the development environment to the Report Server, whereas uploading reports from the Report Manager can be thought of as pulling the reports from the development environment to the Report Server.

You may need to use the Report Manager upload in situations where your report authors do not have rights to deploy reports on the Report Server. The report authors create their reports and test them within Visual Studio. When a report is completed, the report author can place the RDL file for the report in a shared directory or send it as an e-mail attachment to the Report Server administrator. The Report Server administrator can upload the RDL file to a quality assurance Report Server and test the report for clarity, accuracy, and proper use of database resources. Once the report has passed this review, the Report Server administrator can upload the report to the production Report Server.

Uploading Reports in the Chapter06 Project Using the Report Manager

Let's try uploading some of the reports from the Chapter06 report project:

1. Open the Report Manager in your browser. Click the Galactic Delivery Services folder to view its content.
2. Create a new folder called **Chapter 06**.
3. Select the new folder to view its contents.
4. Click the Upload File button in the toolbar on the Content tab. The Upload File page will appear, as shown in Figure 10-9.
5. Click Browse. The Choose File dialog box will appear.

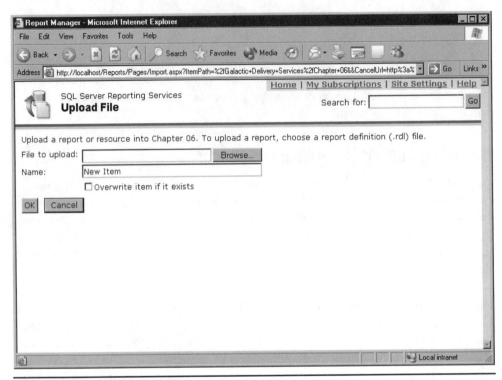

Figure 10-9 *The Upload File page*

6. Navigate to the folder where you created your solution for Chapter 6. If this folder is in the default location, you will find it under the following path:

```
My Documents\Visual Studio Projects\MSSQLRS\Chapter06
```

7. Select the Nametags report (Nametags.rdl) and click Open to exit the Choose File dialog box.

8. Click OK to upload the file.

9. The Nametags report has been uploaded to the Chapter 06 folder.

10. Click the Nametags report to execute it. You will see an error similar to the one in Figure 10-10. You received this because, unlike the deployment in Visual Studio, the upload in Report Manager did not bring the shared data source along with the report.

11. Click the link to the Chapter 06 folder at the top of the page.

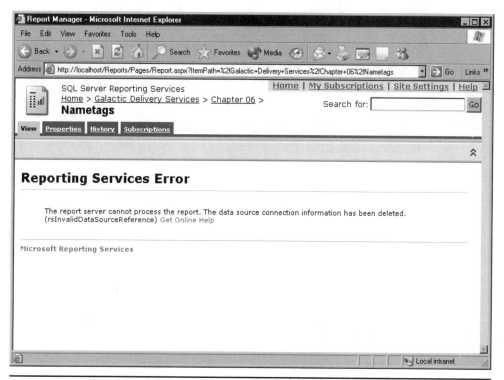

Figure 10-10   *The Reporting Services error page*

Creating a Shared Data Source in the Report Manager

In order to get the Nametags report functioning, we need to provide it with a shared data source. One way to do this is to create a new shared data source using the Report Manager. Follow these steps:

1. Click the New Data Source button in the toolbar on the Content tab. The New Data Source page for a shared data source will appear, as shown in Figure 10-11 and Figure 10-12.

2. Type **Galactic** for Name.

3. Type **Connection to the Galactic Database** for Description.

4. Make sure Microsoft SQL Server is selected in Connection Type. Other options here are OLE DB, Oracle, and ODBC.

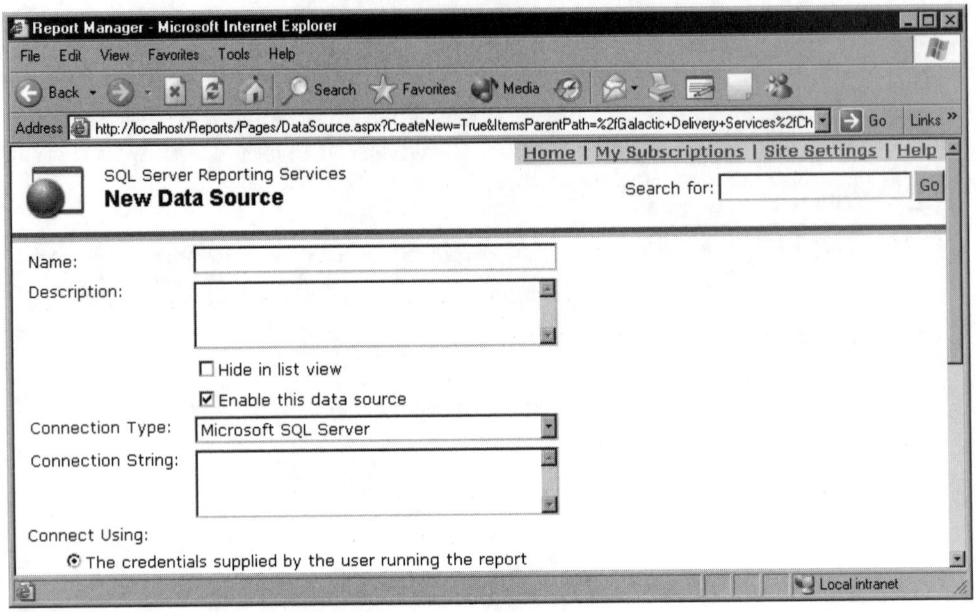

Figure 10-11   *The New Data Source page (top)*

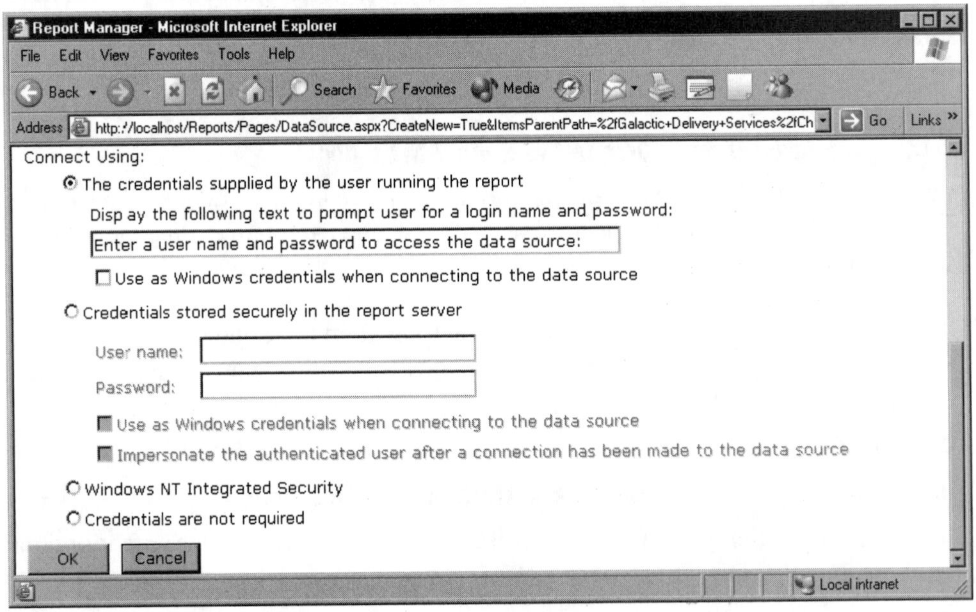

Figure 10-12   *The New Data Source page (bottom)*

5. Type **data source=(local);initial catalog=Galactic** for Connection String. If the Galactic database is not on the Report Server but rather is on a different computer, put the name of that computer in place of "(local)" in the connection string.

NOTE

Do not include the parentheses if you use a computer name in place of "(local)".

6. Select the option Credentials Stored Securely in the Report Server.

7. Type **GalacticReporting** for User Name.

8. Type **gds** for Password.

9. Click OK to save the data source and return to the Chapter 06 folder.

10. Click the Nametags report to execute it. You will receive the same error message page because we have not yet told the report to use our new data source.

11. Select the Properties tab. The properties page for the Nametags report will appear.

12. Click the Data Sources link on the left side of the screen. The Data Sources page for an individual report will appear.

13. A shared data source should be selected. Click Browse. The Select a Shared Data Source page will appear.

14. Expand each folder in the tree view under Location until you can see the Galactic shared data source in the Chapter 06 folder. Click the Galactic shared data source. The path to the Galactic shared data source will be filled in Location. (You can also type this path into Location if you do not want to use the tree view.)

15. Click OK to exit the Select a Shared Data Source page.

16. Click Apply at the bottom of the page.

NOTE

It is very easy to forget to click Apply when making changes to a report's data sources. If you do not click Apply, none of your changes will be saved. This can lead to confusion, frustration, and wasted troubleshooting time. At least, that is what I have been told.

17. Select the View tab to view the report. The report will now generate using the new shared data source. (There will be a red X where the GDS logo is supposed to be. We will deal with this later.)

18. Once the report has completed generating, click the Chapter 06 link at the top of the page.

Hiding an Item

Figure 10-13 shows the list view of the Chapter 06 folder. The Galactic shared data source appears in the left column. Shared data sources have a globe and screen icon. The Nametags report appears in the right column. Reports have an icon showing a piece of paper with two columns.

When users are browsing through folders to find a report, you may not want other items such as shared data sources cluttering things up. It makes more sense to have the shared data sources where the reports can use them, but out of sight of the users. Fortunately, Report Manager provides a way to do just that:

1. Click the Galactic data source. The Data Source Edit page will appear.
2. Check the Hide in List View check box.
3. Click Apply to save this change.
4. Click the Chapter 06 link at the top of the page.

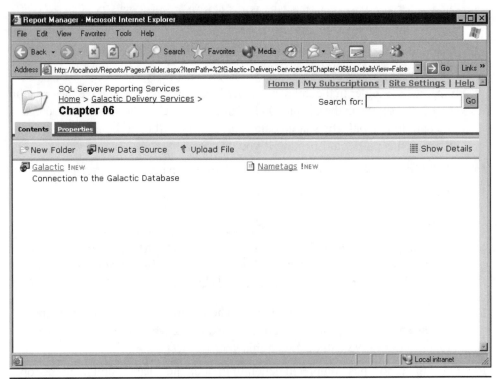

Figure 10-13 *The Chapter 06 folder list view*

The Galactic data source is no longer visible in the list view. You can use this same technique to hide reports you do not want to have generally available to users browsing through the folders.

If you do need to edit the Galactic data source, you can view it by using the detail view of the folder. Follow these steps:

1. Click the Show Details button in the toolbar on the Contents tab. The Galactic data source is now visible in this detail view, as shown in Figure 10-14. By default, the detail view is in alphabetical order by name.

2. Click the Type column heading. The detail view is now sorted by type in ascending order. (In an ascending sort by type, the reports are at the top of the list, with supporting items, such as shared data sources, at the bottom.) Note that the downward, black arrow is now next to the Type column heading on your screen.

3. Click the Type column heading again. The detail view is now sorted by type in descending order. Now the black arrow is pointing upward next to the column heading.

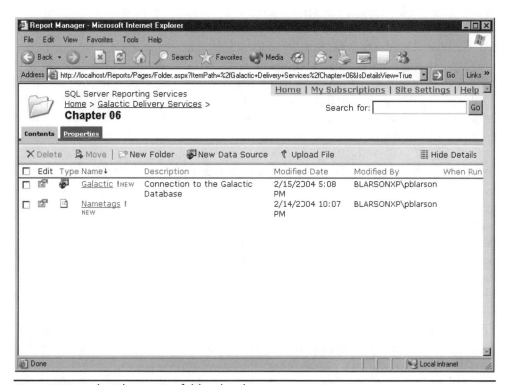

Figure 10-14   *The Chapter 06 folder detail view*

NOTE

The name of the sort order (ascending or descending) and the direction of the black arrow may seem to be opposite to one another. Just remember this: In an ascending sort, you move from smaller values (A, B, C...) to larger values (...X, Y, Z). When you move through the list in the direction of the arrow, you also move from smaller values to larger values.

4. Click the Modified Date column heading. The detail view is sorted by modified date in ascending order. You can sort the detail view by Type, Name, Description, Modified Date, Modified By, or When Run, in either ascending or descending order.

5. Click the Hide Details button in the toolbar on the Contents tab. You are back to the list view.

Connect Using Options

When you are accessing data from a server-based database such as SQL Server or Oracle, you need to provide some type of credentials, usually a user name and password, to show that you have rights to access the data. Keeping these credentials secure is an important concern. The shared data sources created on the Report Server provide several methods for specifying these credentials.

When entering the connection string into a shared data source, it is best not to include the credentials in the connection string itself. The connection string is displayed as plain text to anyone who views the Data Source Edit page. To better protect password information, always enter the credential information under one of the Connect Using options described here.

Credentials Supplied by the User   The first Connect Using option is to have the user enter the credentials required by the data source each time the report is run. This is the Credentials Supplied By the User Running the Report option. You can specify the prompt that will be presented each time the user must enter these credentials. If the Use as Windows Credentials When Connecting to the Data Source check box is checked, the user name and password entered by the user are treated as a Windows login. This means the user name and password provide database access using Windows Integrated security. If this check box is not checked, the user name and password are treated as a database login.

Having the user enter the credentials each time the report is run is the most secure option. There is no login information stored with the data source. However, most users are not pleased with a system where they must enter login information each time they run a report. This option may be appropriate when your organization's security policy forbids storing login information in any way. In most other cases, the other Connect Using options provide a better solution.

Credentials Stored in the Report Server   The next option allows you to have the user name and password stored in the Report Catalog on the Report Server. This is the Credentials Stored Securely in the Report Server option. The user name and password entered with this option are encrypted when they are stored in the Report Catalog. Also, the password is not displayed to the user in the Data Source Edit page.

This Connect Using option is convenient for the user because they do not need to remember and enter credentials to run reports using this data source. It also provides the required security for most situations through the measures noted in the previous paragraph.

As with the first Connect Using option, there is a Use as Windows Credentials When Connecting to the Data Source check box here as well. If this check box is checked, the user name and password stored in the Report Catalog are treated as a Windows login. If this check box is not checked, the user name and password are treated as a database login.

The second check box under this Connect Using option is Impersonate the Authenticated User After a Connection Has Been Made to the Data Source. If this check box is checked, the data source can use these credentials to impersonate this user. Not all database servers support this type of delegation of credentials. Consult the documentation for your specific Report Server for more information.

Integrated Security   If you are not comfortable with storing credentials in the Report Catalog, but you do not want your users entering credentials every time a report is run, integrated security may be the solution for you. The Windows NT Integrated Security option does not require the user to enter credentials. Instead, it takes the Windows login credentials that allowed the user to access the Report Manager and passes them along to the database server. Your database server, of course, needs to be set up to accept these credentials.

Integrated security will always work when the data source exists on the same server as the Report Server. It may run into problems, however, if the data source is on another server. The problems are caused by the way integrated security works between servers.

For a better understanding of the problems with integrated security, let's look at an example of the way integrated security works. The user logs in to their computer. This computer knows everything about this user because the original authentication occurred here.

When the user accesses the Report Manager application, the user's credentials are passed from their computer to the computer hosting the Report Server. However, using standard Windows security, not everything about this login is passed to the Report Server computer; only enough to authenticate the user. Some sensitive information does not make this hop across the network.

When the user runs a report with a data source using integrated security, the Report Server must pass on the credentials to the database server. However, the Report Server does not have the complete credentials to pass along. In fact, it does not know enough about the user to successfully authenticate them on the database server. The authentication on the database server will fail. Using standard Windows security, integrated security only works across one hop, from the original authenticating computer to a second computer. In the case of the Report Manager, this is the hop from the user's computer to the Report Server.

In order to get integrated security to work across more than one hop, your Windows domain must use a special kind of security known as Kerberos, which allows authentication across multiple hops. Using Kerberos security, integrated security will work across any number of servers in the network.

Credentials Not Required   The final Connect Using option is for data sources that do not require any authentication. This option would be used for connection to some Access databases, FoxPro databases, and others that do not require any login or password. This option could also be used if you insist, despite prior warnings here, on putting your credentials right in the connection string.

Uploading Other Items Using Report Manager

In addition to reports and shared data sources, other items can be created in Report Server folders. External images needed as part of the reports can be uploaded, for example, as well as documentation and other supporting materials.

Uploading External Report Images

If you look closely at the Nametags report when it comes up in Report Manager, you will notice that there is a problem with this report. The GDS logo that is supposed to appear in the lower-left corner of each nametag is missing. You will see the broken-link "X" symbol instead of the GDS logo.

This image was stored as an external image in the Chapter06 project. We need to upload this image to the Report Server. Once the image is uploaded into the same folder as the report, the report will be able to find it. Here are the steps to follow to do this:

1. Return to the Chapter 06 folder in the Report Manager.

2. Click Upload File in the Contents tab toolbar. The Upload File page will appear.

3. Click Browse. The Choose File dialog box will appear.

4. Navigate to the folder containing the Chapter06 project. Select the gds.gif file and click Open to exit the Choose File dialog box.

5. Leave the name as gds.gif. The image needs to keep this name so it can be found by the report. Click OK to upload this file.

6. Click the Nametags report to execute it. If the broken-link "X" is still visible, click the Refresh Report button in the Report Viewer toolbar, as shown in Figure 10-15.

NOTE

When you need to have Report Manager refresh a report, always use the Refresh Report button in the Report Viewer toolbar. Do not use the browser's Refresh button. The browser's Refresh button will cause the page to be refreshed, but it will not cause the report to be reexecuted.

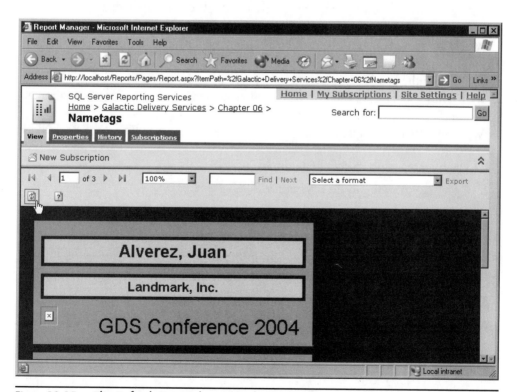

Figure 10-15   *The Refresh Report button in the Report Viewer toolbar*

7. Click the link for the Chapter 06 folder.

8. The entry for the gds.gif image shows in the list view of the Chapter 06 folder. As with the Galactic shared data source, we probably don't want entries for supporting resources cluttering up our list view. Click on the entry for gds.gif. The gds.gif image will be displayed.

9. Click the Properties tab.

10. Check the Hide in List View check box.

11. Click Apply.

12. Click the link for the Chapter 06 folder.

Uploading Supporting Materials

In some cases, you will need to provide your users with documentation on one or more reports in the form of either a text file or a Word or HTML document. There may also be supporting materials created in other applications. For example, you may have a PowerPoint presentation or a Visio diagram that aids in the interpretation and understanding of a set of reports. These materials can be uploaded as a folder item just like report files.

A text file or an HTML document can be displayed right in the browser without any additional software. For other types of documents, if the appropriate application is installed on the user's computer, the documents can be viewed right in the browser as well. These documents can also be downloaded and saved to the user's computer, if desired.

We'll now create a simple text document and then upload it to the Chapter 06 folder:

1. Open Notepad or another text editor.

2. Type the following in the text editor:

   ```
   The items in this folder are for the GDS Conference.
   ```

3. Save this as ReportReadMe.txt in a temporary location on your computer.

4. Return to your browser with the Report Manager viewing the Chapter 06 folder. Click Upload File in the Contents tab toolbar. The Upload File page will appear.

5. Click Browse. The Choose File dialog box will appear.

6. Navigate to the ReportReadMe.txt file and click Open to exit the Choose File dialog box.

7. Click OK to upload this file.

8. Select the ReportReadMe.txt entry in the Chapter 06 folder. You will see the contents of the text file displayed within the Report Manager.

9. Click the link for the Chapter 06 folder.

10. Let's add a second line to our text file. Open up the ReportReadMe.txt file in your text editor and add the following as a second line:

```
These items were created for the GDS Art Department.
```

11. Save the changes and close your text editor.

12. Return to your browser with the Report Manager viewing the Chapter 06 folder. Click Upload File in the Contents tab toolbar. The Upload File page will appear.

13. Click Browse. The Choose File dialog box will appear.

14. Navigate to the ReportReadMe.txt file and click Open to exit the Choose File dialog box.

15. Check the Overwrite Item If It Exists check box. If you fail to check this check box, the new version of the text file will not overwrite the older version on the Report Server.

16. Click OK to upload this file.

17. Select the ReportReadMe.txt entry in the Chapter 06 folder. You will see the new version of the text file.

18. Click the Properties tab.

19. Type **The purpose of these reports**... for the description.

20. Click Apply to save your changes.

21. Click the link for the Chapter 06 folder. The description shows up under the entry for ReportReadMe.txt.

22. Let's make another change to our text file and look at another way to overwrite an entry on the Report Server. Open up the ReportReadMe.txt file in your text editor and add the following as a third line:

```
These items were created for all billing contacts.
```

23. Save the changes and close your text editor.

24. Return to your browser with the Report Manager viewing the Chapter 06 folder. Select the ReportReadMe.txt entry.

25. Click the Properties tab.

26. Click Replace.

27. Click Browse. The Choose File dialog box will appear.

28. Navigate to the ReportReadMe.txt file and click Open to exit the Choose File dialog box.

29. Click OK to upload this file.

30. Click the View tab. You will see the latest version of the text file.

31. Click the link for the Chapter 06 folder.

32. Delete the ReportReadMe.txt file on your computer.

Uploading Reports Using .NET Assemblies

In addition to external images, reports can also reference .NET assemblies. You saw this in the Weather report created in Chapter 8. Let's look at the steps necessary to move this report to the Report Server.

Copying the .NET Assembly to the Report Server

In order for a report to access a .NET assembly, it must be in the application folder of the Report Server. No fancy deployment, upload, or installation routine is required here. Simply copy the assembly's DLL file to the appropriate directory. We will give this a try using the Weather report and its .NET assembly, WeatherInfo.dll. Here are the steps to follow:

1. Locate the WeatherInfo.dll file. If you do not have it anywhere else, it should be in the Report Designer folder on your development computer. The default path for the Report Designer folder is

   ```
   C:\Program Files\Microsoft SQL Server\80\Tools\Report Designer
   ```

2. Copy this file.

3. Paste this file into the Report Server application folder on the computer acting as your Report Server computer. The default path for the Report Server application folder is

   ```
   C:\Program Files\Microsoft SQL Server\MSSQL\Reporting Services\
                                               ReportServer\bin
   ```

Code Access Security

Because Reporting Services is a .NET application, it uses *code access security* to determine what execution permissions are possessed by each assembly. A *code access group* associates assemblies with specific permissions. The criteria for membership in a code access group is determined by a *security class*, and the permissions are determined by *named permission sets*.

Figure 10-16 provides an illustration of code access security. A .NET assembly or web service can gain entry into a code access group only if it matches the criteria specified by the security class. Once the .NET assembly or web service is allowed into a code access group, it can use the named permission set associated with that code access group to gain rights. These rights allow the .NET assembly or web service to perform tasks on a computer. Full trust rights and execution rights are the two types of rights we will use with the Weather report. There are, however, a number of different types of rights that can be included in a named permission set.

Code access groups can be nested one inside another. A .NET assembly or web service can be allowed into a parent group and gain its permissions; then it can try to gain membership in child code access groups to accumulate additional rights. A code access group can be a *first match code group*, where a .NET assembly or web service can only gain membership in one code access group—the first one it matches. Alternatively, a code access group can be a *union code group*, where a .NET assembly or web service is allowed to gain membership in a number of code access groups, joining together the permissions from each group.

In order for our Weather report to execute properly, we will have to create a code access group that provides permissions to the WeatherInfo.dll assembly. Also, we will have to create a second code access group to provide permissions to the web service that we are using to get our weather information. Even though this web service is not executing on our server, our WeatherInfo.dll assembly is executing some if its methods, so it needs to have permission to execute.

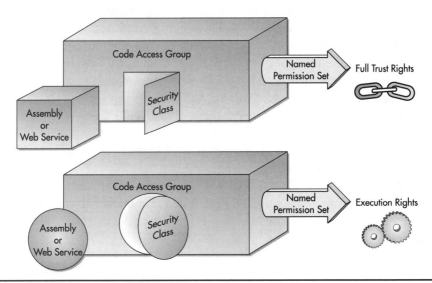

Figure 10-16   *Code access security*

Security Classes   A security class describes the conditions that a .NET assembly or web service needs to meet in order to get into a code access group. We will use two different types of security classes with the Weather report. The UrlMembershipCondition security class will be used with the web service, and the StrongNameMembershipCondition security class will be used with the WeatherInfo.dll assembly.

The UrlMembershipCondition security class says that any assembly or web service that is being executed from a specified URL will be included in a particular code access group. The URL that must be matched is listed in each code access group that is using the UrlMembershipCondition security class. For example, the GDSServer code access group may use UrlMembershipCondition and give "http://GDSServer//*" as the URL that must be matched. Any web service running on the GDSServer would be included in this code access group.

The StrongNameMembershipCondition security class uses the strong name associated with an assembly to identify it. The strong name is assigned to the assembly when it is created. It is a long string of hexadecimal digits that uniquely identifies an assembly. The StrongNameMembershipCondition security class is a good way to ensure that only the intended assembly is allowed into your code access group.

You will see a couple of other security classes in the Report Server security configuration. The AllMembershipCondition security class allows in all .NET assemblies and web services. The ZoneMembershipCondition security class allows in .NET assemblies and web services that originate in a particular zone. Some sample zones are MyComputer, Intranet, and Internet.

Named Permission Sets   Named permission sets group together the permissions that will be assigned by code access groups. The security configuration used by the Report Server contains three named permission sets. The Nothing permission grants no rights. It is used to initially take away all rights from a .NET assembly or web service before specific rights are added back by subsequent code access groups. This ensures that each .NET assembly or web service has only the rights it should have.

The Execution permission grants execution rights to a .NET assembly or web service. This means that the .NET assembly or web service can be run. The .NET assembly or web service does not, however, have rights to access any protected resources, such as the file system or the registry.

The FullTrust permission grants the .NET assembly or web service access to everything. This includes access to all the protected resources. FullTrust permission should only be granted to .NET assemblies and web services that you trust not to mess up your computer!

Modifying the Report Server's Security Configuration

Now that you have a basic understanding of code access security, we can modify the Report Server's security configuration to allow WeatherInfo.dll to run.

CAUTION

Consult with your Reporting Services or network administrator before making any changes to server security.

We need to make some additions to the Report Server's security configuration in order to provide our custom assembly with the rights it needs to execute. The security configuration for the Report Server is in the rssrvpolicy.config file. The default path for this file is

```
C:\Program Files\Microsoft SQL Server\MSSQL\Reporting Services\
                                                    ReportServer
```

This file contains the code access security information in an XML structure.

CAUTION

Make a backup copy of the rssrvpolicy.config file before making any modifications to it. If you accidentally create an invalid XML structure or otherwise cause a problem with the security configuration, the Report Server will not be able to execute any reports.

The XML structure in the rssrvpolicy.config file can be divided into three sections: Security Classes, Named Permission Sets, and Code Groups. We will only need to make changes to the Code Groups section of the document. Here are the steps to follow:

1. Open the rssrvpolicy.config file in Notepad or another text editor.
2. Scroll down until you locate the Code Group portion of the document. The Code Group portion of the document starts on the line after the closing XML tag for the named permission sets:

   ```
   </NamedPermissionSets>
   ```

3. The first code group is the parent code group which makes use of the AllMembershipCondition to assign the Nothing permission to all .NET assemblies and web services. We will add a new child code group right beneath this. Insert this new code group as shown here (add the lines shown in bold):

```
.
.
.
<CodeGroup
        class="FirstMatchCodeGroup"
        version="1"
        PermissionSetName="Nothing">
    <IMembershipCondition
            class="AllMembershipCondition"
            version="1"
    />
    <CodeGroup
            class="UnionCodeGroup"
            version="1"
            PermissionSetName="Execution"
            Name="WeatherWebServiceCodeGroup"
            Description="Code group for the Weather Web Service">
        <IMembershipCondition class="UrlMembershipCondition"
                version="1"
                Url="http://live.capescience.com/*"
        />
    </CodeGroup>
    <CodeGroup
            class="UnionCodeGroup"
            version="1"
            PermissionSetName="Execution"
            Name="Report_Expressions_Default_Permissions"
            Description="This code group grants default permissions for
                        code in report expressions and Code element. ">
.
.
.
```

4. There is another parent code group that uses ZoneMembershipCondition to assign Execute permissions to all .NET assemblies and web services in the MyComputer zone. We will add a new child code group right beneath this.

Insert this new code group as shown here (add the lines shown in bold). Note that the Description and PublicKeyBlob should each be entered on one line.

```
    .
    .
    .

<CodeGroup
      class="FirstMatchCodeGroup"
      version="1"
      PermissionSetName="Execution"
      Description="This code group grants MyComputer code
                                    Execution permission. ">
    <IMembershipCondition
          class="ZoneMembershipCondition"
          version="1"
          Zone="MyComputer" />
    <CodeGroup
          class="UnionCodeGroup"
          version="1"
          PermissionSetName="FullTrust"
          Name="WeatherInfoCodeGroup"
          Description="Code group for the Weather info Custom
                                      Assembly">
        <IMembershipCondition
              class="StrongNameMembershipCondition"
              version="1"
              PublicKeyBlob="0024000004800000940000000602000000
                    2400005253413100040000010000100B9F7
                    4F2D5B0AAD33AA619B00D7BB8B0F767839
                    3A0F4CD586C9036D72455F8D1E85BF635C
                    9FB1DA9817DD0F751DCEE77D9A47959E87
                    28028B9B6CC7C25EB1E59CB3DE01BB516D
                    46FC6AC6AF27AA6E71B65F6AB91B957688
                    6F2EF39417F17B567AD200E151FC744C6D
                    A72FF5882461E6CA786EB2997FA968302B
                    7B2F24BDBFF7A5"
                    />
    </CodeGroup>
    <CodeGroup
          class="UnionCodeGroup"
          version="1"
          PermissionSetName="FullTrust"
          Name="Microsoft_Strong_Name"
          Description="This code group grants code signed with the
                          Microsoft strong name full trust. ">
```

```
<IMembershipCondition
        class="StrongNameMembershipCondition"
        version="1"
        PublicKeyBlob="0024000004800000940000000602000000
                       2400005253413100040000010001007D1
                       FA57C4AED9F0A32E84AA0FAEFD0DE9E8FD
                       6AEC8F87FB03766C834C99921EB23BE79A
                       D9D5DCC1DD9AD236132102900B723CF980
                       957FC4E177108FC607774F29E8320E92EA
                       05ECE4E821C0A5EFE8F1645C4C0C93C1AB
                       99285D622CAA652C1DFAD63D745D6F2DE5
                       F17E5EAF0FC4963D261C8A12436518206D
                       C093344D5AD293"
        />
</CodeGroup>
```

   .
   .
   .

5. Save the modified file and exit your text editor.

NOTE

Looking at the rssrvpolicy.config file, you can see that expressions written within a report are granted Execute permissions. Because the WeatherInfo.GetWeather method is called from a report expression, by default it should only be able to get Execute permissions. .NET Security says that a process cannot get rights that exceed the rights granted to processes further up the stack. The GetWeather method needs FullTrust rights in order to make the web service call. The GetWeather method uses a special process to assert that it needs to exceed the rights of the calling process and gain FullTrust rights. If you downloaded the source code for the WeatherInfo.dll, you can look to see how the assert is accomplished.

Uploading the Report

You are now ready to upload the Weather report. Complete the following steps using the Report Manager:

1. Create a folder called **Chapter 08** in the Galactic Delivery Services folder.

2. Open the Chapter 08 folder and upload the WeatherReport.rdl file from the Chapter08 project folder.

3. Click the report WeatherReport to execute it. The report will produce an error because the shared data source does not exist.

4. Click the Properties tab. The properties page for WeatherReport will appear.

5. Click the Data Sources link on the left side of the screen. The Data Sources page for an individual report will appear.

6. A shared data source should be selected. Click Browse. The Select a Shared Data Source page will appear.

7. Rather than create another shared data source, we are going to use the existing shared data source in the Chapter 06 folder. Expand each folder in the tree view under Location until you can see the Galactic shared data source in the Chapter 06 folder. Click the Galactic shared data source.

8. Click OK to exit the Select a Shared Data Source page.

9. Click Apply at the bottom of the page.

10. Select the View tab to view the report. The report will now generate. (Remember that the .NET assembly calls a web service, so it requires an Internet connection.)

Modifying Reports from the Report Server

In addition to uploading a report definition to the Report Server, it is also possible to download a report definition, modify it, and send your modifications back to the Report Server as an update. You only need to do this if you do not have a copy of the RDL file for a report on the Report Server that needs to be modified. If you already have the report in a report project, you can edit that report using Visual Studio and then redeploy it.

Downloading a Report Definition

For this example, we will imagine that we do not have the RDL file for the SubReportTest report and need to make a change to the report. The first task we need to complete is to download this report's RDL file from the Report Server to our local computer. Follow these steps:

1. Open up the Report Manager in your browser and navigate to the Chapter 09 folder.

2. In the previous section, when we wanted to view the Properties tab for a report, we first executed that report. Now, we will use the Show Details button to get at the Properties tab another way. Click the Show Details button in the Contents tab toolbar. The detail view of the folder's contents will appear.

3. Click the icon in the Edit column next to the SubReportTest report. The Properties tab for the SubReportTest report will appear.

4. There is a Report Definition section on this page just above the buttons at the bottom. Click the Edit link in the Report Definition section. This causes the Report Manager to download a copy of the SubReportTest.rdl file so you can edit it. The File Download dialog box will appear.

5. Click Save. The Save As dialog box will appear.

6. Browse to an appropriate temporary location on your computer. Leave the filename as SubReportTest.rdl. Click Save to exit the Save As dialog box. The file will be downloaded and saved in the specified location.

NOTE

If you have logon credentials stored in one or more data source definitions in the report, these are not saved in the resulting report definition file, for security purposes.

Editing the Report Definition

We now have the report definition file for the SubReportTest report moved from the Report Server to our local computer. However, an RDL file by itself is not very useful. In order to edit it, we have to place it in a report project. Again, remember that, for this example, we are imagining that we do not already have the SubReportTest report in a report project. Here are the steps to follow:

1. Start Visual Studio.

2. Create a new report project in the MSSQLRS folder called EditSubReportTest. (Do not use the Report Wizard.)

3. Create a shared data source called Galactic for the Galactic database using "GalacticReporting" for the user name and "gds" for the password.

4. Right-click the Reports entry in the Solution Explorer and select Add | Add Existing Item from the context menu. The Add Existing Item dialog box will appear.

5. Navigate to the location where you stored the SubReportTest.rdl file in the previous section. Select the SubReportTest.rdl file and click Open to exit the Add Existing Item dialog box.

6. Double-click the SubReportTest report to open it for editing. (If you encounter an error while trying to edit this report, save the project, close Visual Studio, start it back up again, and reopen the EditSubReportTest project.)

7. On the Data tab, add the PurchaseDate to the output.

8. On the Layout tab, put the PurchaseDate in a text box to the right of the SerialNumber. Set the Format property for this text box to "MM/dd/yyyy."

9. Use the Preview tab to make sure your changes were made properly.

10. Click Save All in the toolbar.

11. Close Visual Studio.

Uploading the Modified Report Definition

Now that the report definition changes have been completed, we are ready to upload the modified report:

1. Return to the Report Manager. If you are not already there, navigate to the Properties tab for the SubReportTest report.

2. Click the Update link in the Report Definition section of the page. The Import Report page will appear.

3. Click Browse. The Choose File dialog box will appear.

4. Navigate to the EditSubReportTest folder to find the updated version of the SubReportTest.rdl file.

NOTE

Do not select the copy of SubReportTest.rdl that you originally downloaded. The modified version is in the folder with the EditSubReportTest report project.

5. Select SubReportTest.rdl and click Open to exit the Choose File dialog box.

6. Click OK to upload the file.

7. Click the View tab to view the report, then click the Refesh button in the Report Viewer toolbar. The purchase date is now shown for each transport.

Managing Items in Folders

You now know how to load items into folders on the Report Server. Of course, we live in a dynamic world, so things seldom stay where they are originally put. We need to be able to move items around as we come up with better ways of organizing them. We also need to be able to delete items as they are replaced by something better or are simply not needed anymore. Fortunately, the Report Manager provides ways for us to do this housekeeping in an efficient manner.

Moving Items Between Folders

As an example, let's create a more descriptive folder for our Nametags report and its supporting items. We will begin by moving a single item to this new folder. Then we will look at a method for moving multiple items at the same time.

Moving a Single Item

Here are the steps to follow to move a single item:

1.   Open up the Report Manager in your browser and navigate to the Galactic Delivery Services folder.

2.   Click New Folder. The New Folder page will appear.

3.   Type **2004 Conference** for Name and type **Materials for the 2004 User Conference** for Description.

4.   Click OK to create the new folder.

5.   Click Chapter 06 to view the contents of this folder.

6.   Click Show Details.

7.   Click the icon in the Edit column for the Nametags report. The Nametags report Properties tab will appear.

8.   Click Move. The Move Item page will appear.

9.   Select the 2004 Conference folder in the tree view.

10.   Click OK to move the report to this folder.

11.   Click the 2004 Conference link at the top of the page to view the contents of this folder.

Moving Multiple Items

You can see that the Nametags report has been moved to the 2004 Conference folder. However, the report will not function until the supporting items have also been moved to this folder. Moving each item individually, as we did with the report, is rather time consuming. Fortunately, there is another way:

1.   Click the Galactic Delivery Services link at the top of the page.

2.   Click Chapter 06 to view the contents of this folder.

3.   In the detail view you'll see check boxes next to each item in the folder. These check boxes work with the Delete and Move buttons in the Contents tab toolbar.

When you click Delete, any checked items will be deleted. Likewise, when you click Move, any checked items will be moved.

4. Click the uppermost check box. (The check box to the right of the word "Edit.") Checking this check box will check all items in the folder. Unchecking this check box will uncheck all items in the folder. Because we are moving all the items in the folder, we want all the items to be checked.

5. Click Move in the Contents tab toolbar. The Move Multiple Items page will appear.

6. Select the 2004 Conference folder in the tree view.

7. Click OK to move these items to this folder.

This method works for moving a single item, multiple items, or the entire contents of a folder. Just check the items you want to move and click the Move button. Remember that you need to be in the detail view when using this method.

This section demonstrated moving reports and supporting items. You can also move whole folders using the same techniques.

Deleting a Folder

The Chapter 06 folder is now empty and ready to be deleted. As with the move function, there are two ways to accomplish this. The first way is to view the Properties tab for the folder you want to delete and then click the Delete button. Just for fun, we'll try the second method.

Deleting a Folder Using the Check Boxes and Toolbar

1. Click the Galactic Delivery Services link at the top of the page to view the contents of this folder.

2. Check the Chapter 06 folder.

3. Click Delete. The confirmation dialog box appears.

4. Click OK to confirm your deletion. The Chapter 06 folder has been deleted.

Folders do not need to be emptied before they are deleted. If the Chapter 06 folder had contained reports, supporting items, or even other folders, these would have been deleted along with the folder.

Renaming a Folder

In addition to moving and deleting items, we may also want to rename items. Let's give the Chapter 09 folder a more descriptive name:

1. Click the icon in the Edit column for the Chapter 09 folder. The Chapter 09 Properties tab will appear.

2. Replace the contents of Name by typing **Rendering Test Reports**. Then type **Reports for testing the performance of various rendering types** for Description.

3. Click Apply.

4. Click the Galactic Delivery Services link at the top of the page.

5. Click Hide Details.

   This same technique makes it just as easy to change the names and descriptions for reports and other items. Just because it is easy to make these changes does not mean that it should be done often. Once users become familiar with a folder name, a report name, or a report's location within the folder structure, you should change it only if there is a good reason to do so.

   You may have noted that we could have changed the name of the Chapter 06 folder rather than going through the move-and-delete processes of the previous sections. This is true; we could have simply changed the folder name. However, if we had done that, you would not know how to do moves and deletes!

Seek and Ye Shall Find: Search and Find Functions

The Report Manager provides two features to help users find information. The Search function helps the user locate a report within the Report Server folder structure, and the Find function allows the user to jump to a certain piece of information while viewing a report.

Searching for a Report

First, we will look at the Search function. This function allows the user to enter a portion of a word, a complete word, or a phrase. The Report Manager then searches the names and descriptions of items in the Report Server folder structure for occurrences of this text. The Report Manager does not search the contents of a report or supporting files.

For example, searching for "GDS Report" would find "The GDS Report" and "GDS Reporting." It would not find "Report GDS Income" or "GDS Accounting Report." This is strictly a search for the text just as it is entered. There is no Boolean logic, proximity searching, or other features that you find in Internet search engines. Also, the search is not case sensitive.

Follow these steps to use the Search function:

1. Open up the Report Manager in your browser and navigate to the Home folder.

2. Type **report** for Search For in the upper-right corner of the screen and then click Go. The Search page will be displayed with the search results.

3. The Report Manager will find five items, two folders, a text document, and two reports. There is no weighting or relevance assigned to each result. They are simply displayed in alphabetical order. Click the Galactic Delivery Services folder. You will see the contents of that folder.

4. Click your browser's Back button to return to the search results.

5. Click ReportReadMe.txt. You will see the contents of this file.

6. Click your browser's Back button.

7. Click the SubReportTest report to execute this report. (Keep your browser on this report. We will use it in the Find feature.)

Finding Text Within a Report

Next, we will look at the Find function. This function also allows the user to enter a portion of a word, a complete word, or a phrase. The Report Manager then searches the contents of the current report for occurrences of this text. It then highlights the first occurrence and moves it to the top of the view. The user can use the Next button to move to the next occurrence.

As with the Search function, Find will locate text just as it is entered. There is no Boolean logic or proximity searching. Also, Find is not case sensitive.

We will use the SubReportTest report to demonstrate the Find function. This report should be open in your browser. The SubReportTest report lists all the transports used by GDS. They are listed in transport number order. Suppose we want to look at just the Warp Hauler–type transports sprinkled throughout the report. Rather than skimming through the entire report looking for what we are interested in, here is a better way:

1. Type **warp haul** in the entry area to the left of the words "Find | Next" in the Report Viewer toolbar.

2. Click Find. The first Warp Hauler transport (#1303) will be brought to the top of the viewing area and the "Warp Haul" portion of the transport type will be highlighted.

3. Click Next. (Make sure you do not click Find. Clicking Find simply starts the find operation again from the top of the page.) The next Warp Hauler transport (#1307) will be brought to the top of the viewing area.

4. Click Next. The report jumps to the next Warp Hauler transport (#1310). Click Next once more and the report jumps to the next Warp Hauler transport (#1311) on page 2 of the report.

Managing Reports on the Report Server

Now that you have moved some of your reports to the Report Server, you may be thinking that your job is about done. Actually, it is just beginning. Now you need to manage the reports and supporting materials to ensure the reports can be utilized properly by your users.

Two of the biggest concerns when it comes to managing reports are security and performance. Reports containing sensitive data must be secured so they are only accessed by the appropriate people. Reports must return information to users in a reasonable amount of time without putting undo stress on database resources. Fortunately, Reporting Services provides tools for managing both of these concerns. Security roles and item-level security give you extremely fine control over just who has access to each report and resource. Caching, snapshots, and history allow you to control how and when reports are executed.

Security

In Reporting Services, security was designed with both flexibility and ease of management in mind. Flexibility is provided by the fact that individual access rights can be assigned to each folder and to each item within a folder. An item is either a report or a resource in a folder. You can specify exactly who has rights to each item and exactly what those rights are. Ease of management is provided by security inheritance, security roles, and integration with Windows security. We will begin our discussion with the last entry in this list.

NOTE

It is important to remember that, although we are creating and maintaining these role assignments using the Report Manager, the security rights apply to Reporting Services as a whole. No matter how you access folders and items — through the Report Manager or through the web service — these security rights are enforced.

Integration with Windows Security

Reporting Services does not maintain its own list of users and passwords. Instead, it depends entirely on integration with Windows security. When a user accesses either the Report Manager web application or the web service, that user must authenticate with the Report Server. In other words, the user must have a valid domain user name and password or local user name and password to log on to the Report Server. Both the Report Manager web application and the web service are set up requiring integrated Windows authentication to ensure that this logon takes place.

Once this logon occurs, Reporting Services utilizes the user name and the user's group memberships to determine what rights the user possesses. The user will be able to access only those folders and items they have rights to. In Report Manager, users will not even see the folders they cannot browse and reports they cannot run. There is no temptation for the user to try and figure out how to get into places they are not supposed to go, because they will not even know these places exist.

Local Administrator Privileges

In most cases, rights must be explicitly assigned to folders and items. One exception to this rule, however, is local administrator privileges. Any user who is a member of the local administrators group on the computer hosting the Report Server will have content manager rights to all folders and all items. These automatic rights cannot be modified or removed.

Let's look at the security page:

1. Open up the Report Manager in your browser and navigate to the Home folder.
2. Select the Properties tab. You will see the security page for the Home folder, as shown in Figure 10-17.

The Report Server maintains a security page for each item in the Report Catalog—every folder, every report, and every supporting item. The security page lists all the role assignments for an item. Each role assignment is made up of two things: a Windows user or group and a security role. The rights associated with the security role are assigned to the Windows user or group.

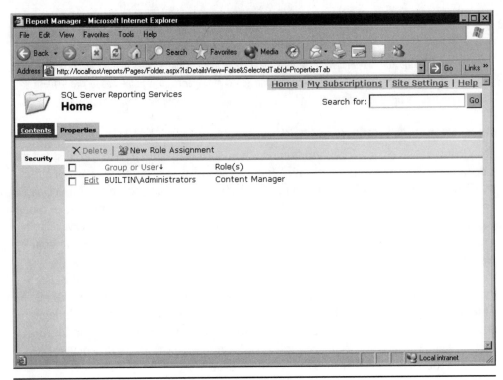

Figure 10-17   *The security page for the Home folder*

Initially, there is one role assignment on the security page for each item. This entry assigns the Content Manager security role to the BUILTIN\Administrators group. This entry is really a reminder that any user who is a member of the local administrators group will have rights to manage the contents of this folder.

NOTE

You could actually delete the role assignment for BUILTIN\Administrators, and the members of the local administrators group would still have rights to manage the contents of this folder. These rights are hardwired into Reporting Services. The BUILTIN\Administrators assignment on the security page is just a reminder of the rights held by anyone in the local administrators group.

Tasks and Rights

You can perform a number of tasks in Reporting Services. Each task has a corresponding right to perform that task. For example, you can view reports.

Therefore, there is a corresponding right to view reports. The tasks within Reporting Services are shown in Table 10-1.

You are probably not familiar with some of these tasks. We will discuss linked reports later in this chapter, and we will discuss report history snapshots and subscriptions in Chapter 11. For now, you simply need to know that these are tasks with associated rights within Reporting Services.

In addition to the tasks listed in Table 10-1 are system-wide tasks with associated rights. These system-wide tasks deal with the management and operation of Reporting Services as a whole. The system-wide tasks within Reporting Services are shown in Table 10-2.

Again, you may not be familiar with all the tasks in this list. We will discuss jobs and shared schedules in Chapter 11.

Roles

The rights to perform tasks are grouped together to create *roles*. Reporting Services includes several predefined roles to help you with security management. In addition,

Task	Description
Create linked reports	Create linked reports and publish them to a folder
Manage all subscriptions	View, modify, and delete any subscription regardless of who owns it
Manage data sources	Create, modify, and delete shared data sources
Manage folders	Create, view, and delete folders; view and modify folder properties
Manage individual subscriptions	Create, view, modify, and delete your own subscriptions
Manage report history	Create, view, and delete report history snapshots; modify report history properties
Manage reports	Create, view, and delete reports; modify report properties
Manage resources	Create, modify, and delete resources; view and modify resource properties
Set security for individual items	View and modify security settings for reports, folders, resources, and shared data sources
View data sources	View shared data sources and their properties
View folders	View folders and their properties
View reports	View reports and linked reports along with their report history snapshots and properties
View resources	View resources and their properties

Table 10-1   *Tasks Within Reporting Services*

Task	Description
Generate events	Provide an application with the ability to generate events within the Report Server
Manage jobs	View and cancel running Report Server jobs
Manage Report Server properties	View and modify configuration properties for the Report Server
Manage Report Server security	View and modify system-wide role assignments
Manage roles	Create, view, modify, and delete role definitions
Manage shared schedules	Create, view, modify, and delete shared schedules used for snapshots and subscriptions
View Report Server properties	View properties that apply to the Report Server
View shared schedules	View a shared schedule

Table 10-2   *System-wide Tasks Within Reporting Services*

you can create your own custom roles, grouping together any combination of rights that you like. The predefined roles and their corresponding rights are listed here.

The Browser Role   The Browser role is the basic role assigned to users who are going to be viewing reports, but will not be creating folders or uploading new reports. The Browser role has rights to perform the following tasks:

► Manage individual subscriptions
► View folders
► View reports
► View resources

The Publisher Role   The Publisher role is assigned to users who will be creating folders and uploading reports. The Publisher role does not have rights to change security settings or manage subscriptions and report history. The Publisher role has rights to perform the following tasks:

► Create linked reports
► Manage data sources
► Manage folders
► Manage reports
► Manage resources

The My Reports Role   The My Reports role is designed to be used only with a special folder called the My Reports folder. Within this folder, the My Reports role gives the user rights to do everything except change security settings. The My Reports role has rights to perform the following tasks:

- ▶ Create linked reports
- ▶ Manage data sources
- ▶ Manage folders
- ▶ Manage individual subscriptions
- ▶ Manage report history
- ▶ Manage reports
- ▶ Manage resources
- ▶ View data source
- ▶ View reports
- ▶ View resources

The Content Manager Role   The Content Manager role is assigned to users who will be managing the folders, reports, and resources. All members of the Windows local administrators group on the computer hosting the Report Server are automatically members of the Content Manager role for all folders, reports, and resources. The Content Manager has rights to perform all tasks, excluding system-wide tasks.

The System User Role   There are also two predefined roles for the system-wide security tasks. The System User role has rights to perform the following system-wide tasks:

- ▶ View Report Server properties
- ▶ View shared schedules

The System Administrator Role   The System Administrator role provides the user with rights to complete any of the tasks necessary to manage the Report Server. All members of the Windows local administrator group on the computer hosting the Report Server are automatically members of the System Administrator role. This role has rights to perform the system-wide tasks listed next.

► Manage jobs

► Manage report server properties

► Manage report server security

► Manage roles

► Manage shared schedules

Creating Role Assignments

As was stated previously, role assignments are created when a Windows user or Windows group is assigned a role for a folder, a report, or a resource. Role assignments are created on the security page for the folder, report, or resource. It is these role assignments that control what the user can see within a folder and what tasks the user can perform on the folder, report, or resource.

Let's try creating role assignments for some of our folders and reports.

NOTE

To complete the next set of activities, you need a user who has rights to log on to the Report Server but is not a member of the local administrators group on that computer. You should know the password for this user so you can log on as that user and view the results of your security settings.

Creating a Role Assignment for a Folder   Let's try creating a new role assignment for the Home folder:

1. Open up the Report Manager in your browser. You should be viewing the contents of the Home folder.

2. Select the Properties tab. You will see the security page for this folder.

3. Click New Role Assignment. The New Role Assignment page will appear, as shown in Figure 10-18.

4. Type the name of a valid user for Group or User Name. If you are using a domain user or domain group, this must be in the format "DomainName\ UserName" or "DomainName\GroupName." If you are using a local user or local group, this must be in the format "ComputerName\UserName" or "ComputerName\GroupName."

5. Check the check box for the Browser role.

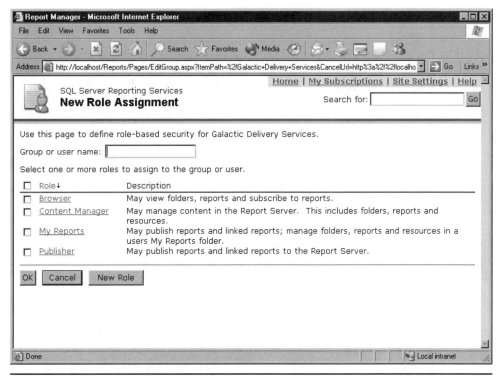

Figure 10-18   *The New Role Assignment page*

6. Click OK to save your role assignment and return to the security page. Reporting Services will check to ensure you entered a valid user or group for the role assignment. If this is not a valid user or group, you will receive an error message and your role assignment will not be saved.

NOTE

A user needs to have at least viewing rights in the Home folder in order to view other folders and navigate to them.

Inherited Role Assignments   By default, folders (other than the Home folder), reports, and resources inherit their role assignments from the folder that contains them. You can think of the nested folders as branches of a tree, with the reports and resources as the leaves. Inherited security means that you can make security changes to one folder and have those changes take effect for all the branches and leaves further along the tree.

This makes managing security very easy. You can maintain security for all the reports and resources within a folder simply by modifying the role assignments for the folder itself. You can maintain security for an entire branch of the tree structure by modifying the role assignments for the folder that forms the base of that branch. Let's take a look at the security for the Galactic Delivery Services folder:

1. Select the Contents tab.
2. Select the Galactic Delivery Services folder to view its contents.
3. Select the Properties tab. You will see the properties page for this folder.
4. Select Security from the left side of the page. You will see the security page for this folder.

The Galactic Delivery Services folder is inheriting its role assignments from the Home folder. You did not add a role assignment giving Browser rights to your user in this folder, and yet there it is. As soon as you added the role assignment to the Home folder, it appeared for all the items within the Home folder.

You gave your user Browser rights in the Home folder so they could view the contents of the Home folder, then navigate into other folders to find the reports they need. You may wish to give this user additional rights in folders further along in the tree. Perhaps the user can manage the content of certain folders that belong to their department, but can only browse when in the Home folder.

In order to accomplish this task, we must first break the inherited security for the Galactic Delivery Services folder:

1. Click Edit Item Security. A dialog box with an inherited security message will appear. The Report Manager is confirming that you want to break that inheritance by creating your own role assignments for this folder.
2. Click OK to confirm that you want to break the inherited security.

Now that you have broken the inherited security, you have new buttons on the toolbar for adding a new role assignment, deleting existing role assignments, and reverting back to inherited security.

Now we can edit the role assignment for your user:

1. Click the Edit link next to the role assignment giving your user Browser rights. The Edit Role Assignment page will appear.
2. Uncheck the check box for the Browser role.

3. Check the check box for the Content Manager role.

4. Click Apply to save the changes to your role assignment and return to the security page. The user now has content manager rights in the Galactic Delivery Services folder.

5. Click the Contents tab.

6. Select the Rendering Test Reports folder to view its content.

7. Select the Properties tab. You will see the properties page for this folder.

8. Select Security from the left side of the page. You will see the security page for this folder.

You can see that the Rendering Test Reports folder is inheriting its role assignments from the Galactic Delivery Services folder.

NOTE

Although we do not do so in these exercises, you can check more than one role when creating or editing a role assignment. The user's rights are then the sum of the rights granted by each role.

Managing Role Assignments for Reports   Now let's try managing role assignments for reports:

1. Select the Contents tab.

2. Click Show Details.

3. Click the icon in the Edit column for the RenderingTest report. The properties page for this report will appear.

4. Click Security on the left side of the page. The security page for this report will appear.

Again, you can see that this report is inheriting its role assignments from the folder that contains it; in this case, the Rendering Test Reports folder. Because the user has Content Manager rights for the folder, the user also has Content Manager rights for the report. This means that the user can change any and all properties of this report and even delete the report altogether.

To continue our security example, we are going to suppose that it is alright for the user to have Content Manager rights for the Rendering Test Reports folder, but not for the Rendering Test report. We will need to edit the role assignment for your user. However, before we can do this, we must break the inheritance, as explained in the following steps.

1. Click Edit Item Security. The confirmation dialog box will appear.

2. Click OK to confirm.

3. Click the Edit link next to the role assignment giving your user Content Manager rights. The Edit Role Assignment page will appear.

4. Uncheck the check box for the Content Manager role.

5. Check the check box for the Browser role.

6. Click Apply to save the changes to your role assignment and return to the security page.

7. Click the Rendering Test Reports link at the top of the page.

Now we will modify the rights granted to this user for the SubReportTest report. In our example, because this is a subreport, we are going to assume that the user should have very limited rights to this report. In fact, they should only be able to review the report. In this case, the predefined Browser role has too many rights. We will have to define our own custom role. To do so, follow these steps:

1. Click the icon in the Edit column for the SubReportTest report. The properties page for this report will appear.

2. Click Security on the left side of the page. The security page for this report will appear.

3. Click Edit Item Security. Click OK to confirm.

4. Click the Edit link next to the role assignment giving your user Content Manager rights. The Edit Role Assignment page will appear.

5. Click New Role.

6. Type **View Report** for Name.

7. Type **View Report Only** for Description.

8. Check View Reports.

9. Click OK to save this new role and return to the Edit Role Assignment page.

10. Uncheck the check box for the Content Manager role.

11. Check the check box for the View Report role.

12. Click Apply to save the changes to your role assignment and return to the security page. The user has rights to view the SubReportTest report, but no other rights with that report.

We will make one more change in order to test security. We will remove all rights assigned to this user for the DrillthroughTest report:

1. Navigate to the Rendering Test Reports folder.

2. Click the icon in the Edit column for the DrillthroughTest report. The properties page for this report will appear.

3. Click Security on the left side of the page. The security page for this report will appear.

4. Click Edit Item Security. Click OK to confirm.

5. Check the check box next to the role assignment giving your user Content Manager rights.

6. Click Delete. The confirmation dialog box will appear.

7. Click OK to confirm the deletion.

You can now close your browser, log out of Windows, and log on with the user name you have been using in the role assignments. Let's test our security changes:

1. Open up the Report Manager in your browser. You should be viewing the contents of the Home folder. Notice that there are no buttons in the Contents tab toolbar for creating folders and data sources or uploading files, as shown in Figure 10-19. That is because the user you are now logged on as has only Browser rights in this folder.

2. Select the Galactic Delivery Services folder to view its contents. When you are in this folder, the New Folder, New Data Source, and Upload File buttons have returned, as shown in Figure 10-20. In this folder, your user has Content Manager rights.

3. Select the Rendering Test Reports folder to view its contents.

4. Click Show Details.

5. Click the icon in the Edit column for the RenderingTest report. The properties page for this report will appear. Note the fact that Security doesn't appear on the left side of the page, as shown in Figure 10-21. Your user has Browser rights to this report, so you can view the report and its history and create subscriptions, but you cannot change its security. (Don't worry about what subscriptions are right now; we will discuss them in Chapter 11.)

6. Click the link for the Rendering Test Reports folder at the top of the page.

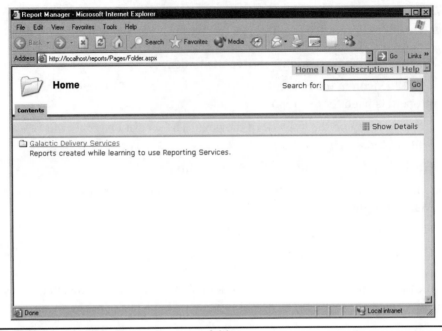

Figure 10-19 Browser rights in the Home folder

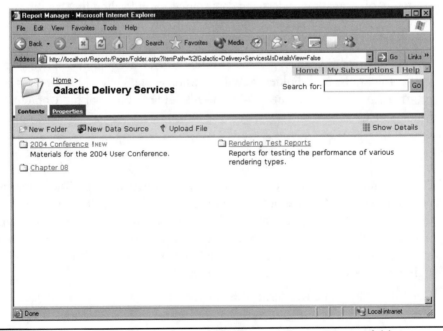

Figure 10-20 Content Manager rights in the Galactic Delivery Services folder

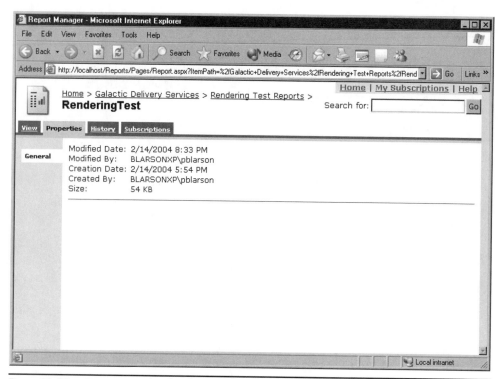

Figure 10-21   *Browser rights for the RenderingTest report*

7. Click the icon in the Edit column for the SubReportTest report. The properties page for this report will appear. Now, the Subscriptions tab is gone, as shown in Figure 10-22. Your user has the rights from our custom View Report role for this report. You can view the report and its history, but you cannot create subscriptions.

8. Click the link for the Rendering Test Reports folder at the top of the page. Notice that the DrillthroughTest report is nowhere to be seen because your user does not have any rights for this report, not even the rights to view it.

9. Click the RenderingTest report to execute it.

10. Go to page 2 of the report. Scroll down to the table below the graph where you see "Custer, Inc."

11. The heading "Custer, Inc." is a link to the DrillthroughTest report. The problem is, your user does not have any rights to the DrillthroughTest report. Clicking this link will result in an "insufficient rights" error message, as shown in Figure 10-23.

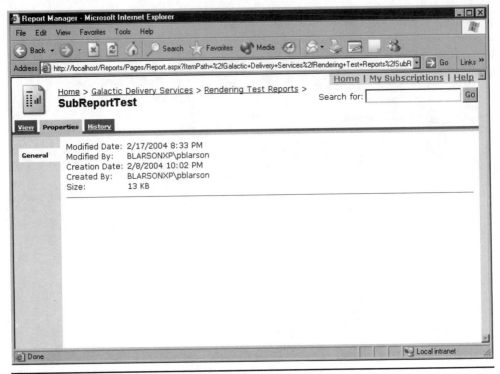

Figure 10-22   *View Report rights for the SubReportTest report*

It is important to give users only the rights they need. This prevents users from viewing data that they should not see or from making modifications or deletions they should not be allowed to make. On the other hand, it is important to provide users with enough rights so that their reports function properly. We don't want users to end up with an error message like the one shown in Figure 10-23 when they are trying to do legitimate work.

Role Assignments Using Windows Groups

As was mentioned previously, role assignments can be made to Windows users or to Windows groups. If you create your role assignments using Windows users, you will need to create a new set of role assignments every time a new user needs to access Reporting Services. This can be extremely tedious if you have a complex set of role assignments for various folders, reports, and resources.

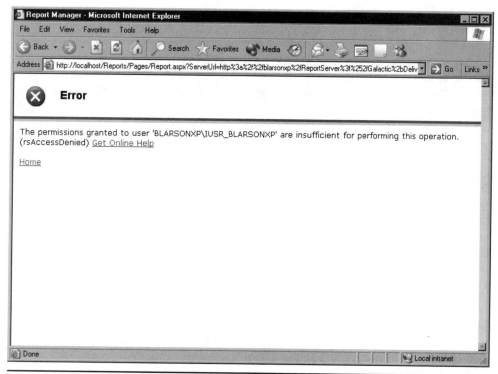

Figure 10-23   *Insufficient rights error*

In most cases, it is better to create role assignments using Windows groups. Then, as new users come along, you simply need to add them to the Windows group that has the appropriate rights in Reporting Services. Much easier!

CAUTION

In some cases, Internet Information Services (IIS), and therefore Reporting Services, will not immediately recognize changes to group membership. This is due to the fact that IIS caches some Windows security information and then works from that cache. Stopping and starting the IIS service will cause the IIS security cache to be reloaded with the latest and greatest group membership information.

Linked Reports

In many cases, the security set up within Reporting Services will restrict the folders that a user can access. The sales department may be allowed to access one set of folders. The personnel department may be allowed to access another set of folders. The personnel department doesn't want to see sales reports, and there will certainly be some personnel reports that should not be seen by everyone in the sales department.

This works very well—a place for everything and everything in its place—until you come to that report that needs to be used by both the sales department and the personnel department. You could put a copy of the report in both places, but this gets to be a nightmare as new versions of reports need to be deployed to multiple locations on the Report Server. You could put the report in a third folder accessed by both the Sales Department and the Personnel Department, but that can make navigation in the Report Manager difficult and confusing.

Fortunately, Reporting Services provides a third alternative: the linked report. With a linked report, your report is deployed to one folder. It is then pointed to by links that are placed elsewhere within the Report Catalog, as shown in Figure 10-24. To the user, the links look just like a report. Because of these links, it appears that the report is in many places. The sales department sees it in their folder. The personnel department sees it in their folder. The fact of the matter is that the report is only deployed to one location, so it is easy to administer and maintain.

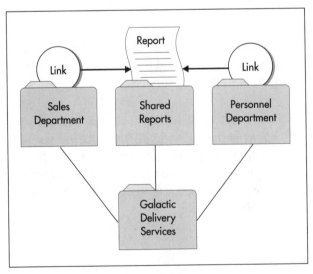

Figure 10-24   *A linked report*

Creating a Linked Report

In order to demonstrate a linked report, we are going to make use of the Invoice-BatchNumberMatrix report from Chapter 4. This report shows the invoice amounts for companies in various cities. Galactic Delivery Services has sales offices in each of these cities. Each sales office will have its own folder within the GDS Report Catalog. A sales office should be able to access the Invoice-BatchNumberMatrix report in their own folder and see the invoices for customers in their city.

Deploying the Report to a Common Folder

We will begin by deploying the report to a common folder. Here are the steps to follow:

1. Log in with a user name and password that has content manager rights in Reporting Services.
2. Start Visual Studio and open the Chapter04 project.
3. Modify the properties of the Chapter04 project as follows:

Property	Value
TargetFolder	Galactic Delivery Services/Shared Reports
TargetServerURL	http://ServerName/ReportServer

Replace "ServerName" with the appropriate server name or with "localhost."

4. Deploy the Invoice-BatchNumberMatrix report.
5. Close Visual Studio.

Creating Linked Reports

Now that the report has been deployed to the Report Catalog, it is time to create our linked reports:

1. Open the Report Manager in your browser and navigate to the Galactic Delivery Services folder.
2. Create a new folder. Type **Axelburg** for Name and **Axelburg Sales Office** for Description.
3. Create another new folder. Type **Utonal** for Name and **Utonal Sales Office** for Description.
4. Navigate to the Shared Reports folder.

5. Click Show Details.

6. Click the icon in the Edit column next to the Invoice-BatchNumberMatrix report.

7. Click Create Linked Report. The create linked report page will appear.

8. Type **Invoice-Batch Number** for Name and **Axelburg invoices in each batch** for Description.

9. Click Change Location. The Folder Location page will appear.

10. Select the Axelburg folder and click OK to return to the create linked report page.

11. Click OK to create and execute this linked report in the Axelburg folder.

12. Type **01/01/2003** for Enter a Start Date and **12/31/2003** for Enter an End Date. Click View Report.

13. Click the link for the Axelburg folder at the top of the page.

14. Click Hide Details. You can see that the linked report we just created looks just like a report.

15. Navigate back to the Shared Reports folder.

16. Click Show Details.

17. Click the icon in the Edit column next to the Invoice-BatchNumberMatrix report.

18. Click Create Linked Report. The create linked report page will appear.

19. Type **Invoice-Batch Number** for Name and **Utonal invoices in each batch** for Description.

20. Click Change Location. The Folder Location page will appear.

21. Select the Utonal folder and click OK to return to the create linked report page.

22. Click OK to create and execute this linked report in the Utonal folder.

23. Select Utonal from the Select a City drop-down list. Type **01/01/2003** for Enter a Start Date and **12/31/2003** for Enter an End Date. Click View Report.

We have now successfully created and tested our two linked reports.

Managing Report Parameters in Report Manager

We have our linked reports, but we have not quite fulfilled all the business needs stated for these linked reports. The Axelburg sales office is supposed to be able to see only their own invoice data. The same is true for the Utonal sales office. We can meet these business needs by managing the report parameters right in the Report Manager. Here are the steps to follow:

1. Navigate to the Axelburg folder. Note the small chain links on the icon for the Invoice-BatchNumber report. This indicates that it is a linked report.

2. Click the icon in the Edit column next to the Invoice-BatchNumber report.

3. Click Parameters on the left side of the screen. The parameter management page will appear. Note that the City parameter has a default of Axelburg. Because this is the Axelburg folder, we will leave that default alone. What we will modify is the user's ability to change this default value.

4. Uncheck the Prompt User check box in the City row. The user will no longer be prompted for a city. Instead, the report will always use the default value. As you may have guessed, you can have a default value, you can prompt the user for the value, or you can do both. You must do at least one of these.

5. Check the Has Default check box in the StartDate row. Type **01/01/2003** for the default value for this row.

6. Check the Has Default check box in the EndDate row. Type **12/31/2003** for the default value for this row.

7. Click Apply to save your changes.

8. Select the View tab.

9. Notice that you can no longer select a city. It is always Axelburg. Also, notice that we now have default values for the date. It is also worth noting that these default values are much easier to modify than the default values that are part of the report.

10. Navigate to the Utonal folder.

11. Click the icon in the Edit column next to the Invoice-BatchNumber report.

12. Click Parameters on the left side of the screen.

13. Change the City field's default parameter to Utonal.

14. Uncheck the Prompt User check box in the City row.

15. Check the Has Default check box in the StartDate row. Type **01/01/2003** for the default value for this row.

16. Check the Has Default check box in the EndDate row. Type **12/31/2003** for the default value for this row.

17. Click Apply to save your changes.

18. Select the View tab.

Now we have the linked reports working just the way we need them. Not only did we simplify things by not deploying the report in multiple places, but we also were able to hardcode parameter values for each linked report.

Delivering the Goods

In this chapter, you saw how to put the reports where our users could come and get them. Our users were set up to pull the reports off of the Report Server. In the next chapter, you will learn how to deliver the goods right to the users. In Chapter 11, the Report Server will push the reports out to the users. The pull and push capabilities combine to give Reporting Services some very powerful tools for putting information in the hands of the users, right where it needs to be.

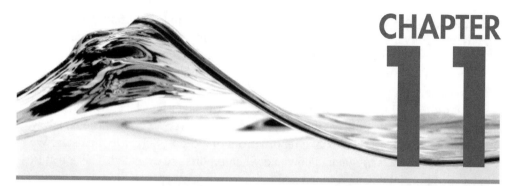

Delivering the Goods:
Report Delivery

433

n the previous chapter, we moved from the development environment to the Report Server. The Report Server allows us to make our reports available to end users. We reviewed the various ways that reports and their supporting resources can be moved from the development environment to the Report Server. We also reviewed the security features that the Report Server provides.

In addition to all this, we looked at the Report Manager interface, which provides users with one method of accessing reports on the Report Server. In this chapter, we will look at additional ways to take reports from the Report Server to the users. We will also look at ways to manage how and when reports are executed. These features can be used to level out server load and to increase user response time.

Caching In

One of the best features of Reporting Services is the fact that the data is requeried each time the report is executed. This is shown in Figure 11-1. The user is not viewing information from a static web page that is weeks or months old. Reporting Services reports include data that is accurate up to the second that the report was run.

This feature can also be the source of one of the drawbacks of Reporting Services. The user is required to wait for the data to be requeried each time a report is run. If your query or stored procedure runs quickly, this may not be a problem. However,

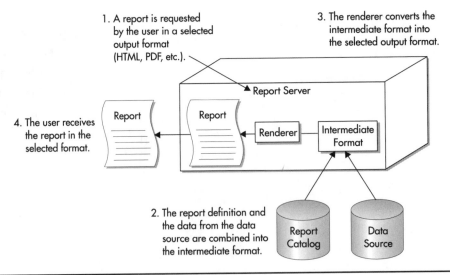

Figure 11-1   *Serving a report without caching*

even fairly quick queries can slow down a server if enough of them are running at the same time.

Fortunately, Reporting Services has a solution to this problem. The solution is report caching.

Report Caching

With many reports, it is not essential to have up-to-the-second data. You may be reporting from a data source that is only updated once or twice a day. The business needs of your users may only require data that is accurate as of the end of the previous day. In these types of situations, it does not make sense to have the data requeried every time a user requests a report. Report caching is the answer.

Report caching is an option that can be turned on for reports on the Report Server. It is turned on individually for each report. When this option is turned on, the Report Server saves a copy, or *instance,* of the report in a temporary location the first time the report is executed, as shown in Figure 11-2.

Upon subsequent executions, with the same parameter values chosen, the Report Server pulls the information necessary to render the report from the report cache rather than requerying data from the database, as shown in Figure 11-3. Because these subsequent executions do not need to requery data, they are, in most cases, faster than the report execution without caching.

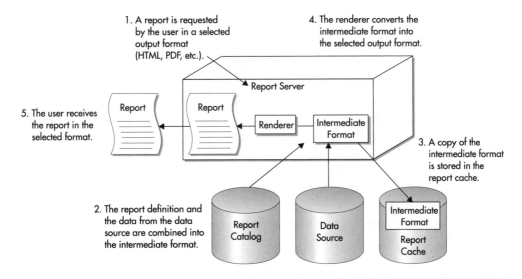

Figure 11-2   *Serving a report with caching, the first time*

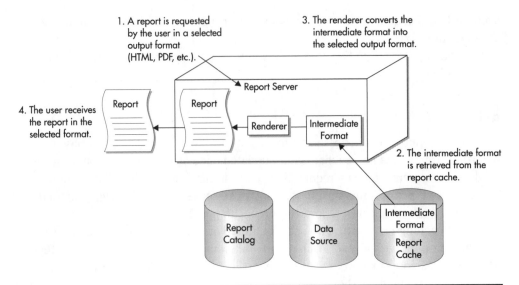

Figure 11-3   *Serving a report with caching, the subsequent times*

Cached Report Expiration

Once an instance of the report is stored in the report cache, it is assigned an expiration date and time. The expiration date and time can be calculated in one of two ways. The expiration date can be calculated based on a certain number of minutes after the creation of the cached instance. For example, the cached instance of the report will exist for 30 minutes and then it will be deleted. Alternatively, the expiration date can be determined by a set schedule. For example, the cached instance of the report will be deleted at 2:00 A.M. every Sunday morning.

The first type of expiration calculation is appropriate for a report that requires a large amount of database resources and is run often, but does not require up-to-the-second data. We can decrease the workload on the database server by fulfilling most of the requests for the report from the report cache. Every 30 minutes we throw the cached report away. The next person who requests the report causes a new instance of the report, with updated data, to be placed in the report cache.

The second type of expiration calculation is appropriate for reports run against data that changes on a scheduled basis. Perhaps you have a report that is being run from your data warehouse. The data warehouse is updated from your transactional database each Sunday at 12:30 A.M. The data in the warehouse remains static in between these loads. The cached report is scheduled to expire right after the data load is completed. The next time the user requests the report after the expiration, a new instance of the report, with the updated data, is placed in the cache. This cached report contains up-to-date data until the next data load.

Cached Reports and Data Source Credentials

In order to create a cached instance of a report, the report must be using stored credentials. These can be credentials for either a Windows logon or a database logon, but they must be stored with the data source. If you think about this from a security standpoint, this is how it has to be.

Suppose for a minute that Reporting Services allowed a cached report to be created with Windows Integrated Security. The Windows credentials of the first person to run the report would be used to create a cached instance of the report. Subsequent users who request this report would receive this cached instance. However, this would mean that the subsequent users are receiving data in the report that was created using the credentials from another user.

If the results of the database query or stored procedure that populates this report vary based on the rights of the database login, we have the potential for a big problem. If the Vice President of Sales is the first person to run the report and create the cached instance, all subsequent users would receive information that was meant only for the VP! Conversely, if a sales representative is the first person to run the report and create the cached instance, when the VP comes along later and requests the report, he will not receive all the information he needs.

The same problem exists if the report prompts for credentials. The first person who runs the report and creates the cached instance is the one who supplies the credentials. Everyone who views the cached instance is essentially using someone else's logon to see this data.

The only way that caching works without creating the potential for a security problem is with credentials stored with the report. In this situation, the same credentials are used to access the database—whether it is the VP or a lowly sales representative running the report. There is no risk that the cached instance of the report will create a breach in database security.

Caching and Report Formats

You can see in Figure 11-2 that the intermediate format of the report, and not the final format of the report, is stored in the report cache. The intermediate format is a combination of the report definition and the data from the datasets. It is not formatted as an HTML page, a PDF document, or other type of rendering format. It is an internal format that is ready for rendering.

Because it is the intermediate format that is stored in the report cache, the cached report can be delivered in any rendering format. The user who first requested the report, and thus caused the cache instance to be created, may have received the report as an HTML document. The next user may receive the cached instance of the report and export it to a PDF document. A third user may receive the cached instance of the report and export it to an Excel file. Caching the intermediate format gives the report cache the maximum amount of flexibility.

Enabling Report Caching

Let's try enabling caching for one of our deployed reports. We actually have a report that is a good candidate for caching. The Weather report takes a long time to execute because of the calls to the web service. Also, the weather conditions that are returned by the web service are not going to change from minute to minute, so it is not essential to retrieve new information every time the report is executed. The Weather report will work just fine if it is retrieved from the cache, as long as we expire the cached instance fairly often, say every 45 minutes.

Enabling Report Caching for the Weather Report

Let's try enabling caching for the Weather report.

1. Open the Report Manager and navigate to the Chapter 08 folder.
2. Click Show Details.
3. Click the icon in the Edit column for the Weather report. The Properties page for the Weather report will appear.
4. Select Execution from the left side of the screen. The Execution Properties page will appear, as shown in Figure 11-4.
5. Select the option "Cache a Temporary Copy of the Report. Expire Copy of Report After a Number of Minutes."
6. Set the number of minutes to 45.
7. Click Apply.
8. Select the View tab. The Weather report will run.

The first time the Weather report runs after caching is turned on, the report needs to perform its regular execution process to gather the data for the intermediate format. This intermediate format is then copied to the report cache before it is rendered for you in the browser. Because the report goes through its regular execution process, it still takes a while to appear.

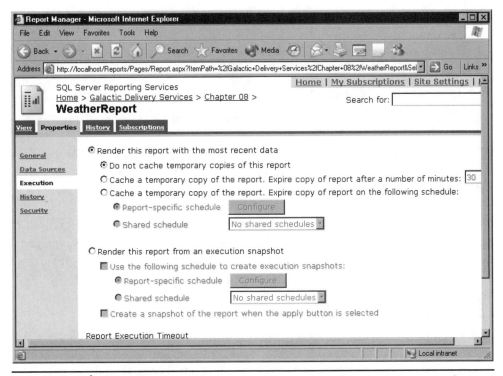

Figure 11-4 *The Execution Properties page*

Viewing the Report from the Report Cache

Now let's run the report. Because there is a cached copy of the report which has not expired, the report will be rendered from the cached copy.

1. Click the Refresh Report button in the toolbar. The report will appear almost immediately. That happened so fast, I bet you don't even believe that it retrieved the report. Let's try it again another way.

2. Click the Chapter 08 link at the top of the page.

3. Click the WeatherReport link in the Name column to run this report.

Pretty slick! The Report Server doesn't need to retrieve any data, execute any expressions, call any assemblies, or create the intermediate format. All it needs to do is convert the intermediate format into the rendered format (in this case, HTML).

What happens if we ask for a different rendering format?

1. Select "Acrobat (PDF) file" from the Select a Format drop-down list.

2. Click Export.

3. If a File Download dialog box appears, click Open.

4. Close the Adobe Acrobat Reader when you are finished viewing the report.

There will be a brief delay as the PDF document is created and your Acrobat Reader is opened. There is no delay to retrieve the information using the web service. Instead, the intermediate format comes from the report cache and is rendered into a PDF document.

If you wait 45 minutes, the cached copy will have expired and the report will again be executed to create the intermediate format. If you want to try this, you can put the book down, go have lunch, and then come back and run the report. It's okay. You go right ahead. I'll be here waiting when you get back.

Cache Expiration on a Schedule

You have just learned that the weather web service we are using for our Weather report is updated every hour on the hour. It makes sense that we set our cached copy of this report to expire on this same schedule. The cached copy should expire at five minutes past the hour, so a new copy of the weather information shows up the next time the report is run after the web service information has been updated.

1. Navigate to the Weather report in the Report Manager, if you are not already there.

2. Select the Properties tab. The Properties page will appear.

3. Select Execution from the left side of the screen. The Execution Properties page will appear.

4. Select "Cache a Temporary Copy of the Report. Expire Copy of Report on the Following Schedule."

5. Report-Specific Schedule will be selected by default. Click Configure next to Report-Specific Schedule. The Schedule page will appear, as shown in Figure 11-5.

6. You can specify hourly, daily, weekly, monthly, or one-time schedules. Select Hour.

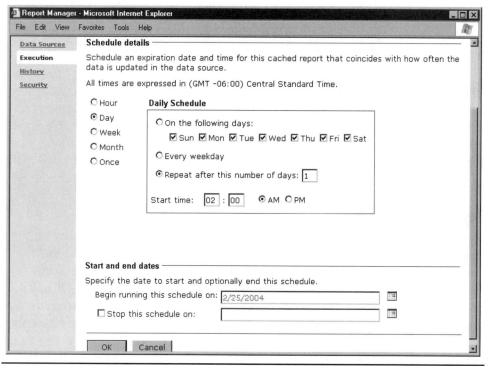

Figure 11-5   *The Schedule page*

7. Leave the Hourly Schedule set to run every 1 hours 00 minutes. Set Start Time to 5 minutes after the next hour. (If it is 2:30 P.M. now, set Start Time to 3:05 P.M.)

8. Select today's date for Begin Running This Schedule On. Leave the field Stop This Schedule On blank. (You change these dates by clicking the calendar icon to the right of the entry area. You cannot type in the date directly.)

> **NOTE**
>
> *Begin Running This Schedule On defaults to tomorrow's date. If you want a schedule to start today, you need to change this from the default setting.*

9. Click OK to return to the Execution Properties page. Note the description of the schedule you just created under Report-Specific Schedule.

10. Click Apply to save your changes to the report cache settings.

11. Select the View tab. The Weather report will run.

Again, the report will take longer to execute the first time as the intermediate format is created and put into the report cache. This cached instance of the report will remain there until 5 minutes past the hour.

Report Cache and Deploying

When a cached report instance expires, either because of a schedule or because it has existed for its maximum length of time, it is removed from the report cache. One other circumstance will cause a cached report instance to be removed from the report cache. If a new copy of a report is deployed from Visual Studio or uploaded using the Report Manager, any cached instances of that report are removed from the report cache.

Report Caching and Report Parameters

Report caching works just fine with reports that are the same each time they are run—that is, reports that do not have any parameters. What about reports whose content changes based on user parameters? Suppose we have a report that requires the user to enter a month as a parameter. One user runs the report for March and creates a cached instance containing the March data. Now a second user runs the report selecting May for the report parameter. Because there is a nonexpired instance of the report in the report cache, it would seem that the report should come from the report cache. If this were to happen, though, the second user would receive the March data instead of the May data.

Fortunately, the Report Server is smart enough to handle this situation. As part of the instance of the report in the report cache, the Report Server stores any parameter values that were used to create that cached instance, as shown in Figure 11-6. The

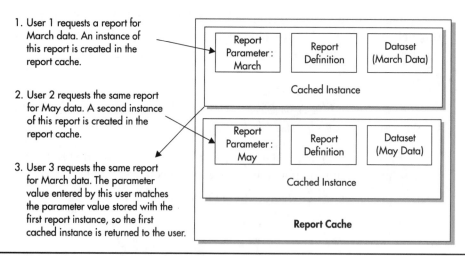

Figure 11-6   *Report caching with parameters*

cached instance is used to satisfy requests made by a subsequent user only if all the parameters used to create the cached instance match the parameters entered by the subsequent user.

Report Caching and Security

Not all users can change report caching properties. In order to change the report caching properties for a report, you must have rights to the Manage Reports task. Of the four predefined security roles, the Content Manager, My Reports, and Publisher roles have rights to this task.

Execution Snapshots

Report caching is a great tool for improving the performance of reports with long execution times. However, there is still one problem. The first user who requests the report after the cached instance has expired has to wait for the report to be created from the underlying data. It would be nice if there was a way to have cached report instances created automatically so that no user has to endure these wait times. Fortunately, Reporting Services can do this as well.

An *execution snapshot* is another way to create a cached report instance. Up to this point, we have discussed situations where cached report instances are created as the result of a user action. A user requests a report, and a copy of that report's intermediate format is placed in the report cache. With execution snapshots, a cached report instance is created automatically.

Execution snapshots can create cached report instances on a scheduled basis, or they can be created as soon as this feature is turned on for a particular report. If a schedule is used, each time the schedule is run, it replaces the current cached instance with a new one. Cached report instances created by an execution snapshot are used to satisfy user report requests the same as any other cached report instance.

Enabling Execution Snapshots

There are two methods for enabling the creation of execution snapshots. We will look at the manual method first.

Manually Creating an Execution Snapshot

Let's try enabling execution snapshots for the Weather report:

1. Navigate to the Weather report in the Report Manager, if you are not already there.
2. Select the Properties tab. The Properties page will appear.

3. Select Execution from the left side of the screen. The Execution Properties page will appear.

4. Select the option Render This Report from an Execution Snapshot.

5. Check the Create a Snapshot of the Report When the Apply Button Is Selected check box.

6. Click Apply. As soon as you click Apply, the Report Server will execute the report and place an instance of the report in the report cache. Allow time for this process to complete.

7. Select the View tab.

The report will be rendered from the cached report instance created by the execution snapshot.

Creating Execution Snapshots on a Schedule

Now let's try the scheduled approach to creating execution snapshots:

1. Select the Properties tab. The Execution Properties page should appear. If not, select Execution from the left side of the page.

2. Check the Use the Following Schedule to Create Execution Snapshots check box.

3. Report-Specific Schedule will be selected by default. Click Configure next to Report-Specific Schedule. The Schedule page will appear.

4. You can specify hourly, daily, weekly, monthly, or one-time schedules. The Day option should be selected by default. Leave this option selected.

5. Select On the Following Days.

6. Uncheck all the days except for today. (If you are reading this on Monday, for example, leave only Monday checked.)

7. Set the start time to 5 minutes from now.

8. Select today's date for Begin Running This Schedule On.

9. Check the box Stop This Schedule On and then select tomorrow's date.

NOTE

I know this schedule does not fit the stated business requirements of refreshing the report at 5 minutes past the hour. However, you probably don't want to waste computer resources generating an execution snapshot of the Weather report, so we will use this schedule for the demonstration.

10. Click OK to return to the Execution Properties page. Note the description of the schedule you just created under Report-Specific Schedule.

11. Click Apply to save your changes to the execution snapshot settings. After 5 minutes, the scheduled execution snapshot will create a cached instance of the report.

12. Select the View tab after 5 minutes. (Go grab some caffeine while you are waiting. You wouldn't want to fall asleep while you are working through all this good stuff!) The Weather report will run and will be rendered from the cached report instance created by your scheduled execution snapshot.

This type of execution snapshot schedule would be appropriate for a report whose underlying data is changed only once per week (again, think of a data warehouse that is updated from a transactional system). The execution snapshot would be scheduled to create a new cached instance of the report right after the new data is available in the warehouse.

Execution Snapshots and Report Parameters

Execution snapshots are created either as soon as the feature is turned on or on a scheduled basis. Because this happens as a background process with no user interface, there is no opportunity to specify parameter values at the time that the execution snapshot creates the cached instance of the report. This fact makes using execution snapshots a little more of a challenge with reports that include parameters.

The way to get around this problem is to specify default values for all the report parameters. When the execution snapshot creates the cached report instance, it will use the default values for each of the report parameters. A side effect of this is that these default values actually become locked in and you can no longer change them.

Execution Snapshots and Security

Not all users can change execution snapshots. In order to change the execution snapshot properties for a report, you must have rights to the Manage Reports task. Of the four predefined security roles, the Content Manager, My Reports, and Publisher roles have rights to this task.

Report History

The report history feature of the Report Manager allows you to keep copies of a report's past execution. This allows you to save the state of your data without having to save copies of the data itself. You can keep documentation of inventory levels, production schedules, or financial records. You can look back in time, using the report history to do trend analysis or to verify past information.

Enabling Report History

In order to demonstrate the report history feature of Reporting Services, we need a report whose results change often. It just so happens we have such a report in our Chapter08 solution. The TransportMonitor report provides different values every time that the report is run. We will move that report to the Report Server and then enable the report history.

1. Open the Report Manager and navigate to the Chapter 08 folder.

2. Use the Upload File button to upload the TransportMonitor report from the Chapter 08 solution.

3. Select Show Details, if it is available in the report viewer toolbar. If it is not available, you are already in Show Details mode.

4. Click the icon in the Edit column for the TransportMonitor report. The Properties page will appear.

5. Click Parameters on the left side of the page. The Parameters page will appear.

6. Click the Has Default check box and type **1304** for Default Value.

7. Click Apply.

8. Click Data Sources on the left side of the page. The Data Sources page will appear.

9. Click Browse. The Data Source page will appear.

10. Use the tree view to find the 2004 Conference folder in the tree structure. The 2004 Conference folder is inside the Galactic Delivery Services folder.

11. Select the Galactic shared data source and click OK.

12. Click Apply.

13. Click History on the left side of the page. The History Properties page will appear, as shown in Figure 11-7.

14. Click the View tab at the top of the page. Remember, this report has autorefresh set. After a few seconds, the report will refresh and new data will be displayed.

15. Make sure the Allow History to Be Created Manually check box is checked. If it is not, check it and click Apply.

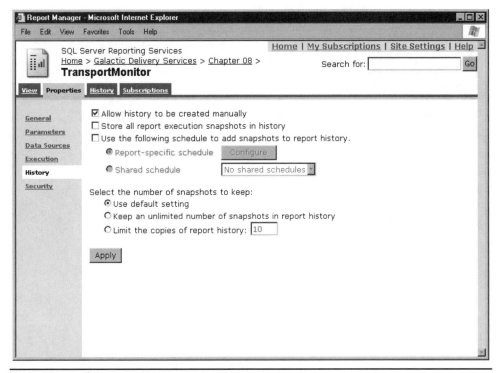

Figure 11-7   *The History Properties page*

Manually Creating a Report History Snapshot

One way to create a report history is to do so manually. We will give this a try in the following example:

1. Select the History tab. (This is the History tab along the top, not the History link on the left side of the page.) The Create/View History page will appear.

2. Click the New Snapshot button in the report viewer toolbar. An entry for a report history snapshot will appear.

3. Click the New Snapshot button two more times to create two more report history snapshots, as shown in Figure 11-8.

4. Click the link in the When Run column to the first report history snapshot you created. This report should appear in a new browser window.

5. Open the other two report history snapshots and compare all three.

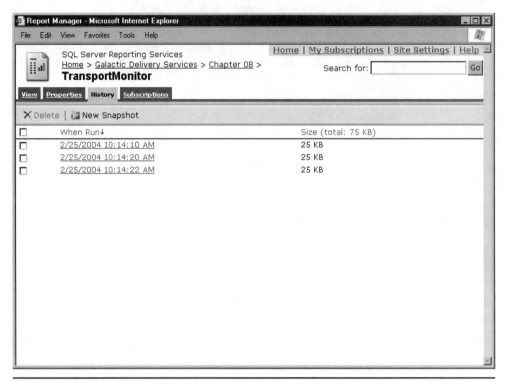

Figure 11-8 *The Create/View History page*

As with the cached report instances, the report history snapshots store the intermediate format of the report. Due to this fact, you can export this report to any of the rendering formats.

1. Select one of your browser windows containing a report history snapshot.

2. Export the snapshot to the Acrobat (PDF) file format and open it in Adobe Acrobat Reader.

3. Close Acrobat Reader and the browser windows containing your report history snapshots.

Report History Snapshots and Report Parameters

To make our TransportMonitor report work with report history snapshots, we had to provide a default value for the transport number parameter. These parameters cannot be changed when each snapshot is created. (They can be changed, however, if the report is run normally through the Report Manager.)

Essentially, we are saving report history snapshots for only one transport. In order to save report history snapshots for other transports, we need to create linked reports with parameters defaulted to the other transport numbers.

1. Select the Properties tab.
2. Click General on the left side of the page.
3. Click Create Linked Report.
4. Type **Transport 1305 Monitor** for Name and **The Transport Monitor Report for Transport 1305** for Description.
5. Click OK. The linked report will execute.
6. Select the Properties tab.
7. Click Parameters on the left side of the page.
8. Change Default Value to **1305**.
9. Click Apply.
10. Click the History tab.
11. Click New Snapshot.
12. Click the entry for the new snapshot to view it. You can see that this is a snapshot for transport number 1305.
13. Close the browser window containing your report history snapshot.

We can create as many linked reports as we need to collect report history snapshots for the different possible parameter values. Remember that linked reports all point back to a single report definition. If the TransportMonitor report is ever updated, it will only need to be deployed in one location, and all the linked reports will have the updated report definition.

Additional Methods for Creating Report History Snapshots

You can create report history snapshots in two other ways, in addition to the manual method just described. You can instruct the Report Server to create a report history snapshot each time it creates an execution snapshot. With this setting turned on, any time the Report Server creates an execution snapshot—either manually or on a scheduled basis—a copy of that execution snapshot is saved as a report history snapshot.

Additionally, you can set up a schedule to create your report history snapshots. Let's give that a try:

1. Click the Chapter 08 link at the top of the page.

2. Click the icon in the Edit column for the TransportMonitor report. (The original report, not the linked copy.)

3. Select the Properties tab.

4. Click History on the left side of the page.

5. Check the Use the Following Schedule to Add Snapshots to Report History check box.

6. Report-Specific Schedule will be selected by default. Click Configure next to Report-Specific Schedule. The Schedule page will appear.

7. Select Hour.

8. Change the Hourly Schedule to run every 0 hours 1 minutes. Set Start Time to 5 minutes from now.

9. Select today's date for Begin Running This Schedule On.

10. Check the Stop This Schedule On check box and set it to tomorrow's date.

11. Click OK to return to the History Properties page. Note the description of the schedule you just created under Report-Specific Schedule.

12. Click Apply to save your changes to the history snapshot settings.

13. Select the History tab.

As each minute passes beyond the time you chose for the schedule to start, a new report history snapshot will be created. You will need to refresh you browser to see the new history snapshots in the list.

Report History Snapshots and Security

Not all users can change report history snapshot properties. In order to change the report history snapshot properties for a report, you must have rights to the Manage Report History task. Of the four predefined security roles, the Content Manager and My Reports roles have rights to this task.

Managing Report History Snapshots

You will not usually have a report that requires a new report history snapshot every minute of the day as we set up in our example. Even so, report history snapshots can start to pile up if you let them. It is important to make business decisions about the number of history snapshots to save for each report. It is then even more important to implement those business decisions and manage the number of history snapshots that are actually being saved on the Report Server.

Setting Limits on the Number of Report History Snapshots

Reporting Services provides a way to limit the number of history snapshots that are saved for any given report. Let's take a look and put a limit on our TransportMonitor report snapshots at the same time.

1. Select the Properties tab.
2. In the Select the Number of Snapshots to Keep section of the page, select the Limit the Copies of Report History option.
3. Set the limit to 5.
4. Click Apply to save your changes to the history snapshot settings.
5. Click OK in response to the warning dialog box.
6. Select the History tab.

If you waited long enough to accumulate more than five report history snapshots, you will see that the list has been reduced to the five most recent history snapshots. The older history snapshots were automatically deleted. As each new history snapshot is created, the oldest history snapshot is deleted, so the total always remains at five. Again, remember that you need to refresh your browser to see these changes as each minute passes.

We chose to set a limit on the number of history snapshots saved for this report. In addition to this option, you have two others to choose from (see Figure 11-7). You can keep an unlimited number of history snapshots, or you can use the default setting for history snapshot retention. You will see how to change this default setting later in this chapter.

Manually Deleting Report History Snapshots

In addition to using the history snapshot limit on the History Properties page, you can also manually delete unwanted history snapshots.

1. Refresh your browser.

CAUTION

If you have reached the limit of five history snapshots, the Report Server is automatically deleting old history snapshots as new ones are created. If your Create/View History page is not up to date, you could try to delete a history snapshot that has already been removed by the Report Server. This will result in an error.

2. Check the check box in the Delete column for three of the snapshot history entries.

3. Click Delete in the History tab toolbar.

4. Click OK to confirm the deletion.

The Report Server will again accumulate history snapshots for this report until it has reached our five snapshot limit. At that point, it will again delete the oldest history snapshot as each new one is created.

Disabling Report History Snapshot Creation

We will now disable the creation of report history snapshots for this report so we are not wasting valuable execution cycles.

1. Select the Properties tab.

2. Uncheck the Use the Following Schedule to Add Snapshots to Report History check box.

3. Click Apply.

4. Select the History tab.

New history snapshots will no longer be created for this report on a scheduled basis. Note, however, that the existing history snapshots were not deleted. These history snapshots are still available for viewing, even though the schedule that created them has been disabled.

Updating Report Definitions and Report History Snapshots

One of the best features of report history snapshots is that they are not lost if the definition of the underlying report is changed. Let's see this in action.

1. Start Visual Studio and open the Chapter08 solution.

2. Open the TransportMonitor report layout.

3. Increase the height of the report body and move the table item down so there is room at the top of the layout area.

4. Place a text box across the top of the layout area.

5. Type the following expression in the text box:

```
="Transport: " & Parameters!TransportNumber.Value
```

6. Click Save All in the toolbar.

7. Right-click the Chapter08 project entry in the Solution Explorer. Select Properties from the context menu. The Chapter08 Property Pages dialog box will appear.

8. Fill in the appropriate values to deploy this report to the Galactic Delivery Services/Chapter 08 folder. (Refer back to Chapter 10 if you need help with this.)

9. Click OK to exit the Chapter08 Property Pages dialog box.

10. Right-click the TransportMonitor report in the Solution Explorer and select Deploy from the context menu.

11. After the deployment has succeeded, close Visual Studio.

12. Return to the Report Manager in your browser.

13. Select the View tab for the TransportMonitor report. Note that the report now includes our change, placing the transport number at the top of the report.

14. Select the History tab. We still have some report history snapshots based on the old report definition.

15. Click New Snapshot to manually create a report history snapshot based on the new report definition. Our five history snapshot limit is still in effect, so one of the old history snapshots may have to be deleted to make room for the new one.

16. Click the most recent history snapshot to view it. It has the transport number at the top because it is based on the new report definition.

17. Close this browser window.

18. Click the oldest history snapshot to view it. It does not have the transport number at the top because it is based on the old report definition.

19. Close this browser window.

Just like the cached report instance, the report history snapshot contains both the report definition and the dataset. Therefore, it is unaffected by subsequent changes to the report definition.

Subscriptions

Up to this point, we have discussed only one way for users to receive reports. They log on to the Report Manager site, find the report they want, and execute it. This is known as *pull* technology. The user pulls the information out of Reporting Services by initiating the execution of the report.

Reporting Services also supports *push* technology for delivering reports. In a push scenario, Reporting Services initiates the execution of the report and then sends the report to the user. This is done through the report *subscription*.

Standard Subscriptions

Reporting Services supports several types of subscriptions. The first is the *standard* subscription. A standard subscription is a request to push a particular report to a particular user or set of users. The standard subscription is usually a self-serve operation. A user logs on to the Report Manager site and finds the report they want. The user then creates the subscription by specifying the schedule for the push delivery and the delivery options.

There are two delivery options for standard subscriptions: e-mail and file share. The e-mail delivery option will, of course, send an e-mail to the specified e-mail addresses with the report either embedded as HTML or as an attached document. The file share option will create a file containing the report in a specified folder on a file share. The file share option can be used to place the report into a document store that is managed and/or indexed by another application such as Microsoft's SharePoint Portal Services.

Creating a Standard E-Mail Subscription with an Embedded Report

You have been hired as the traffic manager for Galactic Delivery Services and are responsible for routing transport traffic. As part of your job, it is important to know what the weather is like at all the hubs. Rather than taking the time to go look at the Weather report on the Report Manager website, you would like to have the report e-mailed to you hourly.

1. Open the Report Manager and navigate to the Chapter 08 folder.

2. Click Show Details.

3. Click the icon in the Edit column for the Weather report.

4. Select the Subscriptions tab. The Create/View Subscriptions page will appear.

5. Click New Subscription. The Subscription Properties page will appear, as shown in Figure 11-9 and Figure 11-10.

6. The Delivered By drop-down list defaults to Report Server E-Mail. Leave this as the default setting.

7. Type your e-mail address for To. Note that you can enter multiple e-mail addresses, separated by a semicolon (;), and you can also enter e-mail addresses for Cc and Bcc.

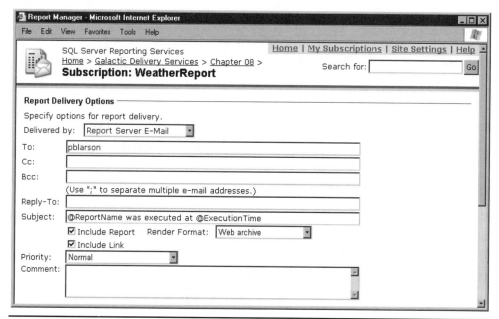

Figure 11-9   *The Subscription Properties page, top*

8. Enter an e-mail address for Reply-To. This can be your own e-mail address, someone else's, or a dummy e-mail address that does not even exist.

9. By default, the subject of the e-mail will be the name of the report followed by the time the report was executed. Change Subject to **@ReportName**.

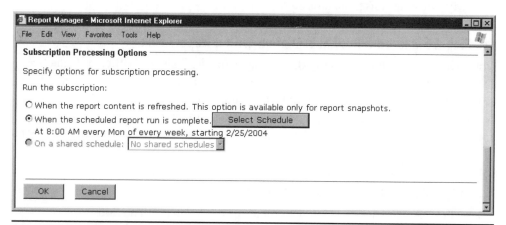

Figure 11-10   *The Subscription Properties page, bottom*

10. Leave the Include Report check box checked. This will include the report in the e-mail. Uncheck the Include Link check box.

11. The Render Format drop-down list will default to Web Archive. Leave this default value.

12. Select High from the Priority drop-down list.

13. For Comment, type **This e-mail was sent from Reporting Services**.

14. For Run the Subscription, select the option When the Scheduled Report Run Is Complete.

15. Click Select Schedule. The Schedule page will appear.

16. Select Hour.

17. Leave the schedule to run every 1 hour and 00 minutes. Set the start time to 5 minutes from now.

18. Select today's date for Begin Running This Schedule On.

19. Check Stop This Schedule On and select tomorrow's date.

20. Click OK to return to the Schedule Properties page.

21. Click OK to create this standard subscription and return to the View/Edit Subscriptions page.

22. After the time specified by your schedule has passed, refresh this page. You should see the time of the execution in the Last Run column and "Mail sent to" followed by your e-mail address in the Status column. You should also have a high-priority e-mail waiting for you in your mailbox.

23. Do not delete this subscription until you have had a chance to look at the My Subscriptions page later in this chapter.

Creating a Standard E-Mail Subscription with a Report Link

You have just been promoted to sales manager for the Axelburg office of Galactic Delivery Services. Congratulations. Being a good manager, you want to keep tabs on how your sales people are doing. In order to do this, you want to view the Invoice-Batch Number report each week to see how much you are invoicing your clients. As a memory aid, you would like to receive an e-mail each week with a link to this report.

1. Open the Report Manager and navigate to the Axelburg folder.

2. Click the Invoice-Batch Number report to execute it.

3. Click New Subscription in the toolbar for the View tab. The Subscription Properties page will appear.

4. Delivered By defaults to Report Server E-Mail. Leave this as the default setting.

5. Type your e-mail address for To.

6. Enter an e-mail address for Reply-To.

7. Change Subject to **@ReportName**.

8. Uncheck the Include Report check box. Leave the Include Link check box checked.

9. Render Format is not used because we are just embedding a link to the report.

10. Select High from the Priority drop-down list.

11. For Comment, type **Remember to check the invoice amounts**.

12. For Run the Subscription, select the option When the Scheduled Report Run Is Complete.

13. Click Select Schedule. The Schedule page will appear.

14. Select Week.

15. Leave Repeat After This Number of Weeks set to 1.

16. Check today for On day(s). For example, Check Mon if today is Monday. Uncheck all the other days.

17. Set the start time to 5 minutes from now.

18. Select today's date for Begin Running This Schedule On.

19. Check Stop This Schedule On and select tomorrow's date.

20. Click OK to return to the Schedule Properties page.

21. At the bottom of the Schedule Properties page, you will see a list of the parameters for the selected report. If necessary, you can specify a set of parameters to use when running this subscription. Leave the default values for the parameters.

22. Click OK to create this standard subscription and return to the Report Viewer page.

When the scheduled time has passed, you will receive an e-mail with a link to this report.

Standard Subscriptions and Execution Snapshots

In addition to creating your own schedule for your standard subscriptions, you can also synchronize your subscriptions with scheduled execution snapshots. For example, the Weather report is set to create an execution snapshot every hour. We want to receive an e-mail with the new version of the report after each new execution snapshot has been created.

One way to do this is to keep the schedule for the execution snapshot synchronized with the schedule for the subscription. The execution snapshot runs, then the subscription runs 1 minute later. This can cause problems if the execution snapshot occasionally takes more than 1 minute to create or if one of the schedules is edited.

A better solution is to let the creation of the execution snapshot drive the delivery of the subscription. The When the Report Content Is Refreshed option does just that (refer back to Figure 11-10). When this option is selected for a subscription, the subscription is sent out every time a new execution snapshot is created. Of course, this option is only available for reports that have execution snapshots enabled.

Multiple Subscriptions on One Report

There is nothing that prevents a user from creating more than one subscription on the same report. Perhaps you want a report delivered every Friday and on the last day of the month. You can't do this with one subscription, but you can certainly do it with two—a weekly subscription for the Friday delivery and a monthly subscription for delivery on the last day of the month.

Another reason for multiple subscriptions is to receive a report run for multiple sets of parameters. You saw, when setting up the subscription for the Invoice-Batch Number report, that you can specify parameter values as part of the subscription properties. Using this feature, you could have one subscription send you a report with one set of parameters and another subscription send you the same report with a different set of parameters.

Embedded Report Versus Attached Report

When you choose to include the report along with the subscription e-mail, the report can either show up embedded in an HTML e-mail or as an attached document. If you select the Web archive format, the report will be embedded. If you select any of the other render formats, the report will be sent as an attached document.

Having the report embedded in the e-mail makes it very convenient for the user to view the report. It is simply part of the body of your e-mail. However, not all e-mail packages support HTML e-mail, so there may be some users who cannot view an embedded report. If a user is not sure of the capabilities of their e-mail package, they should choose the Acrobat (PDF) file format. This format will be sent as an attachment and can be viewed by just about anyone.

Standard Subscriptions and Security

Not all users can create standard subscriptions. In fact, it is possible to view a report but not be able to subscribe to it. In order to subscribe to a report or create a subscription for delivery to others, you must have rights to the Manage Individual Subscriptions task. Of the four predefined security roles, the Browser, Content Manager, and My Reports roles have rights to manage individual subscriptions.

Managing Your Subscriptions

An active user may subscribe to a number of reports scattered throughout a number of folders. Just remembering all the reports you have subscribed to can be a big challenge. Managing all those subscriptions can be even tougher. Fortunately, the Report Manager provides a way to view all your subscriptions in one place.

My Subscriptions

The My Subscriptions page consolidates all your standard subscriptions in one place.

1. Click the My Subscriptions link at the top of the page. The My Subscriptions page will appear, as shown in Figure 11-11.

2. You can click on any heading to sort your list of subscriptions.

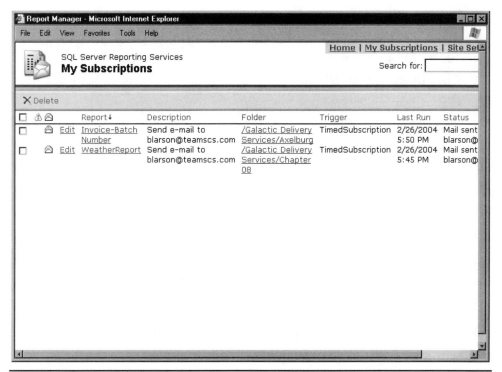

Figure 11-11   *The My Subscriptions page*

3. Click the Edit link next to WeatherReport. The Subscription Properties page will appear.

4. You can make changes to this subscription, if you desire. Click Cancel to return to the My Subscriptions page.

5. Click the WeatherReport link in the Report column. You will jump to the Weather report.

6. Click your browser's Back button.

7. Click the text in the Folder column for the Invoice-Batch Number report. You will jump to the Axelburg folder.

8. Click your browser's Back button.

The My Subscriptions page lists all the standard subscriptions you have created on this Report Server. This makes the subscriptions much easier to manage. You can sort the list several different ways to help you find and manage the subscriptions. You can also use the My Subscriptions page to delete unwanted subscriptions.

Let's delete these subscriptions so you do not waste computing power e-mailing reports.

1. Check the check box in the headings. This will automatically check the check box next to each subscription.

2. Click Delete in the toolbar.

3. Click OK to confirm the deletion.

4. Click the Home link at the top of the page. You will return to the Home folder.

Data-Driven Subscriptions

A better name for a data-driven subscription might be "mass mailing." The data-driven subscription allows you to take a report and e-mail it to a number of people on a mailing list. The mailing list can be queried from any valid Reporting Services data source. The mailing list can contain fields, in addition to the recipient's e-mail address, that are used to control the content of the e-mail sent to each recipient. As mentioned in Chapter 2, the Enterprise Edition of Reporting Services is required in order for you to use data-driven subscriptions.

Creating a Data-Driven Subscription

Transport 1305 has been acting up. GDS wants all of its mechanics to have a good background on the types of problems that this transport is having. To facilitate this, the results from the Transport 1305 Monitor report should be e-mailed to all mechanics every 4 hours. Employees holding the position of Mechanic I should receive the report as a high-priority e-mail. Employees holding the position of Mechanic II should receive the report as a normal-priority e-mail.

1. Open the Report Manager and navigate to the Chapter 08 folder.

2. Click Show Detail.

3. Click the icon in the Edit column for the Transport 1305 Monitor report.

4. Select the Subscriptions tab.

5. Click the New Data-Driven Subscription button. The first page of the Data-Driven Subscription process will appear, as shown in Figure 11-12.

6. Type **Maintenance Watch on Transport 1305** for Description.

7. Select Report Server E-Mail from the Specify How Recipients Are Notified drop-down list.

8. Select the Specify a Shared Data Source option.

9. Click the Next button. The Shared Data Source page will appear, as shown in Figure 11-13.

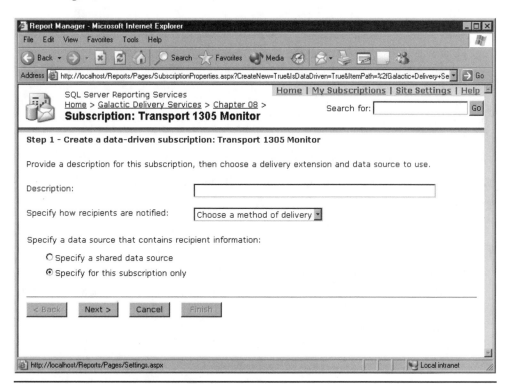

Figure 11-12   *Data-Driven Subscription process, first page*

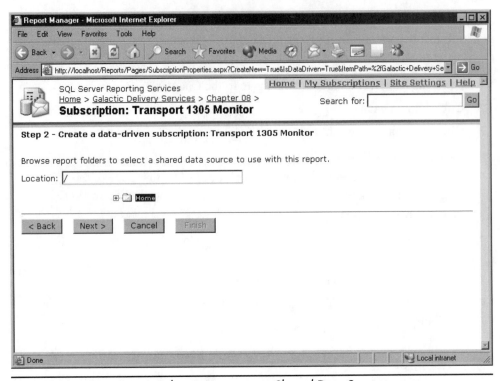

Figure 11-13 *Data-Driven Subscription process, Shared Data Source page*

10. Use the tree view to find the 2004 Conference folder in the Galactic Delivery Services folder.

11. Select the Galactic shared data source in the 2004 Conference folder.

12. Click the Next button. The Query page will appear, as shown in Figure 11-14.

13. Type the following for the query:

    ```
    EXEC stp_MechanicMailingList
    ```

14. Click Validate to make sure there aren't any typos or other problems.

15. If the query does not validate successfully, look for the error in the query you typed. Otherwise, click Next. The Data Association page will appear as shown in Figure 11-15. Here, you will associate columns in the result set with fields in the subscription e-mail.

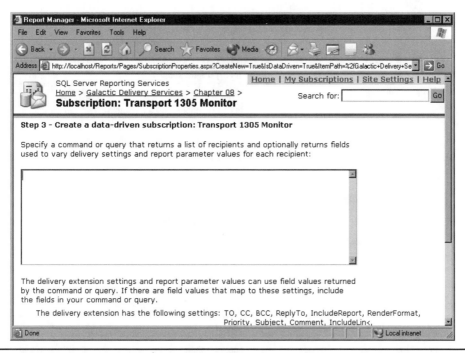

Figure 11-14   *Data-Driven Subscription process, Query page*

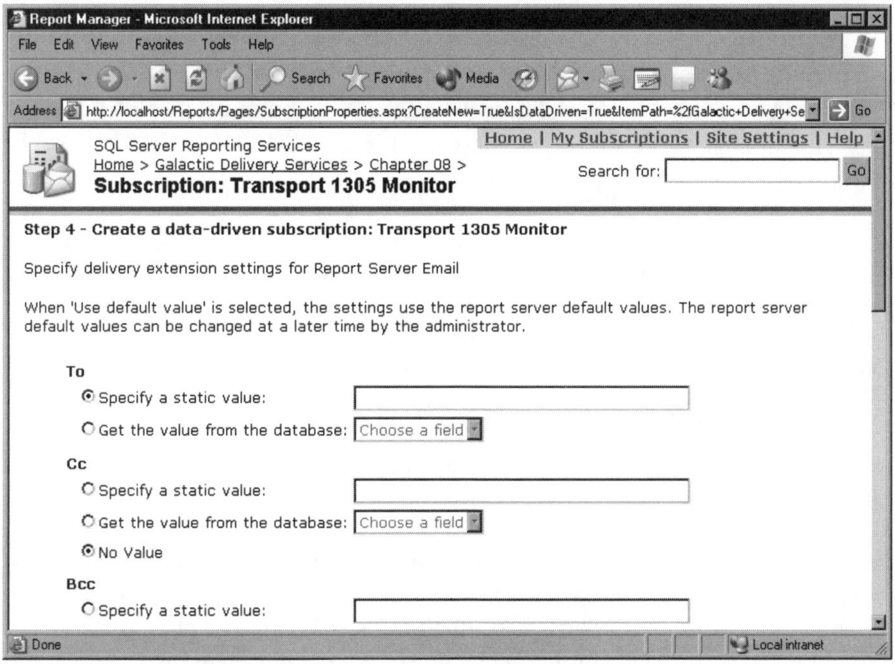

Figure 11-15   *Data-Driven Subscription process, Data Association page*

16. Set the following properties on this page:

Property	Value
To	Specify a static value
Specify a static value (For To)	(Type your e-mail address here. Normally, you would select the e-mail address from a database field, but we want to have a valid e-mail address for our example. Because your system cannot send interplanetary e-mail, we will have to use your e-mail address.)
Reply-To	Specify a static value
Specify a static value (Reply-To)	Reports@Galactic.SRA
Render Format	Specify a static value
Specify a static value (Render Format)	Acrobat (PDF) file
Priority	Get the value from the database
Get the value from the database (Priority)	Priority
Subject	Get the value from the database
Get the value from the database (Subject)	Subject
Include Link	Specify a static value
Specify a static value (Include Link)	False

17. Click the Next button. The Parameter Values page will appear, as shown in Figure 11-16.

18. Leave this page set to the defaults. Click the Next button. The Notify Recipients page will appear, as shown in Figure 11-17.

19. Select the On a Schedule Created for This Subscription option.

20. Click the Next button. The Schedule page will appear.

21. Select the Hour option.

22. Change the schedule to run every 4 hours 00 minutes.

23. Set the start time to 5 minutes from now.

24. Select today's date for Begin Running This Schedule On.

25. Check Stop This Schedule On and select tomorrow's date.

26. Click Finish.

27. Once the scheduled time for your subscription has passed, refresh this page. You should see the time of the execution in the Last Run column and "Done: 8 processed of 8 total; 0 errors." in the Status column. You should also receive eight e-mails (there are eight mechanics in the database, and we sent an e-mail to each one) with the Transport 1305 Monitor report attached.

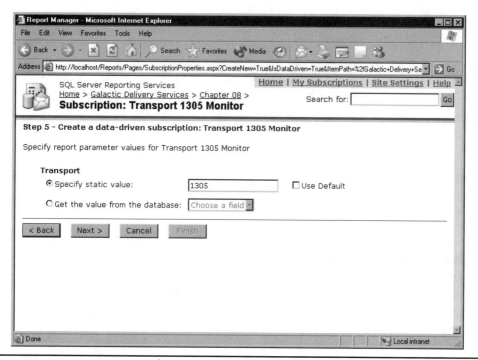

Figure 11-16   *Data-Driven Subscription process, Parameter Values page*

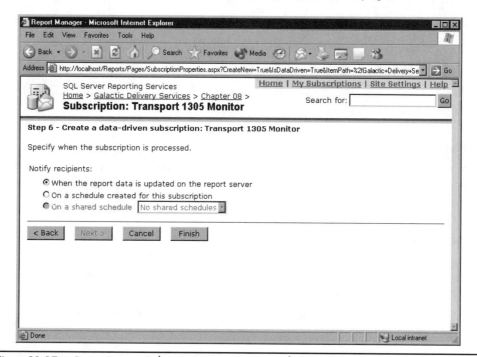

Figure 11-17   *Data-Driven Subscription process, Notify Recipients page*

28. If you do not want to receive eight e-mails every 4 hours for the next day, you can delete this subscription.

Data-Driven Subscriptions and Security

Not all users can create data-driven subscriptions. In order to create a data-driven subscription for a report, you must have rights to the Manage All Subscriptions task. Of the four predefined security roles, only the Content Manager role has rights to this task.

Site Settings

When setting the limit for the number of report history snapshots kept for a given report, we encountered a setting that referred to using a default value. Each time you have the opportunity to specify a schedule for an execution snapshot, a subscription, or other feature, you have an option to select a shared schedule. The report history snapshot default value, the shared schedules, and several other site-wide settings are managed on the Site Settings page.

Configuration Options and Default Values

The main Site Settings page allows you to set several default values and configuration options. This page also acts as a front end for other configuration screens. You can access the Site Settings page by clicking the Site Settings link at the top of the page. The main Site Settings page is shown in Figure 11-18.

We will begin our examination of the site settings by looking at the configuration items and default values on the main Site Settings page.

Name

The value in the Name field appears at the top of each page in the Report Manager. You can change this to the name of your company or some other phrase that will help users identify this report server.

Report History Default

The report history default setting allows you to specify a default value for the maximum number of report history snapshots to keep. This can be set to a specific number or set to allow an unlimited number of snapshots. Each report utilizing report history snapshots can either specify its own maximum number or use this default value.

Report Manager - Microsoft Internet Explorer

File   Edit   View   Favorites   Tools   Help

Home | My Subscriptions | Site Settings | Help

SQL Server Reporting Services
Site Settings

Search for: [   ] [Go]

Settings

Name: [SQL Server Reporting Services   ]

☐ Enable My Reports to support user-owned folders for publishing and running personalized reports.

Choose the role to apply to each user's My Reports folder: [My Reports ▼]

Select the default settings for report history:

⦿ Keep an unlimited number of snapshots in report history

○ Limit the copies of report history: [10]

Report Execution Timeout

○ Do not timeout report execution

⦿ Limit report execution to the following number of seconds: [1800]

☑ Enable report execution logging

☑ Remove log entries older than this number of days: [60]

[Apply]

Security

Configure site-wide security
Configure item-level role definitions
Configure system-level role definitions

Figure 11-18   *The main Site Settings page*

Report Execution Timeout

The default for Report Execution Timeout allows you to specify a default value for the maximum amount of time a report may run before it times out. This can be a specific number of seconds or set to no timeout (unlimited execution time). Each report can either specify its own timeout value or use this default value.

NOTE
The report execution timeout is specified on the Execution Properties page for each report.

Report Execution Logging

The Enable Report Execution Logging option determines whether information about each report execution is placed in the execution log. The execution log that this option refers to is the ExecutionLog table in the ReportServer database. This is not referring to any of the log text files created by the Report Server application. Along with turning logging off and on, you can specify how long the Report Server will keep these log entries.

Your Reporting Services installation includes a DTS package you can use to copy the contents of the ExecutionLog into a set of user-defined tables. You can then use these user-defined tables as a data source and create reports showing the activity occurring on your Report Server. The DTS package is located in:

```
C:\Program Files\Microsoft SQL Server\80\Tools\
                            Reporting Service\ExecutionLog
```

For instructions on using this DTS package, search on "Querying and Reporting on Report Execution Log Data" on www.Microsoft.com.

My Reports

The Enable My Reports option turns on a feature giving each user their own private folder on the Report Server. When this option is enabled, a special folder called "Users Folders" is created in the Home folder. Only users assigned the System Administrator role can see this folder.

CAUTION

You should enable the My Reports option only if you intend to use it. It is a bit tricky to get rid of the Users Folders folder and its content once it is created. If you do create the folder and then need to delete this folder, turn off the My Reports option, then go into each folder in the Users Folders folder and give yourself Content Manager rights. Now you will be able to delete the folders.

Folders Created Through the My Reports Option

As each user logs on for the first time after the My Reports option is enabled, a new folder is created in the Users Folders folder. This new folder has the same name as the domain and logon name of the user signing in. The new folder will be mapped to a folder called "My Reports."

Let's discuss an example to make this clearer. Sally and Jose are two users in the Galactic domain. Shortly after the My Reports option is enabled, Sally accesses the Report Server using the Report Manager. A new folder is created in the Users Folders folder called "Galactic Sally."

Sally is not assigned the System Administrator role, so she cannot see the Users Folders folder or the Galactic Sally folder inside of it. Instead, when Sally views her Home folder, she sees a folder called "My Reports." Sally's My Reports folder is actually a mapping to the Galactic Sally folder.

When Jose accesses the Report Server using the Report Manager, a new folder is created in the Users Folders folder called "Galactic Jose." Jose sees a folder called "My Reports" in his Home folder. Jose's My Reports folder is actually a mapping to the Galactic Jose folder.

Jose is assigned the System Administrator role. In addition to the My Reports folder, Jose can view the Users Folders folder. When Jose opens the Users Folders folder, he can see both the Galactic Sally and the Galactic Jose folders. In fact, he can open the Galactic Sally folder and view its contents.

Security and My Reports

Because the My Reports folder is for each user's personal reports, the users are granted more rights in the My Reports folder than they might be granted anywhere else on the site. On the Site Settings page, you decide which security role to assign to the user in their own My Reports folder. By default, users are assigned the My Reports role in their own My Reports folder.

A user can be granted broader rights in the My Reports folder, because they are the only one who will be using the reports in this folder. No one else will be setting up caching and report history snapshots, for example, because no one else is going to use these reports. You will want to be sure and assign the user to a role that has rights to publish reports; otherwise, each user will not be able to put reports in their own My Reports folder.

When to Enable the My Report Option

There are two situations where the My Reports option can be useful. First of all, if you have a number of individuals who are creating ad hoc reports for their own personal use, the My Reports folder provides a convenient spot for this to take place. If you do use the My Reports folder in this manner, you will want to have some policies in place to ensure that each user's My Reports folder does not become an ad hoc dumping ground.

The second viable use of the My Reports folder is as a quality assurance (QA) testing area for report developers. The report developers can use their individual My Reports folders as a place to test a report in the server environment before it is deployed to a folder available to the users. This is convenient because the system administrator can navigate through the Users Folders folder to access the report, after it has passed QA testing, and move it to its production location. Of course, it is far better to have a dedicated quality assurance server for this purpose, but in situations where this is not feasible, the My Reports folder can be considered as an option.

Other Pages Accessed from the Site Settings Page

In addition to the configuration options and default values managed on the Site Settings page, the page itself serves as a menu to other pages. These pages allow you to manage the security configuration and other site-wide settings. The following is a brief discussion of each area managed from the Site Settings page.

Site-Wide Security

The Site-Wide Security page allows you to assign Windows users and Windows groups to system-level roles. These system-level roles provide users with the rights to view and modify settings for the Report Server, such as those found on the Site Settings page. System Administrator and System User are the two predefined system-level roles.

For more information on system-level roles and system-level tasks, see the "Security" section of Chapter 10.

Item-Level Role Definition

The Item-Level Role Definition page allows you to modify the item-level roles. The predefined item-level roles are Browser, Content Manager, Publisher, and My Reports. You can edit the tasks assigned to these roles or create new roles. If you look at this screen, you will see that it also includes the View Report security role that we defined in Chapter 10.

Take great care before modifying predefined roles. This will make it difficult for anyone else to work with your Reporting Services installation. Rather than modifying a predefined item-level role, copy the predefined role to a new name, make your modifications to this newly created role, and then use the new role to assign rights to users and groups.

For more information on item-level roles and item-level tasks, see the "Security" section of Chapter 10.

System-Level Role Definition

The System-Level Role Definition page allows you to modify the system-level roles. System Administrator and System User are the predefined system-level roles. You can edit the tasks assigned to these roles or create new roles.

Take great care before modifying predefined roles. This will make it difficult for anyone else to work with your Reporting Services installation. Rather than modifying a predefined system-level role, copy the predefined role to a new name, make your modifications to this newly-created role, then use the new role to assign rights to users and groups.

For more information on system-level roles and system-level tasks, see the "Security" section of Chapter 10.

Shared Schedules

Each time you had an option to create a schedule for a feature, such as report cache expiration or execution snapshot creation, it was accompanied by a choice to use a shared schedule. A shared schedule allows you to use a single schedule definition in multiple places. A shared schedule is created using the same page used to create all the other schedules we have been looking at in this chapter.

Shared schedules are beneficial for situations where a number of events should use the same timing. For example, suppose you have ten reports that utilize execution snapshots, all pulling data from a data warehouse. That data warehouse is updated once a week. It makes sense to create one shared schedule that can be used to run the execution snapshots for all these reports.

Not only does this save the time that would otherwise be necessary to create the schedule ten times, but it also makes it easier if the timing of the data warehouse update is changed and the execution snapshot schedule must be changed. If you are using a shared schedule, you only need to make this change once, in the shared location. Without the shared schedule, you would be forced to make this change ten times.

Manage Jobs

Scheduled items in Reporting Services use the SQL Agent to handle their operation. When you create a schedule for a task, such as creating an execution snapshot, you are actually creating a job in the SQL Agent. When one or more of these jobs are executing, they can be managed on the Manage Jobs page. You can use the Manage Jobs page to view the status of executing jobs and to cancel a job that is not executing properly.

NOTE

Jobs appear on the Manage Jobs page only when they are actually executing on the server. In fact, a job must be running for more than 30 seconds before it will appear on this page.

Building On

In this chapter, we looked at ways to deliver reports and control their execution from within the Report Manager. In the next chapter, we will look at ways to customize report delivery by building on to Reporting Services. These techniques will allow you to integrate Reporting Services reports with your own websites and custom applications.

Extending Outside the Box: Customizing Reporting Services

U p to this point, we have been using Reporting Services just as it comes out of the box (or off of the installation CD, if you want to get technical). All of our management of Reporting Services features and all of our report execution have been through the Report Manager. Reporting Services and the Report Manager do, after all, provide a very feature-rich environment in their default configuration.

One of the best features of Reporting Services, however, is the ability to extend it beyond its basic operation. In this chapter, we will do just that. We will look at ways to execute reports without using the Report Manager interface. We will also look at ways to manage Reporting Services without using the Report Manager interface. Finally, we will work through an example showing how to change the security mechanism used by Reporting Services.

All of this will give you a brief taste of what Reporting Services can do when you start extending outside the box.

Using Reporting Services Without the Report Manager

The Report Manager provides a very nice interface for finding and executing reports. There will be times, however, when the Report Manager is not the best way to deliver a report to your users. Perhaps the user is browsing your website or using a custom application and needs to view a report. In these situations, it does not make sense to force the user to jump to Report Manager and begin navigating folders. We want to deliver the report to the user right where they are. In this section, we will explore several ways to do just that.

URL Access

One way to execute a report without using Report Manager is through URL access. URL access allows a browser or a program capable of issuing HTTP requests to specify a URL and receive a report in the HTML report viewer. This URL can be built into a standard HTML anchor tag to allow a report to be displayed with one mouse click.

Basic URL Access

The basic URL used to access a report has two parts. The first part is the URL of the Report Server web service. In a default installation, this is

```
http://{computername}/ReportServer
```

where {computername} is the name of the computer hosting the Report Server. This is followed by a question mark and the path through the Reporting Services virtual folders to the report you wish to execute. The Home folder is the root of this path, but it's not included in the path itself. The path must begin with a forward slash (/).

Let's try an example. We will execute the Invoice-Batch Number report for the Axelburg office. This report is in the Axelburg folder inside of the Galactic Delivery Services folder.

NOTE

In the examples used throughout the rest of this chapter, it is assumed that Reporting Services is installed on your computer. The localhost name is used to access IIS information on this computer. If you have Reporting Services installed on a different computer, substitute the name of that computer in place of "localhost" in the following examples.

1. Start Internet Explorer.

2. Enter the following URL in the address bar:

   ```
   http://localhost/ReportServer?/Galactic Delivery Services/Axelburg/
                                                  Invoice-Batch Number
   ```

3. Click Go. The Invoice-Batch Number report will appear in the browser inside of the Report Viewer.

NOTE

When your URL is submitted, it will be URL encoded. Some of the characters in your URL may be replaced by other characters or by hexadecimal strings such as %20. This ensures that the URL can be interpreted correctly when it is sent to the web server.

As with Report Manager, Windows Integrated security is being used when a user executes a report through URL access. The user must have rights to execute the report; otherwise, an error will result. However, because the user is not browsing through the folder structure to get to the report, the user does not need to have any rights to the folder containing the report. You can use this fact to hide a report from non-administrative users who are browsing through folders in the Report Manager, while still making the report accessible to someone using URL access.

In addition to executing reports, you can also view the contents of folders, resources, and shared data sources. Try the following:

1. Enter this URL in the address bar:

   ```
   http://localhost/ReportServer?/Galactic Delivery Services
   ```

2. Click Go. The contents of the Galactic Delivery Services folder will appear.

3. Click the link for the 2004 Conference folder. The contents of the 2004 Conference folder will appear, as shown in Figure 12-1.

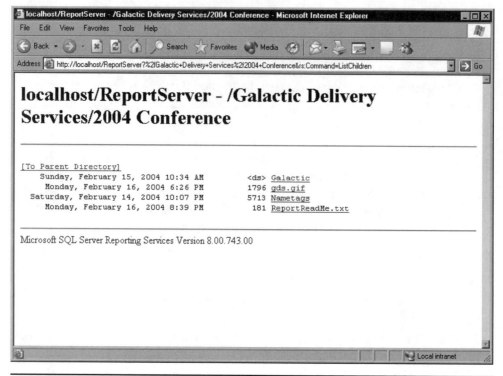

Figure 12-1   *Browsing folder contents using URL access*

Command Parameters

Look at the URL in the address bar. You will see that something has been added to the URL, namely "&rs:Command=ListChildren." This is called a *command parameter*. It tells Reporting Services what to do with the item pointed to by the URL. The four possible values for the command parameter are listed in Table 12-1.

Command Parameter	Applies To	Result
GetDataSourceContents	Data Source	Displays the data source definition as an XML structure
GetResourceContents	Resource Item	Displays the contents of the resource item in the browser
ListChildren	Folder	Lists the contents of the folder with links to each content item
Render	Report	Displays the report in the Report Viewer

Table 12-1   *Values for the Command Parameter*

Looking at this table, you will quickly realize that only one command parameter value applies to each type of item you can encounter in the Reporting Services virtual folders. Attempting to use a command parameter with the wrong type of item will result in an error. If you do not include the command parameter, Reporting Services will simply perform the one and only command that applies to the type of item you are targeting in your URL. Because specifying the command parameter is completely unnecessary, one can only assume that this was put in place to allow for future growth.

Passing Parameters

When you executed the Invoice-Batch Number report through URL access, you received the default values for the start date and end date. You can change these dates in the Report Viewer, but only after waiting for the report to execute with the default values. It would be much better to get exactly what you want the first time around.

Fortunately, there is a way to do just that. You can pass the values for report parameters as part of the URL. On the URL, include an ampersand (&) followed by the name of the report parameter, an equals sign, and the parameter value.

Try the following:

1. Enter the following URL in the address bar:

    ```
    http://localhost/ReportServer?/Galactic Delivery Services/Axelburg/
              Invoice-Batch Number&StartDate=11/1/2003&EndDate=11/30/2003
    ```

2. Click Go. The Invoice-Batch Number report will appear with data for November, 2003.

Controlling the Report Viewer

In addition to specifying report parameters in the URL, you can also include parameters to control the format of the response from Reporting Services. You can specify which rendering format should be used for the report. Rather than using the export drop-down list in the Report Viewer to export the report to a particular format, you can have it delivered in that format straight from Reporting Services.

Give this a try:

1. Enter the following URL in the address bar:

    ```
    http://localhost/ReportServer?/Galactic Delivery Services/
                      2004 Conference/Nametags&rs:Format=PDF
    ```

2. Click Go.
3. Click Open, if you are prompted whether to open or save the file.
4. The Nametags report will appear in PDF format in Adobe Acrobat Reader.

5. Close Adobe Acrobat Reader. The valid format parameters are as follows:

  ▶ HTML3.2

  ▶ HTML4.0

  ▶ MHTML

  ▶ PDF

  ▶ IMAGE

  ▶ EXCEL

  ▶ CSV

  ▶ XML

You can also specify what portion of the Report Viewer interface you want visible. Here's an example:

1. Enter the following URL in the address bar:

```
http://localhost/ReportServer?/Galactic Delivery Services/Axelburg/
        Invoice-Batch Number&StartDate=11/1/2003&EndDate=11/30/2003
        &rc:Parameters=false
```

2. Click Go. The Invoice-Batch Number report will appear with data for November, 2003. The parameter portion of the Report Viewer is not visible, so the user cannot change the parameter values.

You can even get rid of the entire Report Viewer interface as follows:

1. Enter the following URL in the address bar:

```
http://localhost/ReportServer?/Galactic Delivery Services/Axelburg/
        Invoice-Batch Number&StartDate=11/1/2003&EndDate=11/30/2003
        &rc:Toolbar=false
```

2. Click Go. The Invoice-Batch Number report will appear with data for November, 2003.

3. Expand the 445 row heading and the Axelburg column heading.

Even when we expand the row and column headings, causing a new page to be sent from the Report Server, the Report Viewer does not reappear.

The major settings that can be passed as URL parameters and their possible values are listed in Table 12-2.

Setting	Valid Values	Function
BookmarkID	{BookmarkID}	Jumps to the specified Bookmark ID in the report.
DocMap	True False	Specifies whether the document map is shown.
DocMapID	{DocMapID}	Jumps to the specified Document Map ID.
EndFind	{PageNumber}	The last report page to be searched when executing a Find from the URL (see FindString).
FallbackPage	{PageNumber}	The report page to go to if the Find is unsuccessful or a jump to a Document Map ID fails.
FindString	{TextToFind}	Searches for this text in the report and jumps to its first location.
HTMLFragment	True False	When this is set to true, the report is returned as a table rather than a complete HTML page. This table can then be placed inside your own HTML page.
LinkTarget	{TargetWindowName} _blank _self _parent _top	Specifies the target window to use for any links in the report.
Parameters	True False	Specifies whether to show the parameters section of the Report Viewer.
Section	{PageNumber}	The page number of the report to render.
StartFind	{PageNumber}	The first report page to be searched when executing a Find from the URL (see FindString).
StreamRoot	{URL}	The path used to prefix the value of the src attribute of any IMG tags in an HTML rendering of the report.
Toolbar	True False	Specifies whether the Report Viewer toolbar is visible.
Zoom	Page Width Whole Page 500 200 150 100 75 50 25 10	The zoom percentage to use when displaying the report.

Table 12-2 *URL Parameters and Their Possible Values*

Web Service Access

In addition to URL access, you can also access reports by using the web service interface. This is the same interface used by the Report Manager web application to interact with Reporting Services. This means that anything you can do in Report Manager you can also do through the web service interface.

The web service interface provides additional functionality not available through URL access. For example, the web service interface allows you to specify a set of credentials to use when executing a report. This allows your custom application to use a set of hard-coded credentials to access reports through the web service interface. This can be a big benefit in situations where you want Reporting Services reports to be exposed on an Internet or extranet site where each user does not have a domain account.

Using a Web Service Call to Execute a Report

This example will take you through the steps necessary to execute a report using the web service interface. In this example, you will build a web application that acts as a front end for the Axelburg Invoice-Batch Number report.

NOTE

Some basic knowledge of ASP.NET programming is assumed in the following discussion.

Creating a Project and a Web Reference   First we need to create an ASP.NET project with a reference to the Reporting Services web service.

1. Start up Visual Studio .NET 2003.
2. Create a new project.
3. Select Visual Basic Projects in the Project Types area.
4. Select ASP.NET Web Application from the Templates area.
5. Enter **http://localhost/AxelburgFrontEnd** for Location.
6. Click OK.
7. When the new project has been created, right-click the project folder for this new project in the Solution Explorer and select Add Web Reference from the context menu. The Add Web Reference dialog box will appear.
8. Select the link for Web Services on the Local Machine.

NOTE

Again, if Reporting Services is not on your computer, do not use this link. Instead, look for the web service on the computer where Reporting Services is installed.

9. When the list of web services on the local machine appears, click the link for ReportService.

10. When the Reporting Service description appears in the dialog box, click Add Reference.

In order to use a web service, you need to create code that knows how to send data to and retrieve data from that web service. Fortunately, this code is generated for you by Visual Studio through the process of creating a web reference. Once the web reference is in place, you can call the methods of the web service the same way you call the methods of a local .NET assembly.

When you clicked the link for Web Services on the Local Machine, a URL beginning with "http://localhost" was used to locate the web services on the local machine. Because of this, the Reporting Services web service will use "localhost.ReportingService" as its namespace.

Creating the Web Form   Now, we need to create the web form that will serve as our user interface.

1. Change the name of WebForm1.aspx to **ReportFrontEnd.aspx**.

2. Place three labels, two calendar controls, and a button on the web form, as shown in Figure 12-2.

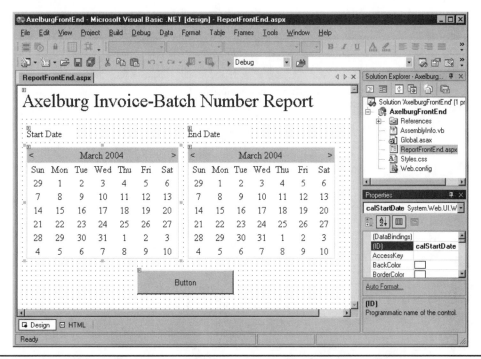

Figure 12-2   *The Axelburg Invoice-Batch Number report front end*

3. Change the Text property of each label as shown.

4. Change the ID property of the left calendar control to **calStartDate**.

5. Set the SelectedDate property and the VisibleDate property of calStartDate to **November 1, 2003**.

6. Change the ID property of the right calendar control to **calEndDate**.

7. Set the SelectedDate property and the VisibleDate property of calEndDate to **December 31, 2003**.

8. Change the ID property of the button to **cmdExecute**.

9. Change the Text property of the button to **Execute**.

10. Double-click the cmdExecute button to open the code window.

11. Enter the following code for cmdExecute_Click.

```
Private Sub cmdExecute_Click(ByVal sender As System.Object, _
                        ByVal e As System.EventArgs) _
                        Handles cmdExecute.Click
    Dim report As Byte() = Nothing

    ' Create an instance of the Reporting Services
    ' Web Reference.
    Dim rs As localhost.ReportingService _
                        = New localhost.ReportingService

    ' Create the credentials that will be used when accessing
    ' Reporting Services. This must be a logon that has rights
    ' to the Axelburg Invoice-Batch Number report.
    ' *** Replace "LoginName", "Password", and "Domain" with
    '     the appropriate values. ***
    rs.Credentials = New _
            System.Net.NetworkCredential("LoginName", _
        "Password", "Domain")
            rs.PreAuthenticate = True

    ' The Reporting Services virtual path to the report.
    Dim reportPath As String = _
        "/Galactic Delivery Services/Axelburg/Invoice-Batch Number"

    ' The rendering format for the report.
    Dim format As String = "HTML4.0"

    ' The devInfo string tells the report viewer
    ' how to display with the report.
    Dim devInfo As String = _
        "<DeviceInfo>" + _
        "<Toolbar>False</Toolbar>" + _
        "<Parameters>False</Parameters>" + _
        "<DocMap>True</DocMap>" + _
        "<Zoom>100</Zoom>" + _
        "</DeviceInfo>"

    ' Create an array of the values for the report parameters
```

```
Dim parameters(1) As localhost.ParameterValue
Dim paramValue As localhost.ParameterValue _
                        = New localhost.ParameterValue
paramValue.Name = "StartDate"
paramValue.Value = calStartDate.SelectedDate
parameters(0) = paramValue
paramValue = New localhost.ParameterValue
paramValue.Name = "EndDate"
paramValue.Value = calEndDate.SelectedDate
parameters(1) = paramValue

' Create variables for the remainder of the parameters
Dim historyID As String = Nothing
Dim credentials() As localhost.DataSourceCredentials = Nothing
Dim showHideToggle As String = Nothing
Dim encoding As String
Dim mimeType As String
Dim warnings() As localhost.Warning = Nothing
Dim reportHistoryParameters() As _
                    localhost.ParameterValue = Nothing
Dim streamIDs() As String = Nothing

Dim sh As localhost.SessionHeader = _
                    New localhost.SessionHeader
rs.SessionHeaderValue = sh

Try
    ' Execute the report.
    report = rs.Render(reportPath, format, historyID, _
                    devInfo, parameters, credentials, _
                    showHideToggle, encoding, mimeType, _
                    reportHistoryParameters, warnings, _
                    streamIDs)

    sh.SessionId = rs.SessionHeaderValue.SessionId

    ' Flush any pending response.
    Response.Clear()

    ' Set the HTTP headers for a PDF response.
    HttpContext.Current.Response.ClearHeaders()
    HttpContext.Current.Response.ClearContent()
    HttpContext.Current.Response.ContentType = "text/html"
    ' filename is the default filename displayed
    ' if the user does a save as.
    HttpContext.Current.Response.AppendHeader( _
      "Content-Disposition", _
      "filename=""Invoice-BatchNumber.HTM""")

    ' Send the byte array containing the report
    ' as a binary response.
    HttpContext.Current.Response.BinaryWrite(report)
    HttpContext.Current.Response.End()
Catch ex As Exception
    If ex.Message <> "Thread was being aborted." then
        HttpContext.Current.Response.ClearHeaders()
        HttpContext.Current.Response.ClearContent()
```

```
                        HttpContext.Current.Response.ContentType = "text/html"
                        HttpContext.Current.Response.Write( _
                            "<HTML><BODY><H1>Error</H1><br><br>" & _
                                        ex.Message & "</BODY></HTML>")
                        HttpContext.Current.Response.End()
                End If
            End Try
        End Sub
```

12. Click Save All in the toolbar.

13. Select Debug | Start from the main menu. This will execute your program.

14. When the browser window appears with the web application front-end page, click Execute. The report will appear using the dates selected on the front-end page.

15. Switch back to Visual Studio and select Debug | Stop Debugging from the main menu.

You can refer to the comments in the code sample for information on the purpose of each section of code. For additional information, refer to Appendix B.

Managing Reporting Services Through Web Services

In addition to executing reports through the web service interface, you can also manage Reporting Services using the web services. If you had a mind to, you could write an application that completely replaces the Report Manager web application for controlling Reporting Services. Refer to Appendix B for more information on management capabilities of the web services interface.

Reporting Services Utilities

In addition to URL access and the web services interface, you can also interact with Reporting Services through several command-line utility programs. Like the other methods, these command-line utilities allow you to manage Reporting Services. These utilities allow you to start up or activate Reporting Services as well as control encryption keys and encrypted values. The most capable of the utilities, the RS utility, allows you to script and automate just about any Reporting Service activity.

Each utility program will be described here briefly. For more information, you can execute any of the utility programs followed by /? to view a listing of the valid parameters.

CAUTION

Even though the parameter listing for each utility program uses a dash before the parameter character (as in −a), you may need to use a forward slash (as in /a) in order for the utility program to function.

The RSActivate Utility

As the name implies, the RSActivate utility activates a new Reporting Services installation. This only needs to be done once when Reporting Services is newly installed. The activation process creates the encryption key that Reporting Services will use to encrypt sensitive information, such as user names and passwords, stored in the configuration files.

Usually, activation occurs automatically as part of the Reporting Services installation process. In most cases, you will not need to use the RSActivate utility unless a problem occurs during installation. See "Manually Activating Reporting Services" in Chapter 2 for more information on using the RSActivate utility to manually activate a Reporting Services installation.

The RSKeyMgmt Utility

The RSKeyMgmt utility is used to administer the encryption key used by Reporting Services. You can use the RSKeyMgmt utility to back up the encryption key. You can also use RSKeyMgmt to delete encrypted data in case of a problem.

When Reporting Services is installed, sensitive information stored in the configuration files, such as logon credentials, is encrypted for security. Also, any user names and passwords stored in reports or shared data sources are also encrypted. The encryption key used to decrypt the information is stored in the Report Catalog (ReportServer) database. Making certain changes can cause problems with the Reporting Services installation. These changes include the following:

▶ Modifying the user account used by the Reporting Services web service

▶ Modifying the name of the SQL Server used to store the Report Catalog

▶ Modifying the name of the computer hosting Reporting Services

A backup copy of the encryption key made with the RSKeyMgmt utility helps recover your Reporting Services installation in these situations.

The backup copy of the encryption key is protected by a password. You specify this password as a parameter to the RSKeyMgmt utility when you create the backup. You must have this password when you use the backup copy of the key.

Creating a Backup of the Report Server Encryption Key   To make a backup of the Report Server encryption key, do the following:

1. Insert a disk in the Report Server's floppy drive.

2. Open a command window.

3. Enter the following at the command prompt, where {password} is the password used to protect the encryption key:

```
rskeymgmt /e /f a:\rsdbkey.txt /p {password}
```

4. Press ENTER.

5. When the backup process is complete, store the disk in a safe location.

Recovering a Reporting Services Installation   If your Reporting Services installation becomes disabled due to one of the situations described previously and you have a backup of the encryption key, follow this procedure:

1. Insert the disk containing the backup of your encryption code into the Report Server's floppy drive.

2. Open a command window.

3. Enter the following at the command prompt, where {password} is the password used to protect the encryption key:

```
rskeymgmt /a /f a:\rsdbkey.txt /p {password}
```

4. Press ENTER.

5. When the process completes, enter the following at the command prompt:

```
iisreset
```

6. Press ENTER.

If your Reporting Services installation becomes disabled due to one of the situations described previously and you do not have a backup of the encryption key, follow this procedure:

1. Open a command window.

2. Enter the following at the command prompt:

```
rskeymgmt /d
```

3. Press ENTER.

4. When the process completes, enter the following at the command prompt:

```
iisreset
```

5. Press ENTER.

6. Use the RSConfig utility to specify the connection information to the Report Catalog.

7. Reenter the user names and passwords for all reports and shared data sources stored on this Report Server that used stored credentials.

The RSConfig Utility

The RSConfig utility is used to change the credentials used by Reporting Services to access the Report Catalog (ReportServer) database. These credentials are encrypted in the configuration file, so they cannot be edited directly.

The following example changes the credentials used to access the Report Catalog on a SQL Server called RSServer to use a SQL Server logon called "RSCatLogon" with a password of "rscat37":

```
rsconfig /c /s RSServer /d ReportServer /a Sql /u RSCatLogon
                                               /p rscat37
```

The RS Utility

The RS utility is used to execute script that can interact with Reporting Services. The scripting language supported by the RS utility is Visual Basic .NET. This scripting language supports the complete web service interface to Reporting Services.

The RS utility automatically creates a reference to the web service interface. This predefined reference, called *rs,* means you do not need to instantiate the web service interface; it is simply ready to go. All the Reporting Services classes and data types are also available.

The following sample code lists the contents of the Galactic Delivery Services virtual folder:

1. Enter the following into Notepad or some other text editor:

```
Public Sub Main()
    Dim items() As CatalogItem
    items = rs.ListChildren("/Galactic Delivery Services", False)

    Dim item As CatalogItem
    For Each item In items
        Console.WriteLine(item.Name)
    Next item
End Sub
```

2. Save this to a file called rstest.rss in a convenient folder on the Report Server.

3. Open a command window.

4. Change to the folder where you stored the rstest.rss file.

5. Enter the following at the command prompt, where {userID} is a logon with administrative rights on the Report Server and {password} is the password for that logon:

```
rs /i rstest.rss /s http://localhost/ReportServer
                    /u {userID} /p {password}
```

6. Press ENTER. A list of the folders in the Galactic Delivery Services folder will appear in the command window.

Log Files

Along with the Reporting Services utilities, the logs created by Reporting Services can be helpful for managing and troubleshooting. These logs are text files that can be viewed with Notepad or any other text editor. In a default installation, the log files created by Reporting Services are stored in the following folder:

```
C:\Program Files\Microsoft SQL Server\MSSQL\
                                    Reporting Services\LogFiles
```

Four different types of log files are created, as listed in the following table.

File Name	Created By
ReportServer_{timestamp}.log	Report Server Engine
ReportServerService_{timestamp}.log ReportServerService_main_{timestamp}.log	Report Server Windows Service
ReportServerWebApp_{timestamp}.log	Report Manager

In addition to these log files is an ExecutionLog table in the Report Catalog (ReportServer) database. A record is created in this table each time a report is executed. The date and time of the execution as well as the user name of the logged on user are recorded. Unfortunately, the report that is being executed is identified by a globally unique identifier (GUID) rather than by the report name. Fortunately, Microsoft provides a DTS package for converting the information in the ExecutionLog table into something far more useable, including report names.

For more information on the Execution Log and the conversion DTS package, view "Execution Log" in the index of Reporting Services Books Online. (Reporting Services Books Online is available in your Program menu under Microsoft SQL Server | Reporting Services | Reporting Services Books Online.)

Custom Security

Another way to customize Reporting Services is through its security extension. By default, Reporting Services uses Windows Integrated Security. As you have seen, this means that a user must have valid credentials (a user name and password) for either a local logon on the Report Server or for a domain logon on the domain containing the Report Server.

There are times, however, when creating Windows credentials for each Reporting Services user is not desirable or even feasible. You may want to expose reports on an Internet or extranet site. You may want to use the Report Manager as part of a web application that makes use of a different security model, such as forms authentication. In these situations, you can consider using the Reporting Services security extension to implement a security mechanism for the Report Manager and the Report Server web service that better fits your needs. As noted in Chapter 2, the Enterprise Edition of Reporting Services is required to use the Reporting Services security extension.

Authentication and Authorization

Before we discuss the security extension, we need to look at the way security functions in Reporting Services. There are actually two parts to security in Reporting Services: *authentication* and *authorization*. Authentication determines whether or not you can come in. Authorization determines what you can do once you are inside.

Authentication

Think of security like a trip to an amusement park. If you are a big amusement park fan like me (I can't get enough of those rollercoasters!), you probably purchase the multiday pass. Because the pass can only be used by the person who originally purchased it, you must prove that you are the rightful owner of that pass when you get to the main gate. You may even have to show a picture ID to prove you are who you say you are.

This is the process of authentication. You must prove that you have the appropriate credentials to gain access. At the amusement park gate, you needed two things to gain entrance: a pass and some type of identification to prove that you have the right to use that pass. The same is true for authentication in the computer world. First, you need some type of pass that has rights to get you in the gate. This usually takes the form of a user name, or more accurately, a user account identified by a user name. You must have a valid user account in order to log on.

Second, you must have some way to prove that you are the rightful owner of that user account. This is often done by specifying a password along with the user name. In areas where security needs to be tighter, this proof of ownership might take the form of an electronic card or a thumbprint scan.

In the default setup for Reporting Services, we are essentially outsourcing the main gate operations. Windows takes care of authenticating the user for us. If Windows says the user is okay, they must be okay. As you will see in a moment, when we implement custom security, we will take back this job of authentication for ourselves.

Persisting Authentication

Because we are dealing with web interfaces—the Report Manager web application and the Report Server web service—we have one more authentication issue to deal with. Each time a user makes a request through either of these interfaces, the authentication has to be done again. This is just the nature of the HTTP requests we use with both web applications and web services. It is a bit like having to come in through the main gate of the amusement park every time you want to go on a different ride.

When we are using Windows authentication, the authentication process is completely transparent to the users. Because of this, having to redo the authentication each time a user requests a different Report Manager screen or executes a different report is not a big deal. However, if you create a logon screen as part of your custom security, this will be a different story. No user wants to reenter their user name and password each time they execute a report or navigate from one folder to another.

What we need is some way to remember that we have already authenticated a particular user. We need the electronic equivalent of the ultraviolet-light-sensitive hand stamp used at the amusement park for exit and reentry. In computer terms, we need to *persist* the authentication.

For the custom security extension created later in this chapter, we will use a browser cookie to persist the authentication. If the cookie is not present in an HTTP request, the logon screen will be displayed. This should happen only at the beginning of a user session. Once we have authenticated the user, we will send the cookie information to the user's browser and instruct it to create a cookie. The browser will send this cookie along with all subsequent HTTP requests made to Reporting Services. If the cookie is present, the logon information will be taken from the cookie and the user will not see the logon screen.

Authorization

Let's return to our amusement park analogy. You have passed through the main gate and are ready to ride that killer coaster. However, there are some limitations on just who can go on each ride. You must be taller than a certain height to go on the wild rides. You must be shorter than a certain height to go on the kiddie rides.

This is the process of authorization. You must prove that you have rights to perform a certain activity before you can actually do that activity. At the amusement park, you must prove to the ride operator that you are taller or shorter than the height marking painted on the sign. If your head does not come above the line, you do not have the right to perform the activity of riding the rollercoaster.

As you saw in Chapter 11, Reporting Services uses role-based authorization. Your logon account is assigned to a certain role for each folder, report, or resource. This role includes rights to perform certain activities on that item. Being assigned to the Browser role for a report means you are authorized to view that report.

The role assignments are stored in the Report Catalog within Reporting Services. When using the default security setup, Reporting Services checks the role assignments in the Report Catalog each time you try to perform a task. It determines from these role assignments whether or not you are authorized to perform that task and then either lets you proceed or brings the process to a screeching halt.

When we implement custom security, you must perform this authorization check yourself. Fortunately, Reporting Services allows you to continue to use the role information stored in the Report Catalog. Therefore, if you wish, you can still use the screens in the Report Manager to create and edit role assignments and have those changes stored in the Report Catalog. Your custom security implementation can then use the information in the Report Catalog to determine authorization. If this does not fit your needs, you can create your own method for determining what a user is authorized to do.

Issues with Custom Security

Before we look at how to create and deploy a custom security extension, we need to discuss several issues related to custom security. Changing the security mechanism for an enterprise application should not be done lightly. Before implementing a custom security extension, make sure you cannot fulfill your business needs without it, then look at each of the following issues.

Tried and True

Windows Integrated security is the default security model for Reporting Services and is, in fact, the only security model that comes with the product. Reporting Services was designed with Windows Integrated security in mind. Therefore, it is the only security model that has been thoroughly tested and proven to provide a secure environment.

If you implement your own custom security extension, you are taking the responsibility of creating a secure environment on your own shoulders. You are responsible for the design, testing, and implementation of an environment that will ensure the proper security for your Report Server. Remember that a custom security extension includes both authentication and authorization. Not only do you need to keep out those people who are not allowed to enter your Report Server environment, but you also have to restrict the activities of those users you do let in.

All or Nothing

When you implement a custom security extension, you completely replace the security mechanism on a Reporting Services installation. You cannot use your custom security extension for some users and the default behavior for others. This is an all-or-nothing proposition. Once you replace the default security mechanism, *all* authentication and *all* authorization comes through your custom code.

Validate All User Input

Care should be taken to validate all user input to prevent problems. This is especially true when you are creating a security interface. You should take steps to ensure that your custom security extension is not vulnerable to invalid characters and buffer overruns as a means of gaining unauthorized entry.

In addition to serving as the means for a security attack, special characters can also cause a problem if you are using the MyReports feature. As we discussed in Chapter 11, when the MyReports feature is enabled, a virtual user folder is created from the user name of each Reporting Services user. The MyReports folder is then mapped to the appropriate user folder as each user logs on. User names containing any of the following characters can cause problems with these virtual user folders:

```
: ? ; @ & = + $ , \ * > < | . " / '
```

Using the Secure Sockets Layer

Anytime you are transmitting authentication information, you should use Secure Sockets Layer (SSL) to protect that transmission. When you use SSL, your data is encrypted before it is transmitted between the client and host computers. This helps prevent any interception or tampering with the authentication information while it is in transit.

To use SSL, simply use "https://" rather than "http://" at the beginning of your URL. In addition, there is an SSL setting in the web application file and an SSL setting in the Internet Information Services management utility. These settings can be used to require all users to utilize an SSL connection when accessing the Reporting Services web application and web service.

Changing Security Models

Changing security models on your Reporting Services installation is not something to be done lightly. Any role assignments you created under a previous security model will be removed when you change to a new model. Only the default system administration rights will be present.

Changing back from a custom security extension to the default Windows Integrated security, although possible, is not generally recommended. If you do so, you may experience errors when accessing items that had security roles assigned to them under your custom security extension. In addition, if you cannot successfully change back to Windows Integrated security, you will have to reinstall Reporting Services.

Creating a Custom Security Extension

To demonstrate custom security in Reporting Services, we need to create our own code for both authentication and authorization. This code will take the form of several custom classes that implement Reporting Services interfaces. In addition, we will create an override for some of the methods in the web service wrapper class in order to implement the cookie processing and persist our authentication.

If the previous paragraph sounds like Greek to you, then the custom security extension is probably not for you. You need a firm grasp of object-oriented programming (OOP) to understand the code samples in this section. Don't feel bad if OOP is not your thing—many people lead happy and productive lives without knowing how to implement an interface or override a constructor!

We will be looking at a sample security extension that implements forms security for Reporting Services. Forms security allows you to present the user with a form on which they can enter their user name and password. You can then validate that user name and password against a database table or other data store where you are maintaining a list of valid user credentials. This sample will help you become familiar with the workings of a security extension in Reporting Services. The sample is based on Microsoft's Forms Authentication Sample for Reporting Services. The original sample was written in C#. I have translated it into Visual Basic for consistency with the other examples in this book. Some revisions were also made to better fit with the Galactic Delivery Services examples.

CAUTION

The code provided here is merely a sample to aid in your understanding of the custom security extension. It is not intended to be used in a production environment. Discuss any intended security changes with your organization's security manager, system administrator, or network administrator before proceeding.

Preparing the Sample Code

The forms security sample consists of a single solution called FormsSecurity. This solution contains two projects—the FormsSecurity project and the StoreRSLogon project. The FormsSecurity project contains all the classes that implement the security extension along with the logon screens. The StoreRSLogon project contains code for a Windows application that allows you to assign user names and passwords to employees of Galactic Delivery Services.

First, a couple things need to be taken care of before we are ready to look through this sample code. Therefore, complete the following steps:

1. Download the FormsSecurity solution files and copy them to a test computer that contains both Reporting Services and Visual Studio .NET 2003 with Visual Basic .NET.

2. Open the FormsSecurity solution.

3. Add a reference in the FormsSecurity project to the Microsoft.ReportingServices .Interfaces.dll file. The default location for this file is

```
C:\Program Files\Microsoft SQL Server\MSSQL\Reporting Services\
                                                ReportServer\bin
```

NOTE

In this example, it is assumed that you are using a copy of Visual Studio .NET 2003 that is running on your Report Server.

4. Add a web reference to the ReportService web service on this computer. Name this web reference **RSWebService**. (Use the computer name rather than localhost when adding this reference. Testing has shown some unexpected results when using localhost for the web reference when building a custom security extension.)

5. Select Save All in the toolbar.

The AuthenticationExtension Class

The AuthenticationExtension class implements a Reporting Services interface called IAuthenticationExtension. The AuthenticationExtension class, along with a second class called CheckAuthentication, handles the authentication responsibilities. Some of the code from the AuthenticationExtension class is listed here (see the downloaded sample code for a complete listing):

```
Imports System
Imports System.Data
Imports System.Data.SqlClient
Imports System.Security.Principal
Imports System.Web
Imports Microsoft.ReportingServices.Interfaces

Namespace MSSQLRS.FormsSecurity
Public Class AuthenticationExtension : Implements _
                                        IAuthenticationExtension
```

```vb
' This function determines whether a user logon is valid.
Public Function LogonUser(ByVal userName As String, _
                          ByVal password As String, _
                          ByVal authority As String) _
    As Boolean Implements IAuthenticationExtension.LogonUser
    Return CheckAuthentication.VerifyPassword(userName, password)
End Function


' GetUserInfo is required by the implementation of
' IAuthenticationExtension.
' The Report Server calls the GetUserInfo method for each request to
' retrieve the current user identity.
Public Sub GetUserInfo(ByRef userIdentity As IIdentity, _
            ByRef userId As IntPtr) _
            Implements IAuthenticationExtension.GetUserInfo
    ' If the current user identity is not null,
    ' set the userIdentity parameter to that of the current user.
    If (Not (HttpContext.Current Is Nothing)) And _
       (Not (HttpContext.Current.User.Identity Is Nothing)) Then
        userIdentity = HttpContext.Current.User.Identity
    Else
        userIdentity = Nothing
    End If

    userId = IntPtr.Zero
End Sub


' This function is called by the Report Server when it sets
' security on an item. The function calls VerifyUser to make
' sure this is a valid user name.
Public Function _
            IsValidPrincipalName(ByVal principalName As String) _
            As Boolean Implements _
            IAuthenticationExtension.IsValidPrincipalName
    Return VerifyUser(principalName)
End Function


' Look up the user name in the database to make sure it is valid.
Public Shared Function VerifyUser(ByVal userName As String) _
            As Boolean
    Dim isValid As Boolean = False
    Dim conn As SqlConnection = New SqlConnection(ConnectionString)
    Dim cmd As SqlCommand = New SqlCommand("stp_LookupUser", conn)
    Dim sqlParam As SqlParameter
    Dim reader As SqlDataReader
```

```
    ' Look up the user name in the Employee table
    ' in the Galactic database.
    cmd.CommandType = CommandType.StoredProcedure
    sqlParam = cmd.Parameters.Add("@UserName", SqlDbType.VarChar, 255)
    sqlParam.Value = username

    Try
      conn.Open()
      reader = cmd.ExecuteReader

      ' If a row was returned, the user is valid.
      If reader.Read() Then
        isValid = True
      End If
    Catch ex As Exception
      Throw New Exception("Exception verifying password. " & _
                                                      ex.Message)

    Finally
      conn.Close()
    End Try


    Return isValid
  End Function
End Class
End Namespace
```

GetUserInfo Method   The GetUserInfo method of the AuthenticationExtension class is called by Reporting Services to determine the identity of the current user. This method reads the user's credentials that are being persisted in the cookie. Going back to our amusement park analogy, the GetUserInfo method puts our user's hand under the ultraviolet light to see if it has been stamped.

If GetUserInfo does not find a cookie with credential information, it returns an empty identity. When this occurs, the user is redirected to the logon page. The user then supplies the credentials and the authorization process can continue. If everything is working correctly, this should only occur once, at the beginning of the session.

Remember, GetUserInfo is simply extracting the credentials from the cookie. It is not determining the validity of those credentials. That is left to the LogonUser method.

LogonUser Method   Once we have the credentials, either from the cookie or from the logon page, they must be verified. Reporting Services calls the LogonUser method to do this verification. In our implementation, LogonUser calls the VerifyPassword method in the CheckAuthentication class.

VerifyPassword looks up the user name in the Employee table of the Galactic database. It encrypts the password supplied as part of the user's credentials and compares it with the encrypted password stored in the Employee table. If the two encrypted passwords match, the logon is valid. The result of this password match is returned to the LogonUser method and then returned to Reporting Services.

IsValidPrincipalName and VerifyUser Methods   The IsValidPrincipalName and VerifyUser methods are used to determine whether a user name is valid. The IsValidPrincipalName method simply calls the VerifyUser method to perform this task. The VerifyUser method looks for the user name in the Employee table of the Galactic database. If the user name is found in the table, it is valid.

The VerifyUser method is called by a method in the AuthorizationExtension class. This is done to validate the user name in a configuration file. The IsValidPrincipalName method is called from Reporting Services whenever you create a new role assignment. This is done to validate the user name entered for that role assignment, before the assignment is saved in the Report Catalog.

The AuthorizationExtension Class

The AuthorizationExtension class implements a Reporting Services interface called IAuthorizationExtension. The AuthorizationExtension class handles the authorization responsibilities. Some of the code from the AuthorizationExtension class is listed here (see the downloaded sample code for a complete listing):

```
Imports System
Imports System.IO
Imports System.Collections
Imports System.Collections.Specialized
Imports System.Globalization
Imports System.Runtime.Serialization
Imports System.Runtime.Serialization.Formatters.Binary
Imports Microsoft.ReportingServices.Interfaces
Imports System.Xml

Namespace MSSQLRS.FormsSecurity
Public Class AuthorizationExtension : Implements _
                                  IAuthorizationExtension

  Private Shared m_adminUserName As String

  Public Function CheckAccess(ByVal userName As String, _
            ByVal userToken As IntPtr, _
```

```
                    ByVal secDesc() As Byte, _
                    ByVal requiredOperation As FolderOperation) _
        As Boolean Implements IAuthorizationExtension.CheckAccess
    Dim acl As AceCollection
    Dim ace As AceStruct
    Dim aclOperation As FolderOperation

    ' If the user is the administrator, allow unrestricted access.
    ' Because SQL Server defaults to case-insensitive, we have to
    ' perform a case insensitive comparison.
    If String.Compare(userName, m_adminUserName, True, _
                        CultureInfo.CurrentCulture) = 0 Then
        Return True
    End If


    acl = DeserializeACL(secDesc)
    For Each ace In acl
      ' First check to see if the user has an access control
      ' entry for the item.
      If String.Compare(userName, ace.PrincipalName, True, _
                          CultureInfo.CurrentCulture) = 0 Then
        ' If an entry is found, return true if the given
        ' required operation is contained in the ACE structure
        For Each aclOperation In ace.FolderOperations
          If aclOperation = requiredOperation Then
            Return True
          End If
        Next
      End If
    Next


    Return False
End Function


' Overload for an array of folder operations
Public Function CheckAccess(ByVal userName As String, _
                ByVal userToken As IntPtr, _
                ByVal secDesc() As Byte, _
                ByVal requiredOperations As FolderOperation()) _
        As Boolean Implements IAuthorizationExtension.CheckAccess

    Dim operation As FolderOperation

    For Each operation In requiredOperations
      If Not CheckAccess(userName, userToken, secDesc, operation) Then
        Return False
```

```
      End If
   Next


   Return True
End Function


' This subroutine implements SetConfiguration as required
' by IExtension
Public Sub SetConfiguration(ByVal configuration As String) _
           Implements IAuthorizationExtension.SetConfiguration
   ' Retrieve the admin user and password from the config settings
   ' and verify it.
   Dim doc As XmlDocument = New XmlDocument
   Dim child As XmlNode

   doc.LoadXml(configuration)

   If doc.DocumentElement.Name = "AdminConfiguration" Then
     For Each child In doc.DocumentElement.ChildNodes
       If child.Name = "UserName" Then
         m_adminUserName = child.InnerText
       Else
         Throw New Exception("Unrecognized configuration element.")
       End If
     Next

     If _
   MSSQLRS.FormsSecurity.AuthenticationExtension.VerifyUser( _
                                        m_adminUserName) _
                                        = False Then
       Throw New Exception("An attempt was made to load an " & _
"Administrative user for the Report Server that is not valid.")
     End If
   Else
     Throw New Exception("Error loading config data.")
   End If
End Sub

End Class
End Namespace
```

SetConfiguration Method   The SetConfiguration method reads a section of XML from the RSReportServer.config file. This XML information specifies the user name of the administrative user. This user name is stored in the m_adminUserName property of the AuthorizationExtension class.

The CheckAccess methods give this user all rights to all items. This ensures that there is at least one user with rights to administer Reporting Services. This is necessary because, when you initially switch to your custom security extension, there are no role assignments for any of the items in Reporting Services.

CheckAccess Method   The AuthorizationExtension class actually has several CheckAccess methods. These methods are overloaded based on the last parameter, requiredOperation. The correct method is called depending on which type of access is being checked.

For example, if the user is trying to delete a folder, the CheckAccess method will be called with a requiredOperation parameter of type FolderOperation. The version of CheckAccess that checks rights on folder operations is executed. If the user is using the check boxes on the Report Manager View Details page to delete several folders at once, the CheckAccess method will be called with a requiredOperation parameter that is an array of the FolderOperation type. The version of CheckAccess that checks rights on an array of folder operations is executed.

Only two of the CheckAccess methods—the method for a folder operation and the method for an array of folder operations—are printed here. The CheckAccess methods for reports, resources, and other types of report items are very similar to the CheckAccess methods shown here for folder operations. You can refer to the source code to view the other overloads of the CheckAccess methods.

The CheckAccess method is called by Reporting Services to verify the user's right to perform operations. It may be called once if the user is performing a specific operation. In other cases, the CheckAccess method may be called many times during the painting of a single screen. For example, if the user is viewing the Home folder, the CheckAccess method must be called for each item in the Home folder to determine if the user has rights to view that item.

The CheckAccess method first determines if the current user is the administrative user. If they are, the CheckAccess method returns true, indicating that this user has rights to do whatever operation is being requested. The operation is then completed by Reporting Services.

If this is not the administrative user, the CheckAccess method walks through the security descriptor collection until it finds an entry for this particular user. It then walks through a second collection, which contains the rights assigned to this user. If it finds the rights to the requested operation, it returns true, allowing the operation to be completed. If it does not find the rights to the requested operation, it returns false, causing the operation to be aborted.

Deploying a Custom Security Extension

This section contains a process for deploying a custom security extension on a Report Server. If you wish to complete this process solely for educational purposes, you should do so on a test installation of Reporting Services. That way, if anything goes wrong, either in deploying the custom security extension or in reverting back to Windows Integrated security, you can reinstall Reporting Services without harming a production environment.

This process should not be tested on a production installation of Reporting Services with the intent to revert back to Windows Integrated security at its conclusion. As stated earlier, changing to a custom security extension and then changing back to Windows Integrated security is not generally recommended. You have been warned. Don't come crying to me if you screw up your production server!

Preparation

CAUTION

Create a backup of all configuration files as directed in the following procedure. Without these backups, you may not be able to return to a working environment if the custom security extension fails.

To create a backup for all configuration files, follow these steps:

1. Add the reference and the web reference as instructed in the "Preparing the Sample Code" section of this chapter.

2. Create a folder called RSSecurityBackup on the ReportServer. This folder can be anywhere it will not be accidentally deleted. This folder will hold a backup copy of your Reporting Services configuration files for backing up your custom security extension.

3. In the RSSecurityBackup folder, create a folder called ReportServer and a folder called ReportManager.

4. Copy the following files from the Reporting Services\ReportManager folder to the RSSecurityBackup\ReportManager folder:

    ```
    rsmgrpolicy.config
    RSWebApplication.config
    Web.config
    ```

    The default location for the Reporting Services\ReportManager folder is

    ```
    C:\Program Files\Microsoft SQL Server\MSSQL\Reporting Services\
                                                    ReportManager
    ```

5. Copy the following files from the Reporting Services\ReportServer folder to the RSSecurityBackup\ReportServer folder:

    ```
    RSReportServer.config
    rssrvpolicy.config
    Web.config
    ```

The default location for the Reporting Services\ReportServer folder is

```
C:\Program Files\Microsoft SQL Server\MSSQL\Reporting Services\
                                                  ReportServer
```

Compiling and Deploying the Custom Security Assembly and Logon Pages

Now that you have created backup copies of your Reporting Services configuration files, you can compile and deploy the custom security assembly and the logon pages.

1. Open the FormsSecurity solution in Visual Studio .NET 2003.

2. Select Build | Build Solution from the main menu to build the assembly and the executable in this solution.

3. Copy the resulting MSSQLRS.FormsSecurity.dll assembly and the MSSQLRS .FormsSecurity.pdb debug database to the ReportManager\bin folder. The default location for this folder is

```
C:\Program Files\Microsoft SQL Server\MSSQL\Reporting Services\
                                                  ReportManager\bin
```

4. Copy the same MSSQLRS.FormsSecurity.dll assembly and the MSSQLRS .FormsSecurity.pdb debug database to the ReportServer\bin folder. The default location for this folder is

```
C:\Program Files\Microsoft SQL Server\MSSQL\Reporting Services\
                                                  ReportServer\bin
```

5. Copy the UILogon.aspx file to the ReportManager\Pages folder. The default location for this folder is

```
C:\Program Files\Microsoft SQL Server\MSSQL\Reporting Services\
                                                  ReportManager\Pages
```

6. Copy the Logon.aspx file to the ReportServer folder. The default location for this folder is

```
C:\Program Files\Microsoft SQL Server\MSSQL\Reporting Services\
                                                  ReportServer
```

Modifying the Reporting Services Configuration

In addition to placing the assembly and the logon pages in the appropriate location, you need to modify several Reporting Services configuration files and the IIS configuration to enable your custom security extension.

1. You will begin by modifying three Report Manager configuration files. These three files can all be found in the following folder:

```
C:\Program Files\Microsoft SQL Server\MSSQL\Reporting Services\
                                                  ReportManager
```

2. Open the rsmgrpolicy.config file in a text editor such as Notepad. This file contains the code access security configuration for the Report Manager.

3. Find the code group for the MyComputer zone. Change the permission set from Execution to FullTrust, as shown here:

```
<CodeGroup
        class="FirstMatchCodeGroup"
        version="1"
        PermissionSetName="FullTrust"
        Description="This code group grants MyComputer code Execution
                                                permission. ">
        <IMembershipCondition
            class="ZoneMembershipCondition"
            version="1"
            Zone="MyComputer" />
```

This change is necessary to allow the custom security extension to access the database and look up user information.

CAUTION

As with all XML documents, the config files are case sensitive. Pay close attention to the case of each entry you make in these configuration files.

4. Save your changes.

5. Open the RSWebApplication.config file in your text editor. This file contains custom configuration information for the Report Manager web application.

6. Find the <UI> entry and add the following, replacing {computername} with the name of your Report Server computer:

```
<UI>
 <CustomAuthenticationUI>
        <loginUrl>/Pages/UILogon.aspx</loginUrl>
        <UseSSL>False</UseSSL>
 </CustomAuthenticationUI>
 <ReportServerUrl>http://{computername}/ReportServer</ReportServerUrl>
</UI>
```

This entry tells the Report Manager where to redirect a user who has not been authenticated. If you have SSL available on this server, change the <UseSSL> setting from False to True.

7. Save your changes.

8. Open the Web.config file in your text editor. This file contains the standard configuration information for the Report Manager web application.

9. Locate the <identity impersonate="true"/> entry. Change this entry to "false", as shown:

```
<identity impersonate="false"/>
```

10. Save your changes.

11. Next you will modify three Report Server configuration files. These three files can all be found in the following folder:

```
C:\Program Files\Microsoft SQL Server\MSSQL\Reporting Services\
                                                    ReportServer
```

12. Open the RSReportServer.config file in your text editor. This file contains custom configuration information for the Report Server web service.

13. Find the <Security> and <Authentication> entries and modify them as shown:

```
<Security>
        <Extension Name="Forms"
                Type="MSSQLRS.FormsSecurity.AuthorizationExtension,
                                        MSSQLRS.FormsSecurity">
                <Configuration>
                        <AdminConfiguration>
                                <UserName>Stanley</UserName>
                        </AdminConfiguration>
                </Configuration>
        </Extension>
</Security>
<Authentication>
        <Extension Name="Forms"
                Type="MSSQLRS.FormsSecurity.AuthenticationExtension,
                                        MSSQLRS.FormsSecurity"/>
</Authentication>
```

These entries tell the Report Server web service what classes to use for authentication and authorization and which assembly contains those classes. The <Configuration> entry here contains the configuration information read by the SetConfiguration method, as discussed previously. Stanley will be the administrative user.

14. Save your changes.

15. Open the rssrvpolicy.config file in your text editor. This file contains the code access security configuration for the Report Server.

16. Add a code group for the custom security assembly, as shown here:

```
<CodeGroup
        class="UnionCodeGroup"
        version="1"
        PermissionSetName="FullTrust">
    <IMembershipCondition
            class="UrlMembershipCondition"
            version="1"
            Url="$CodeGen$/*"
    />
</CodeGroup>
```

```
<CodeGroup
      class="UnionCodeGroup"
      version="1"
      Name="SecurityExtensionCodeGroup"
      Description="Code group for the sample security extension"
      PermissionSetName="FullTrust">
   <IMembershipCondition
         class="UrlMembershipCondition"
         version="1"
         Url="C:\Program Files\Microsoft SQL Server\MSSQL\Reporting
              Services\ReportServer\bin\MSSQLRS.FormsSecurity.dll"
   />
</CodeGroup>
```

This code group uses URL membership to assign Full Trust rights to the custom security assembly. Change the URL path as necessary, if Reporting Services is not installed in the default location.

17.   Save your changes.

18.   Open the Web.config file in your text editor. This file contains the standard configuration information for the Report Server web service.

19.   Locate the <identity impersonate="true"/> entry. Change this entry to "false", as shown:

```
<identity impersonate="false"/>
```

20.   Locate the <authentication mode="Windows" /> entry. Replace it with the following:

```
<authentication mode="Forms">
  <forms loginUrl="logon.aspx" name="sqlAuthCookie" timeout="60"
                                            path="/"></forms>
</authentication>
```

21.   Add the following <authorization> entry immediately below the <authentication> entry:

```
<authorization>
  <deny users="?" />
</authorization>
```

22.   Save your changes and close your text editor.

23.   From the Administrative Tools area of the Control Panel, start the Internet Information Services management console.

24.   Navigate to the entry for the Reports virtual directory. This virtual directory should be located under Default Web Site.

25.   Right-click the Reports virtual directory and select Properties from the context menu. The Reports Properties dialog box will appear.

26. Select the Directory Security tab.

27. Click Edit in the Anonymous Access and Authentication Control area. The Authentication Methods dialog box appears.

28. Check the Anonymous Access check box.

29. Click OK to exit the Authentication Methods dialog box.

30. Click OK to exit the Reports Properties dialog box.

31. Right-click the ReportServer virtual directory and select Properties from the context menu. The ReportServer Properties dialog box will appear.

32. Select the Directory Security tab.

33. Click Edit in the Anonymous Access and Authentication Control area. The Authentication Methods dialog box appears.

34. Check the Anonymous Access check box.

35. Click OK to exit the Authentication Methods dialog box.

36. Click OK to exit the ReportServer Properties dialog box.

37. Close the Internet Information Services management console.

Reporting Services is now configured to use the custom security extension.

Restarting IIS

Anytime you make a change to the Reporting Services configuration files or to the custom security assembly, you need to restart IIS in order for these changes to take effect. Do not restart IIS if you have users in the middle of online sessions on your IIS server. You can restart IIS by using the following procedure:

1. Open a command window.

2. Type **iisreset** at the command prompt and press ENTER. The iisreset utility will stop and restart IIS.

3. Once IIS has restarted, close the command window.

Using the Custom Security Extension

To test the custom security extension, simply open your browser and go to the Report Manager. Rather than seeing the Report Manager, you will see the logon page. Enter a user name and password and click Logon to log on to Reporting Services.

Two logons are set up in the Employee table of the Galactic database:

User Name	Password	Administrative User
Stanley	SR	Yes
Ellen	EH	No

The logon for Ellen will not have any security role assignments. Use the Stanley administrative logon to assign security roles to the Ellen logon.

NOTE

In order for the cookie to function properly, you need to access the Report Manager using the computer name rather than using localhost.

Creating Logons

You can create additional non-administrative logons using the StoreRSLogon application. You created this executable when you built the FormsSecurity solution. To create a new logon, do the following:

1. Run StoreRSLogon.exe.

2. Select a Galactic Delivery Services employee from the Employee drop-down list.

3. Enter a user name and password for this employee.

4. Click Save to save these credentials in the Employee table of the Galactic database. The password is stored in the Employee table as an encrypted value.

5. Exit the StoreRSLogon program.

Debugging the Custom Security Assembly

In some cases, the custom security code will not work perfectly on the first try. Hard to believe, but true. You have two tools to help you in this situation. The log files and the Visual Studio debugger.

The log files are very helpful because they record any exceptions that might occur. Because we deployed the debug database file (PDB) along with the assembly file (DLL), the log file will even contain the method name and line number where the exception occurred. If an exception occurs, you should check the most recent log file for the Report Server, the Report Manager web application, and the Report Server web services.

You can also use the Visual Studio debugger to set breakpoints and step through the custom assembly code. Debugging should only be done on a test or development server, never on a production server. To use the debugger, do the following:

1. Start Visual Studio .NET 2003 and open the FormsSecurity solution.

2. Open Internet Explorer and navigate to the Report Manager. The logon page will appear. Do not log on yet.

3. Return to Visual Studio and set the desired breakpoints in your code.

4. Select Debug | Processes from the main menu. The Processes dialog box will appear.

5. From the list of processes, select the aspnet_wp.exe process (or the w3wp.exe process if you are using IIS 6.0) and then click Attach. The Attach to Process dialog box will appear.

6. Check the Common Language Runtime and Native check boxes.

7. Click OK to exit the Attach to Process dialog box.

8. Click Close to exit the Processes dialog box.

9. Switch to Internet Explorer, enter the user name and password, and click Logon.

10. When one of your breakpoints is encountered, the debugger will stop execution and change focus to Visual Studio.

11. You can now view variables and step through the code as you do with any other Visual Basic program.

12. When you have completed your debugging session, click Stop Debugging in Visual Studio and then close Internet Explorer.

Changing Back to Windows Integrated Security

If your custom security extension does not function properly or if, despite all the warnings, you want to change from your custom security extension back to Windows Integrated security, use the following procedure:

1. Remove all role assignments you created using the forms security user names.

2. Copy all the files in the RSSecurityBackup\ReportManager folder to the ReportManager folder. Replace the existing files. The default location of the ReportManager folder is

```
C:\Program Files\Microsoft SQL Server\MSSQL\Reporting Services\
                                                 ReportManager
```

3. Copy all the files in the RSSecurityBackup\ReportServer folder to the ReportServer folder. Replace the existing files. The default location of the ReportServer folder is

```
C:\Program Files\Microsoft SQL Server\MSSQL\Reporting Services\
                                                 ReportServer
```

4. Use the Internet Information Services management console to remove Anonymous access from both the Reports and the ReportServer virtual directories.

5. Use the iisreset utility program to restart IIS.

Other Extensions

In addition to the custom security extension, Reporting Services offers other APIs that allow you to extend its default functionality. You can develop your own data access extensions, rendering extensions, and delivery extensions. Examples showing how to utilize some of these extensions are included with Reporting Services. A number of third-party developers are using these APIs to create some very capable add-ons for Reporting Services.

Best Practices

Before finishing up, we will consider a few items that can make Reporting Services more efficient and easier to manage. These best practices are general rules of thumb that help things run smoother in most Reporting Services installations. As with all rules of thumb, there are always exceptions. However, as you create your Reporting Services installation and the business practices to go with it, consider these practices and the benefits that go with them.

Report-Authoring Practices

The following practices can make your report-authoring process more efficient and more consistent. A standard look and feel is usually desirable as users move from one report to the next. The ability to be responsive to your users and create reports in a timely manner is always a plus.

Use Report Templates

A number of tasks in report authoring can be repetitive, such as placing the company name and logo at the top of the page and placing the page number and date of execution at the bottom. Rather than wasting time creating these items afresh on each report, use one or more report templates. The report templates allow you to start your report layout with these redundant items already present.

In addition, the report templates allow you to provide a common look and feel to your reports. Templates can help ensure that certain style elements, such as a logo image or a page number in a certain location, are always present. The templates can help to enforce this common look and feel across a number of report authors.

Use Visual SourceSafe

Because the report-authoring environment for Reporting Services is also a development environment, seamless support for Visual SourceSafe is built right in. Use it! It takes very little additional time and effort to store your reports in Visual SourceSafe.

Visual SourceSafe has two advantages: First, there is no more wondering who has the latest source code for a report. This is especially important when modifying and then deploying reports to the Report Server. You do not want to have a report author deploy an old version of a report on top of a newer version.

Second, Visual SourceSafe provides versioning of your report source code. If you decide you really don't like the latest changes to a report, you can roll back to an older version. If an older version of an RDL file is pulled off of the Report Server on top of your newer version, Visual SourceSafe can save the day.

Use Shared Data Sources

Shared data sources can really help cut down on management headaches. They centralize the storage of database credentials. If a database is moved to a new server, there are fewer places to change the connection information. If the database logon credentials are changed, there are fewer locations to be modified.

Shared data sources also facilitate the use of production and development database servers. Report development can be done using a shared data source pointing to the development database server. A shared data source with the same name can exist on the production Report Server pointing to the production database server. With the Overwrite Data Sources option turned off, the shared data source from the development environment will not overwrite the shared data source in the production environment. Instead, the report will seamlessly go from querying development data in the development environment to querying production data in the production environment. Isn't that the way it's supposed to work?

Use Views and Stored Procedures

Give your report authors rights to query views and execute stored procedures. Avoid giving them rights to the underlying tables. Having them operate with views and stored procedures makes it easier to enforce security and maintain privacy. It also prevents accidental data modifications and deletions.

Report Deployment Practices

The practices listed here will help you move reports from the development environment to the production Report Server. You need to make sure there is some level of control over which reports can access your production data. You also need to control who can do what on your production Report Server.

Review Reports Before Deploying

It is generally a good idea to have reports reviewed before they are put into production. This is especially true if you have non-developers creating their own reports. You need to make sure that efficient queries were used to extract the data so that there is not an undue burden placed on the database server. You also need to have some level of assurance the information the report claims to present is actually the information that is being pulled from the database.

Use Linked Reports

Rather than deploying duplicate copies of the same report to your Report Server, use linked reports. Each linked report can have its own default parameters and its own security. At the same time, updates to that report are done in one centralized location. This helps prevent the confusion that can arise from having multiple versions of the same report running in the production environment at the same time.

Assign Security at the Folder Level

Make your security role assignments at the folder level. Let the reports inherit their security from the folders they reside in. Assigning individual security roles to individual reports is cumbersome and easily leads to errors. Your security practices should be relatively easy to implement; otherwise, they will not be followed.

Assign Security to Domain Groups

By the same token, it makes more sense to assign roles to domain groups than to try to assign roles to each individual user. Just as with assigning security at the report level, making assignments at the user level causes things to become very complex very rapidly. The simpler security policy is usually better, because it is the one that is more likely to be followed.

Assign Only the Rights Needed

Only give each user the rights they need to complete their required tasks. It is easier to assign broad rights rather than narrow, but this can lead to security breaches and problems managing the Report Server. Take the time to create custom security roles that provide users with only those rights they really need. Then use these custom roles as you are granting access to domain groups. The additional time taken during setup will be more than made up for in the time saved not having to clean up after users who were doing things that they shouldn't have been able to do in the first place.

Use Caching and Snapshots

Use caching and snapshots to reduce the load on your Report Server and increase performance. Set up scheduled snapshots to execute long-running reports during off hours. Believe me, users will not care if their data is eight hours old when they can get their reports back in seconds!

Where Do We Go from Here?

As Reporting Services matures over the next year or two, there is little doubt that it will remain a very exciting product. With a new version of Reporting Services due out with the next release of SQL Server and third parties releasing alternative report-authoring environments and Reporting Services extensions, it is safe to say that Reporting Services will continue to be in the news for some time to come. Based on the interest seen in the first weeks after the product launch, it also looks like Reporting Services will have a rapidly growing user community.

It may be difficult to say exactly where Reporting Services is going from here, but I think all the signs point in a positive direction. It might be easier to answer the question, Where does my business information go from here? With a tool as capable, flexible, and extensible as Reporting Services, the answer is, anywhere you need it to go!

Appendixes

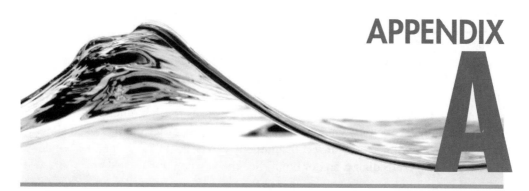

Report Item Reference

Report Objects

The first section of this appendix lists the report objects available in Reporting Services. These include the layout areas, the data regions and the remaining report items. This section describes each object, including whether the object has its own custom properties dialog box, and lists all the properties for that object. Properties can be set in the Properties window or in the custom properties dialog box. The font of each property will let you know if the property can be set in the Properties Window, the custom properties dialog box or both. (See the key below.)

Layout Areas

KEY:

Property in Properties Window Only

Property in Properties Window and Custom Properties Dialog Box

Property in Custom Properties Dialog Box Only

Body

Description: The layout area containing the bulk of the report content

Custom Properties Dialog Box: No (The Columns and ColumnSpacing properties can be found in the custom properties dialog box for the Report.)

Properties: BackgroundColor, BackgroundImage, BorderColor, BorderStyle, BorderWidth, **Columns**, **ColumnSpacing**, Size

Notes: If the Size: Width of the Body item added to the Margins: Left and Margins: Right of the Report item is wider than the PageSize: Width of the Report item, your report will span multiple pages horizontally.

Page Header

Description: The layout area repeated at the top of each page. Can be enabled and disabled in the Report Properties dialog box or on the Report menu.

Custom Properties Dialog Box: No (The PrintOnFirstPage and PrintOnLastPage properties can be found in the custom properties dialog box for the Report.)

Properties: BackgroundColor, BackgroundImage, BorderColor, BorderStyle, BorderWidth, **PrintOnFirstPage**, **PrintOnLastPage**, Size

Notes: You cannot include field values in the Page Header.

Page Footer

Description: The layout area repeated at the bottom of each page. Can be enabled and disabled in the Report Properties dialog box or on the Report menu.

Custom Properties Dialog Box: No (The PrintOnFirstPage and PrintOnLastPage properties can be found in the custom properties dialog box for the Report.)

Properties: BackgroundColor, BackgroundImage, BorderColor, BorderStyle, BorderWidth, **PrintOnFirstPage**, **PrintOnLastPage**, Size

Notes: You cannot include field values in the Page Footer.

Report

Description: The report is not a layout area itself but rather is a container for the other layout areas.

Custom Properties Dialog Box: Yes

Properties: Author, **AutoRefresh**, **Classes**, *CustomCode*, **DataElementName**, **DataElementStyle**, **DataSchema**, **DataTransform**, **Description**, **DrawGrid**, **EmbeddedImages**, **GridSpacing**, Language, **Margins**, **PageSize**, **References**, **ReportParameters**, **SnapToGrid**

Notes: If the Size: Width of the Body item added to the Margins: Left and Margins: Right of the Report item is wider than the PageSize: Width of the Report item, your report will span multiple pages horizontally.

Data Regions

KEY:

Property in Properties Window Only

Property in Properties Window and Custom Properties Dialog Box

Property in Custom Properties Dialog Box Only

Chart

Description: A business graphic such as a line graph or a pie chart. The chart is the only data region that cannot contain other report items.

Custom Properties Dialog Box: Yes

Properties: BackgroundColor, BackgroundImage, Bookmark, BorderColor, BorderStyle, BorderWidth, Calendar, *ChartAreaBorderAndLineStyle*, *ChartAreaFillStyle*, *Clustered*, Color, *Cylinder*, DataElementName, DataElementOutput, **DataSetName**, Direction, *DisplayChartWith3-DVisualEffect*, *DisplayLegendInsidePlotArea*, **Filters**, Font, Format, *HorizontalRotation*, Label, Language, *LegendBorderAndLineStyle*, *LegendFillStyle*, *LegendFontStyle*, *LegendLayout*, *LegendPosition*, LineHeight, Location, **Name**, NoRows, NumeralLanguage, NumeralVariant, *Orthographic*, Padding, PageBreakAtEnd, PageBreakAtStart, **Palette**, Parent, *Perspective*, *PlotAreaBorderAndLineStyle*, *PlotAreaFillStyle*, *Shading*, *ShowLegend*, Size, **Subtype**, TextAlign, TextDecoration, *Title*, *TitleFontStyle*, ToolTip, **Type**, UnicodeBiDi, VerticalAlign, *VerticalRotation*, Visibility, *WallThickness*, WritingMode, *X-AxisFormatting, Y-AxisFormatting*

Chart Category Group

Description: Controls the category groupings on the chart. These usually form the x-axis of the chart.

Custom Properties Dialog Box: Yes

Properties: *DataElementCollection, DataElementName, DataElementOutput, Filters, Group On, Label, Name, Parent Group, Sorting*

Chart Series Group

Description: Controls the series groupings on the chart. The series comes into play when there is more than one data point for each category grouping.

Custom Properties Dialog Box: Yes

Properties: *DataElementCollection, DataElementName, DataElementOutput, Filters, Group On, Label, Name, Parent Group, Sorting*

Chart Value

Description: Controls the values placed on the chart

Custom Properties Dialog Box: Yes

Properties: *Action, Angle, DataElementName, DataElementOutput, DataLabel, Format, JumpToBookmark, JumpToReport, JumpToReportParameters, JumpToURL, LabelFontStyle, MarkerSize, MarkerType, PlotDataAsLine, Position, SeriesLabel, ShowMarkers, ShowPointLabels, Value*

List

Description: A freeform layout area that can be tied to a dataset

Custom Properties Dialog Box: Yes

Properties: BackgroundColor, BackgroundImage, **Bookmark**, BorderColor, BorderStyle, BorderWidth, Calendar, Color, **DataElementName**, **DataElementOutput**, **DataInstanceElementOutput**, **DataInstanceName**, **DataSetName**, Direction, **Filters**, Font, Format, **Grouping**, **KeepTogether**, **Label**, Language, LineHeight, Location, **Name**, NoRows, NumeralLanguage, NumeralVariant, Padding, **PageBreakAtEnd**, **PageBreakAtStart**, Parent, Size, *Sorting*, TextAlign, TextDecoration, **ToolTip**, UnicodeBiDi, VerticalAlign, **Visibility**, WritingMode

List Details Group

Description: Grouping at the detail level in a list

Custom Properties Dialog Box: Yes

Properties: *DataElementCollection, DataElementName, DataElementOutput, Filters, Group On, Label, Name, Parent Group, Visibility*

Matrix

Description: A pivot table for viewing row and column data
Custom Properties Dialog Box: Yes
Properties: BackgroundColor, BackgroundImage, **Bookmark**, BorderColor, BorderStyle, BorderWidth, Calendar, **CellDataElementName**, **CellDataElementOutput**, Color, **DataElementName**, **DataElementOutput**, **DataSetName**, Direction, **Filters**, Font, Format, **GroupsBeforeRowHeaders**, **KeepTogether**, **Label**, Language, **LayoutDirection**, LineHeight, Location, **Name**, NoRows, NumeralLanguage, NumeralVariant, Padding, **PageBreakAtEnd**, **PageBreakAtStart**, Parent, Size, TextAlign, TextDecoration, **ToolTip**, UnicodeBiDi, VerticalAlign, **Visibility**, WritingMode

Matrix Column

Description: Defines the appearance of a column in a matrix
Custom Properties Dialog Box: No
Properties: BackgroundColor, BackgroundImage, BorderColor, BorderStyle, BorderWidth, Calendar, Color, Direction, Font, Format, Language, LineHeight, NumeralLanguage, NumeralVariant, Padding, TextAlign, TextDecoration, UnicodeBiDi, VerticalAlign, Width, WritingMode

Matrix Column Group

Description: Defines the data that makes up each column in a matrix
Custom Properties Dialog Box: Yes
Properties: *DataElementCollection, DataElementName, DataElementOutput, Filters, GroupOn, Label, Name, ParentGroup, Sorting, Visibility*

Matrix Row

Description: Defines the appearance of a row in a matrix
Custom Properties Dialog Box: No
Properties: BackgroundColor, BackgroundImage, BorderColor, BorderStyle, BorderWidth, Calendar, Color, Direction, Font, Format, Height, Language, LineHeight, NumeralLanguage, NumeralVariant, Padding, TextAlign, TextDecoration, UnicodeBiDi, VerticalAlign, WritingMode

Matrix Row Group

Description: Defines the data that makes up each row in a matrix
Custom Properties Dialog Box: Yes
Properties: *DataElementCollection, DataElementName, DataElementOutput, Filters, GroupOn, Label, Name, ParentGroup, Sorting, Visibility*

Matrix Subtotal

Description: Defines the formatting for a subtotal cell in a matrix
Custom Properties Dialog Box: No
Properties: BackgroundColor, BackgroundImage, BorderColor, BorderStyle, BorderWidth, Calendar, Color, DataElementName, DataElementOutput, Direction, Font, Format, Language, LineHeight, NumeralLanguage, NumeralVariant, Padding, Position, TextAlign, TextDecoration, UnicodeBiDi, VerticalAlign, WritingMode

Table

Description: A table for viewing columnar data
Custom Properties Dialog Box: Yes
Properties: BackgroundColor, BackgroundImage, **Bookmark**, BorderColor, BorderStyle, BorderWidth, Calendar, Color, **DataElementName**, **DataElementOutput**, **DataSetName**, **DetailDataCollectionName**, **DetailDataElementName**, **DetailDataElementOutput**, Direction, **Filters**, Font, Format, **KeepTogether**, **Label**, Language, LineHeight, Location, **Name**, NoRows, NumeralLanguage, NumeralVariant, Padding, **PageBreakAtEnd**, **PageBreakAtStart**, Parent, **RepeatFooterOnNewPage**, **RepeatHeaderOnNewPage**, Size, *Sorting*, TextAlign, TextDecoration, **ToolTip**, UnicodeBiDi, VerticalAlign, **Visibility**, WritingMode

Table Column

Description: Defines the appearance of a column in a table
Custom Properties Dialog Box: No
Properties: BackgroundColor, BackgroundImage, BorderColor, BorderStyle, BorderWidth, Calendar, Color, Direction, Font, Format, Language, LineHeight, NumeralLanguage, NumeralVariant, Padding, TextAlign, TextDecoration, UnicodeBiDi, VerticalAlign, Visibility, Width, WritingMode

Table Details Group

Description: Grouping at the detail level in a table
Custom Properties Dialog Box: Yes
Properties: *DataElementCollection, DataElementName, DataElementOutput, Filters, GroupOn, Label, Name, ParentGroup, Visibility*

Table Group

Description: Defines the data that makes up a group in the table
Custom Properties Dialog Box: Yes

Properties: *DataElementCollection, DataElementName, DataElementOutput, Filters, GroupOn, IncludeGroupFooter, IncludeGroupHeader, Label, Name, PageBreakAtEnd, PageBreakAtStart, ParentGroup, RepeatFooterOnNewPage, RepeatHeaderOnNewPage, Sorting, Visibility*

Table Row

Description: Defines the appearance of a row in a table
Custom Properties Dialog Box: No
Properties: BackgroundColor, BackgroundImage, BorderColor, BorderStyle, BorderWidth, Calendar, Color, Direction, Font, Format, Grouping, Grouping/Sorting, Height, Language, LineHeight, NumeralLanguage, NumeralVariant, Padding, RepeatOnNewPage, TextAlign, TextDecoration, UnicodeBiDi, VerticalAlign, Visibility, WritingMode
Notes: The Grouping property appears for the detail table row. The Grouping/Sorting property appears for the other types of table rows. The Grouping/Sorting property displays the correct information but it displays it in the Details Grouping dialog box rather than the Grouping and Sorting Properties dialog box. (This is a bug.) The RepeatOnNewPage property does not appear for a detail table row.

Report Items

KEY:

Property in Properties Window Only
Property in Properties Window and Custom Properties Dialog Box
Property in Custom Properties Dialog Box Only

Image

Description: Places a graphic on the report
Custom Properties Dialog Box: Yes
Properties: Action, Bookmark, BorderColor, BorderStyle, BorderWidth, **JumpToBookmark, JumpToReport, JumpToReportParameters, JumpToURL, Label**, Location, MIMEType, **Name**, Padding, Parent, **RepeatWith**, Size, Sizing, Source, **ToolTip**, Value, **Visibility**

Line

Description: Places a line on the report
Custom Properties Dialog Box: Yes
Properties: Bookmark, EndPoint, **Label**, LineColor, LineStyle, LineWidth, Location, **Name**, Parent, **RepeatWith**, *ToolTip*, **Visibility**

Rectangle

Description: Places a rectangle on the report
Custom Properties Dialog Box: Yes
Properties: BackgroundColor, BackgroundImage, **Bookmark**, BorderColor, BorderStyle, BorderWidth, **DataElementName**, **DataElementOutput**, **Label**, LinkToChild, Location, **Name**, **PageBreakAtEnd**, **PageBreakAtStart**, Parent, **RepeatWith**, Size, **ToolTip**, **Visibility**

Subreport

Description: Inserts one report into another
Custom Properties Dialog Box: Yes
Properties: Bookmark, BorderColor, BorderStyle, BorderWidth, Calendar, Color, **DataElementName**, **DataElementOutput**, Direction, Font, Format, **Label**, Language, LineHeight, Location, MergeTransactions, **Name**, NoRows, NumeralLanguage, NumeralVariant, Padding, **Parameters**, Parent, **ReportName**, Size, TextAlign, TextDecoration, **ToolTip**, UnicodeBiDi, VerticalAlign, **Visibility**, WritingMode

Text Box

Description: Places a text box on the report
Custom Properties Dialog Box: Yes
Properties: Action, BackgroundColor, BackgroundImage, **Bookmark**, BorderColor, BorderStyle, BorderWidth, Calendar, **CanGrow**, **CanShrink**, Color, **DataElementName**, **DataElementOutput**, **DataElementStyle**, **Direction**, **Font**, **Format**, **HideDuplicates**, **InitialToggleState**, **JumpToBookmark**, **JumpToReport**, **JumpToReportParameters**, **JumpToURL**, **Label**, Language, **LineHeight**, Location, **Name**, NumeralLanguage, NumeralVariant, **Padding**, Parent, **RepeatWith**, Size, TextAlign, **TextDecoration**, **ToolTip**, UnicodeBiDi, **Value**, VerticalAlign, **Visibility**, **WritingMode**

Property Reference

This section describes the properties of the report objects. The property is listed only once even if it is a property of several objects. If the property can be set in a custom properties dialog box, the explanation notes the tab where this property appears.

Some properties serve as a summary of several properties in the Properties window. BackgroundImage and BorderColor are two examples of these summary properties. A plus sign to the left of a property in the Properties window tells you that it is a summary property and has several detail properties beneath it. Click the plus sign to expand the summary property so you can view and change the value of the detail properties.

In this section, the **Detail Properties:** entry signals that this property is a summary property, which contains several detail properties. The detail properties are explained in the **Notes:** entry for the summary property.

Properties

Action

Description: Specifies which type of hyperlink action this item will execute

When to Use: The report item is to cause the Report Viewer to navigate to a bookmark in this report, to another report, or to a website.

Notes: Linking to a bookmark or to another report works only in the Report Viewer or in the HTML and MHTML rendering formats. Linking to a website works only in the Report Viewer and the HTML, MHTML, PDF, and Excel rendering formats.

Property Of: Chart Value, Image, Text Box

Custom Properties Dialog Box Location: Navigation tab (Action tab for a chart value.)

Angle

Description: Adjusts the angle of the point labels on a chart

When to Use: A chart is to include labels on each data point, and the labels need to be rotated to an orientation other than horizontal.

Notes: Rotating data point labels to a 90-degree angle or a –90-degree angle helps fit more information in a tight space.

Property Of: Chart Value

Custom Properties Dialog Box Location: Edit Chart Value dialog box – Point Labels tab

Author

Description: Records the author of the report

When to Use: The author's name is to be stored with the report.

Property Of: Report

Custom Properties Dialog Box Location: Report Properties – General tab

AutoRefresh

Description: Sets the number of seconds for the report to automatically re-execute when being displayed in the Report Viewer

When to Use: The report shows constantly changing information and will be viewed in the Report Viewer.

Notes: AutoRefresh only works in the Report Viewer in Report Manager. AutoRefresh does not work on the Visual Studio Preview tab or in any of the export formats.

Property Of: Report

Custom Properties Dialog Box Location: Report Properties – General tab

BackgroundColor

Description: Sets the fill color for the item

When to Use: An item is to have its own fill color.

Property Of: Body, Chart, List, Matrix, Matrix Column, Matrix Row, Matrix Subtotal, Page Header, Page Footer, Rectangle, Table, Table Column, Table Row, Text Box

BackgroundImage

Description: Selects a graphic to fill the background of an item

When to Use: An item is to have its own fill from a graphic.

Notes: The Source detail property specifies whether the image is embedded, external or in a database. The Value detail property contains the name of the image. The MIMEType detail property contains the MIME type of the image. The BackgroundRepeat detail property specifies how the image is repeated, if it does not fill the entire report object.

Property Of: Body, Chart, List, Matrix, Matrix Column, Matrix Row, Matrix Subtotal, Page Header, Page Footer, Rectangle, Table, Table Column, Table Row, Text Box

Detail Properties: Source, Value, MIMEType, BackgroundRepeat

Bookmark

Description: Creates a named bookmark in a report

When to Use: There is to be a Chart Value, Image, or Text Box serving as a hyperlink to this report item.

Notes: The Bookmark serves as the target for a hyperlink jump within the same report. Clicking a Chart Value, Image, or Text Box whose JumpToBookmark property matches this report item's Bookmark property will cause the Report Viewer to jump to this report item. Bookmarks work only in the HTML and MHTML rendering formats.

Property Of: Chart, Image, Line, List, Matrix, Rectangle, Subreport, Table, Text Box
Custom Properties Dialog Box Location: Navigation tab

BorderColor

Description: The color of the border around the outside of the report item
When to Use: There is to be a non-black border around this report item.
Notes: The value in the Default detail property is used as the value for the Left, Right, Top, and Bottom detail properties unless a value is specified for the detail property itself. The Left, Right, Top, and Bottom detail properties control the color for the individual sides of the report object.
Property Of: Body, Chart, Image, List, Matrix, Matrix Column, Matrix Row, Matrix Subtotal, Page Header, Page Footer, Rectangle, Subreport, Table, Table Column, Table Row, Text Box
Detail Properties: Default, Left, Right, Top, Bottom

BorderStyle

Description: The style (none, solid, dotted, dashed, etc.) of the border around the outside of the report item
When to Use: There is to be a border around this report item.
Notes: A border is displayed only when the BorderStyle property is set to a value other than None. Some of the more complex border styles, such as double and groove, are not clearly visible unless the corresponding BorderWidth property is set to a value larger than 1 point. The value in the Default detail property is used as the value for the Left, Right, Top, and Bottom detail properties unless a value is specified for the detail property itself. The Left, Right, Top, and Bottom detail properties control the style for the individual sides of the report object.
Property Of: Body, Chart, Image, List, Matrix, Matrix Column, Matrix Row, Matrix Subtotal, Page Header, Page Footer, Rectangle, Subreport, Table, Table Column, Table Row, Text Box
Detail Properties: Default, Left, Right, Top, Bottom

BorderWidth

Description: The width of the border around the outside of the report item
When to Use: There is to be a border around this report item with a width other than 1 point.
Notes: The value in the Default detail property is used as the value for the Left, Right, Top, and Bottom detail properties unless a value is specified for the detail property itself. The Left, Right, Top, and Bottom detail properties control the width for the individual sides of the report object.

Property Of: Body, Chart, Image, List, Matrix, Matrix Column, Matrix Row, Matrix Subtotal, Page Header, Page Footer, Rectangle, Subreport, Table, Table Column, Table Row, Text Box

Detail Properties: Default, Left, Right, Top, Bottom

Calendar

Description: The calendar to use when dealing with date values in this report item

When to Use: A calendar other than the Gregorian calendar is to be used with date values in this report item.

Property Of: Chart, List, Matrix, Matrix Column, Matrix Row, Matrix Subtotal, Subreport, Table, Table Column, Table Row, Text Box

CanGrow

Description: Specifies whether or not a text box can grow vertically to display the entire contents of the Value property

When to Use: The expected length of the Value property contents is not known or may vary.

Notes: Text boxes can grow in the vertical direction, but not in the horizontal direction.

Property Of: Text Box

Custom Properties Dialog Box Location: Text Box Properties, Basic or Text Box Properties, Advanced – Format tab

CanShrink

Description: Specifies whether or not a text box can shrink vertically to remove any blank lines after the contents of the Value property is displayed

When to Use: The expected length of the Value property contents is not known or may vary.

Property Of: Text Box

Custom Properties Dialog Box Location: Text Box Properties, Basic or Text Box Properties, Advanced – Format tab

CellDataElementName

Description: The name to be used for the element or attribute used to identify the cell data when exporting to the XML rendering format

When to Use: The report is to be exported using the XML rendering format.

Property Of: Matrix

Custom Properties Dialog Box Location: Matrix Properties – Data Output tab

CellDataElementOutput

Description: Specifies whether the cell data is output when exporting to the XML rendering format

When to Use: The report is to be exported using the XML rendering format.

Property Of: Matrix

Custom Properties Dialog Box Location: Matrix Properties – Data Output tab

ChartAreaBorderAndLineStyle

Description: The format of the line surrounding the entire chart item

When to Use: There is to be a line around the entire chart item.

Notes: The Style detail property controls the style, the Width detail property controls the width, and the Color detail property controls the color of the line.

Property Of: Chart

Custom Properties Dialog Box Location: Chart Properties – General tab

Detail Properties: Style, Width, Color

ChartAreaFillStyle

Description: The fill behind the entire chart area

When to Use: The Chart item is to have its own fill color.

Notes: The fill can be a single color or a two-color gradient. The Color detail property contains the color of the area or is the first color in a two-color gradient when the Gradient detail property is true. The Gradient detail property specifies whether this is a single color fill (false) or a two-color gradient (true). The EndColor detail property contains the second color in a two-color gradient.

Property Of: Chart

Custom Properties Dialog Box Location: Chart Properties – General tab

Detail Properties: Color, Gradient, End Color

Classes

Description: The classes (assemblies) referenced by this report that include nonshared properties or methods

When to Use: Nonshared properties or methods from an assembly are to be referenced by one or more expressions in the report.

Notes: The ClassName detail property contains a list of classes, contained in external assemblies, that are referenced by this report. The InstanceName detail property contains the name of an object (or instance) created from this class.

Property Of: Report

Custom Properties Dialog Box Location: Report Properties – References tab

Detail Properties: ClassName, InstanceName

Clustered

Description: Specifies that a series in a 3-D chart is to be shown front-to-back rather than side-to-side

When to Use: Depth is to be added to a 3-D chart to aid analysis or add interest.

Property Of: Chart

Custom Properties Dialog Box Location: Chart Properties – 3D Effect tab

Color

Description: The foreground color

When to Use: A foreground color other than black is to be used.

Property Of: Chart, List, Matrix, Matrix Column, Matrix Row, Matrix Subtotal, Subreport, Table, Table Column, Table Row, Text Box

Columns

Description: The number of columns in the report body

When to Use: The report body is to have multiple columns.

Property Of: Body

ColumnSpacing

Description: The amount of space between multiple columns

When to Use: The report body is to have multiple columns with a separation other than 0.5 inch.

Property Of: Body

CustomCode

Description: Visual Basic functions and subroutines to be embedded in the report

When to Use: The report requires Visual Basic code too complex to put in a property value.

Property Of: Report

Cylinder

Description: Specifies that bars and columns in a 3-D chart are to be cylinders rather than rectangular solids

When to Use: Interest and variety is to be added to a 3-D chart.

Property Of: Chart

Custom Properties Dialog Box Location: Chart Properties – 3D Effect tab

DataElementCollection

Description: The name of the element that is to contain all instances of this group when exporting to the XML rendering format

When to Use: This group is to be included when exporting to the XML rendering format.

Property Of: Chart Category Group, Chart Series Group, List Details Group, Matrix Column Group, Matrix Row Group, Table Details Group, Table Group

Custom Properties Dialog Box Location: Data Output tab

DataElementName

Description: The name to be used for the element or attribute used when exporting to the XML rendering format

When to Use: The report is to be exported using the XML rendering format.

Property Of: Chart, Chart Category Group, Chart Series Group, Chart Value, List, List Details Group, Matrix, Matrix Column Group, Matrix Row Group, Matrix Subtotal, Rectangle, Report, Subreport, Table, Table Details Group, Table Group, Text Box

Custom Properties Dialog Box Location: Data Output tab

DataElementOutput

Description: Specifies whether this item is output when exporting to the XML rendering format

When to Use: The report is to be exported using the XML rendering format.

Property Of: Chart, Chart Category Group, Chart Series Group, Chart Value, List, List Details Group, Matrix, Matrix Column Group, Matrix Row Group, Matrix Subtotal, Rectangle, Subreport, Table, Table Details Group, Table Group, Text Box

Custom Properties Dialog Box Location: Data Output tab

DataElementStyle

Description: Specifies whether this item is output as an element or an attribute when exporting to the XML rendering format

When to Use: The report is to be exported using the XML rendering format.

Property Of: Report, Text Box

Custom Properties Dialog Box Location: Data Output tab

DataInstanceElementOutput

Description: Specifies whether the list instances are output when exporting to the XML rendering format

When to Use: The report is to be exported using the XML rendering format.
Property Of: List
Custom Properties Dialog Box Location: List Properties – Data Output tab

DataInstanceName

Description: The name to be used for the element used when exporting to the XML rendering format
When to Use: The report is to be exported using the XML rendering format.
Property Of: List
Custom Properties Dialog Box Location: List Properties – Data Output tab

DataLabel

Description: The label to be used for data points on the chart
When to Use: The data points on the chart are to be labeled.
Property Of: Chart Value
Custom Properties Dialog Box Location: Edit Chart Value – Point Labels tab

DataSchema

Description: The schema name used when exporting to the XML rendering format
When to Use: The report is to be exported using the XML rendering format.
Property Of: Report
Custom Properties Dialog Box Location: Report Properties – Data Output tab

DataSetName

Description: The name of the dataset to be used with the data region
When to Use: There is a dataset to be used with a data region.
Property Of: Chart, List, Matrix, Table
Custom Properties Dialog Box Location: General tab (For chart, it is on the Data tab.)

DataTransform

Description: The name of a transform (XSLT document) to be applied after the report has been exported using the XML rendering format
When to Use: The XML document created by the export is to be transformed into another document format.
Property Of: Report
Custom Properties Dialog Box Location: Report Properties – Data Output tab

Description

Description: The description of the report

When to Use: The report's description is to be stored with the report.

Property Of: Report

Custom Properties Dialog Box Location: Report Properties – General tab

DetailDataCollectionName

Description: The name of the element that is to contain all instances of this group when exporting to the XML rendering format

When to Use: This group is to be included when exporting to the XML rendering format.

Property Of: Table

Custom Properties Dialog Box Location: Table Properties – Data Output tab

DetailDataElementName

Description: The name to be used for the element or attribute used to identify the detail data when exporting to the XML rendering format

When to Use: The report is to be exported using the XML rendering format.

Property Of: Table

Custom Properties Dialog Box Location: Table Properties – Data Output tab

DetailDataElementOutput

Description: Specifies whether this item is output when exporting to the XML rendering format

When to Use: The report is to be exported using the XML rendering format.

Property Of: Table

Custom Properties Dialog Box Location: Table Properties – Data Output tab

Direction

Description: The writing direction to be used with this item, either left-to-right or right-to-left

When to Use: A character set which is written right-to-left is being used in this item.

Property Of: Chart, List, Matrix, Matrix Column, Matrix Row, Matrix Subtotal, Subreport, Table, Table Column, Table Row, Text Box

Custom Properties Dialog Box Location: Text Box Properties, Advanced – Format tab (for text box)

DisplayChartWith3-DVisualEffect

Description: Specifies whether to make a chart 3-D
When to Use: Readability or interest is to be added by making a chart three-dimensional.
Property Of: Chart
Custom Properties Dialog Box Location: Chart Properties – 3D Effect tab

DisplayLegendInsidePlotArea

Description: Specifies whether to display the chart legend inside the chart plotting area
When to Use: Space can be saved by placing the chart's legend in an unused portion of the plotting area.
Property Of: Chart
Custom Properties Dialog Box Location: Chart Properties – Legend tab

DrawGrid

Description: Specifies whether the layout grid is shown on the Layout tab
When to Use: The layout grid dots are not desired on the Layout tab.
Property Of: Report
Custom Properties Dialog Box Location: Report Properties – General tab

EmbeddedImages

Description: The collection of graphics embedded in the report
When to Use: Images are to be embedded in the report.
Property Of: Report

EndPoint

Description: The coordinates of the end of the line
When to Use: A line is to be positioned on the report.
Notes: The Horizontal and Vertical detail properties specify the location of the end of the line.
Property Of: Line
Detail Properties: Horizontal, Vertical

Filters

Description: One or more expressions to exclude certain records from the dataset
When to Use: The dataset contains records that are not desired in the data region, and these records cannot or should not be removed by the dataset query.

Notes: The detail properties combine to build a set of filter expressions. Only records in the dataset that satisfy this set of filter expressions are included in the data region or grouping.

Property Of: Chart, Chart Category Group, Chart Series Group, List, List Details Group, Matrix, Matrix Column Group, Matrix Row Group, Table, Table Details Group, Table Group

Custom Properties Dialog Box Location: Filters tab

Detail Properties: Expression, Operator, Value, And/Or

Font

Description: The specification of the font to be used to render text within this item

When to Use: A font other than Normal, Arial, 10 point is desired.

Notes: The FontStyle detail property specifies whether the font is normal or italicized. The FontFamily detail property contains the name of the font. The FontSize detail property specifies the size of the font in points. The FontWeight detail property specifies the thickness of the font and is used to create bold text. (Underlining is controlled by the TextDecoration property.)

Property Of: Chart, List, Matrix, Matrix Column, Matrix Row, Matrix Subtotal, Subreport, Table, Table Column, Table Row, Text Box

Detail Properties: FontStyle, FontFamily, FontSize, FontWeight

Format

Description: A formatting string to control the appearance of a value

When to Use: An appearance other than the default appearance of a value is required for better readability.

Property Of: Chart, Chart Value, List, Matrix, Matrix Column, Matrix Row, Matrix Subtotal, Subreport, Table, Table Column, Table Row, Text Box

Custom Properties Dialog Box Location: Text Box Properties, Basic or Text Box Properties, Advanced – Format tab (for text box) or Edit Chart Value – Point Labels tab (for chart value)

GridSpacing

Description: The distance between layout grid points

When to Use: A distance other than 0.125 inch is desired between grid points.

Property Of: Report

Custom Properties Dialog Box Location: Report Properties – General tab

Grouping

Description: The grouping information for the detail level of the data region

When to Use: The detail level of this data region is to be a group.

Property Of: List, Table Row
Notes: This property displays the Detail Grouping dialog box.

Grouping/Sorting

Description: The grouping and sorting information for a header-level or footer-level table row
When to Use: Data is to be grouped or sorted.
Property Of: Table Row
Notes: This property displays the Detail Grouping dialog box. (This is a bug.)

GroupOn

Description: The grouping expression
When to Use: Data is to be grouped when displayed by this data region.
Property Of: Chart Category Group, Chart Series Group, List Details Group, Matrix Column Group, Matrix Row Group, Table Details Group, Table Group
    Custom Properties Dialog Box Location: General tab

GroupsBeforeRowHeaders

Description: The number of columns that are to appear to the left of the row headers. (Reverse this if you're using a right-to-left matrix.)
    When to Use: The row headers are to appear in the matrix rather than to the left (or right) of it.
    Property Of: Matrix
    Custom Properties Dialog Box Location: Matrix Properties – General tab

Height

Description: The height of the row
When to Use: The row height is to be modified.
Property Of: Matrix Row, Table Row

HideDuplicates

Description: Specifies whether to hide duplicate values when the text box is repeated in a table column
    When to Use: The value in the text box is to act as a group header, even though it is within the table detail rather than the group header.
    Property Of: Text Box
    Custom Properties Dialog Box Location: Basic Table Properties or Advanced Table Properties – General tab

HorizontalRotation

Description: The horizontal rotation applied to a 3-D chart
When to Use: The horizontal rotation must be adjusted to provide the user with the optimum view of the chart data.
Property Of: Chart
Custom Properties Dialog Box Location: Chart Properties – 3D Effect tab

IncludeGroupFooter

Description: Specifies whether a footer row is to be included for this group
When to Use: Totals or other concluding information is to be displayed at the end of the table group.
Property Of: Table Group
Custom Properties Dialog Box Location: Grouping and Sorting Properties – General tab

IncludeGroupHeader

Description: Specifies whether a header row is to be included for this group
When to Use: Headers or other introductory information is to be displayed at the beginning of the table group.
Property Of: Table Group
Custom Properties Dialog Box Location: Grouping and Sorting Properties – General tab

InitialToggleState

Description: The initial state of the toggle graphic associated with this text box
When to Use: This text box is being used to control the visibility of another report item.
Property Of: Text Box
Custom Properties Dialog Box Location: Advanced Text Box Properties – Visibility tab

JumpToBookmark

Description: The name of the bookmark to which this report item is to hyperlink
When to Use: This report item is to cause the Report Viewer to navigate to a bookmark in this report.
Notes: Linking to a bookmark works only in the Report Viewer or in the HTML and MHTML rendering formats.
Property Of: Chart Value, Image, Text Box
Custom Properties Dialog Box Location: Navigation tab (Action tab for a chart value.)

JumpToReport

Description: The name of the report to which this report item is to hyperlink

When to Use: This report item is to cause the Report Viewer to navigate to another report.

Notes: Linking to another report works only in the Report Viewer or in the HTML and MHTML rendering formats.

Property Of: Chart Value, Image, Text Box

Custom Properties Dialog Box Location: Navigation tab (Action tab for a chart value.)

JumpToReportParameters

Description: The parameters required by the report to which the item is to hyperlink

When to Use: This report item is to cause the Report Viewer to navigate to another report, and the target report requires report parameters.

Notes: The Parameter Name detail property contains a list of parameters for the hyperlinked report. The Parameter Value detail property contains a list of values to be assigned to each of those parameters.

Property Of: Chart Value, Image, Text Box

Custom Properties Dialog Box Location: Navigation tab (Action tab for a chart value.)

Detail Properties: Parameter Name, Parameter Value

JumpToURL

Description: The URL to which this report item is to hyperlink

When to Use: This report item is to cause the Report Viewer to navigate to a website.

Notes: Linking to a website works only in the Report Viewer and the HTML, MHTML, PDF, and Excel rendering formats.

Property Of: Chart Value, Image, Text Box

Custom Properties Dialog Box Location: Navigation tab (Action tab for a chart value.)

KeepTogether

Description: Specifies whether to attempt to keep this data region on one page

When to Use: The data region is to be kept on one page for better readability and analysis.

Property Of: List, Matrix, Table

Custom Properties Dialog Box Location: General tab

Label

Description: The document map label for this item

When to Use: The report is to include a document map, and this item is to be linked to one item in the document map.

Notes: The document map works only in the Report Viewer and in the PDF and Excel rendering formats.

Property Of: Chart, Chart Category Group, Chart Series Group, Image, Line, List, List Details Group, Matrix, Matrix Column Group, Matrix Row Group, Rectangle, Subreport, Table, Table Details Group, Table Group, Text Box

Custom Properties Dialog Box Location: General tab or Navigation tab

LabelFontStyle

Description: The font style of a chart point label

When to Use: The chart values are to have their own textual labels.

Notes: The FontFamily detail property contains the name of the font. The FontSize detail property specifies the size of the font in points. The FontStyle detail property specifies whether the font is normal or italicized. The FontWeight detail property specifies the thickness of the font and is used to create bold text. The Color detail property specifies the color of the type. The TextDecoration detail property specifies whether the text is underlined, linedthrough, or overlined.

Property Of: Chart Value

Custom Properties Dialog Box Location: Edit Chart Value – Point Labels tab

Detail Properties: FontFamily, FontSize, FontStyle, FontWeight, Color, TextDecoration

Language

Description: The language being used to display values within this report item

When to Use: The language being used is something other than the default language on the computer.

Property Of: Chart, List, Matrix, Matrix Column, Matrix Row, Matrix Subtotal, Report, Subreport, Table, Table Column, Table Row, Text Box

LayoutDirection

Description: The direction in which matrix columns are built, either left-to-right or right-to-left

When to Use: A matrix must be built from right-to-left.

Property Of: Matrix

Custom Properties Dialog Box Location: Matrix Properties – General tab

LegendBorderAndLineStyle

Description: The border and line style for the chart legend
When to Use: The chart legend is to have a non-default border.
Notes: The Style detail property controls the style of the line. The Width detail property controls the width of the line. The Color detail property controls the color of the line.
Property Of: Chart
Custom Properties Dialog Box Location: Chart Properties – Legend tab
Detail Properties: Style, Width, Color

LegendFillStyle

Description: The fill style for the chart legend
When to Use: The chart legend is to have its own fill style.
Notes: The fill can be a single color or a two-color gradient. The Color detail property contains the color of the area or is the first color in a two-color gradient when the Gradient detail property is true. The Gradient detail property specifies whether this is a single color fill (false) or a two-color gradient (true). The EndColor detail property contains the second color in a two-color gradient.
Property Of: Chart
Custom Properties Dialog Box Location: Chart Properties – Legend tab
Detail Properties: Color, Gradient, End Color

LegendFontStyle

Description: The font style for the chart legend
When to Use: The chart legend is to have a non-default font style.
Notes: The FontFamily detail property contains the name of the font. The FontSize detail property specifies the size of the font in points. The FontStyle detail property specifies whether the font is normal or italicized. The FontWeight detail property specifies the thickness of the font and is used to create bold text. The Color detail property specifies the color of the type. The TextDecoration detail property specifies whether the text is underlined, linedthrough, or overlined.
Property Of: Chart
Custom Properties Dialog Box Location: Chart Properties – Legend tab
Detail Properties: FontFamily, FontSize, FontStyle, FontWeight, Color, TextDecoration

LegendLayout

Description: Specifies whether the chart legend is laid out in columns, rows, or as a table

When to Use: The chart legend is to have a non-default layout for better readability.
Property Of: Chart
Custom Properties Dialog Box Location: Chart Properties – Legend tab

LegendPosition

Description: The position of the chart legend relative to the plot area
When to Use: The chart legend is to have a nonstandard position.
Property Of: Chart
Custom Properties Dialog Box Location: Chart Properties – Legend tab

LineColor

Description: The color of the line
When to Use: The line is to have a color other than black.
Property Of: Line

LineHeight

Description: The height of a line of text within this report item
When to Use: The report item is to use a nonstandard line height.
Property Of: Chart, List, Matrix, Matrix Column, Matrix Row, Matrix Subtotal, Subreport, Table, Table Column, Table Row, Text Box

LineStyle

Description: The style of the line (solid, dashed, dotted, etc.)
When to Use: The line is to have a style other than solid.
Property Of: Line

LineWidth

Description: The width of the line in points
When to Use: The line is to have a width other than 1 point.
Property Of: Line

LinkToChild

Description: The report item within the rectangle that will be the ultimate target of a document map entry that points to the rectangle
When to Use: A rectangle containing several report items is the target of a document map entry.
Property Of: Rectangle

Location

Description: The location of the report item within the layout area
When to Use: Every time an item is placed in a layout area.
Notes: The Left and Top detail properties specify the position of the upper-left corner of the report item in the layout area.
Property Of: Chart, Image, Line, List, Matrix, Rectangle, Subreport, Table, Text Box
Detail Properties: Left, Top

Margins

Description: The size of the margins on the report page
When to Use: The margins are to be something other than 1 inch.
Notes: If the body width plus the left and right margins are greater than the report page width, the report will span more than one page horizontally. The Left, Right, Top, and Bottom detail properties specify the size of each margin in inches.
Property Of: Report
Custom Properties Dialog Box Location: Report Properties – Layout tab
Detail Properties: Left, Right, Top, Bottom

MarkerSize

Description: The size of the marker placed for each data value on a chart
When to Use: Each data value is to be highlighted with a shape to mark its position.
Property Of: Chart Value
Custom Properties Dialog Box Location: Edit Chart Value – Appearance tab

MarkerType

Description: The shape used to mark each data value on a chart
When to Use: Each data value is to be highlighted with a shape to mark its position.
Property Of: Chart Value
Custom Properties Dialog Box Location: Edit Chart Value – Appearance tab

MergeTransactions

Description: Combines any transactions from a subreport with the transactions of the parent report
When to Use: The queries in both the parent report and the subreport initiate data modifications that should be committed only if both are successful.
Notes: Both reports must use the same data source.
Property Of: Subreport

MIMEType

Description: The MIME type of the graphic used to populate the image item
When to Use: The MIME type must be selected only when using an external image source such as a database. The MIME type is automatically detected for embedded images.
Property Of: Image

Name

Description: The name of the report item
When to Use: The report item will be referenced by another item in the report (e.g. to control visibility).
Notes: Report item names must be unique within a report.
Property Of: Chart, Chart Category Group, Chart Series Group, Image, Line, List, List Details Group, Matrix, Matrix Column Group, Matrix Row Group, Rectangle, Subreport, Table, Table Details Group, Table Group, Text Box
Custom Properties Dialog Box Location: General tab

NoRows

Description: The message displayed in place of a data region when that data region's dataset contains no rows
When to Use: A data region's dataset may be empty.
Property Of: Chart, List, Matrix, Subreport, Table

NumeralLanguage

Description: The language to use when applying formatting to numeric output
When to Use: The numeral language is to be something other than the default for the computer.
Property Of: Chart, List, Matrix, Matrix Column, Matrix Row, Matrix Subtotal, Subreport, Table, Table Column, Table Row, Text Box

NumeralVariant

Description: The variant of the numeral language to use when applying formatting to numeric output
When to Use: The numeral language variant is to be something other than the default for the computer.
Property Of: Chart, List, Matrix, Matrix Column, Matrix Row, Matrix Subtotal, Subreport, Table, Table Column, Table Row, Text Box

Orthographic

Description: Specifies whether to present a 3-D chart as an orthographic projection

When to Use: An orthographic projection of a 3-D chart is to be used to provide the best view for analysis.

Notes: An orthographic projection represents the three dimensions as perpendicular to one another. The Perspective property is ignored when the Orthographic property is selected.

Property Of: Chart

Custom Properties Dialog Box Location: Chart Properties – 3D Effect tab

Padding

Description: The amount of empty space left around the sides of an item

When to Use: The amount of empty space is to be changed to improve the report's presentation and readability.

Notes: The Left, Right, Top, and Bottom detail properties specify in points the white space on each side of the report item.

Property Of: Chart, Image, List, Matrix, Matrix Column, Matrix Row, Matrix Subtotal, Subreport, Table, Table Column, Table Row, Text Box

Custom Properties Dialog Box Location: Advanced Text Box Properties – Format tab (only for text box)

Detail Properties: Left, Right, Top, Bottom

PageBreakAtEnd

Description: Specifies whether a forced page break is to be inserted at the end of this report item

When to Use: A page break is to be forced to meet report-formatting needs.

Property Of: Chart, List, Matrix, Rectangle, Table, Table Group

Custom Properties Dialog Box Location: General tab

PageBreakAtStart

Description: Specifies whether a forced page break is to be inserted at the beginning of this report item

When to Use: A page break is to be forced to meet report-formatting needs.

Property Of: Chart, List, Matrix, Rectangle, Table, Table Group

Custom Properties Dialog Box Location: General tab

PageSize

Description: The size of the report page

When to Use: The report will be printed or exported to the PDF or TIFF rendering formats.

Notes: The Width detail property specifies the width of the report in inches. The Height detail property specifies the height of the report in inches.

Property Of: Report

Custom Properties Dialog Box Location: Report Properties – Layout tab

Detail Properties: Width, Height

Palette

Description: The color scheme to use for a chart

When to Use: A non-default set of colors is to be used when creating a chart.

Property Of: Chart

Custom Properties Dialog Box Location: Chart Properties – General tab

Parameters

Description: The parameter values to be passed to a subreport

When to Use: The subreport is to receive values from the parent report to control the subreport's content.

Notes: The Parameter Name detail property contains a list of parameters for the selected subreport. The Parameter Value detail property contains a list of values to be assigned to each of those parameters.

Property Of: Subreport

Custom Properties Dialog Box Location: Subreport Properties – Parameters tab

Detail Properties: Parameter Name, Parameter Value

Parent

Description: The report item that contains this item

When to Use: This is a read-only property controlled by the item's location on the report layout.

Property Of: Chart, Image, Line, List, Matrix, Rectangle, Subreport, Table, Text Box

Parent Group

Description: The group that contains this group

When to Use: This is a read-only property maintained automatically by the group hierarchy.

Property Of: Chart Category Group, Chart Series Group, List Details Group, Matrix Column Group, Matrix Row Group, Table Details Group, Table Group

Custom Properties Dialog Box Location: General tab

Perspective

Description: The amount of perspective applied to a 3-D chart

When to Use: The default perspective of a 3-D chart is to be changed to improve readability or interest.

Property Of: Chart

Custom Properties Dialog Box Location: Chart Properties – 3D Effect tab

PlotAreaBorderAndLineStyle

Description: The format of the line surrounding the chart's plot area

When to Use: The format of the chart's plot area is to be changed from the 1-point, solid, black line.

Notes: The Style detail property controls the style of the line. The Width detail property controls the width of the line. The Color detail property controls the color of the line.

Property Of: Chart

Custom Properties Dialog Box Location: Chart Properties – General tab

Detail Properties: Style, Width, Color

PlotAreaFillStyle

Description: The fill behind the chart's plotting area

When to Use: The chart's plotting area is to have a fill color other than light gray.

Notes: The fill can be a single color or a two-color gradient. The Color detail property contains the color of the area or is the first color in a two-color gradient when the Gradient detail property is true. The Gradient detail property specifies whether this is a single color fill (false) or a two-color gradient (true). The EndColor detail property contains the second color in a two-color gradient.

Property Of: Chart

Custom Properties Dialog Box Location: Chart Properties – General tab

Detail Properties: Color, Gradient, End Color

PlotDataAsLine

Description: Specifies whether the chart data is to be represented by a line

When to Use: The chart data is to be represented by a line.

Property Of: Chart Value

Custom Properties Dialog Box Location: Edit Chart Value – Appearance tab

Position

Description: The position of the chart value labels or the matrix subtotal

When to Use: The chart value label is to be placed in a position other than directly above the data point, or the matrix subtotal is to be placed above or before the detail rather than below or after it.

Property Of: Chart Value, Matrix Subtotal

Custom Properties Dialog Box Location: Edit Chart Value – Point Labels tab. (This property does not appear in a custom properties dialog box for a Matrix Subtotal.)

PrintOnFirstPage

Description: Specifies whether the page header or page footer should print on the first page of the report

When to Use: The report contains a page header or footer that is not to be printed on the first page of the report.

Property Of: Page Header, Page Footer

Custom Properties Dialog Box Location: Report Properties – General tab

PrintOnLastPage

Description: Specifies whether the page header or page footer should print on the last page of the report.

When to Use: The report contains a page header or footer that is not to be printed on the last page of the report.

Property Of: Page Header, Page Footer

Custom Properties Dialog Box Location: Report Properties – General tab

References

Description: The custom assemblies referenced by the report

When to Use: A report expression is to make use of a property or method in a custom assembly.

Notes: The AssemblyName detail property contains a list of assemblies that are referenced by the report.

Property Of: Report

Custom Properties Dialog Box Location: Report Properties – References tab

Detail Properties: AssemblyName

RepeatFooterOnNewPage

Description: Specifies whether a footer should be repeated on each new page spanned by the table

When to Use: A table or table group contains a footer that is to be repeated on every page spanned by the table.

Property Of: Table, Table Group

Custom Properties Dialog Box Location: General tab

RepeatHeaderOnNewPage

Description: Specifies whether a header should be repeated on each new page spanned by the table

When to Use: A table or table group contains a header that is to be repeated on every page spanned by the table.

Property Of: Table, Table Group

Custom Properties Dialog Box Location: General tab

RepeatOnNewPage

Description: This table row should repeat on each page of the report

When to Use: One or more table rows should repeat on each page of the report for better report clarity.

Property Of: Table Row (Not a property of a detail table row.)

RepeatWith

Description: The data region this report item should repeat with across multiple pages

When to Use: This report item is part of a heading that is to be repeated with a data region that spans multiple pages.

Property Of: Image, Line, Rectangle, Text Box

Custom Properties Dialog Box Location: General tab

ReportName

Description: The name of the report to be displayed in this subreport item

When to Use: The report name is always required when using a subreport item.

Property Of: Subreport

Custom Properties Dialog Box Location: Subreport Properties – General tab

ReportParameters

Description: The parameters used by this report

When to Use: User input is to be used in determining the content of this report.

Notes: The AllowNullValue detail property specifies whether each parameter can have a null value. The AllowBlankValue detail property specifies whether each parameter can have a blank value. The AvailableValues detail property contains a list of the valid values for each property, either as a list of constants or as a reference to a dataset. The DataType detail property specifies the data type of each parameter. The DefaultValues detail property contains a default value for each property, either as a constant value or as a reference to a dataset. The Name detail property contains the name of each property. The Prompt detail property contains the prompt string for each property.

Property Of: Report
Custom Properties Dialog Box Location: Report Parameters
Detail Properties: AllowNullValue, AllowBlankValue, AvailableValues, DataType, DefaultValues, Name, Prompt

SeriesLabel

Description: A portion of the label applied to the series on the chart
When to Use: The series label is to include information from the data value.
Notes: The series label is made up of the expression specified in the series grouping concatenated with the expression specified with the chart value.
Property Of: Chart Value
Custom Properties Dialog Box Location: Edit Chart Value – Values tab

Shading

Description: The type of shading used in a 3-D chart
When to Use: Shading other than simple shading is to be used with a 3-D chart to increase readability or enhance interest.
Property Of: Chart
Custom Properties Dialog Box Location: Chart Properties – 3D Effect tab

ShowLegend

Description: Specifies whether to show the chart legend
When to Use: The chart is to include a data series that must be identified by the legend.
Property Of: Chart
Custom Properties Dialog Box Location: Chart Properties – Legend tab

ShowMarkers

Description: Specifies whether to place a marker for each data value on a chart
When to Use: Each data value on a chart is to be highlighted with a shape to mark its position.
Property Of: Chart Value
Custom Properties Dialog Box Location: Edit Chart Value – Appearance tab

ShowPointLabels

Description: Specifies whether to label each data value on a chart
When to Use: Each data value on a chart is to be labeled to improve readability or analysis.
Property Of: Chart Value
Custom Properties Dialog Box Location: Edit Chart Values – Point Labels tab

Size

Description: The size of the report item

When to Use: Every time an item is placed in a layout area.

Notes: The Width detail property contains the width of the report object in inches. The Height detail property contains the height of the report object in inches.

Property Of: Body, Chart, Image, List, Matrix, Page Header, Page Footer, Rectangle, Subreport, Table, Text Box

Detail Properties: Width, Height

Sizing

Description: The technique used to size a graphic within an image report item

When to Use: The graphic is to be sized using a technique other than the fit technique.

Notes: The AutoSize technique changes the size of the image report item so the graphic completely fills it at its normal size. The Fit technique stretches the graphic to fit the dimensions of the image report item. The FitProportional technique shrinks or magnifies the graphic to fit the image report item but retains its proportions of height to width. The Clip technique displays as much of the graphic, at its normal size, as will fit within the image report item; the remainder is clipped off.

Property Of: Image

SnapToGrid

Description: Specifies whether report item corner points are aligned with the grid when they are placed on the report layout

When to Use: The report layout is not to be constrained by the grid.

Property Of: Report

Custom Properties Dialog Box Location: Report Properties – General tab

Sorting

Description: The expression used to order the dataset or data grouping

When to Use: The dataset or data grouping is to be presented in a sort order that is not provided by the dataset query.

Notes: The Expression detail property contains a list of expressions used to sort the contents of the data region or grouping. The Direction detail property specifies whether each sort is in ascending order or descending order.

Property Of: Chart Category Group, Chart Series Group, List, Matrix Column Group, Matrix Row Group, Table, Table Group

Custom Properties Dialog Box Location: Sorting tab

Detail Properties: Expression, Direction

Source

Description: The source of the graphic

When to Use: A source must be specified for each image report item.

Notes: A Database image is extracted from a binary large object (BLOB). An Embedded image is stored in the report itself. An External image is stored in the report project and deployed to the Report Manager with the report.

Property Of: Image

Custom Properties Dialog Box Location: Image Wizard

Subtype

Description: The specific type of chart

When to Use: A chart subtype must be specified for all chart types except a bubble chart.

Property Of: Chart

Custom Properties Dialog Box Location: Chart Properties – General tab

TextAlign

Description: The horizontal position of the text within a report item

When to Use: The text is to be centered or right-justified.

Property Of: Chart, List, Matrix, Matrix Column, Matrix Row, Matrix Subtotal, Subreport, Table, Table Column, Table Row, Text Box

TextDecoration

Description: The decoration (underline, overline, or line through) applied to the text

When to Use: The text is to be underlined, overlined, or struck through.

Property Of: Chart, List, Matrix, Matrix Column, Matrix Row, Matrix Subtotal, Subreport, Table, Table Column, Table Row, Text Box

Custom Properties Dialog Box Location: Text Box Properties, Advanced – Font tab (only for text box)

Title

Description: The title of the chart

When to Use: The chart is to be given a title to provide better understanding of the data it contains.

Property Of: Chart

Custom Properties Dialog Box Location: Chart Properties – General tab

TitleFontStyle

Description: The font style of the chart title

When to Use: The chart is to have a title.

Notes: The FontFamily detail property contains the name of the font. The FontSize detail property specifies the size of the font in points. The FontStyle detail property specifies whether the font is normal or italicized. The FontWeight detail property specifies the thickness of the font and is used to create bold text. The Color detail property specifies the color of the type. The TextDecoration detail property specifies whether the text is underlined, linedthrough, or overlined.

Property Of: Chart

Custom Properties Dialog Box Location: Chart Properties – General tab

Detail Properties: FontFamily, FontSize, FontStyle, FontWeight, Color, TextDecoration

ToolTip

Description: The tool tip displayed for this report item

When to Use: The user is to be provided with additional information concerning a report item when interacting with the report.

Property Of: Chart, Image, Line, List, Matrix, Rectangle, Subreport, Table, Text Box

Custom Properties Dialog Box Location: General tab

Type

Description: The general type of chart

When to Use: A general chart type must be specified for all charts.

Property Of: Chart

Custom Properties Dialog Box Location: Chart Properties – General tab

UnicodeBiDi

Description: The technique used for handling text rendered right-to-left embedded in a line of text rendered left-to-right, or vice versa

When to Use: Multiple languages are to be included in the same text box, with one language rendered left-to-right and the other rendered right-to-left.

Property Of: Chart, List, Matrix, Matrix Column, Matrix Row, Matrix Subtotal, Subreport, Table, Table Column, Table Row, Text Box

Value

Description: Chart Value—An expression to determine the values to be charted; Image—The name of the graphic to be placed in the image item; Text Box—The text to be displayed in the text box.

When to Use: A value is required for a chart value, an image, or a text box.

Property Of: Chart Value, Image, Text Box

Custom Properties Dialog Box Location: Chart Value: Edit Chart Value – Values tab; Image: Image Wizard; Text Box: Basic Text Box Properties or Advanced Text Box Properties – General tab

VerticalAlign

Description: The vertical position of the text within a report item
When to Use: The text is to be located in the middle or at the bottom.
Property Of: Chart, List, Matrix, Matrix Column, Matrix Row, Matrix Subtotal, Subreport, Table, Table Column, Table Row, Text Box

VerticalRotation

Description: The vertical rotation applied to a 3-D chart
When to Use: The vertical rotation must be adjusted to provide the user with the optimum view of the chart data.
Property Of: Chart
Custom Properties Dialog Box Location: Chart Properties – 3D Effect tab

Visibility

Description: Specifies whether a report item is visible on the report
When to Use: The report item is not to be visible on the report, or the report item's visibility is to be toggled by another report item.
Notes: The Hidden detail property specifies whether this report item is visible or hidden. The ToggleItem detail property is a reference to another report item that will toggle the visibility of this report item.
Property Of: Chart, Image, Line, List, List Details Group, Matrix, Matrix Column Group, Matrix Row Group, Rectangle, Subreport, Table, Table Column, Table Details Group, Table Group, Table Row, Text Box
Custom Properties Dialog Box Location: Visibility tab
Detail Properties: Hidden, ToggleItem

WallThickness

Description: The thickness of the walls surrounding a 3-D chart
When to Use: The thickness of the walls surrounding a 3-D chart is to be adjusted to create the most pleasing chart representation.
Property Of: Chart
Custom Properties Dialog Box Location: Chart Properties – 3D Effect tab

Width

Description: The width of a column
When to Use: The column width is to be adjusted to the appropriate size for the data it contains.
Property Of: Matrix Column, Table Column

WritingMode

Description: Indicates whether the text is written left-to-right/top-to-bottom or top-to-bottom/right-to-left

When to Use: A character set that is written top-to-bottom/right-to-left is to be used.

Property Of: Chart, List, Matrix, Matrix Column, Matrix Row, Matrix Subtotal, Subreport, Table, Table Column, Table Row, Text Box

X-AxisFormatting

Description: The formatting for the x-axis of a chart

When to Use: A chart type with an x-axis is to be rendered.

Notes: The detail properties control the look of each aspect of the x-axis.

Property Of: Chart

Custom Properties Dialog Box Location: Chart Properties – X-Axis tab

Detail Properties: CrossAt, FormatCode, FormatCodeStyle, InterlacedStrips, LogarithmicScale, MajorGridlines, MajorGridlinesInterval, MajorGridlinesStyle, MajorTickMark, MinorGridlines, MinorGridlinesInterval, MinorGridlinesStyle, MinorTickMark, NumericOrTime-scaleValues, Reversed, ScaleMaximum, ScaleMinimum, ShowLabels, SideMargins, Title, TitleAlign, TitleStyle

Y-AxisFormatting

Description: The formatting for the y-axis of a chart

When to Use: A chart type with a y-axis is to be rendered.

Notes: The detail properties control the look of each aspect of the y-axis.

Property Of: Chart

Custom Properties Dialog Box Location: Chart Properties – Y-Axis tab

Detail Properties: CrossAt, FormatCode, FormatCodeStyle, Interlaced Strips, Logarithmic Scale, MajorGridlines, MajorGridlinesInterval, MajorGridlinesStyle, MajorTickMark, MinorGridlines, MinorGridlinesInterval, MinorGridlinesStyle, MinorTickMark, Reversed, ScaleMaximum, ScaleMinimum, ShowLabels, SideMargins, Title, TitleAlign, TitleStyle

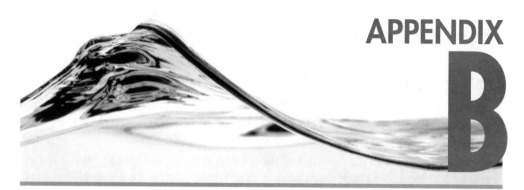

APPENDIX
B

Web Service
Interface Reference

IN THIS APPENDIX:

ReportingService Web Service

ReportingService Web Service

Creating a Web Reference to ReportingService

In order to use a web service, you need to create code that knows how to send data to and retrieve data from that web service. Fortunately, this code is generated for you by Visual Studio through the process of creating a web reference. Once the web reference is in place, you can call the methods of the web service the same way you call the methods of a local .NET assembly. Here are the steps for creating a web reference:

1. In your Visual Basic .NET or C# project (not a Report project), right-click the project entry in the Solution Explorer and select Add Web Reference from the context menu. The Add Web Reference dialog box will appear.

2. Select the link for Web Services on the Local Machine.

3. When the list of web services on the local machine appears, click the link for ReportService.

4. When the Reporting Service Description appears in the dialog box, click Add Reference.

When you click the link for Web Services on the Local Machine, a URL beginning with "http://localhost" is used to locate the web services on the local machine. Because of this, the Reporting Services web service will use "localhost.ReportingService" as its namespace.

Credentials and the ReportingService Web Service

Most ReportingService methods require logon credentials to be authenticated prior to their execution. This is accomplished by creating a network credential object and assigning it to the Credentials property of the ReportingService object. In the following code, a logon is accomplished prior to the execution of the ListChildren method. The ListChildren method returns an array with one element for each report item found in the specified folder (the Home folder in this example). The array will only contain those items that the specified credentials have the right to view.

```
Dim rs As localhost.ReportingService
Dim LogonCredentials As System.Net.NetworkCredential
Dim items As localhost.CatalogItem()

rs = New localhost.ReportingService
LogonCredentials = New _
    System.Net.NetworkCredential("LogonName", "Password", "Domain")
```

```
rs.Credentials = LogonCredential
rs.PreAuthenticate = True

items = rs.ListChildren("/", False)
```

Of course, if you were to use this sample code, you would need to replace LogonName, Password, and Domain with the appropriate logon name, password, and domain name for a valid domain logon. Also, this code sample assumes that you have created a web reference to the ReportingService web service called localhost.ReportingService, as described in the previous section.

When the PreAuthenticate property is true, the credentials are sent with the first web service request. When the PreAuthenticate property is false, the credentials are not sent to the server until the server issues an authentication challenge. In other words, when the PreAuthenticate property is false, the credentials are not sent to the server until the server requires a login. Setting the PreAuthenticate property to true can save one roundtrip between the server and the client, but as long as you have the Credentials property initialized to a valid logon, either setting for the PreAuthenticate property (true or false) will work.

Code Sample

Unfortunately, space restrictions prevent the inclusion of code samples for each of the ReportingService web service properties, methods, and classes. A sample program incorporating all these items is available for download from the web page for this book. Go to http://www.osborne.com and locate the book's page using the ISBN 0072232161.

ReportingService Properties

BatchHeaderValue
Description: This property is used to hold a unique, system-generated batch ID. This batch ID serves to group multiple method calls from the ReportingService web service into a single batch. The batch ID is created by calling the CreateBatch method. The batch is committed by calling the ExecuteBatch method. The batch is rolled back by calling the CancelBatch method.

Credentials
Description: This property is used to hold the logon credentials used by the client application to authenticate on the ReportingService web service. Most ReportingService methods require authentication before they will execute.

PreAuthenticate

Description: When the PreAuthenticate property is true, the credentials are sent with the first web service request. When the PreAuthenticate property is false, the credentials are not sent to the server until the server issues an authentication challenge.

ReportingService Methods

CancelBatch

Description: This method cancels the current batch of ReportingService method calls. The current batch is specified by the BatchHeader object and must be assigned to the BatchHeaderValue property of the ReportingService object. If the batch is cancelled, none of the method calls in the batch is executed.

This method does not return a value.

Parameters: None

CancelJob

Description: This method cancels an executing job. This method returns true if the job was cancelled; otherwise, it returns false.

Parameters:

Name	Type	Description
JobID	String	The ID of the job to cancel

CreateBatch

Description: This method creates a batch ID that can be used to group ReportingService method calls into a batch. If an error occurs in one of the method calls in the batch, all previous operations performed by the batch are rolled back and subsequent operations are not attempted. This is useful when you have one ReportingService method call that depends on the successful completion of a prior ReportingService method call. For instance, you may call the CreateFolder method to create a new folder, and then call the CreateReport method to create a report in your new folder. You do not want to attempt to create the report if the folder cannot be created.

This method returns a batch ID string. This batch ID must be assigned to the batchID property of a BatchHeader object. The BatchHeader object must be assigned to the BatchHeaderValue property of the ReportingService object. The methods in the batch are not executed until the ExecuteBatch method is called to commit the batch.

Parameters: None

CreateDataDrivenSubscription

Description: This method creates a data-driven subscription for a report. This method returns a string containing the subscription ID.

Parameters:

Name	Type	Description
Report	String	The folder path and name of the report to which to subscribe
ExtensionSettings	ExtensionSettings Object	An object containing the settings for the delivery extension (for example, e-mail delivery) used by this subscription
DataRetrievalPlan	DataRetrievalPlan Object	An object containing the information necessary to connect to and retrieve the data used for the data-driven subscription
Description	String	The description of this subscription
EventType	String	Either "TimedSubscription" for a subscription triggered by a schedule or "SnapshotUpdated" for a subscription triggered by the updating of a snapshot
MatchData	String	Information used to implement the event type
Parameters	An Array of ParameterValueOrFieldReference Objects	An array of the values used for the report's parameters

CreateDataSource

Description: This method creates a new shared data source. This method does not return a value.

Parameters:

Name	Type	Description
DataSource	String	The name of the data source
Overwrite	Boolean	True if this data source should overwrite an existing data source; otherwise, false
Parent	String	The path to the folder where the shared data source is created
Definition	DataSourceDefinition Object	An object containing the connection information for the shared data source
Properties	An Array of Property Objects	An array of property settings for the shared data source

CreateFolder

Description: This method creates a new Reporting Services folder in the specified folder. This method does not return a value.

Parameters:

Name	Type	Description
Folder	String	The name of the new folder
Parent	String	The path to the folder where the new folder is created
Properties	An Array of Property Objects	An array of property settings for the folder

CreateLinkedReport

Description: This method creates a new linked report in the specified folder. This method does not return a value.

Parameters:

Name	Type	Description
Report	String	The name of the new linked report
Parent	String	The path to the folder where the new linked report is created
Link	String	The folder path and name of the report to which the new linked report should be linked
Properties	An Array of Property Objects	An array of property settings for the new linked report

CreateReport

Description: This method creates a new report in the specified folder. This method returns an array of Warning objects.

Parameters:

Name	Type	Description
Report	String	The name of the new report
Parent	String	The path to the folder where the new report is created
Overwrite	Boolean	True if an existing report with the same name in the same folder is to be replaced with the new report; otherwise, false
Definition	An Array of Bytes	The Report Definition Language (RDL) defining the new report in base-64 binary
Properties	An Array of Property Objects	An array of property settings for the report

CreateReportHistorySnapshot

Description: This method creates a history snapshot of a specified report. The snapshot is created immediately, not at a scheduled time. This method call will fail if report history is not enabled for the specified report.

This method returns a string representing the data and time at which the history snapshot was created.

Parameters:

Name	Type	Description
Report	String	The Reporting Services folder and the report name of the report from which the history snapshot is created
Warnings	An Array of Warning Objects	An array of warning messages generated when creating this report history snapshot. (This parameter must be called ByRef.)

CreateResource

Description: This method creates a new resource entry in the specified folder. This method does not return a value.

Parameters:

Name	Type	Description
Resource	String	The name of the new resource
Parent	String	The path to the folder where the new resource is created
Overwrite	Boolean	True if an existing resource with the same name in the same folder is to be replaced with the new resource; otherwise, false
Contents	An Array of Bytes	The contents of the resource in base-64 binary
MimeType	String	The MIME type of the resource (260 characters maximum)
Properties	An Array of Property Objects	An array of property settings for the resource

CreateRole

Description: This method creates a new Reporting Services security role. This method does not return a value.

Parameters:

Name	Type	Description
Name	String	The name of the new role
Description	String	The description of the new role
Tasks	An Array of Task Objects	An array of Reporting Services tasks that may be executed by this role

CreateSchedule

Description: This method creates a new shared schedule. This method returns a string containing the schedule ID.

Parameters:

Name	Type	Description
Name	String	The name of the schedule
ScheduleDefinition	ScheduleDefinition Object	An object containing the information necessary to define a schedule

CreateSubscription

Description: This method creates a new subscription for a report. This method returns a string containing the subscription ID.

Parameters:

Name	Type	Description
Report	String	The folder path and name of the report to which to subscribe
ExtensionSettings	ExtensionSettings Object	An object containing the settings for the delivery extension (for example, e-mail delivery) used by this subscription
Description	String	The description of this subscription
EventType	String	Either "TimedSubscription" for a subscription triggered by a schedule or "SnapshotUpdated" for a subscription triggered by the updating of a snapshot
MatchData	String	Information used to implement the event type
Parameters	An Array of ParameterValue Objects	An array of the values used for the report's parameters

DeleteItem

Description: This method removes an item from a Reporting Services folder. This can be a report, a resource, a shared data source, or a Reporting Services folder. If a report is deleted, any subscriptions and snapshots associated with that report are also deleted. This method does not return a value.

You cannot use this method to delete the My Reports folder or the Users folders created when the My Reports option is enabled.

Parameters:

Name	Type	Description
Item	String	The folder path and name of the item to be deleted

DeleteReportHistorySnapshot

Description: This method removes a specified history snapshot. This method does not return a value.

Parameters:

Name	Type	Description
Report	String	The folder path and name of the report from which the history snapshot is to be deleted
HistoryID	String	The ID of the history snapshot to delete

DeleteRole

Description: This method removes a Reporting Services security role. This will also remove all security assignments involving the deleted security role. This method does not return a value.

Parameters:

Name	Type	Description
Name	String	The name of the security role to delete

DeleteSchedule

Description: This method removes a shared schedule. In addition, any snapshots or subscriptions using this schedule are also deleted. This method does not return a value.

Parameters:

Name	Type	Description
ScheduleID	String	The schedule ID of the schedule to delete

DeleteSubscription

Description: This method removes a subscription from a report. This method does not return a value.

Parameters:

Name	Type	Description
SubscriptionID	String	The subscription ID of the subscription to delete

DisableDataSource

Description: This method disables a shared data source. Any reports and data-driven subscriptions that use this shared data source will not execute. This method does not return a value.

Parameters:

Name	Type	Description
DataSource	String	The folder path and name of the shared data source to be disabled

EnableDataSource

Description: This method enables a shared data source. This method does not return a value.

Parameters:

Name	Type	Description
DataSource	String	The folder path and name of the shared data source to be enabled

ExecuteBatch

Description: This method executes all method calls that have been associated with the current batch. (See the CreateBatch method.) The method calls in the batch are not executed until the ExecuteBatch method is called. This method does not return a value.

Parameters: None

FindItems

Description: This method finds reports, resources, shared data sources, and folders whose name or description satisfies the search conditions. The contents of the specified folder and all the folders contained within that folder will be searched. This method returns an array of CatalogItem objects that satisfy the search conditions.

Parameters:

Name	Type	Description
Folder	String	The folder path and name of the folder that serves as the root of the search
BooleanOperator	BooleanOperatorEnum	Either **AND** if all of the search conditions must be true; otherwise, **OR** if only one of the search conditions must be true
Conditions	An Array of SearchCondition Objects	An array containing the search conditions

FireEvent

Description: This method triggers a Reporting Services event. You can use the ListEvents method to get an array of valid events and their parameters. This method does not return a value.

Parameters:

Name	Type	Description
EventType	String	The name of the event
EventData	String	The values for the parameters associated with this event

FlushCache

Description: This method clears any cached copies of the specified report. This includes cached copies created both by caching and by execution snapshots. It will not clear history snapshots. This method does not return a value.

Parameters:

Name	Type	Description
Report	String	The folder path and name of the report whose cache is to be flushed

GetCacheOptions

Description: This method checks whether there is a cached copy of the specified report. If there is a cached copy of the report, the expiration time or the scheduled expiration information for the cached copy is returned in the Item parameter. This method returns a boolean, which is true if caching is enabled for the report; otherwise, it returns false.

Parameters:

Name	Type	Description
Report	String	The folder path and name of the report whose cache options are to be checked.
Item	ExpirationDefinition Object	An object containing the expiration information for the cached copy of the report. (This parameter must be called ByRef.)

GetDataDrivenSubscriptionProperties

Description: This method gets the information from the specified data-driven subscription. The data-driven subscription information is returned in several reference parameters. This method returns a string containing the ID of the owner of the specified data-driven subscription.

Parameters:

Name	Type	Description
DataDrivenSubscriptionID	String	The data-driven subscription ID of the data-driven subscription whose information is to be returned.
ExtensionSettings	ExtensionSettings Object	An object containing the extension settings. (This parameter must be called ByRef.)
DataRetrievalPlan	DataRetrievalPlan Object	An object containing the data source and query used to select data for the data-driven subscription. (This parameter must be called ByRef.)
Description	String	The description of the data-driven subscription. (This parameter must be called ByRef.)
Active	ActiveState Object	An object containing the active state of the data-driven subscription. (This parameter must be called ByRef.)
Status	String	The status of the data-driven subscription. (This parameter must be called ByRef.)
EventType	String	The event type associated with the data-driven subscription. (This parameter must be called ByRef.)
MatchData	String	The parameter data for the event type associated with the data-driven subscription. (This parameter must be called ByRef.)
Parameters	An Array of ParameterValueOrFieldReference Objects	An array of parameter information for the report associated with the data-driven subscription. (This parameter must be called ByRef.)

GetDataSourceContents

Description: This method gets the information for the specified shared data source. This method returns a DataSourceDefinition object containing the information for the shared data source.

Parameters:

Name	Type	Description
DataSource	String	The folder path and name of the shared data source whose information is to be returned

GetExecutionOptions

Description: This method gets the execution options for the specified report. This method returns an ExecutionSettingEnum value of either "Live," indicating the report will be executed, or "Snapshot," indicating the report will be rendered from a history snapshot.

Parameters:

Name	Type	Description
Report	String	The folder path and name of the report whose execution option is to be returned.
Item	ScheduleDefinitionOrReference Object	An object containing a schedule definition or a reference to a shared schedule. (This parameter must be called ByRef.)

GetExtensionSettings

Description: This method gets the parameter information for the specified delivery extension. This method returns an array of ExtensionParameter objects containing the parameter information.

Parameters:

Name	Type	Description
Extension	String	The name of the delivery extension

GetItemType

Description: This method gets the type of the specified Reporting Services item. This method returns an ItemTypeEnum value as shown here:

Value	Description
Unknown	Invalid Item Path or Item of Unknown Type
Folder	This item is a folder
Report	This item is a report
Resource	This item is a resource
LinkedReport	This item is a linked report
DataSource	This item is a shared data source

Parameters:

Name	Type	Description
Item	String	The folder path and name of the item whose type is to be returned

GetPermissions

Description: This method gets the tasks that may be executed on the specified Reporting Services item by the logon credentials currently being used to access the ReportingService web service. This method returns an array of strings, with each string containing the name of one task that the logon credentials have permission to execute.

Parameters:

Name	Type	Description
Item	String	The folder path and name of the item whose permissions are to be returned

GetPolicies

Description: This method gets the Reporting Services security policies associated with the specified Reporting Services item. This method returns an array of Policy objects.

Parameters:

Name	Type	Description
Item	String	The folder path and name of the item whose policies are to be returned.
InheritParent	Boolean	True if the policies are inherited from the parent folder; otherwise, false. (This parameter must be called ByRef.)

GetProperties

Description: This method gets the values of each specified property of the Reporting Services item. This method returns an array of Property objects.

Parameters:

Name	Type	Description
Item	String	The folder path and name of the item whose properties are to be returned
Properties	An Array of Property Objects	An array of the properties whose values you want returned

GetRenderResource

Description: This method gets a resource for the specified rendering extension. This method returns a byte array containing a base-64 encoding of the requested resource.

Parameters:

Name	Type	Description
Format	String	The rendering extension format (for example, PDF or XML).
DeviceInfo	String	A device-specific setting for the specified rendering format.
MimeType	String	The MIME type of the resource. (This parameter must be called ByRef.)

GetReportDataSourcePrompts

Description: This method gets the prompt strings for all the data sources tied to the specified report. This method returns an array of DataSourcePrompt objects.

Parameters:

Name	Type	Description
Report	String	The folder path and name of the report whose data source prompts are to be returned

GetReportDataSources

Description: This method gets the data sources tied to the specified report. This method returns an array of DataSource objects.

Parameters:

Name	Type	Description
Report	String	The folder path and name of the report whose data sources are to be returned

GetReportDefinition

Description: This method gets the definition for the specified report. This method returns a byte array with the report definition as a base-64 encoded RDL structure.

Parameters:

Name	Type	Description
Report	String	The folder path and name of the report whose definition is to be returned

GetReportHistoryLimit

Description: This method gets the maximum number of history snapshots that may be saved for the specified report. This method returns an integer representing the history snapshot limit.

Parameters:

Name	Type	Description
Report	String	The folder path and name of the report whose snapshot history limit is to be returned.
IsSystem	Boolean	True if the report history snapshot limit comes from the system limit; otherwise, false. (This parameter must be called ByRef.)
SystemLimit	Integer	The system limit for report history snapshots. (This parameter must be called ByRef.)

GetReportHistoryOptions

Description: This method gets the report history snapshot options and properties for the specified report. This method returns a boolean value that is true if a history snapshot is enabled and is false otherwise.

Parameters:

Name	Type	Description
Report	String	The folder path and name of the report whose snapshot history options are to be returned.
KeepExecutionSnapshots	Boolean	True if a history snapshot is enabled; otherwise, false. (This parameter must be called ByRef.)
Item	ScheduleDefinitionOrReference Object	An object that contains information about a schedule definition or a reference to a shared schedule that is used to create the history snapshot. (This parameter must be called ByRef.)

GetReportLink

Description: This method gets the name of the report to which the specified linked report is tied. This method returns a string containing the folder path and the name of the report.

Parameters:

Name	Type	Description
Report	String	The folder path and name of the linked report whose underlying report is to be returned

GetReportParameters

Description: This method gets the report parameter properties for the specified report. This method returns an array of ReportParameter objects.

Parameters:

Name	Type	Description
Report	String	The folder path and name of the report whose parameter properties are to be returned.
HistoryID	String	Set this parameter to a history ID to retrieve the parameters for a history snapshot; otherwise, set it to Nothing (Null for C#).
ForRendering	Boolean	Set this parameter to true to return the parameter properties used during the creation of the specified history snapshot; otherwise, set it to false.
Values	An Array of ParameterValue Objects	An array of the values that will be validated for the report.
Credentials	An Array of DataSourceCredential Objects	An array specifying data source credentials to be used when validating parameters.

GetResourceContents

Description: This method gets the contents of a Reporting Services resource. This method returns a byte array containing the base-64 encoded contents of the resource.

Parameters:

Name	Type	Description
Resource	String	The folder path and name of the resource whose contents are to be returned.
MimeType	String	This is the MIME type of the resource. (This parameter must be called ByRef.)

GetRoleProperties

Description: This method gets a description of the specified role, along with the tasks this role is able to complete. This method returns an array of Task objects.

Parameters:

Name	Type	Description
Name	String	The name of the role whose description and tasks are to be returned.
Description	String	The description of the role. (This parameter must be called ByRef.)

GetScheduleProperties

Description: This method gets the properties of the specified shared schedule. This method returns a Schedule object.

Parameters:

Name	Type	Description
ScheduleID	String	The schedule ID of the schedule to be returned

GetSubscriptionProperties

Description: This method gets the properties of the specified subscription. This method returns a string containing the ID of the owner of this subscription.

Parameters:

Name	Type	Description
SubscriptionID	String	The subscription ID of the subscription whose properties are to be returned.
ExtensionSettings	An ExtensionSettings Object	An object containing the settings for the delivery extension associated with this subscription. (This parameter must be called ByRef.)
Description	String	The description of the subscription. (This parameter must be called ByRef.)
Active	An ActiveState Object	An object containing the active state of the subscription. (This parameter must be called ByRef.)
Status	String	The status of the subscription. (This parameter must be called ByRef.)
EventType	String	Either "TimedSubscription" for a subscription triggered by a schedule or "SnapshotUpdated" for a subscription triggered by the updating of a snapshot. (This parameter must be called ByRef.)
MatchData	String	Information used to implement the event type. (This parameter must be called ByRef.)
Parameters	An Array of ParameterValue Objects	An array of the values used for the report's parameters. (This parameter must be called ByRef.)

GetSystemPermissions

Description: This method gets the system permissions assigned to the logon credentials currently being used to access the ReportingService web service. This method returns an array of strings that contain the system permissions.

Parameters: None

GetSystemPolicies

Description: This method gets the system role assignments for this Reporting Services installation. This method returns an array of Policy objects.

Parameters: None

GetSystemProperties

Description: This method gets the value of each specified system property. This method returns an array of Property objects.

Parameters:

Name	Type	Description
Properties	An Array of Property Objects	An array of properties and their values

InheritParentSecurity

Description: This method sets the Reporting Services item to inherit its security from its parent folder. As a result, any role assignments made specifically for this item will be deleted. This method does not return a value.

Parameters:

Name	Type	Description
Item	String	The folder path and name of the item whose security is to be inherited

ListChildren

Description: This method lists all the Reporting Services items that are children of the specified folder. The list includes only those items that the logon credentials currently being used to access the ReportingService web service have a right to view. This method returns an array of CatalogItem objects.

Parameters:

Name	Type	Description
Item	String	The folder path and name of the folder whose children are to be listed
Recursive	Boolean	True if the list should recurse down the folder tree; otherwise, false

ListEvents

Description: This method lists the events supported by this Reporting Services installation. This method returns an array of Event objects.

Parameters: None

ListExtensions

Description: This method lists the extensions of the specified type that have been defined for this Reporting Services installation. This method returns an array of Extension objects.

Parameters:

Name	Type	Description
ExtensionType	ExtensionTypeEnum	Either **Delivery** for delivery extensions, **Render** for rendering extensions, **Data** for data access extensions, or **All** for all of the above

ListJobs

Description: This method lists the jobs that are currently running on this Reporting Services installation. This method returns an array of Job objects.

Parameters: None

ListLinkedReports

Description: This method lists the linked reports tied to a specific report. This method returns an array of CatalogItem objects.

Parameters:

Name	Type	Description
Report	String	The folder path and name of the report whose linked reports are to be listed

ListReportHistory

Description: This method lists the history snapshots and their properties for the specified report. This method returns an array of ReportHistorySnapshot objects.

Parameters:

Name	Type	Description
Report	String	The folder path and name of the report whose history snapshots are to be listed

ListReportsUsingDataSource

Description: This method lists the reports using the specified shared data source. This method returns an array of CatalogItem objects.

Parameters:

Name	Type	Description
DataSource	String	The folder path and name of the shared data source whose reports are to be listed

ListRoles

Description: This method lists the roles defined for this Reporting Services installation. This method returns an array of Role objects.

Parameters: None

ListScheduledReports

Description: This method lists the reports using the specified shared schedule. This method returns an array of CatalogItem objects.

Parameters:

Name	Type	Description
ScheduleID	String	The schedule ID of the shared schedule whose reports are to be listed

ListSchedules

Description: This method lists all the shared schedules. This method returns an array of Schedule objects.

Parameters: None

ListSecureMethods

Description: This method lists all the ReportingService web service methods that require a secure connection. This method returns an array of strings containing the method names.

Parameters: None

ListSubscriptions

Description: This method lists the subscriptions that a specified user has created for a specified report. This method returns an array of Subscription objects.

Parameters:

Name	Type	Description
Report	String	The folder path and name of the report whose subscriptions are to be listed
Owner	String	The name of the owner whose subscriptions are to be retrieved

ListSubscriptionsUsingDataSource

Description: This method lists the subscriptions using the specified shared data source. This method returns an array of Subscription objects.

Parameters:

Name	Type	Description
DataSource	String	The folder path and name of the shared data source whose subscriptions are to be listed

ListSystemRoles

Description: This method lists the system roles defined for this Reporting Services installation. This method returns an array of Role objects.

Parameters: None

ListSystemTasks

Description: This method lists the system tasks defined for this Reporting Services installation. This method returns an array of Task objects.

Parameters: None

ListTasks

Description: This method lists the tasks defined for this Reporting Services installation. This method returns an array of Task objects.

Parameters: None

MoveItem

Description: This method moves the specified Reporting Services item to the specified folder path. This method does not return a value.

Parameters:

Name	Type	Description
Item	String	The folder path and name of the item to be moved
Target	String	The folder path to which this item is to be moved

PauseSchedule

Description: This method pauses the execution of the specified schedule. This method does not return a value.

Parameters:

Name	Type	Description
ScheduleID	String	The ID of the schedule to pause

PrepareQuery

Description: This method determines the fields that will be returned by the specified query running against the specified data source. This information can be used by the CreateDataDrivenSubscription and SetDataDrivenSubscriptionProperties methods. This method returns a DataSetDefinition object.

Parameters:

Name	Type	Description
DataSource	DataSource Object	An object containing the data source information.
DataSet	DataSetDefinition Object	An object containing the query to return the fields for the data-driven subscription.
Changed	Boolean	True if the dataset passed in the DataSet parameter is different from the dataset returned in the DataSetDefinition object; otherwise, false. (This parameter must be called ByRef.)

Render

Description: This method renders the specified report. This method returns a byte array containing the rendered report.

Parameters:

Name	Type	Description
Report	String	The folder path and name of the report to be rendered.
Format	String	The rendering format to be used.

Name	Type	Description
HistoryID	String	The ID of the history snapshot from which to render the report. (Set this to Nothing if the report should not be rendered from a history snapshot.)
DeviceInfo	String	An XML structure to control the behavior of the Report Viewer.
Parameters	An Array of ParameterValue Objects	An array of values for the report parameters.
Credentials	An Array of DataSourceCredentials Objects	An array of credentials to use when accessing the data sources.
ShowHideToggle	String	The Show/Hide Toggle ID. (Set this to Nothing when not used.)
Encoding	String	The encoding used for the contents of the report. (This parameter must be called ByRef.)
MimeType	String	The MIME type of the rendered report. (This parameter must be called ByRef.)
ParametersUsed	An Array of ParameterValue Objects	If the report is rendered from a history snapshot, this will contain an array of the parameter values used to create the history snapshot. (This parameter must be called ByRef.)
Warnings	An Array of Warning Objects	An array containing any warnings that resulted from the rendering of the report. (This parameter must be called ByRef.)
StreamIDs	String	A stream identifier used by the RenderStream method. This is used to render an external resource such as an image. (This parameter must be called ByRef.)

RenderStream

Description: This method obtains the contents of an external resource used by a rendered report. This method returns a byte array containing the external resource.

Parameters:

Name	Type	Description
Report	String	The folder path and name of the report associated with the specified resource.
Format	String	The rendering format to be used.
StreamID	String	The ID of the stream for the main report.

Name	Type	Description
HistoryID	String	The ID of the history snapshot from which to render the report. (Set this to Nothing if the report should not be rendered from a history snapshot.)
DeviceInfo	String	An XML structure to control the behavior of the Report Viewer.
Parameters	An Array of ParameterValue Objects	An array of values for the report parameters.
Encoding	String	The encoding used for the contents of the report. (This parameter must be called ByRef.)
MimeType	String	The MIME type of the rendered report. (This parameter must be called ByRef.)

ResumeSchedule

Description: This method resumes a schedule that has been paused. This method does not return a value.

Parameters:

Name	Type	Description
ScheduleID	String	The ID of the schedule to resume

SetCacheOptions

Description: This method sets the caching options for the specified report. This method does not return a value.

Parameters:

Name	Type	Description
Report	String	The folder path and name of the report whose caching options are to be set
CacheReport	Boolean	True if each execution of the report is to be cached; otherwise, false
Item	ExpirationDefinition Object	An object containing information telling when the cached report is to expire

SetDataDrivenSubscriptionProperties

Description: This method sets the properties of a data-driven subscription. This method does not return a value.

Parameters:

Name	Type	Description
DataDrivenSubscriptionID	String	The ID of the data-driven subscription whose properties are to be set
ExtensionSettings	ExtensionSettings Object	An object containing the settings for the delivery extension (for example, e-mail delivery) used by this subscription
DataRetrievalPlan	DataRetrievalPlan Object	An object containing the information necessary to connect to and retrieve the data used for the data-driven subscription
Description	String	The description of this subscription
EventType	String	Either "TimedSubscription" for a subscription triggered by a schedule or "SnapshotUpdated" for a subscription triggered by the updating of a snapshot
MatchData	String	Information used to implement the event type
Parameters	An Array of ParameterValueOrFieldReference Objects	An array of the values used for the report's parameters

SetDataSourceContents

Description: This method sets the properties of a shared data source. This method does not return a value.

Parameters:

Name	Type	Description
DataSource	String	The name of the data source
Definition	DataSourceDefinition Object	An object containing the connection information for the shared data source

SetExecutionOptions

Description: This method sets the execution options of the specified report. This method does not return a value.

Parameters:

Name	Type	Description
Report	String	The folder path and name of the report whose execution option is to be set.
ExecutionSetting	ExecutionSettingEnum	Either **Live** if the report is to be executed from the data sources or **Snapshot** if the report is to come from an execution snapshot.
Item	ScheduleDefinitionOrReference Object	An object containing the information for a schedule or a reference to a shared schedule. This schedule is used to create the execution snapshot and is valid only if the ExecutionSetting is Snapshot.

SetPolicies

Description: This method sets the security policies for the specified report. This method does not return a value.

Parameters:

Name	Type	Description
Item	String	The folder path to the Reporting Services item for which the security policies are to be set
Policies	An Array of Policy Objects	An array of security policy information

SetProperties

Description: This method sets the properties of the specified Reporting Services item. This method does not return a value.

Parameters:

Name	Type	Description
Item	String	The folder path to the Reporting Services item for which the properties are to be set
Properties	An Array of Property Objects	An array of properties and their values

SetReportDataSources

Description: This method sets the properties for data sources associated with the specified report. This method does not return a value.

Parameters:

Name	Type	Description
Report	String	The folder path to the report for which the data source properties are to be set
DataSources	An Array of DataSource Objects	An array of data sources and their properties

SetReportDefinition

Description: This method sets the report definition of the specified report. This method returns an array of Warning objects containing any warning messages that may result from this operation.

Parameters:

Name	Type	Description
Report	String	The folder path to the report for which the report definition is to be set
Definition	An Array of Bytes	A byte array containing the Report Definition Language (RDL) in base-64 binary

SetReportHistoryLimit

Description: This method sets the limit for the number of history snapshots that may be saved for the specified report. This method does not return a value.

Parameters:

Name	Type	Description
Report	String	The folder path to the report for which the history snapshot limit is to be set
UseSystem	Boolean	True if the system default history snapshot limit is to be used with this report; otherwise, false
HistoryLimit	Integer	The limit for the number of history snapshots saved for this report

SetReportHistoryOptions

Description: This method sets the options specifying when a history snapshot is created for the specified report. This method does not return a value.

Parameters:

Name	Type	Description
Report	String	The folder path to the report for which the history snapshot options are to be set.
EnableManualSnapshotCreation	Boolean	True if snapshots can be created using the CreateReportHistorySnapshot method; otherwise, false.
KeepExecutionSnapshots	Boolean	True if execution snapshots are saved as history snapshots; otherwise, false.
Item	ScheduleDefinitionOrReference Object	An object containing the information for a schedule or a reference to a shared schedule. This schedule is used to create the history snapshot.

SetReportLink

Description: This method sets the report to which the specified linked report should be linked. This method does not return any value.

Parameters:

Name	Type	Description
Report	String	The folder path and name of the linked report
Link	String	The folder path and name of the report to which this should be linked

SetReportParameters

Description: This method sets the parameter property for the specified report. This method does not return a value.

Parameters:

Name	Type	Description
Report	String	The folder path and name of the report whose parameter property should be set
Parameters	An Array of ReportParameter Objects	An array of information on report parameter properties

SetResourceContents

Description: This method sets the contents of a Reporting Services resource. This method does not return a value.

Parameters:

Name	Type	Description
Resource	String	The folder path and name of the resource whose contents is to be set
Contents	An Array of Bytes	The contents of the resource in base-64 binary
MimeType	String	The MIME type of the resource

SetRoleProperties

Description: This method sets the properties of a security role. This method does not return a value.

Parameters:

Name	Type	Description
Name	String	The folder path and name of the security role whose properties are to be set
Description	String	The description of the security role
Tasks	An Array of Task Objects	An array of Reporting Services tasks that may be executed by this role

SetScheduleProperties

Description: This method sets the properties of a shared schedule. This method does not return a value.

Parameters:

Name	Type	Description
Name	String	The name of the shared schedule
ScheduleID	String	The ID of the shared schedule whose properties are to be set
ScheduleDefinition	ScheduleDefinition Object	An object containing the information necessary to define a schedule

SetSubscriptionProperties

Description: This method sets the properties of a subscription. This method does not return a value.

Parameters:

Name	Type	Description
SubscriptionID	String	The ID of the subscription whose properties are to be set
ExtensionSettings	ExtensionSettings Object	An object containing the settings for the delivery extension (for example, e-mail delivery) used by this subscription
Description	String	The description of this subscription
EventType	String	Either "TimedSubscription" for a subscription triggered by a schedule or "SnapshotUpdated"for a subscription triggered by the updating of a snapshot
MatchData	String	Information used to implement the event type
Parameters	An Array of ParameterValue Objects	An array of the values used for the report's parameters

SetSystemPolicies

Description: This method sets the system role assignments for this Reporting Services installation. This method does not return a value.

Parameters:

Name	Type	Description
Policies	An Array of Policy Objects	An array of the values used to set the system policies

SetSystemProperties

Description: This method sets the specified system properties. This method does not return a value.

Parameters:

Name	Type	Description
Properties	An Array of Property Objects	An array of properties and their values

UpdateReportExecutionSnapshot

Description: This method updates the report execution snapshot for the specified report. This method does not return a value.

Parameters:

Name	Type	Description
Report	String	The folder path and name of the report whose execution snapshot is to be updated

ValidateExtensionSettings

Description: This method validates the settings for a Reporting Services extension. This method returns an array of ExtensionParameter objects.

Parameters:

Name	Type	Description
Extension	String	The name of the extension
ParameterValues	An Array of ParameterValueOrFieldReference Objects	An array of parameter values that are to be validated

ReportingService Web Service Classes

The Namespace for ReportingService Web Service Classes

The namespace for ReportingService web service classes is the same as the namespace used for ReportingService itself. If the ReportingService has a namespace of

```
localhost.ReportingService
```

then the namespace for each ReportingService web service class would be

```
localhost.{ClassName}
```

where {ClassName} is the name of one of the classes.

The "Specified" Properties

Many of the properties for these classes have a corresponding property by the same name, with "Specified" on the end. These properties are used to let any code using the class know if a value has been specified for this property or if it has been left with no value specified. In most cases, these "specified" properties are added to correspond to class properties with data types of boolean, date, and others that cannot easily represent an empty state.

For example, the DataSourceDefinition class has a property named Enabled. When this property is set to true, the data source is enabled. When this property is set to false, the data source is disabled. If you do not specify a value for this property, it will default to false and the data source will be disabled. To prevent this from happening, a property called EnabledSpecified of type boolean has been added to the DataSourceDefinition class. This additional property lets the code using this class know whether the value for the Enabled property should be used because it has been specified by the user or if it should be ignored because it has not been specified.

It is up to you as the developer to make sure that these "specified" properties are set properly. Any time you provide a value for a property that has a corresponding "specified" property, you need to set that "specified" property to true. If you do not take care of this in your code, these property values will be ignored by the methods that are using these classes.

In some cases, "specified" properties have been added for class properties that are read-only. This would seem to make no sense because you cannot specify a value for a property that is read-only. Nevertheless, there they are. In these cases, the "specified" properties can be safely ignored.

ActiveState

Description: An object of the ActiveState class type is returned by the GetSubscriptionProperties method to provide information on various error conditions that may be present in a specified subscription. In addition to the properties listed here, this class includes a "specified" property for each of the properties shown. These "specified" properties can be ignored.

Properties:

Property	Type	Description
DeliveryExtensionRemoved	Boolean	True if the delivery extension used by the subscription has been removed; otherwise, false. (Read-only.)
InvalidParameterValue	Boolean	True if a parameter value saved with a subscription is invalid; otherwise, false. (Read-only.)
MissingParameterValue	Boolean	True if a required parameter value is not saved with a subscription; otherwise, false. (Read-only.)
SharedDataSourceRemoved	Boolean	True if a shared data source used with a subscription has been removed; otherwise, false. (Read-only.)
UnknownReportParameter	Boolean	True if a parameter name saved with a subscription is not recognized as a parameter for this report; otherwise, false.

BatchHeader

Description: This class contains the Batch ID for a batch of web service method calls.

Properties:

Property	Type	Description
BatchID	String	The identifier for a batch

CatalogItem

Description: This class contains information about a single item in the Report Catalog. This may be a Reporting Services folder, a report, a shared data source, or a resource.

Properties:

Property	Type	Description
CreatedBy	String	The name of the user who created the item.
CreationDate	Date	The date and time that the item was created.
CreationDateSpecified	Boolean	True if a value for CreationDate is specified; otherwise, false.
Description	String	The description of the item.
ExecutionDate	Date	The date and time that a report item was last executed. (Valid only for report items.)
ExecutionDateSpecified	Boolean	True if a value for ExecutionDate is specified; otherwise, false.
Hidden	Boolean	True if the item is hidden; otherwise, false.
HiddenSpecified	Boolean	True if a value for Hidden is specified; otherwise, false
ID	String	The ID of the item.
MimeType	String	The MIME type of a resource item. (Valid only for resource items.)
ModifiedBy	String	The name of the user who last modified the item.
ModifiedDate	Date	The date and time that the item was last modified.
ModifiedDateSpecified	Boolean	True if a value for ModifiedDate is specified; otherwise, false.
Name	String	The name of the item.
Path	String	The folder path to the item.
Size	Integer	The size of the item in bytes.
SizeSpecified	Boolean	True if a value for Size is specified; otherwise, false.
Type	ItemTypeEnum	The type of the item. Valid values are Unknown, Folder, Report, Resource, LinkedReport, and Datasource.
VirtualPath	String	The virtual path to the item. This is populated only when viewing items under the MyReports folder.

DailyRecurrence

Description: This class contains the time that must elapse, in days, before a schedule recurs. This class inherits from RecurrencePattern.

Properties:

Property	Type	Description
DaysInterval	Integer	The number of days before a schedule recurs

DataRetrievalPlan

Description: This class is used to define the data that will be selected for a data-driven subscription.

Properties:

Property	Type	Description
DataSet	DataSetDefinition	Defines the dataset to use with the data-driven subscription
Item	DataSourceDefinitionOrReference	Defines the data source to use with the data-driven subscription

DataSetDefinition

Description: This class contains the information necessary to define a dataset.

Properties:

Property	Type	Description
AccentSensitivity	SensitivityEnum	True if this dataset is sensitive to accents, False if this dataset is not sensitive to accents, or Auto if the sensitivity setting should be determined from the data provider.
AccentSensitivitySpecified	Boolean	True if a value for AccentSensitivity has been specified; otherwise, false.
CaseSensitivity	SensitivityEnum	True if this dataset is case sensitive, False if this dataset is not case sensitive, or Auto if the sensitivity setting should be determined from the data provider.
CaseSensitivitySpecified	Boolean	True if a value for CaseSensitivity has been specified; otherwise, false.
Collation	String	The locale used when sorting the data in the dataset. (Uses the SQL Server collation codes.)
Fields	An Array of Field Objects	An array containing the field information.
KanatypeSensitivity	SensitivityEnum	True if this dataset is kanatype sensitive, False if this dataset is not kanatype sensitive, or Auto if the sensitivity setting should be determined from the data provider. (This is used only for some Japanese character sets.)
KanatypeSensitivitySpecified	Boolean	True if a value for KanatypeSensitivity has been specified; otherwise, false.
Name	String	The name of the dataset.
Query	QueryDefinition Object	An object containing the query used to retrieve the data.

Property	Type	Description
WidthSensitivity	SensitivityEnum	True if this dataset is width sensitive, False if this dataset is not width sensitive, or Auto if the sensitivity setting should be determined from the data provider.
WidthSensitivitySpecified	Boolean	True if a value for WidthSensitivity has been specified; otherwise, false.

DataSource

Description: This class contains either a reference to a shared data source or an object with the information necessary to define a data source.

Properties:

Property	Type	Description
Item	A DataSourceReference Object or a DataSourceDefinition Object	If the data source is referencing a shared data source, this will be a DataSourceReference object; otherwise, this will be a DataSourceDefinition object.
Name	String	The name of the data source.

DataSourceCredentials

Description: This class contains the credentials used to access a data source.

Properties:

Property	Type	Description
DataSourceName	String	The name of the data source that will use these credentials
Password	String	The password used to connect to the data source
UserName	String	The user name used to connect to the data source

DataSourceDefinition

Description: This class contains the information necessary to define a data source. This class inherits from DataSourceDefinitionOrReference.

Properties:

Property	Type	Description
ConnectString	String	The connection string.
CredentialRetrieval	CredentialRetrievalEnum	Prompt if the user is to be prompted for credentials when accessing this data source, Store if the credentials are stored in the data source definition, Integrated if Windows Authentication is to be used to access the data source, or None if no credentials are required.
Enabled	Boolean	True if the data source is enabled; otherwise, false.
EnabledSpecified	Boolean	True if a value for Enabled has been specified; otherwise, false.
Extension	String	The name of the data source extension. Valid values include SQL, OLEDB, ODBC, and a custom extension.
ImpersonateUser	Boolean	True if the report server is to impersonate the user after a connection has been made to the data source; otherwise, false.
ImpersonateUserSpecified	Boolean	True if a value for ImpersonateUser has been specified; otherwise, false.
Password	String	The password when the credentials are stored in the data source definition.
Prompt	String	The message used when prompting the user for credentials.
UserName	String	The user name when the credentials are stored in the data source definition.
WindowsCredentials	Boolean	True if the stored credentials are Windows credentials or False if the stored credentials are database credentials.

DataSourceDefinitionOrReference

Description: This class serves as a parent class. Any class that inherits from the DataSourceDefinitionOrReference class can be used where a DataSourceDefinitionOrReference type object is required.

Classes Inheriting from This Class:

Class Name	Description
DataSourceDefinition	Used when a data source definition is to be specified
DataSourceReference	Used when a reference to a shared data source is to be specified

DataSourcePrompt

Description: This class contains information about the message displayed to the user when prompting for data source credentials.

Properties:

Property	Type	Description
DataSourceID	String	The unique ID of a data source
Name	String	The name of the data source
Prompt	String	The prompt message

DataSourceReference

Description: This class contains a reference to a shared data source. This class inherits from DataSourceDefinitionOrReference.

Properties:

Property	Type	Description
Reference	String	The folder path and name of the shared data source

DaysOfWeekSelector

Description: This class contains information for the days of the week on which a schedule runs.

Properties:

Property	Type	Description
Friday	Boolean	True if the schedule is to run on Friday; otherwise, false.
Monday	Boolean	True if the schedule is to run on Monday; otherwise, false.
Saturday	Boolean	True if the schedule is to run on Saturday; otherwise, false.
Sunday	Boolean	True if the schedule is to run on Sunday; otherwise, false.
Thursday	Boolean	True if the schedule is to run on Thursday; otherwise, false.
Tuesday	Boolean	True if the schedule is to run on Tuesday; otherwise, false.
Wednesday	Boolean	True if the schedule is to run on Wednesday; otherwise, false.

ExpirationDefinition

Description: This class serves as a parent class. Any class that inherits from the ExpirationDefinition class can be used where an ExpirationDefinition type object is required.

Classes Inheriting from This Class:

Class Name	Description
ScheduleExpiration	Used when a date and time is to be specified for the expiration
TimeExpiration	Used when an elapsed time, in minutes, should be specified for the expiration

Extension

Description: This class represents a Reporting Services extension.

Properties:

Property	Type	Description
ExtensionType	ExtensionTypeEnum	Delivery for a delivery extension, Render for a rendering extension, Data for a data-processing extension, or All to represent all extension types. (Read-only.)
LocalizedName	String	The localized name of the extension for display to the user. (Read-only.)
Name	String	The name of the extension. (Read-only.)
Visible	Boolean	True if the extension is visible to the user interface; otherwise, false.

ExtensionParameter

Description: This class contains information about a setting for a delivery extension.

Properties:

Property	Type	Description
DisplayName	String	The name of the extension parameter.
Encrypted	Boolean	True if the Value property should be encrypted; otherwise, false. (Read-only.)
Error	String	An error message describing a problem with the value specified for this extension parameter. (Read-only.)
IsPassword	Boolean	True if the value for this parameter should not be returned in SOAP responses (this prevents passwords from being sent in clear text); otherwise, false. (Read-only.)
Name	String	The name of the device information setting. (Read-only.)
ReadOnly	Boolean	True if this extension parameter is read-only; otherwise, false. (Read-only.)
Required	Boolean	True if this extension parameter is required; otherwise, false. (Read-only.)
RequiredSpecified	Boolean	True if a value for Required has been specified; otherwise, false.
ValidValues	An Array of ValidValue Objects	An array of valid values for this extension parameter.
Value	String	The value of this extension parameter.

ExtensionSettings

Description: This class contains information for a delivery extension.

Properties:

Property	Type	Description
Extension	Extension Object	An object representing a Reporting Services extension
ParameterValues	An Array of ParameterValueOfFieldReference Objects	An array of parameter values for this extension

Field

Description: This class contains information for a field within a dataset.

Properties:

Property	Type	Description
Alias	String	The alias of a field in a report
Name	String	The name of a field in a query

MinuteRecurrence

Description: This class contains the time that must elapse, in minutes, before a schedule recurs. This class inherits from RecurrencePattern.

Properties:

Property	Type	Description
MinutesInterval	Integer	The number of minutes before a schedule recurs

MonthlyDOWRecurrence

Description: This class contains the days of the week, the weeks of the month, and the months of the year on which a schedule runs. This class inherits from RecurrencePattern.

Properties:

Property	Type	Description
DaysOfWeek	DaysOfWeekSelector Object	An object that determines the days of the week on which the schedule runs
MonthsOfYear	MonthsOfYearSelector	An object that determines the months of the year on which the schedule runs

Property	Type	Description
WhichWeek	WeekNumberEnum	FirstWeek if the schedule is to run the first week of the month, SecondWeek if the schedule is to run the second week of the month, ThirdWeek if the schedule is to run the third week of the month, FourthWeek if the schedule is to run the fourth week of the month, or LastWeek if the schedule is to run the last week of the month
WhichWeekSpecified	Boolean	True if a value for WhichWeek has been specified; otherwise, false

MonthlyRecurrence

Description: This class contains the days of the month and the months of the year on which a schedule runs. This class inherits from RecurrencePattern.

Properties:

Property	Type	Description
Days	String	The days of the month on which the schedule recurs
MonthsOfYear	MonthsOfYearSelector	An object that determines the months of the year on which the schedule recurs

MonthsOfYearSelector

Description: This class contains information on the months of the year in which a schedule runs.

Properties:

Property	Type	Description
April	Boolean	True if the schedule is to run in April; otherwise, false.
August	Boolean	True if the schedule is to run in August; otherwise, false.
December	Boolean	True if the schedule is to run in December; otherwise, false.
February	Boolean	True if the schedule is to run in February; otherwise, false.
January	Boolean	True if the schedule is to run in January; otherwise, false.
July	Boolean	True if the schedule is to run in July; otherwise, false.
June	Boolean	True if the schedule is to run in June; otherwise, false.
March	Boolean	True if the schedule is to run in March; otherwise, false.
May	Boolean	True if the schedule is to run in May; otherwise, false.

Property	Type	Description
November	Boolean	True if the schedule is to run in November; otherwise, false.
October	Boolean	True if the schedule is to run in October; otherwise, false.
September	Boolean	True if the schedule is to run in September; otherwise, false.

NoSchedule

Description: This class is used when no schedule is associated with an execution snapshot or a history snapshot. This class inherits from ScheduleDefinitionOrReference. It does not contain any properties.

ParameterFieldReference

Description: This class represents a field in a dataset used to supply the value for a parameter. This class inherits from ParameterValueOrFieldReference.

Properties:

Property	Type	Description
FieldAlias	String	The alias of a field
ParameterName	String	The name of a field

ParameterValue

Description: This class represents the actual value for a parameter. This class inherits from ParameterValueOrFieldReference.

Properties:

Property	Type	Description
Label	String	The label used for this parameter
Name	String	The name of the parameter
Value	String	The value of the parameter

ParameterValueOrFieldReference

Description: This class serves as a parent class. Any class that inherits from the ParameterValueOrFieldReference class can be used where a ParameterValueOrFieldReference type object is required.

Classes Inheriting from This Class:

Class Name	Description
ParameterFieldReference	Used when a reference to a field is to be specified
ParameterValue	Used when a parameter value is to be specified

Policy

Description: This class represents a domain user or domain group and the security roles assigned to that user or group.

Properties:

Property	Type	Description
GroupUserName	String	The name of a domain user or domain group
Roles	An Array of Role Objects	An array of security roles

Property

Description: This class represents a property of a Reporting Services item.

Properties:

Property	Type	Description
Name	String	The name of the property
Value	String	The value of the property

QueryDefinition

Description: This class contains information to define a query used for a dataset or a data-driven subscription.

Properties:

Property	Type	Description
CommandText	String	The query text (usually a SELECT statement).
CommandType	String	The type of query supplied in the CommandText property. (For data-driven subscriptions, this will always have a value of Text.)
Timeout	Integer	The number of seconds the query may execute before it times out.
TimeoutSpecified	Boolean	True if a value for Timeout has been specified; otherwise, false.

RecurrencePattern

Description: This class serves as a parent class. Any class that inherits from the RecurrencePattern class can be used where a RecurrencePattern type object is required.

Classes Inheriting from This Class:

Class Name	Description
MinuteRecurrence	Used when the schedule is to recur in minutes
DailyRecurrence	Used when the schedule is to recur on a daily basis
WeeklyRecurrence	Used when the schedule is to occur on certain days of the week and to recur on a weekly basis
MonthlyRecurrence	Used when the schedule is to occur on certain days of the month and certain months of the year
MonthlyDOWRecurrence	Used when the recurrence is to occur on a day of the week, week of the month, and month of the year

ReportHistorySnapshot

Description: This class contains information defining a history snapshot.

Properties:

Property	Type	Description
CreationDate	Date	The date and time that the history snapshot was created. (Read-only.)
HistoryID	String	The ID of the history snapshot. (Read-only.)
Size	Integer	The size (in bytes) of the history snapshot. (Read-only.)

ReportParameter

Description: This class contains information about a report parameter.

Properties:

Property	Type	Description
AllowBlank	Boolean	True if this report parameter can be empty; otherwise, false. (Read-only.)
AllowBlankSpecified	Boolean	True if a value for AllowBlank was specified; otherwise, false.
DefaultValues	String	The default value of the report parameter.
DefaultValuesQueryBased	Boolean	True if the default value comes from a query; otherwise, false. (Read-only.)
DefaultValuesQueryBasedSpecified	Boolean	True if a value for DefaultValuesQueryBased is specified; otherwise, false.
Dependencies	An Array of Strings	An array showing which other report parameters are depended on by the query used to provide the default value and the query used to provide valid values. Used only if the default value or the valid values come from a parameterized query. (Read-only.)

Property	Type	Description
ErrorMessage	String	Any error messages describing errors with this report parameter.
MultiValue	Boolean	True if the parameter can be a multivalued parameter. (Read-only.)
MultiValueSpecified	Boolean	True if a value for MultiValue is specified; otherwise, false.
Name	String	The name of the parameter. (Read-only.)
Nullable	Boolean	True if the report parameter may be null; otherwise, false.
NullableSpecified	Boolean	True if a value for Nullable is specified; otherwise, false.
Prompt	String	The message displayed to the user when prompting for a value for this parameter.
PromptUser	Boolean	True if the user is to be prompted for this report parameter; otherwise, false.
PromptUserSpecified	Boolean	True if a value for PromptUser has been specified; otherwise, false.
QueryParameter	Boolean	True if this parameter is used in a data source query; otherwise, false. (Read-only.)
QueryParameterSpecified	Boolean	True if a value for QueryParameter is specified; otherwise, false.
State	Parameter StateEnum	HasValidValue if the report parameter has a valid value, MissingValidValue if a valid value for the report parameter does not exist, HasOutstandingDependencies if other report parameters that are depended on by this report parameter have not yet been specified, or DynamicValuesUnavailable if no values were returned by a query designated to provide the list of valid values. (Read-only.)
StateSpecified	Boolean	True if a value for State is specified; otherwise, false.
Type	Parameter TypeEnum	Boolean if type boolean, DateTime if type datetime, Float if type float, Integer if type integer, or String if type string. (Read-only.)
TypeSpecified	Boolean	True if a value for Type is specified; otherwise, false.
ValidValues	An Array of ValidValue Objects	An array of the valid values for this report parameter.
ValidValuesQueryBased	Boolean	True if the valid values come from a query; otherwise, false.
ValidValuesQueryBasedSpecified	Boolean	True if a value for ValidValuesQueryBased is specified; otherwise, false.

Role

Description: This class contains information about a security role.

Properties:

Property	Type	Description
Description	String	The description of the role
Name	String	The name of the role

Schedule

Description: This class contains information about a schedule.

Properties:

Property	Type	Description
Creator	String	The name of the user who created the schedule. (Read-only.)
Definition	ScheduleDefinition Object	The definition of the schedule.
Description	String	The description of the schedule.
LastRunTime	Date	The date and time the schedule was last run. (Read-only.)
LastRunTimeSpecified	Boolean	True if a value for LastRunTime is specified; otherwise, false.
Name	String	The name of the schedule.
NextRunTime	Date	The date and time the schedule will run next. (Read-only.)
NextRunTimeSpecified	Boolean	True if a value for NextRunTime is specified; otherwise, false.
ReferencesPresent	Boolean	True if this is a shared schedule and it is referenced by reports and subscriptions.
ScheduleID	String	The ID of the schedule. (Read-only.)
State	ScheduleStateEnum	Running if one or more reports associated with this schedule are currently running, Ready if one or more reports associated with this schedule are ready to run, Paused if the schedule is paused, Expired if the end date for this schedule has passed, or Failing if an error has occurred and the schedule has failed.

ScheduleDefinition

Description: This class contains information for defining a schedule. This class inherits from ScheduleDefinitionOrReference.

Properties:

Property	Type	Description
EndDate	Date	The end date and time for the schedule
EndDateSpecified	Boolean	True if a value for EndDate has been specified; otherwise, false

Property	Type	Description
Item	RecurrencePattern Object	An object containing information about when the schedule should run
StartDateTime	Date	The start date and time for the schedule

ScheduleDefinitionOrReference

Description: This class serves as a parent class. Any class that inherits from the ScheduleDefinitionOrReference class can be used where a ScheduleDefinitionOrReference type object is required.

Classes Inheriting from This Class:

Class Name	Description
NoSchedule	Used when no schedule is to be specified
ScheduleDefinition	Used when a schedule definition is to be specified
ScheduleReference	Used when a reference to a shared schedule is to be specified

ScheduleExpiration

Description: This class defines when a cached copy of a report should expire. This class inherits from ExpirationDefinition.

Properties:

Property	Type	Description
Item	ScheduleDefinitionOrReference Object	Either a schedule definition or a reference to a shared schedule

ScheduleReference

Description: This class contains a reference to a shared schedule. This class inherits from ScheduleDefinitionOrReference.

Properties:

Property	Type	Description
Definition	ScheduleDefinition Object	The definition of the schedule
ScheduleID	String	The ID of the shared schedule

SearchCondition

Description: This class provides information on a search within the Report Catalog.

Properties:

Property	Type	Description
Condition	ConditionEnum	Contains if the search must match only a portion of the property's value to be considered a match or Equals if the search must match all of the property's value to be considered a match
ConditionSpecified	Boolean	True if a value for Condition has been specified; otherwise, false
Name	String	The name of the property being searched
Value	String	The value to find

Subscription

Description: This class contains information to define a subscription.

Properties:

Property	Type	Description
Active	ActiveState Object	The active state of the subscription. (Read-only.)
DeliverySettings	ExtensionSettings Object	The settings specific to the delivery extension.
Description	String	A description of the format and the delivery method.
EventType	String	The type of event that triggers the subscription.
IsDataDriven	Boolean	True if the subscription is data-driven; otherwise, false.
LastExecuted	Date	The date and time the subscription was last executed. (Read-only.)
LastExecutedSpecified	Boolean	True if a value for LastExecuted is specified; otherwise, false.
ModifiedBy	String	The name of the user who last modified the subscription. (Read-only.)
ModifiedDate	Date	The date and time of the last modification to the subscription. (Read-only.)
Owner	String	The user name of the owner of the subscription. (Read-only.)
Path	String	The full path and name of the report associated with the subscription.
Report	String	The name of the report associated with the subscription.
Status	String	The status of the subscription. (Read-only.)
SubscriptionID	String	The ID of the subscription.
VirtualPath	String	The virtual path to the report associated with the subscription. This is populated only if the associated report is under the MyReports folder.

Task

Description: This class contains information about a Reporting Services task.

Properties:

Property	Type	Description
Description	String	The description of this task. (Read-only.)
Name	String	The name of this task. (Read-only.)
TaskID	String	The ID for this task. (Read-only.)

TimeExpiration

Description: This class contains the time that must elapse, in minutes, before a cached copy of a report expires. This class inherits from ExpirationDefinition.

Properties:

Property	Type	Description
Minutes	Integer	The number of minutes before expiration

ValidValue

Description: This class contains information on a valid value for an extension parameter or a report parameter.

Properties:

Property	Type	Description
Label	String	The label for the valid value
Value	String	The valid value for the setting

Warning

Description: This class contains information on a warning message or an error message.

Properties:

Property	Type	Description
Code	String	The error or warning code. (Read-only.)
Message	String	The error or warning message. (Read-only.)
ObjectName	String	The name of the object associated with the warning or error. (Read-only.)
ObjectType	String	The type of the object associated with the warning or error. (Read-only.)
Severity	String	Warning if this is a warning or Error if this is an error.

WeeklyRecurrence

Description: This class contains the days of the week on which a schedule runs and the number of weeks to elapse before each recurrence. This class inherits from RecurrencePattern.

Properties:

Property	Type	Description
DaysOfWeek	DaysOfWeekSelector Object	An object that determines the days of the week on which the schedule runs.
WeeksInterval	Integer	The number of weeks before a schedule runs again.
WeeksIntervalSpecified	Boolean	True if a value for WeeksInterval is specified; otherwise, false.

C

Report Definition
Language Reference

IN THIS APPENDIX:
Report Definition Language

Report Definition Language

The Report Definition Language (RDL) is an XML structure defined by Microsoft for storing Reporting Services reports. RDL is an element-centric XML structure. That is to say, RDL primarily uses elements to store information, rather than attributes.

The two types of elements within RDL are parent elements and property elements. Parent elements contain other elements, whereas property elements define a property of the parent element. The name of the property is the same as the name of the element. The value of the property is the contents of the element. For example, if the LeftMargin property of the report is set to 1 inch, the element containing that property would look like this:

```
<LeftMargin>1in</LeftMargin>
```

Property elements do not contain other elements.

Default Values

In order to keep the RDL files from becoming unwieldy, properties that are set to a default value will not be included in the RDL file. For example, the default value for the PageHeight property of a report is 11 inches. If the PageHeight of a report is set to 11 inches, the RDL file for that report will not contain a PageHeight element. The programs that read (or consume) the RDL file need to know these default values and fill them in automatically.

RDL Structure

NOTE

In the following illustrations, the single arrows indicate a one-to-zero-or-one relation between the parent element and the child element. For example, the Report element may contain zero or one PageHeader elements. The arrows with shading indicate a one-to-zero-or-many relation between the parent element and the child elements. For example, the DataSources element may contain zero or many DataSource elements.

Report

The entire report definition is contained within the Report element. The structure of the parent elements within the Report element is shown here:

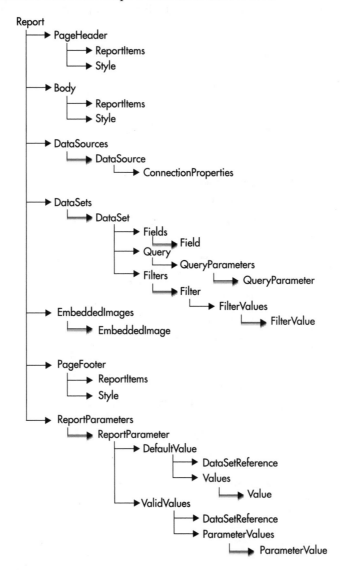

ReportItems

The report layout is made up of report items. As you saw in the previous illustration, report items can be placed in the PageHeader, the Body, and the PageFooter elements. The structure of the parent elements within the ReportItems element is shown here:

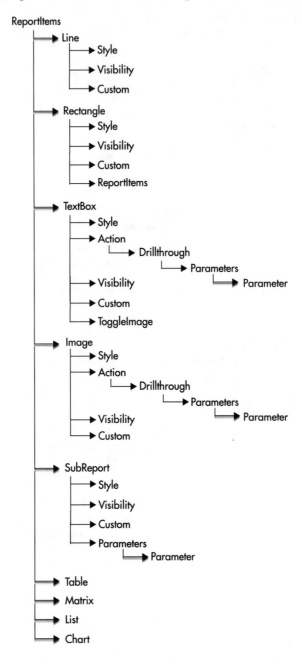

The structure of each of the data regions is shown in the following sections.

Table

The structure of the parent elements within the Table element is shown here:

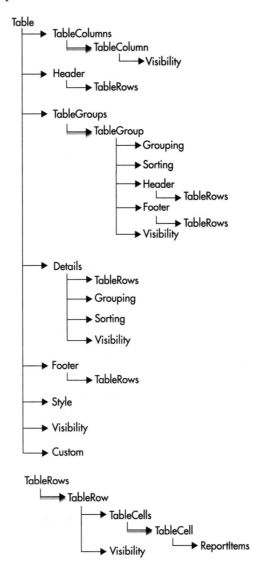

Matrix

The structure of the parent elements within the Matrix element is shown here:

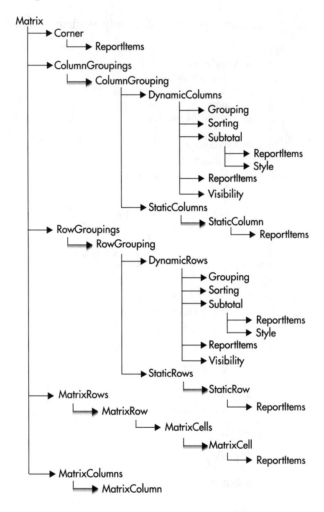

List

The structure of the parent elements within the List element is shown here:

Chart

The structure of the parent elements—Chart, Axis, and ChartSeries—within the Chart element is shown here and on the following page:

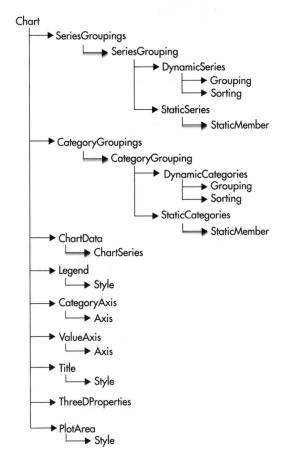

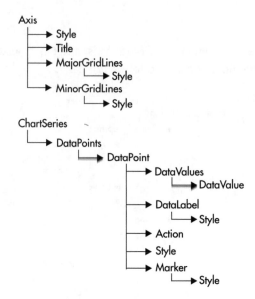

Grouping, Sorting, and Style

Last, but not least, the structure of the Grouping, Sorting, and Style elements is shown here:

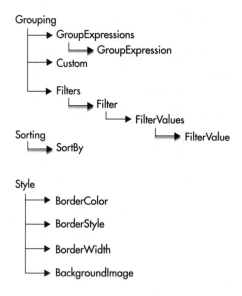

These items are used within a number of the other elements.

Index

INTERNATIONAL CONTACT INFORMATION

AUSTRALIA
McGraw-Hill Book Company
Australia Pty. Ltd.
TEL +61-2-9900-1800
FAX +61-2-9878-8881
http://www.mcgraw-hill.com.au
books-it_sydney@mcgraw-hill.com

CANADA
McGraw-Hill Ryerson Ltd.
TEL +905-430-5000
FAX +905-430-5020
http://www.mcgraw-hill.ca

**GREECE, MIDDLE EAST, & AFRICA
(Excluding South Africa)**
McGraw-Hill Hellas
TEL +30-210-6560-990
TEL +30-210-6560-993
TEL +30-210-6560-994
FAX +30-210-6545-525

MEXICO (Also serving Latin America)
McGraw-Hill Interamericana Editores
S.A. de C.V.
TEL +525-1500-5108
FAX +525-117-1589
http://www.mcgraw-hill.com.mx
carlos_ruiz@mcgraw-hill.com

SINGAPORE (Serving Asia)
McGraw-Hill Book Company
TEL +65-6863-1580
FAX +65-6862-3354
http://www.mcgraw-hill.com.sg
mghasia@mcgraw-hill.com

SOUTH AFRICA
McGraw-Hill South Africa
TEL +27-11-622-7512
FAX +27-11-622-9045
robyn_swanepoel@mcgraw-hill.com

SPAIN
McGraw-Hill/
Interamericana de España, S.A.U.
TEL +34-91-180-3000
FAX +34-91-372-8513
http://www.mcgraw-hill.es
professional@mcgraw-hill.es

**UNITED KINGDOM, NORTHERN,
EASTERN, & CENTRAL EUROPE**
McGraw-Hill Education Europe
TEL +44-1-628-502500
FAX +44-1-628-770224
http://www.mcgraw-hill.co.uk
emea_queries@mcgraw-hill.com

ALL OTHER INQUIRIES Contact:
McGraw-Hill/Osborne
TEL +1-510-420-7700
FAX +1-510-420-7703
http://www.osborne.com
omg_international@mcgraw-hill.com

Sound Off!

Visit us at **www.osborne.com/bookregistration** and let us know what you thought of this book. While you're online you'll have the opportunity to register for newsletters and special offers from McGraw-Hill/Osborne.

We want to hear from you!

Sneak Peek

Visit us today at **www.betabooks.com** and see what's coming from McGraw-Hill/Osborne tomorrow!

Based on the successful software paradigm, Bet@Books™ allows computing professionals to view partial and sometimes complete text versions of selected titles online. Bet@Books™ viewing is free, invites comments and feedback, and allows you to "test drive" books in progress on the subjects that interest you the most.